SPSS for Social Scientists

SPSS for Social Scientists

**Robert L. Miller, Ciaran Acton, Deirdre A. Fullerton
and John Maltby**

Consultant editor: Jo Campling

First published 2002 by
PALGRAVE MACMILLAN
Houndmills, Basingstoke, Hampshire RG21 6XS and
175 Fifth Avenue, New York, N.Y. 10010
Companies and representatives throughout the world

PALGRAVE MACMILLAN is the global academic imprint of the Palgrave
Macmillan division of St. Martin's Press, LLC and of Palgrave Macmillan Ltd.
Macmillan® is a registered trademark in the United States, United Kingdom
and other countries. Palgrave is a registered trademark in the European
Union and other countries.

ISBN 0–333–92286–7

This book is printed on paper suitable for recycling and made from fully
managed and sustained forest sources.

A catalogue record for this book is available from the British Library.

A catalogue record for this book is available from the Library of Congress.

10   9   8   7   6   5   4   3   2   1
11   10   09   08   07   06   05   04   03   02

Typeset in Great Britain by
Aarontype Ltd, Easton, Bristol

Printed and bound in Great Britain by
Antony Rowe Ltd, Chippenham and Eastbourne

CONTENTS

LIST OF FIGURES

PREFACE

Statistics and quantitative methods courses in the social sciences often suffer from an inability to make a link between the skills they seek to impart and present-day society. They can be made more attractive to students by illustrating analytic methods with examples from the contemporary world and involving students in computer analyses of real data. As teachers of statistics and quantitative methods courses in three universities in the British Isles, we were aware of the need for locally interesting datasets that would be available to students in the social sciences. The availability of the British Social Attitudes (BSA) Survey brought with it the possibility of utilising the research data that had been collected in teaching.[1] This use is particularly appropriate given the commitment of the organisers of the BSA surveys to disseminating the results of the survey to the widest possible audiences.

As well as providing 'raw material' for statistical analysis exercises on a research methods training course, the four datasets − 'Crime', 'Health', 'Welfare' and 'Politics' − constitute significant bodies of information about contemporary British society. The data provide the basis for the substantive consideration of attitudes and social structure in Britain and could be used to great effect on social science courses in disciplines such as Criminology, Health Studies, Sociology, Social Policy and Political Science.

Layout and scope of the book

The text begins with two introductory chapters. The 'Introduction' chapter places 'the quantitative perspective' within the landscape of the social sciences and then moves on to discuss the logic underlying statistical analysis. This is followed by an 'Orientation' chapter that gives information about the British Social Attitudes Survey and explains the Windows 'environment' as it relates to SPSS. This chapter tells the student about the general layout of SPSS and gives advice about general 'housekeeping' that will ensure that carrying out practical work with the program is efficient and trouble-free. SPSS has built-in features for advising and helping users. How to access and use these is explained in this 'Orientation' chapter.

The two introductory chapters are followed by ten modules that provide instruction about the practicalities of carrying out statistical analyses with SPSS. This begins with Module 1 on 'Data Input', moves through procedures for looking at individual variables in Module 2, 'Listing and Exploring Data', to the important topic of data refinement in Module 3, 'Data Selection and Manipulation', and then on to seven modules that present the practicalities of different types of statistical analysis with SPSS. The text ends with a 'Conclusion' chapter that provides advice about the procedures for selecting appropriate statistical tests.

---

[1] Note that the four datasets have been adapted from the BSA for use as *teaching datasets*. While the data are of high quality, changes have been made to make them more suitable for student use − most notably the simplification of the missing values codes used in the survey and the construction of additional scales for teaching purposes. This different treatment of missing values means that some of the percentage tabulations given in Appendix 3 may not agree precisely with those found in the teaching datasets. Academics wishing to use the BSA data for research purposes *must* make use of the original BSA datasets.

The four practice datasets are integral to the successful use of this textbook and it is essential that students have a genuine understanding of the contents of these datasets. To make this understanding possible, three Appendixes are provided:

- Appendix 1 – *The Dataset Variables Quick Look-up Guides.* A comprehensive listing and brief description of all the variables in the datasets so that students can locate the variables they need when carrying out exercises.
- Appendix 2 – *Scales.* Descriptions of each of the scales contained in the datasets, including details of their meaning and construction.
- Appendix 3 – *Questions Used to Generate Variables Used in the Practice Datasets.* A reproduction of the exact wordings and response options used in the actual questions asked by the British Social Attitudes interviewers are given so that students can have a genuine understanding of the meaning of the variables they are using in their analyses.

Finally, the text is intended as an introduction to the main data features of SPSS and provides careful step-by-step instruction in the practical details of carrying out statistical procedures and the interpretation of SPSS output. While this necessarily requires the discussion of the logic underlying many of the statistical procedures, this book is not intended to be a 'stand-alone' statistical text. It should be used on a course of study in conjunction with a statistics textbook and/or a program of lectures and readings provided by the instructor.

ACKNOWLEDGEMENTS

The organisers of the British Social Attitudes Survey located in the National Centre for Social Research have overall responsibility for the BSA series. We are grateful for their support and interest in the development of the textbook and that they made the data available for the construction of the practice datasets that accompany this text and allowed us to duplicate portions of the BSA interview schedule and questionnaires.

SPSS, Inc. has allowed us to reproduce windows and output generated by the SPSS programme. This obviously was essential for this text and we are most appreciative of their permission.

Finally, the students at the Queen's University, Belfast, the University of Ulster and Sheffield Hallam University who used a draft version of the workbook during the academic year 1999– 2000 provided essential feedback that allowed us to identify areas where the text could be improved. Again, we are grateful for their tolerance and good humour.

Introduction

The use and analysis of numeric data in the social sciences has a chequered history. During a period from the latter decades of the nineteenth century through to the middle of the twentieth, the quantification of social data and the development of means of analysis were crucial in the efforts of the social sciences to secure acceptance as legitimate academic disciplines. From the end of the Second World War and coincident with academic recognition, the quantitative perspective in the social sciences enjoyed a golden period that reached its culmination in the late 1960s and early 1970s when the computerised analysis of social data became generalised. The advent of computerisation in the social sciences had a transforming effect, greatly expanding both the scope of issues that could be investigated using quantitative issues and the depth of investigation that could be carried out. Computer 'packages' – sets of computer programs for the statistical analysis of social data with special 'user-friendly' interfaces to allow social scientists to run the programs without a special knowledge of their mathematical construction – were instrumental in the expansion of computerised data analysis beyond a small set of specialists. SPSS, then known as the Statistical Package for the Social Sciences, was the most popular of these. It remains so today.

The schism between quantitative and qualitative perspectives

Ironically (or perhaps predictably), the point in time when the quantitative perspective was at its most hegemonic also was the period that saw the beginnings of a serious backlash as qualitative methods began to reassert themselves. From this period, a schism developed between quantitative and qualitative practitioners that ran across all of the social sciences. In some disciplines such as geography, quantification dominated, in others such as anthropology, qualitative research reigned, while in other disciplines, such as sociology, the split was roughly even. A characteristic across social science disciplines throughout the decades of the 1970s and 1980s, however, was a lack of contact across the schism that was common to all.

Thankfully, this period of mutual incomprehension seems to be drawing to an end. At the beginning of the new millennium, practitioners of both quantitative and qualitative methods have begun to develop a mutual appreciation of the 'opposing' camp. This is driven by developments of both perspective and technology.

In the recent past, the mainstream of quantitative research maintained a condescending view of qualitative research. Qualitative research was tolerated as useful for carrying out preliminary exploratory investigations of social phenomena, but only as a precursor to 'serious' quantitative hypothesis-testing investigation. However, more thoughtful quantitative researchers have begun to realise that, while quantitative analysis can answer many types of questions very well – establishing *when* and *how who* did *what* and *where* – it tends to fall down over the crucial question of *why*. To put it another way, quantitative methods are very effective at establishing the *veracity* of empirical social facts but are less effective at establishing the *motivations* or *reasoning* employed by social actors. As a result, triangulated research designs, in which qualitative methods are seen not just as a preliminary but also as a crucial final stage necessary to add context to empirical quantitative findings, are becoming common.

For its part, qualitative research has become more tolerant of the quantitative perspective. Qualitative researchers laboured under a dominant quantitative perspective during the 1960s and 1970s. Part of their reaction to their second-class status was aggressive anti-quantification. As they became established in positions of power and status equal to those of their quantitative counterparts, qualitative researchers felt more secure and became in turn more tolerant of quantitative information.

Technological innovation has promoted the accommodation of the two perspectives. Only a few decades ago computers were seen as hostile and esoteric devices for use only by mathematical specialists. The effects of the spread of computer use to the general population, and especially the universal take-up of wordprocessing technology with a resultant loss of computer phobia among qualitative social scientists, should not be underestimated.

Of more direct salience is the recent impact of computerisation upon *qualitative* analysis. The advent of specialist qualitative data management and analysis packages has transformed qualitative research since 1990. Today it would be difficult to find a serious qualitative researcher who does not have firsthand experience of the practical benefits of computerisation for their own analysis. A side effect of this take-up of computers by qualitative researchers has been to render them more open to quantification.

A happy irony of technological innovation has been that as computing power and complexity has increased, the human–machine interface has simplified. This applies as much to quantitative data analysis packages in the social sciences as elsewhere. The use of a quantitative computer package today does not require any special mathematical expertise or ability, with the result that the constituency of academics with at least some capacity for social science computing has expanded. Increased ease of access has meant that more social scientists are able to 'cross over' between qualitative and quantitative techniques. SPSS, the most popular and widely used social science data analysis package, with its Windows format and extensive online Help facilities, is a prime example of the more accessible packages of the new millennium.

The end result of all these changes has been that the recent mutual suspicion and incomprehension between quantitative and qualitative social scientists has abated greatly, being replaced with a more relaxed and tolerant atmosphere.

Two quantitative perspectives

The empirical

It is a misnomer to speak of a single quantitative perspective. Instead, the use of quantitative data in the social sciences can be seen to fall into two broad modes of working. While these perspectives overlap, they in fact are based upon quite different premises. The first perspective, which can be termed the *empirical*, has beginnings which can be traced at least as far back as the first modern censuses carried out at the beginning of the nineteenth century. The advent of the industrial revolution and the rise of bureaucratic state apparatuses brought about the first modern collations of information drawn from the general population.

The core features of this empirical perspective are the control, manipulation, depiction and presentation of large amounts of data. Its clearest present-day examples would be the published tabulation tables of a large-scale census or a multi-coloured three-dimensional graph or chart that depicts similar tabular information in a figurative form. The basic task of the empirical perspective is relatively simple, making use of gross computing power to carry out the reliable processing of bulk information into manageable formats. Information is sorted using common-sense sets of categories. Care is taken in the presentation of the resulting sorts to facilitate the recognition of patterns by the scanning human eye. There is no data analysis in the sense of seeking to depict linkages or associations between bits of information statistically or attempting to model social processes. At its most advanced in the empirical mode, the clever presentation of information allows the researcher to see or notice features that are not readily apparent in raw data or in less ingenious presentation. SPSS has the capacity to carry out analyses in the empirical mode with great efficiency through its procedures for generating tables in a variety of formats, its facilities for data manipulation, its multiple classification analysis procedures and its variety of ways for generating graphs and charts and using exploratory data analysis (EDA) techniques to depict data.

The positivist

The second perspective, which can be termed the *positivist*, has beginnings in the writings of Emile Durkheim and the first attempts to depict social processes through the modelling of social data. While in practice there is much overlap between the positivist and empirical approaches to data analysis, they in fact employ quite different 'logics' of discovery. All statistical testing which gives its results in the form of probability or significance levels or in terms of an hypothesised relationship or association being found or not confirmed by data is making use of the positivist mode of analysis. The basic perspective underpinning the positivist model of data analysis stretches from quite basic statistical procedures that can be done easily by a beginning student up through sophisticated statistical modelling at the frontiers of social science.

The exact steps involved in positivist statistical testing will be introduced in detail in Module 4, *t-tests*, and then applied in many of the other modules in this text, but here let us here consider the general ideas behind the perspective. The positivist view at its most extreme can be found in the idea of the *social fact* as propounded by Emile Durkheim. Durkheim began by noting that much social behaviour which seems be highly individualistic and idiosyncratic from the point of view of a lone individual in fact conforms to quite regular and predictable patterns if the occurrence of the behaviour is looked at for a large aggregate of people. The example of individual behaviour that he chose to examine was suicide, collecting information on suicide rates from different countries and noting how the rates varied in regular ways (for instance, that single people were more likely to commit suicide than married people). However, let us pick something a bit more cheerful – love.

Popularly, falling in love is seen as almost random. Images abound such as of Cupid firing his darts randomly or of love at first sight when two strangers' eyes meet across a crowded room. Lonely people long for the one perfect soulmate that exists somewhere for them. Perhaps we are being a bit cynical and mocking here, but the point holds – people fall in love and the experience is by definition an intensely personal one. At the same time, oddly, falling in love conforms to very definite patterns of age and social groupings. If we take a cohort of 'typical' university students – those who entered straight from their secondary education – they will be aged between about nineteen and twenty-two and, even though they have been socially active for almost a decade, most will not be in love or in a permanent partnership that is intended to last a lifetime. If we follow up the same cohort a decade later, most will be in a permanent relationship, probably marriage, and probably with children or expecting children soon. If we look at the characteristics of the partners that go to make up each couple, by and large we will find congruence across a wide variety of social characteristics. 'Like' will have paired with 'like' with regard to general social background, education, race, ethnic group, religion and so on. There will have been a typical sequence of events in the life course that led up to the forming of the partnership – completion of education, followed by employment and financial independence and, *then and only then*, falling in love and forming the permanent relationship. The women will tend to have fallen in love at the same age or a few years younger than their male partners. There will of course be many exceptions – people who remain single or break the sequence by having children while single or marry before attaining financial independence and so on – or people who cross the barriers of age, class or ethnicity to find a partner; but these will be 'exceptions that prove the rules' of endogamy and sequence. If love really were blind, we should not find these regularities: the choice of partner should have been more random with partnerships that cross barriers of race, ethnicity, social class, gender or age as likely as those that do not. The age of falling in love should not be clustered in the twenties, but should be scattered equally from the early teens through to old age and the pronounced sequence of falling in love shortly after obtaining secure employment should not exist.

Much of the explanation for these aggregate patterns in love and marriage can of course be found at quite mundane, commonsensical levels. Permanent relationships between couples, especially if they intend to have children, become much more practical once financial independence is attained. Patterns of social and residential endogamy mean that people of similar class and ethnic backgrounds are likely to interact with each other more often so that, by chance, they have more opportunities for pairing off. Nevertheless (assuming that most of these people are pairing off owing to love rather than calculation or arranged marriages) events that are being experienced as intensely individual experiences *are* conforming to socially regular patterns. (That increasing numbers of these partnerships may be dissolving later on in life does not constitute disproof. Instead, rises in divorce and/or single parent families are only complications – further intensely individually experienced phenomena that in fact also conform to predictable patterns at the aggregate level.)

But the positivist perspective is more than simply an aggregate view. As well as noting that phenomena can display regular patterns at a group level, the positivist perspective goes further and posits a genuine level of reality *beyond* that of individuals or their aggregation. This hypothesised meta-reality is the core of the idea of the *social fact*. For instance, with regard to suicide, Durkheim proposed the idea of integration as a feature of a society as a whole, a feature that existed at the societal level but then worked downward to affect individuals. He suggested that variations in suicide could be related to the way in which individuals were integrated or not integrated within society and proposed a typology of three kinds of suicide:

- *Altruistic* suicide, in which the individual is so integrated in society that the will to live can be overwhelmed by the social. The cases of the Japanese samurai who commits ritual suicide or the soldier who throws himself or herself on a grenade in order to save the rest of the squad are examples.
- *Egoistic* suicide, in which individuals who lack day-to-day networks of social support and are less integrated in society are more likely to fall prey to psychological mood swings. The above-noted propensity for single people to be more likely to commit suicide is perhaps the clearest example.
- *Anomic* suicide, in which societal integration drops during a time of social change when established mores of correct social behaviour become unclear. Durkheim predicted that suicide rates should rise during times of both economic depression *and* economic boom as an expression of anomic suicide.

The reliability and validity of Durkheim's analysis of suicide has been debated ever since it was proposed, but that is beside the point here. What is of relevance here is that Durkheim deliberately chose an intensively individualistic act – suicide – and then used his analysis of it to present the idea of social facts and an approach to quantitative analysis.

Similarly, with regard to love, one can suggest that there are features of the whole society that can affect the individual's likelihood to fall or not fall in love. Concerning the uncanny regular timing of the point at which one forms a permanent relationship with a member of the opposite sex, societies develop a set of conventional age-related behaviours as a common organising principle that can be termed the *life course*. Love and forming a partnership is a set point on this general life course that is determined by the social milestones such as securing employment that preceed it and those that follow, such as beginning to produce the next generation. Marital endogamy can be seen as a special case of general principles of inclusion and exclusion on the basis of ethnic identity and religion that translate into individual differences in choices of life partners. Similarly, general principles of stratification – social class – also translate into patterns of endogamy in the individual choice of life partners. From the positivist point of view, these constraints and propensities are operating meta-socially, independently of individual reality. It is this meta-social level, which has its full expression only at a level beyond that of individual consciousness and motivation, that constitutes what Durkheim meant by social facts.

The positivist paradigm in statistical analysis

This idea of the social fact forms the deep background that is the rationale underpining hypothesis-testing statistical analysis. If group regularities in social behaviour are just the simple amalgamation of individuals, description – the *empirical* approach – would be sufficient. Hypothesis-based statistical testing goes a step further. All probability-based statistics, no matter how basic, are assuming that there are regularities in the data that exist at a level beyond that of the individual. The collection of information from *groups* causes the idiosyncratic differences between single individuals to be mutually cancelled out, allowing the meta-level relationships to emerge. In effect, the 'trees' blur together, allowing us to see 'the forest'. To propose that there is a link between two features of a group of people and then to test for the reality of that proposed link means that one is assuming that the link exists in a way that transcends any single individual – one is positing that a social fact exists.

The positivist approach to social science data analysis can be depicted in a diagram (see below). In the 'positivist paradigm', the researcher begins with a general theory or set of abstract

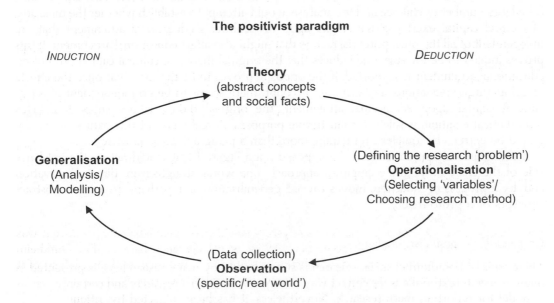

The positivist paradigm

INDUCTION   *DEDUCTION*

Theory
(abstract concepts
and social facts)

Generalisation
(Analysis/
Modelling)

(Defining the research 'problem')
Operationalisation
(Selecting 'variables'/
Choosing research method)

(Data collection)
Observation
(specific/'real world')

concepts. 'A *theory* is defined here as a set of interrelated propositions, some of which can be empirically tested. Thus, a theory has three important characteristics: (1) it consists of a set of propositions; (2) these propositions are interrelated; and (3) some of them are empirically testable' (Lin, 1976, p. 17). These general propositions can be applied to a specific situation in order to *deduce* a likely relationship or set of concrete phenomena in the real world. (In *deduction*, one moves from general, abstract principles to specific, concrete situations.) The conceptual ideas of the theory are applied to specific instances in the real world through a process called *operationalisation*. An *hypothesis* is constructed, which is a statement of association or difference between concrete phenomena. The hypothesis is tested in the real world to see whether the expected association or difference actually occurs in the manner which has been predicted. If the predicted association or difference does occur as expected, the hypothesis is considered to have been supported (or at least not disproven) and, through a process called *generalisation*, the researcher is led to *induce* that the general theory that he or she began with seems to have been confirmed in the real world. (In *induction*, one moves from specific, concrete observations to general, abstract principles.) If the predicted association or relationship is *not* found, the researcher is led to induce the opposite, that the general theory appears not to have been confirmed when tested against real facts.

In Module 4, on *t-tests*, specific examples of this hypothesis-testing approach will be introduced. Here, using 'the causes of high educational attainment', let us present a general example in order to illustrate the positivist approach to data analysis. There are a large variety of competing explanations of educational attainment. One type of explanation is that the educational attainment of individuals can be attributed in part to the level of educationally relevant cultural knowledge present in a child's home. This fund of cultural knowledge is sometimes termed *cultural capital*. The concepts of cultural capital and educational attainment could be operationalised by developing specific measures for each — say, the number of 'quality' periodical or magazine subscriptions that a home takes as an operationalisation of cultural capital and final secondary school exam results as a measure of educational attainment. At the same time, there are a myriad of other competing explanations for educational attainment. These also could be operationalised — say, a child's IQ score to indicate innate academic ability, household income to indicate the material capital of the family, a rating of the child's secondary school to indicate the effect of good versus bad teaching and so on. Information on all these factors could be taken for a large number of children and the analysis would attempt to establish whether the measures of cultural capital exert positive effects upon the children's educational attainment that are independent of all the other potential factors that might also affect educational attainment. If this proves indeed to be the case, one induces that the original theory of cultural capital promoting educational attainment is supported. If the opposite proves to be the case, that once the effects of competing explanations are taken into account, there seems to be no independent effect of cultural capital upon educational attainment, the original theory is not supported. (This hypothetical example is solely for illustrative purposes. A real study of this nature obviously would be extremely complex and require more than a paragraph to summarise.)

If the empirical approach had to be imposed upon Figure I.1, it would fall on the left-hand side of the chart only. In the empirical approach, one works straight from direct observation and, by a process of induction, moves toward generalisation and, perhaps, to a set of abstract concepts or a proto-theory.

Critiques of the positivist paradigm

The positivist paradigm of social research is subscribed to by many researchers, is presented in many research textbooks as *the* correct way of carrying out social research, and certainly acts as a model for reporting much research. Nevertheless, it has been subjected to critiques.

The 'scientific revolution' critique

Critiques of the positivist paradigm fall into two broad types. The first of these was laid out initially in Thomas Kuhn's *The Structure of Scientific Revolutions* (1962). The theory-testing approach of positivist social science research purports to have its origins in natural science practice. Kuhn, however, pointed out that the cycle of operationalisation, testing hypotheses against data, and then using the results to confirm or disconfirm theory was, at best, an 'after-the-fact' logic. If a set of observations is found to disconfirm theory, rather than the theory being rejected as the paradigm would indicate, the most likely result is that the research results will be questioned. That is, instead of the theory being rejected, the operationalisation of the concepts or the accuracy of the data generation, collection or analysis, or even the competence or veracity of the researcher, may be questioned. This reluctance to reject theory out of hand stems partly from the inherent complexity of social science research. Ensuring complete control of a social process conflicts directly with the need to maintain a natural context. In fact, a controlled experiment is usually impossible, not feasible owing to expense or time span, or unethical. Researchers have to work in natural situations and impose statistical controls that at best only mimic a true experimental design. So many parameters are left uncontrolled or fluid that a single negative result cannot be taken as grounds for the definitive rejection of a whole theory or body of concepts. To put it another way, in the event of a negative result, the researcher is more likely in the first instance to question the data and analysis rather than the theory being tested.

The reluctance to reject existing theory is, however, only partly based in methodological considerations. Existing theories are not neutral constructs. They are soundly based in scientific establishments and in the careers of the dominant academics in a given discipline. To cast doubt upon an existing theory is to threaten a discipline's academic status quo. The result, Kuhn argues, is that *political* considerations affect the dissemination and take-up of contrary research results. For example, problematic results may not appear in the mainstream journals of a discipline and their proponents may be less likely to obtain secure professional appointments. Change in dominant theoretical perspectives does take place eventually, but more by attrition than by impartial academic debate. The proponents of a new theoretical viewpoint gradually gain adherents and work in to the centre from the periphery of academic respectability. With time, the 'old guard' quite literally will die out and be supplanted by a new generation whose careers are not dependent upon outmoded conceptual views.

A concrete example of this process could be the impact of feminism upon social stratification research. Up until the beginning of the 1970s, the study of social stratification concentrated solely upon the positions of men. The situation was not so much that women were relegated to a position of secondary importance in stratification studies but rather that the position of women was completely absent from debates on stratification and that this was not even seen as an issue or problem. At that point, feminist social scientists began to develop a critique of this male bias, making points that seem obvious now: for instance, that women make up slightly more than half of the population; that most adults live as part of a couple in which their social position in a system of social stratification is determined by both partners; that both the father *and* the mother have profound effects upon as individual's social mobility; and so on. The issue was bitterly debated from the mid-1970s, beginning in peripheral, radical publications and only gradually penetrating into mainstream outlets. The conclusion that one would draw from the literature that was published is that proponents of the 'male-only' view of social stratification were able to defend their position quite effectively. Based upon a review of the published literature of that time, one would have to conclude that at best the outcome was that women are now incorporated into social stratification literature, but that both their position within that literature and their perceived significance in systems of social stratification were secondary relative to men. Despite this, a generation has turned over during the interim so that, aside from a few retrograde chauvinistic pockets of resistance, no serious student of social stratification working today would fail to treat women as having significance equal to men.

Hence, from this viewpoint, while positivist methods of concept-testing may serve to refine or secure minor modifications to existing theories, they cannot secure a profound shift in scientific paradigms. Instead, such shifts occur through social mechanisms that are essentially political in which the assessment of the scientific validity of competing arguments plays only an oblique role – changing the opinions of a younger, replacement generation.

The 'interpretive' critique

The 'scientific revolution' critique centres upon questioning the mechanisms of proof and disproof that are used to generate and refine social science conceptual systems. In contrast, the 'interpretive' critique centres upon the nature of social data, questioning whether social phenomena actually are stable and replicable. The 'interpretive' critique has its origin in qualitative social science. Its core is the assertion that social phenomena are qualitatively different in their nature from the types of phenomena studied by other scientific disciplines. Social phenomena are produced by conscious actors – human beings – and what is observed can be only the outward manifestations of inner meaningful intentions. The problems arise because we may observe *what* people do, but we can never be totally sure of the reasons *why* they do what they do. Even if we question them directly and they are willing to answer, we can be neither sure that they are capable of giving us a complete and accurate explanation of their reasoning and motivation nor can we even assume that the reasons they do provide are truthful. Any explanations that the researcher attaches to explain phenomena are in fact the researcher's own constructs and can never be considered definitive.

Furthermore, unlike inanimate objects, human beings are *conscious social actors*. People who are the objects of research can react to the experience; for example, altering their behaviour once they realise they are being observed, reacting emotionally to the person carrying out an intensive in-depth interview, or modifying their answers to a questionnaire in order to provide answers they feel are socially acceptable (or, alternatively, giving deliberately provocative responses). Hence, social phenomena must be considered inherently unreliable. This social version of the Heisenburg Uncertainty Principle means that almost all social data must be considered potentially 'contaminated' in some way by a human's subjective reactions to being the object of research.

The implication of the 'interpretive' critique is to call into question the assumption of the positivist approach that there are stable regularities existing at a level beyond that of the individual – social facts – that can be measured. While regularities may appear to have a stable existence, this may be a chimera. The phenomena being recorded may be in part solely an artefact of the research itself. The subject's reaction to being researched may be so unpredictable as to be for all intents and purposes random. What appears to be a generalisable regularity could break down at any moment.

Parallels between this general view of social research phenomena as being inherently malleable and unstable can be found with two other perspectives that provide essentially the same criticisms of a positivist approach to social research – a *postmodernist* view and a *'chaotic'* view.

Postmodernism argues that any social situation can be depicted by *multiple explanations*. Each participant can hold one, or several, different views of what is going on. Any or all of these stances may be equally correct and there is no valid means of choosing between them – nor need there be. The 'interpretive' critique of social research can be seen as a special case of this general 'postmodern' view of social reality.

Chaos theory asserts that apparently trivial events can have profound effects upon large, apparently stable, complex system and that identifying which trivial event will have an effect or what the nature of that effect will be is beyond calculation. In practical terms, chaos theory implies that a complex system can exist for a long time in an apparent state of equilibrium but that this equilibrium can break down unexpectedly at any time. Predictable relationships that appear to be stable do exist, *but their permanence is an illusion.* Since social systems are complex systems, the seemingly stable relationships that the researcher is observing and then using to validate sets of concepts can break down at any moment in a manner that cannot be anticipated by a social theory.

Assessment

We presented these critiques of the positivist perspective with some trepidation in case students were put off quantitative analysis before ever beginning. However, we concluded that it would have been remiss if we had set out quantification as a totally accepted and unchallenged viewpoint in the social sciences. The existence of criticisms of the quantitative perspective do not in themselves automatically invalidate that perspective. Many quantitative researchers would take exception to at least some of the criticisms and assert the alternative, that quantification has a legitimate and valued role to play in the social sciences that cannot be neglected. Others who work with quantitative data do take the criticisms seriously, but take them as cautions about how to make the best and most valid use of quantified information. A keen awareness of the potential effects of researchers upon the nature of the data they are collecting, instead of pointing to rejection, can lead to a more valid and realistic assessment of the findings of a quantitative analysis. As you turn to the ten very specific and detailed Modules that follow after the Orientation chapter, we hope that this brief introduction will help to set your efforts in context.

Orientation

The British Social Attitudes Survey

The British Social Attitudes (BSA) Survey was established in 1983 and is conducted annually by the National Centre for Social Research (formerly SCPR). The primary function of the survey is to measure the changing attitudes, values and beliefs of the British public across a range of subjects including crime, health, education, employment, civil liberties and moral values. (The British Social Attitudes Survey has been conducted every year since 1983, with the exception of 1988 and 1992 when core funding was devoted to conducting post-election studies of political attitudes and political behaviour in the British Election Study (BES) survey series.)

The survey is designed to yield a representative sample of adults, although for practical reasons the sample is confined to those living in private households. Since 1993, the Postcode Address File has been used as the sampling frame, whereas prior to this the sample was drawn from the electoral register. Data are weighted to take account of the fact that not all the units covered in the survey have the same probability of selection and these weights have been applied to each of the four datasets that accompany this book. For further details on the weighting procedures employed in this survey you should consult *British Social Attitudes: the 16th Report* (Jowell *et al.*, 1999).

The data that constitutes an integral part of this book is drawn from the 1998 British Social Attitudes Survey. Three different versions of the 1998 questionnaire (A, B and C) were administered and each 'module' of questions is asked either of the full sample (around 3600 respondents) or of a random two-thirds or one-third of the sample. The 1998 British Social Attitudes survey has been edited for the purposes of this book and four separate teaching datasets (centred on the topics: Crime, Health, Politics and Welfare) have been created.

The datasets

1. **The Crime dataset** focuses on a variety of topics relating to crime, moral values and sexual mores. It contains details on respondents' attitudes to issues such as pre-marital sex, abortion, religious belief and the extent of crime in their local area. The Crime dataset is used as the source for most of the examples contained in this book.
2. **The Health dataset** contains variables dealing with a wide range of health-based issues. Information is provided on respondents' attitudes to topics such as the NHS, genetic research and disability.
3. **The Politics dataset** contains a range of variables relating to political attitudes, beliefs and activity. Questions relate to local, national and European issues and the topics covered include taxation, the monarchy, electoral reform and voting behaviour.
4. **The Welfare dataset** includes a range of interesting variables relating to social welfare. Information is provided on respondents' attitudes to issues such as the Welfare State, wealth redistribution, the benefits system and unemployment.

Each dataset has been specially adapted and contains a number of common *core* variables. These core variables include basic demographic details on the respondents to the questionnaire, such

10

as age, religion, educational qualifications, social class, marital status and so on. With certain exceptions (the declaration of missing value codes, some modifications to correct coding errors and make the use of the data easier for students, and the construction of some scales for teaching purposes), the variables that make up the four teaching datasets are the same as those contained in the original 1998 British Social Attitudes dataset available to the academic public. (Note that the four datasets are intended for teaching purposes only. Researchers intending to carry out secondary analysis for publication are strongly advised to access the original BSA data.)

Additional information on all the variables in the four datasets can be found in the three Appendixes at the end of the workbook. These should allow the reader to carry out informed analyses of the data with minimal supervision.

Obtaining the practice datasets

As you can see, the four practice datasets taken from the BSA Survey are an important feature of this book. You will need to have them on your computer before you begin to work your way through the modules and exercises in the textbook. You obtain the datasets by downloading them directly from the Palgrave web site located at ⟨http//:www.palgrave.com/ sociology/miller⟩. Detailed instructions for downloading the data are given on this website.

Alternatively, the instructor on your course may already have obtained the datasets and set them up for student use. If so, your instructor will tell you how to access the datasets at your institution.[1]

Introduction to the workbook

This workbook has been designed as a step-by-step guide to data analysis using SPSS. It comprises two introductory chapters and ten substantive modules which together serve to acquaint the reader with the key aspects of statistical analysis and data modification using SPSS. We began by examining the main features of the 'quantitative perspective' and considered some of the strengths (and weaknesses) of this approach to social research. The current chapter adopts a much sharper focus. Its main purpose is to provide a brief introduction to some of the basic features of SPSS and the Windows environment within which this version of SPSS operates. Subsequent chapters fit into a modular structure and take the reader through the various stages of quantitative analysis using SPSS, including data input, data modification, data exploration and statistical testing. The general pattern is for each module to focus on a single statistical procedure, beginning with an explanation of its underlying logic. This is followed by step-by-step instructions for the successful execution of the procedure using SPSS, and the resulting SPSS output is reproduced in the form of tables or charts and carefully analysed and explained. This structure should enable students to complete the modules successfully with minimum supervision. An Exercise or Exercises at the end of each chapter will help to consolidate learning.

---

[1] Instructors wishing to download the datasets and install them on systems within their institutions for the use of students who are using this textbook have our permission to do so. This may be the most practical way of providing the datasets when student access to computing facilities and SPSS is through a central server.

Introduction to SPSS for Windows

This workbook is based upon the personal computer version of SPSS, SPSS for Windows. One of the advantages of using the Windows version of SPSS is that many of the features will be familiar to users of other programs which operate in a Windows environment, such as the wordprocessing package Word for Windows or the spreadsheet package Excel for Windows.

SPSS is a computer software package that is specifically designed to perform statistical operations and facilitate data analysis and is by far the most popular statistical package used by social scientists. It is worth pointing out at this stage that one of the best sources of information and help about SPSS and its various functions is literally at your fingertips, and can be accessed through the comprehensive **Help menu** within the SPSS program. Some of the important features of this Help menu include:

The Online Tutorial

This provides a good introduction to the program and adopts a clear step-by-step approach to the various features of SPSS.

The Statistics Coach

This provides some basic assistance with many of the statistical procedures available in SPSS. For more detailed statistical explanations you are advised to consult the SPSS applications guide or any good introductory statistics text.

The Contextual Help System

This provides information on specific features of SPSS. Pointing the mouse at the specific particular feature or control you want to know more about and clicking the right mouse key activates this help facility.

Getting started on SPSS

The SPSS program (assuming, of course, that it is installed on your computer) is accessed by clicking on the **Start** button situated on the bottom left-hand side of the computer screen and selecting **SPSS for Windows** from the **Programs** menu.

(You should note that the menu system may be configured slightly differently on the computer you are using and therefore the location of SPSS may not be identical to that illustrated in Figure O.1a.)

This will start SPSS (the SPSS icon will appear in the Windows **Task bar** at the bottom of the screen) and the **Data Editor** window will open up automatically.

Once opened, there are a number of ways to begin using the SPSS package. The opening dialog box (shown in Figure O.1b) offers five options and you can proceed by clicking on the required option button and then on **OK**.

Figure O.1a   Starting SPSS

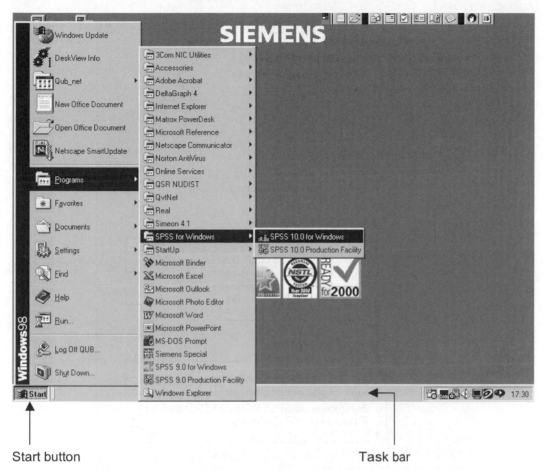

Start button   Task bar

It is worth pointing out that this dialog box may not always appear when you open SPSS (for example, if the previous user has clicked on the **'Don't show this dialog box in the future'** option). Fortunately, all of the options available in the opening dialog box can be accessed through the SPSS menu system.

The opening dialog box can also be removed by clicking on **Cancel** and, as we want to take a closer look at the Data Editor window, you can do this now.

The Data Editor window is blank at this stage and contains no data (see Figure O.2). You will need to become familiar with the window in Figure O.2 if you are to navigate around SPSS successfully. Some of its main features are explained below.

(1) The Title bar

The top section of the window is known as the **Title bar** and by clicking and dragging on this you can reposition the window anywhere on the screen. On the right-hand side of the Title bar are three small squares:

Figure O.1b SPSS for Windows 'opening dialog box'

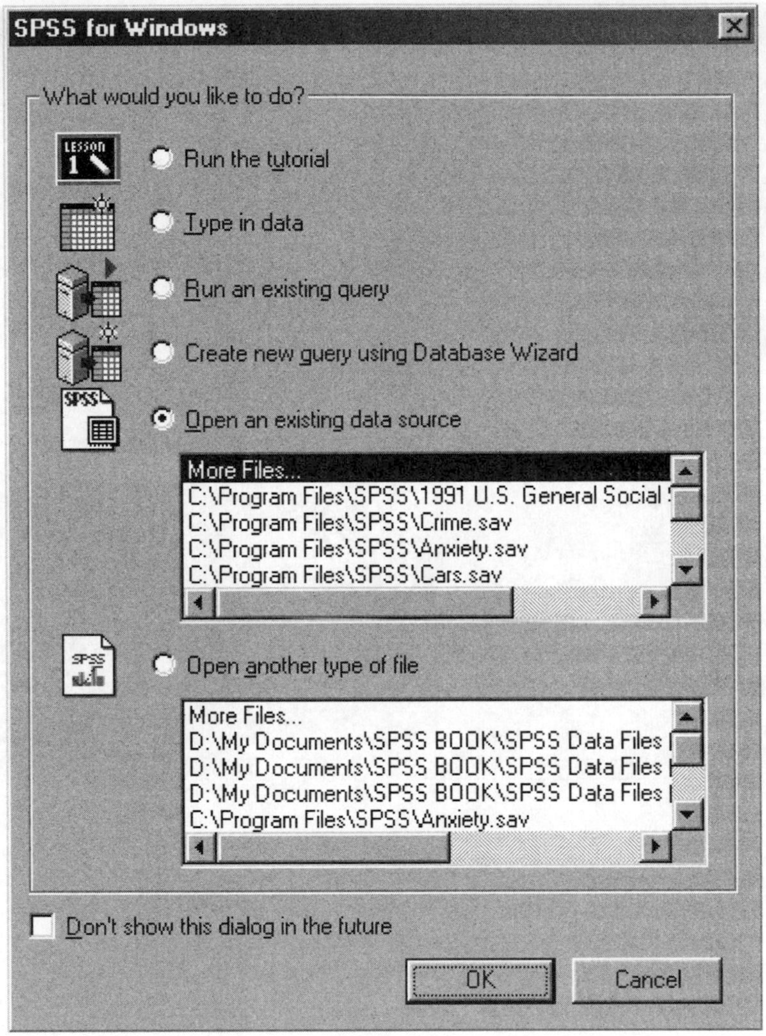

❑ The first is the **Minimize** button and clicking on this reduces the window to an icon in the Windows **Task bar** at the bottom of the screen. Try this, but don't panic when the window disappears. This window is still open and you simply click on the SPSS icon in the Windows **Task bar** to restore it to its original size.

❑ The second square represents the **Maximize** button and if you click on this the Data Editor window will fill the screen. To restore the window to its original size click on this button again.

❑ Clicking on the third square in the top right hand corner of the Data Editor window closes the SPSS program down altogether. If you have made any changes to the dataset or produced any output you will be asked if you want to **Save** them (there will be more on saving SPSS files later in this chapter).

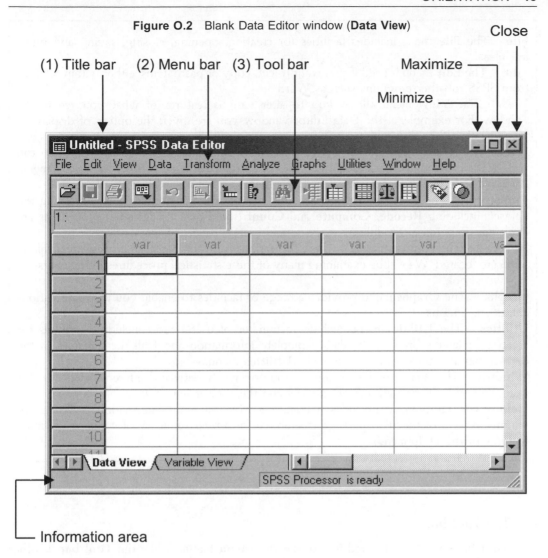

Figure O.2 Blank Data Editor window (**Data View**)

(1) Title bar   (2) Menu bar   (3) Tool bar

Close

Maximize

Minimize

Information area

You can also resize the Data Editor window by clicking and dragging the sides or the corners of the window.

(2) The Menu bar

Underneath the **Title bar** you will find the **Menu bar** which is the primary means of getting SPSS to carry out the tasks you require.

As can be seen from Figure O.2, the **Menu bar** contains ten broad menu headings, beginning with **File** and ending with **Help**. If you click the mouse on any of these headings a variety of options relating to this topic will appear in a drop-down menu. Figure O.3, for instance (p. 17), displays the **Edit** drop-down menu. To get rid of the drop-down menu simply click anywhere outside it.

A brief summary of some of the main functions associated with each of these ten menus is appropriate at this stage.

File – The **File** menu includes facilities for creating, opening, closing, saving and printing files.

Edit – The **Edit** menu is used if you want to cut, copy or paste items, either within SPSS or from SPSS to other programs such as Word.

View – The **View** menu allows you to alter various features of what you see in the window. For example, in the Data Editor window you are given the option of displaying value labels rather than number codes or removing grid lines.

Data – The **Data** menu allows you to manipulate the dataset in various ways. You can weight the dataset, insert additional variables or merge two datasets together via this menu. Also available in this menu is the facility for selecting out a subset of the data.

Transform – The **Transform** menu contains facilities for transforming and modifying the dataset, including **Recode**, **Compute** and **Count** (these data modification procedures are explained in detail in Module 3).

Analyze – The **Analyze** menu is where the various forms of statistical analysis available in SPSS are located. We will be examining many of these statistical procedures in the course of this workbook.

Graphs – The **Graphs** menu provides a range of facilities to enable you to create various charts and graphs.

Utilities – The **Utilities** menu includes a number of useful tools including facilities for creating smaller subsets of the data. Complete information about all the variables in the dataset can also be accessed through the **Utilities** menu.

Window – The **Window** menu allows you to switch between different windows (for example between the Data Editor window and the Viewer window).

Help – The **Help** menu provides a comprehensive range of information and help on various aspects of the SPSS package (see above for a brief summary of some of the main features of the **Help** menu).

(3) The Tool bar

The **Tool bar** in SPSS is located just below the **Menu bar** and, like the **Tool bar** in other Windows-based applications, provides a number of shortcuts for commonly used procedures or tasks. For instance, the first three icons in the Data Editor **Tool bar** perform the functions of opening a file, saving a file and printing a file. If you place the mouse pointer on any of the icons in the **Tool bar** a brief description of the function it performs will appear directly underneath the icon (and also in the information area at the bottom left-hand side of the screen). *Do not click the mouse unless you want to carry out the procedure in question!*

Some minor adjustments to SPSS

Before we proceed any further there are a couple of changes that we recommend you make to the *default options* in SPSS. You will find that resetting these options has two main advantages: (1) variables will be much easier to locate; (2) the results of your analysis will be labelled more fully. Moreover, you should find this workbook easier to follow if your SPSS settings are identical to ours.

Resetting variable lists

Before you carry out any kind of analysis in SPSS you need to select the *variables you are interested* in from a list of all the variables in your dataset. This selection process is much easier if the variables are displayed *alphabetically*, using *variable names* rather than variable labels. However, in order to achieve this we need to change the **Variable Lists** default options.

Click on **Edit** to open up the **Edit** drop-down menu (see Figure O.3) and select **Options** by clicking on it.

Figure O.3 **Edit** drop-down menu

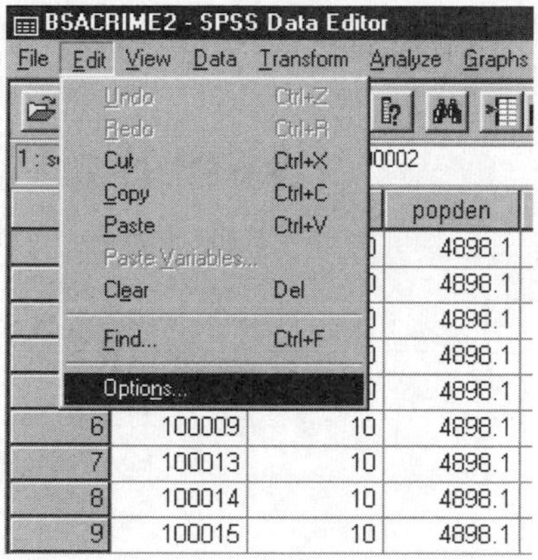

This will open up the **Options** dialog box shown in Figure O.4. Click on the **General** tab to ensure that the **Variable Lists** options are displayed and then select **Alphabetical** and **Display names** by clicking on them. Finally click on **OK**.

These changes will be implemented the next time you open a data file (this is covered in the following section, 'Loading a Data File') and their effect can be observed in Figure O.9 (p. 22). You will notice in Figure O.9 that *variable names*, rather than variable labels, appear in the variable list and that this is ordered *alphabetically* (see Module 1 for more details on the distinction between variable names and variable labels).

Resetting output labels

The second change we want to make to the SPSS default settings relates to the *output* or *results* of our analysis. In general, we want our results to contain as much information as possible about the variables we used. We therefore need to change the output settings in SPSS so that our output includes the variable names and labels and also the *category codes* (values) and their labels.

Click on **Edit** to open up the **Edit** drop-down menu (see Figure O.3 again) and select **Options** as before.

This time, however, we need to click on the **Output Labels** tab in the **Options** dialog box and then change the settings in the four boxes to either **Names and Labels** or **Values and Labels** (see Figure O.5).

These adjustments to the output labels will take effect immediately, and when you come to produce your first frequency table (see Module 2) your output should contain not just the

Figure O.4   Edit   Options: General dialog box

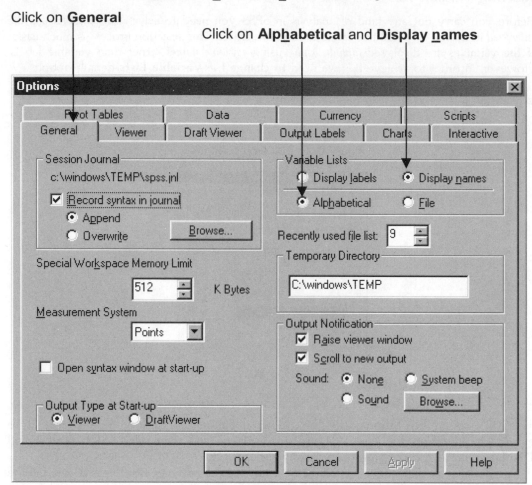

Click on **General**

Click on **Alphabetical** and **Display names**

variable names and category codes, but also a description of what these represent (i.e. variable and value labels).

Loading a data file

So far we have been looking at a Data Editor window which contains no data! There are two main ways of rectifying this situation. The first is to create a data file by inputting your own data (this process will be examined in detail in Module 1), while the alternative option is to open a previously created SPSS data file. Here we will go through the steps for opening an already existing SPSS data file, the Crime dataset.

First, click on **File** from the Menu bar and then on **Open** from the drop-down menu that appears (see Figure O.6). This will give you the option of opening different types of files. As we want to open a data file, click on **Data**.

Figure O.5 <u>E</u>dit: Option<u>s</u>: Output Labels dialog box

Click on **Output Labels**

Select **Names and Labels/ Values and Labels**

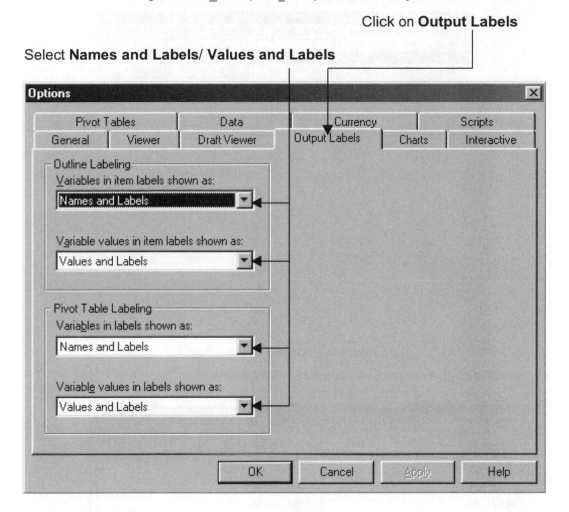

This will bring up the **Open File** dialog box (see Figure O.7). You now need to select the appropriate location of the SPSS file you wish to open (the relevant *drive* and *folder*).

For example, I have saved the British Social Attitudes **Crime** dataset (**BSACrime**) in a folder entitled SPSS. To open this dataset I simply locate the SPSS folder and double click on **BSACrime**, as illustrated in Figure O.7.

After a few moments the Data Editor window will reappear, but this time complete with the **Crime** data from the British Social Attitudes Survey (see Figure O.8). It is important to note that the Data Editor provides two different views of the data, the **Data View** and the **Variable View**. The Data View displays the actual data values (or value labels) in a spreadsheet format, while the Variable View displays variable information including variable and value labels, level of measurement and missing values (see Module 1 for more details on these). You can switch between these two views by clicking the **Data View** and **Variable View** buttons at the bottom left-hand corner of the screen (see Figure O.8).

Figure O.6 Opening a data file

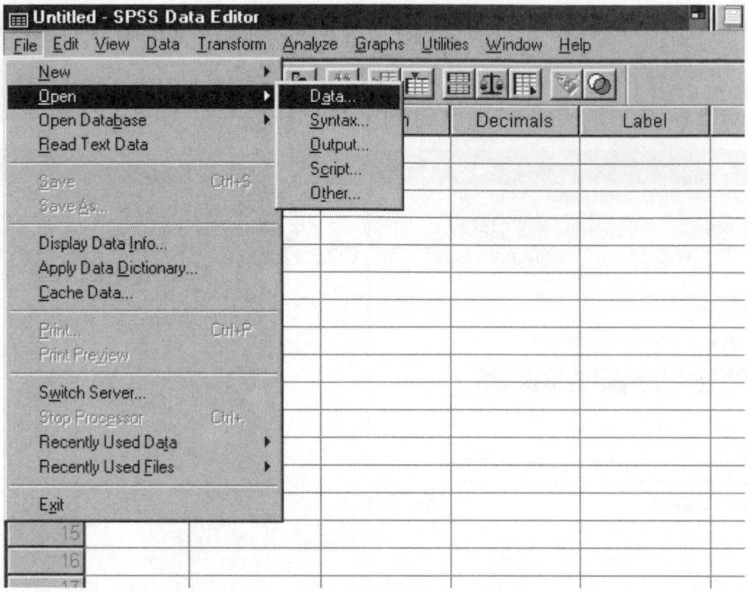

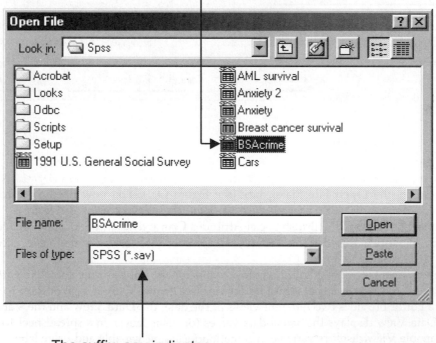

Figure O.7 **Open File** dialog box

Double click to open SPSS data file, **BSAcrime**

The suffix **.sav** indicates
that this is an SPSS **data** file

Figure O.8 Data Editor window

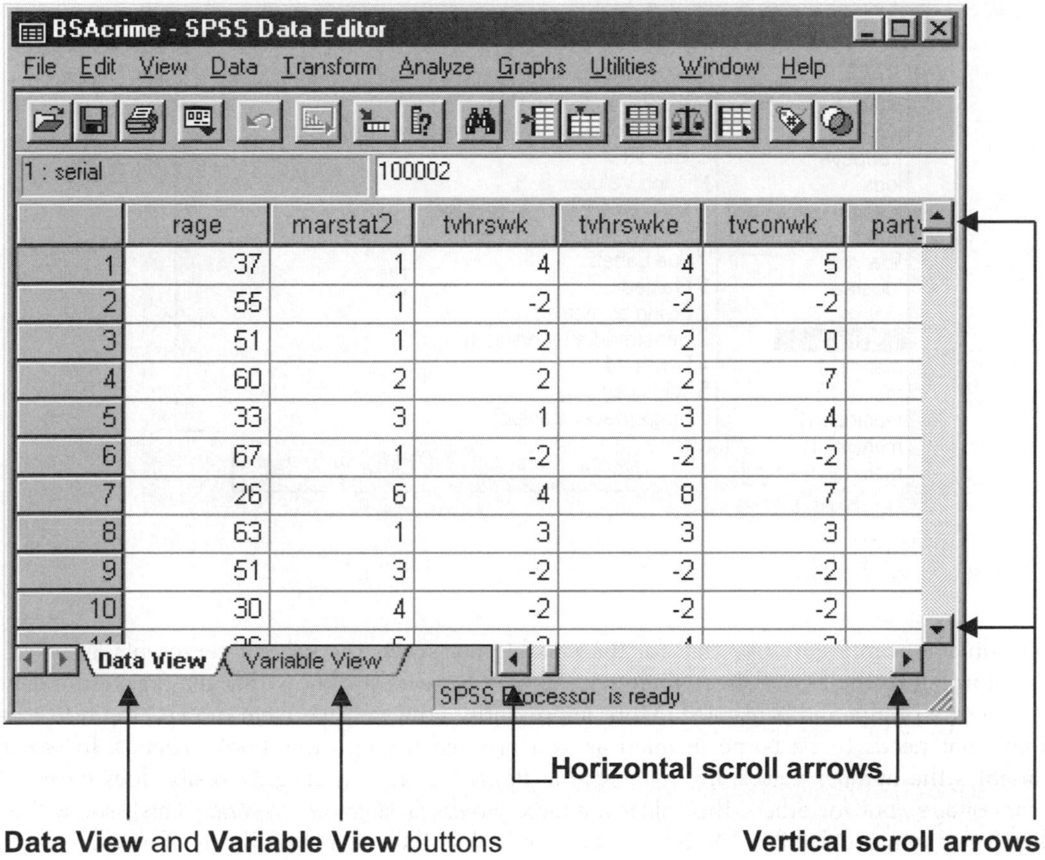

If you are not currently in Data View, click on the **Data View** button now. You will see that the data grid is now full of numbers (referred to as *values*) which represent the various responses to the survey questions. A different column is allocated to each variable and a separate row for each case (respondent). As there is far too much information for it all to fit on the screen, we can use the **vertical scroll arrows** to scroll up or down through the cases and the **horizontal scroll arrows** to scroll back and forward through the different variables.

If we look at the first column in Figure O.8, for instance, we can see that it is labelled **rage** (this is a variable that provides us with information on the respondents' age). The first cell in the grid (where the first row and the first column intersect) contains the number 37, which informs us that the first respondent is aged 37. Moving down the first column, we can see that the second respondent is aged 55, the third 51, the fourth 60 and so on.

However, if we look at the cell immediately to the right of the first cell, we see the number 1, which tells us that the first respondent has been allocated a value of 1 on the variable **marstat2** (respondent's marital status). To find out exactly what this means, click on **Utilities** in the Menu bar and then on **Variables**. This will open up the **Variables** dialog box shown in Figure O.9. Click on **marstat2** in the variable list and information on **marstat2** will appear in the right-hand box.

Figure O.9   Variables dialog box

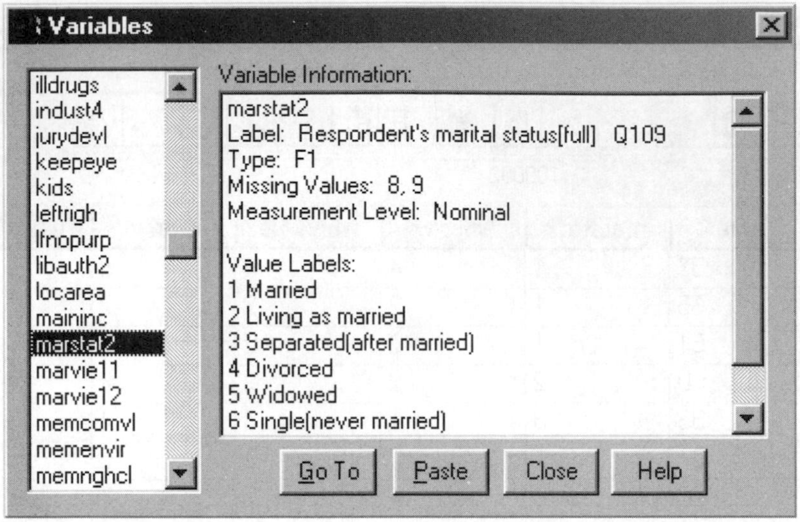

We can see from Figure O.9 that for the variable **marstat2**, the value 1 represents 'Married'.

Returning to the Data Editor window in Figure O.8, we now know that the first respondent is 37 years of age and is married. More importantly, however, we have drawn attention to a point that needs to be borne in mind as you proceed through this book. That is, for some variables the number values are *meaningful in themselves* (for instance 37 really does mean 37 years of age), but for others, the values are merely *codes for different categories*. This issue will be developed in more detail in Module 2 when we look at the concept of 'levels of measurement'.

It is worth noting at this point, however, that SPSS provides a facility for displaying value labels (rather than the actual values themselves) in the Data Editor Window.

Click on **View** in the Menu bar and then click on **Value Labels** in the drop-down menu. As you can see from Figure O.10, the values have now been replaced by *labels*. So, for instance, on the variable **marstat2** the word 'Married' replaces the value 1, 'Living as married' replaces the value 2, and so on. You will also notice that some variables (**rage**, for example) remain unchanged. Because the values for these 'quantitative' variables are meaningful in themselves there is no need for value labels.

You can also 'switch' the value labels 'on' or 'off' by clicking on the **Value Labels** icon in the tool bar.

The Viewer window

When you begin any kind of statistical analysis in SPSS a second window, the Viewer window, opens up. This is where all the *output* from your analysis is located (all the tables and charts you ask SPSS to produce). The information in the Viewer window reproduced in Figure O.11 is the outcome of a request that SPSS produce a frequency table and a bar chart for the variable **rsex** (detailed instructions on how to get SPSS to produce frequency tables and various charts will be given in Module 2). As you can see from Figure O.11, the top part of this window is almost

Figure O.10 Data Editor window with **Value Labels** displayed

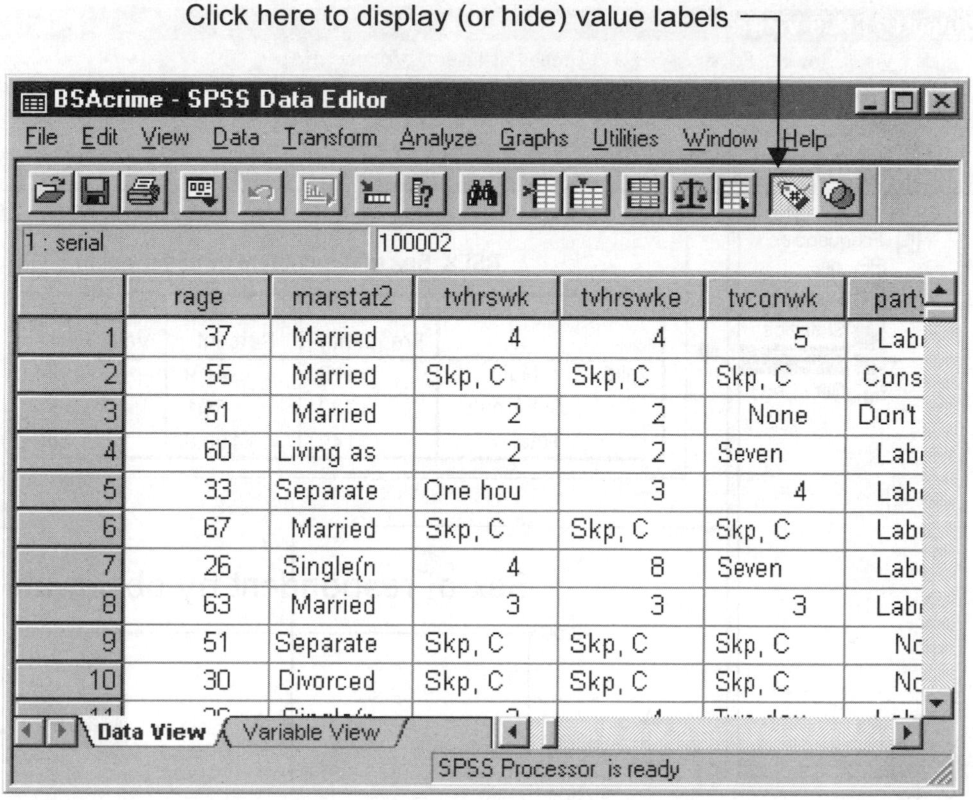

Click here to display (or hide) value labels ⎤

	rage	marstat2	tvhrswk	tvhrswke	tvconwk	part
1	37	Married	4	4	5	Lab
2	55	Married	Skp, C	Skp, C	Skp, C	Cons
3	51	Married	2	2	None	Don't
4	60	Living as	2	2	Seven	Lab
5	33	Separate	One hou	3	4	Lab
6	67	Married	Skp, C	Skp, C	Skp, C	Lab
7	26	Single(n	4	8	Seven	Lab
8	63	Married	3	3	3	Lab
9	51	Separate	Skp, C	Skp, C	Skp, C	Nc
10	30	Divorced	Skp, C	Skp, C	Skp, C	Nc

identical to the Data Editor window, while the bottom part is divided into two sections or **panes**. The left-hand pane is known as the *outline* pane and this contains an outline view or summary of all the items that are included in the Viewer Window. The right-hand pane is the *display* pane (sometimes referred to as the *contents* pane) and contains the output itself, although only part of this output is visible at any one time. To gain a better understanding of how the Viewer Window operates we need to examine Figure O.11 in a bit more detail.

The outline pane contains a number of icons, the first of which is labelled **Output**. This is the container for all the output in the Viewer Window and if you double click on this icon the entire output disappears (double click on it again and it returns).

The second icon in the outline pane in Figure O.11 is labelled **Frequencies** and this refers to the statistical procedure we requested SPSS to carry out. All the other icons in the outline pane are represented by *book symbols* and relate to the different parts of the output which appear in the display pane. The first of these book symbols is labelled **Title** and simply refers to the title of the output. This is not visible in the Display pane in Figure O.11 because the output has been scrolled down to the middle of the table. The icon below this is entitled **Notes** and refers to technical information associated with the procedure. Such information is usually hidden from view and the *closed book symbol* confirms this. Double clicking on a closed book symbol reveals the information (the output appears in the display pane) and double clicking on an open book

Figure O.11 Viewer window

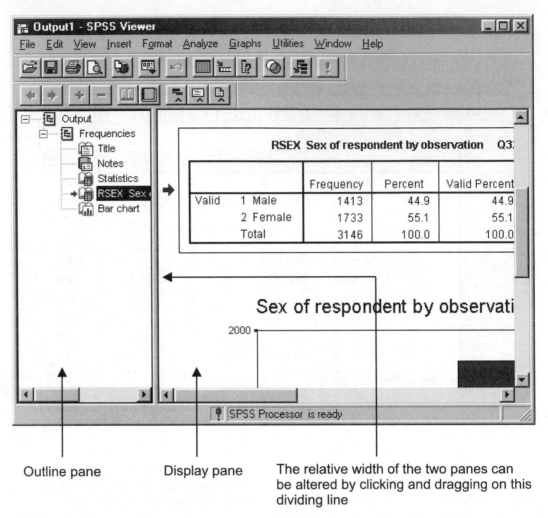

Outline pane   Display pane   The relative width of the two panes can
be altered by clicking and dragging on this
dividing line

symbol conceals it. The next icon is labelled **Statistics** and refers to a table which reports the number of cases produced by the **Frequency** procedure we carried out on the variable **rsex**. Although represented by an open book icon, this table is not visible in Figure O.11 because the output has been scrolled down past it.

The fourth book icon in the outline pane is labelled **RSEX** which represents the actual frequency table for the variable **rsex**. The arrow to the side of this icon (and the fact that **RSEX** is highlighted) indicates that the output associated with it is currently the focus of the display pane. Clicking on any of the other book icons will shift the focus of the display screen to their associated output. The different elements of a frequency table will be examined in detail in Module 2. The final icon in the outline pane represents the bar chart for **rsex** and the top of this chart is just visible in the display window shown in Figure O.11.

Saving to a disk

One of the most important things you will need to know before you begin analysing data is how to *save* SPSS files. While there are many different types of SPSS files, the two you are most likely to want to save are *data files* and *output files*. If you are using SPSS in a centralised computer facility you may not be able to save onto the hard drive or server and should therefore ensure that you have a formatted floppy disk before you begin.

Saving the data file

Under normal circumstances you will not need to save the data file. This is automatically saved in its original form when you exit from SPSS. However, if you have made any *modifications* to the data file you may want to save these for later use (see Module 3 for examples of the kinds of modifications that SPSS allows you to perform on the data).

To protect the original version of the data you should save the modified version under a different name. The procedures for saving a data file onto a floppy disk are as follows.

Ensure that the Data Editor window is the active window (that is, it should be the front window on the screen and you should be able to see the data grid unobstructed). Then click on **File** in the Menu bar and on **Save As** in the drop-down menu (see Figure O.12).

This will open up the **Save Data As** dialog box shown in Figure O.13.

To save to a floppy disk you need to change to the A:drive. Click the downward arrow to the right of the **Save in** box to access the different drives and then select the A:drive by clicking on **3½ Floppy [A:]**. All that remains to do now is to give your data file a name (MYDATAFILE, for example) and click on **Save**.

Figure O.12 Saving a data file

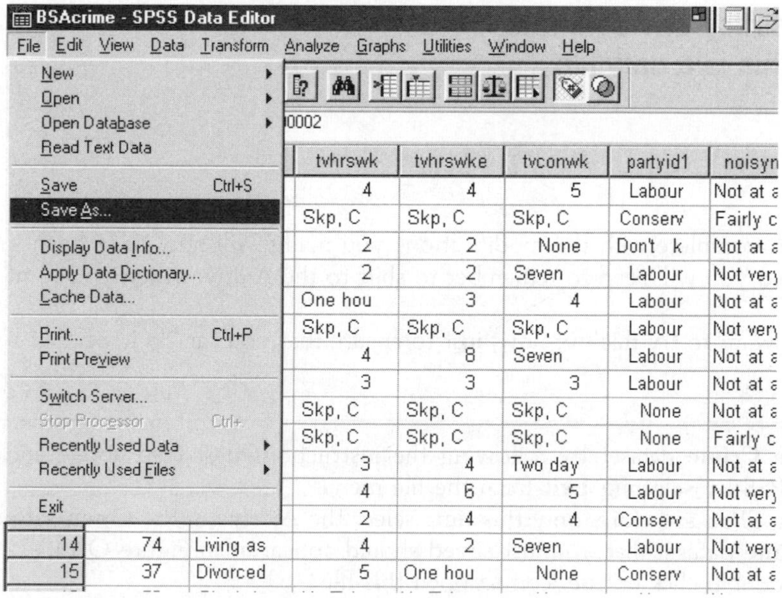

Figure O.13 Save Data As dialog box

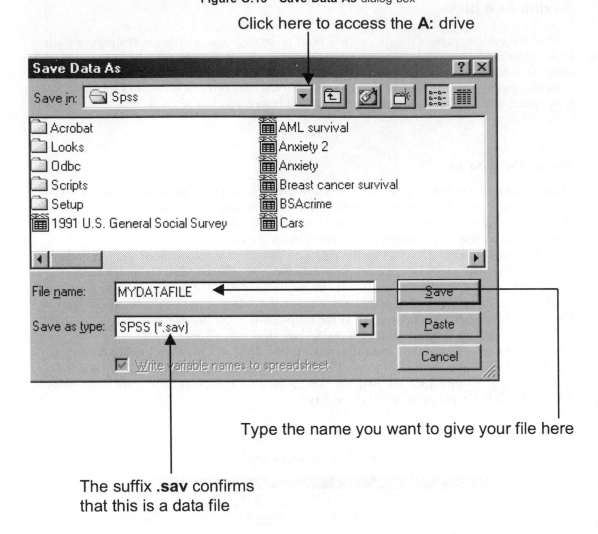

Click here to access the **A:** drive

Type the name you want to give your file here

The suffix **.sav** confirms
that this is a data file

The data set, complete with the modifications you made, will now have been saved to your floppy disk so you will need to remember to shift to the **A:**drive when you want to open this file again.

You may want to try this out now, just to ensure that you can do it when it really matters.

- Save the **Crime** dataset by following the instructions described above and then close down SPSS by selecting **Exit** from the file menu.
- Open up SPSS as before, only this time select the A:drive in the **Open File** dialog box. The **Crime** dataset that you just saved should appear as in Figure O.14.
- Simply double click on the icon to open this file.

Figure O.14 Open File dialog box

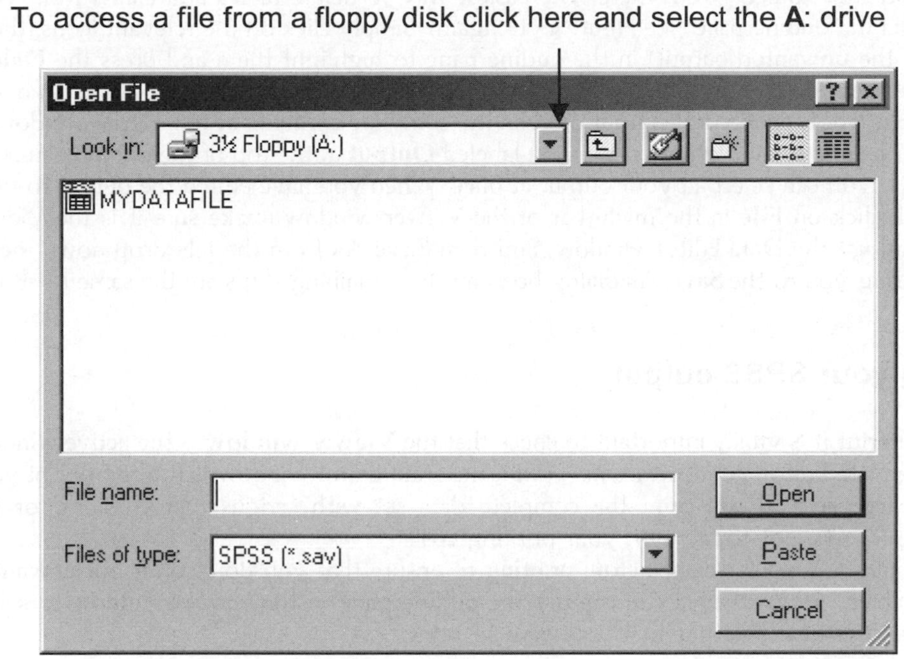

To access a file from a floppy disk click here and select the **A**: drive

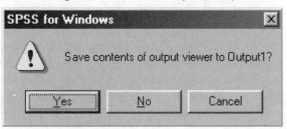

Saving your output file

Saving output when you exit SPSS

In addition to saving the SPSS data file you may also want to save the *results* of your SPSS analysis (the various tables and charts that you produce during a session). If you have produced any output at all during a session, SPSS will produce the prompt in Figure O.15 when you go to close down the program:

Figure O.15 Save output prompt

- Click **Yes** to open up the **Save As** dialog box. This is almost identical to the **Save Data As** dialog box (see Figure O.13) and the same procedures are followed to save the output file. So you need to change to the **A**:drive, give the output file a name, and click on **Save**.
- Saving your output in this way means that all the output that appears in the Viewer Window will be saved.

If you want to be more selective you can edit out the unwanted tables or charts in the Viewer window and save directly from there. The easiest way to delete tables and charts from your output is via the outline pane (see Figure O.11 again). Simply click on the relevant icons (those relating to the unwanted output) in the outline pane to highlight them and press the **Delete** key on your keyboard. Note that by clicking on the appropriate icons in the outline pane you can highlight whole sections of output or even the complete contents of the output window in one go. For example, by clicking on the icon labeled **Output** at the top of the outline pane (see Figure O.11) you can select all your output at once. When you have edited the output to your satisfaction, click on **File** in the menu bar of the Viewer window (make sure it is the Viewer window and *not* the Data Editor window) and then **Save As** from the File drop-down menu. This will bring you to the **Save As** dialog box and the remaining steps are the same as above.

Printing your SPSS output

Before you print it is vitally important to check that the **Viewer window** is the active window and *not* the Data Editor Window. *Do not print* if the Data Editor window is to the front of your screen. Otherwise you will print the complete data set with serious repercussions for the world's rainforests, not to mention your printing costs!

You should edit your output before printing to ensure that you don't print out unwanted charts or tables. Alternatively, you can use the outline pane of the Viewer window to select only those parts of the output that you want to print.

Figure O.16   Print dialog box

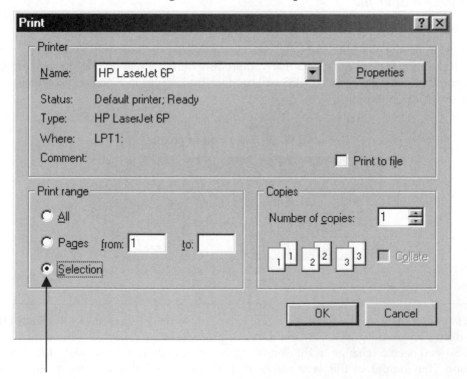

Selection button

To print, click on **File** in the menu bar of the Viewer window and then select **Print** from the File drop-down menu. The **Print** dialog box (shown in Figure O.16) will then open up.

If you have used the outline pane to select only part of the total output, the **Selection** button will be highlighted (as in Figure O.16). If you click **OK** now, only that part of the output that you selected will be printed. However, if you didn't make a selection the **All visible output** button will be highlighted and clicking **OK** will result in all the output in the display pane being printed.

Finally, if you are using a centralised computing facility a 'queue' may develop as print jobs 'stack up' (especially if several users are trying to print their SPSS output at once). Print jobs can also 'stack up' if the printer is temporarily off-line or if it runs out of paper. If your output doesn't appear immediately, check to see if your output is waiting to be printed *before* resubmitting a **Print** command as every time you do this you are requesting another copy of the output!

Now that you are familiar with some of the basic features of SPSS you should be in a position to begin the first module of this workbook, which deals with the important task of inputting data.

1 Data Input

Raw data can come in a variety of sources. One of the most common data collection methods is *social surveys* which can be administered using formal interview schedules or self-completion questionnaires such as the example in Appendix 1 (p. 57). Other forms of data collection are *proforma* that are filled out (for example, job or college applications) and *personal records* (for example, a company's personnel records, medical records or academic transcripts). The possible sources of data can be almost infinite, depending upon circumstances and the ability of the researcher to recognise a source of good data when it presents itself.

In data input to SPSS, the task is to take the information which has been collected (*raw data*), organise it and move it to a working SPSS datafile.

The process of inputting data can be broken into three stages.

- *Coding*
- The mechanics of *transferring* coded information into a SPSS file
- *Configuring* the data within SPSS.

Cases and variables

For a computer package to be able to receive information in the form of data; these data must be put into a regular, predictable format.

A complete individual record is usually called a *case*. A short questionnaire is provided in Appendix 1 at the end of this module. You will need to complete this *now*, as it will form the basis of much of the explanation that will follow. Once you have completed it, *you* become a *case* and your responses to this questionnaire make up a single complete *record*. Each other person who answers the questionnaire would also become a case in the data. (You may find in some manuals that the words 'record' or 'observation' are sometimes used in the place of 'case'.)

Cases, such as survey respondents, personnel records or medical files, often correspond to individual people. Cases, however, can also refer to *organisations* or *timespans*. For instance, in household survey, the information obtained relates to the entire household rather than to individuals within the house. In this instance the case would be the household, not the individual. It is also possible to have, for example, a database of hospitals (where each case is the information held on a complete hospital) or a geographically based dataset (where information on complete cities makes up the cases). A historian might have a database where the cases are timespans — say, decades. The point is that, in each instance, the case is the information recorded on a single unit of analysis.

For each *Case*, the specific bits of information recorded for the case are called *Variables*. In the 'Drinking questionnaire' (Appendix 1), each separate answer you gave is a response to a **variable** in the dataset. For instance, **age**, where you said you are __X__ years old is a variable; and your response to Question 5, where you said you *never drink alcohol/drink rarely/drink moderately/drink frequently/drink heavily* is another variable. Your particular answers to these questions are the *values* that these variables have for you. A different person answering the questionnaire would give responses to the same questions/variables but their values for those variables could be different. For instance their name, age, faculty and drinking habits could be different from yours.

Here are two additional examples.

> - A medical admission being the *case*, with *variables* being things like the cause of admission, the GP who attended, etc.
> - If a household was the *case*, *variables* could be things like the number of people living in the house, tenure of housing, household income, the type of heating in the house, etc.

These concepts (cases, variables and values) are fundamental for any kind of data analysis. Think about them one more time, and make sure you understand how they relate to one another. The questions you ask, or the types of information you record, are variables. Each individual answer or piece of information is a value. The people or things you test in the study are cases ... For each case, you have one value for each variable. (Norusis, 1988, p. 61)

'Rectangular' format

Computers keep track of the bits of information on cases by always having a variable's information (*codings*) appear in the same location. For most datasets, the data usually appear in what we can call a 'grid' of *cases* by *variables*. Each *case*, or record, makes up one complete 'line' of data and the *variables* appear as columns. We can show how this would look for the answers some other people gave to the 'Drinking questionnnaire' (Figure 1.1)

Figure 1.1 Responses to the 'Drinking questionnaire' in grid format

001	Robert	1	45	1	3	1	8	3	3	2	30.33
002	Margaret	2	23	2	1	1	2	2	0	0	0.00
003	Fred	1	52	3	2	1	2	0	2	1	4.55
004	Paddy	1	36	5	3	1	16	6	10	0	15.45

Robert's responses to the questionnaire are presented in a row format. Each respondent is given a unique *identifier*. Robert for example has been allocated 001, and Margaret has been allocated 002. The third column contains details of the respondent's gender. The first case, Robert, is male which has the value 1, and the second respondent, Margaret, is female which has the value 2.

All cases reserve 'space' for each variable. In responding to the questionnaire, respondents may not answer all the questions, thus some information may be *missing* for some variables. For example, someone answering the 'Drinking questionnaire' may not be able to remember how much they spent on alcohol last weekend or might refuse to tell how much they drank. It is important to record this data as *missing*. In some instances it may be that the question is *not relevant*. For example, if the respondent did not drink alcohol during the previous weekend (Question 6) they did not need to complete Questions 7 and 8 about types of alcohol consumed and the amount spent. In this instance a 'not relevant' code might be used for Questions 7 and 8. (We will return to this below.)

Exercise

As an exercise, try transferring *your* responses to the questionnaire on to 'line 005' of the grid in Figure 1.1.

Inputting data into SPSS

It is possible to input data into SPSS in a number of ways. Since the SPSS 'data grid' is in the form of a spreadsheet, the normal conventions for using a spreadsheet apply. This means that data can be brought into SPSS in one of four ways:

1. Imported from SPSS on another computer as an *SPSS Portable file* (**.por*)
2. Imported from *database spreadsheets* (for example, Excel, dBase, Foxpro, Access)
3. Imported from *text files* (ascii files)
4. Entered directly onto the *SPSS Data Editor* window.

Option 1: importing an SPSS portable file

Often we will want to transfer a SPSS data file from one computer to another. This is accomplished by putting the data file that is to be transferred into a special form – a *SPSS*

Figure 1.2a Importing a SPSS portable file (**BSACrime**) using **File Open Data**

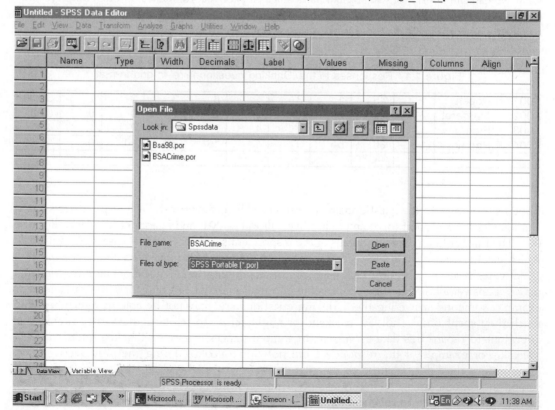

portable file. The data is read from the portable file and immediately saved as a normal SPSS data file. (The reason we do this is that the 'internal architecture' of computers can differ and there is no guarantee that a SPSS data file that works fine on one computer will always work automatically on another.) Below, we have an example of importing the BSA **Crime** dataset. (Note that before you begin, you already have to have downloaded the SPSS portable file for the **Crime** dataset from the Palgrave web site onto the hard disk of your computer. Instructions on how to do this are given at the Palgrave web site ⟨http//:www.palgrave.com/sociology/miller⟩ and in the Appendix to the Orientation chapter, p. 30.)

Click on the **File** menu, then on **Open** and then choose **Data**... A window like that in Figure 1.2a will open up. Go to the '**Look in**' box in the *Open File* window and select the folder on your hard disk where you have saved the BSACrime portable file. (In our example the name of the folder is *'Spssdata'*.) Open the 'pull down' menu for '**Files of type**', scroll down and select '**SPSS portable [*.por]**'. Now, highlight the file named *'BSACrime.por'* (it may be the only *.por file appearing on your computer screen). The file's name should appear in '**File name**' box. Now, click on the '**Open**' button and the data for the Crime dataset should fill the data grid.

You now need to save the imported data as a normal SPSS data file. It is quite easy to do this: click on the **File** menu again and then on **Save As**... A window like that in Figure 1.2b should appear. Click on the '**Save**' button and the data grid will be saved as a normal SPSS data file (*BSACrime.sav*). Later on, when you want to analyse the Crime dataset, you always will call up the SPSS *.sav file, *BSACrime.sav.*

Figure 1.2b   Saving an imported SPSS portable file (**BSACrime**) as a SPSS*.**sav** file

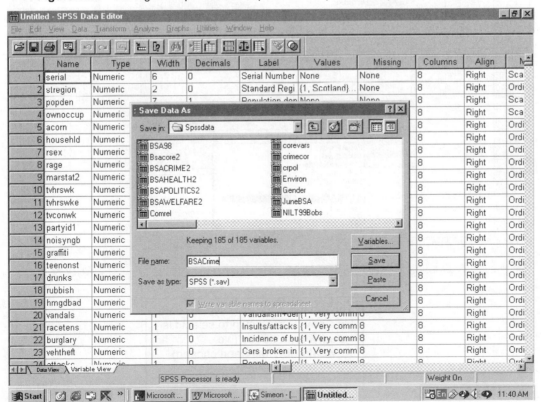

Option 2: importing data from spreadsheets

Those of you that have used a spreadsheet package probably will have noticed that the SPSS 'grid' which consists of rows of 'cases' and 'columns' of variables corresponds to the way a spreadsheet configures data. Spreadsheet users sometimes find that a convenient way to input data into SPSS is to type the data into your favourite spreadsheet programme and then import the data to SPSS. SPSS has facilities for handling data from the more commonly-used spreadsheets. It is possible to use the **File Open** option to import a spreadsheet file. Click on the **File** menu, then on **Open** and then choose **Data**. A window like that in Figure 1.2c will open up. Select the location and scroll down to select appropriate file type, then click **OK**. Here, we have selected a dBase file called *'Newdata.dbf'*.

Figure 1.2c   Importing files from other spreadsheets using **File Open Data**

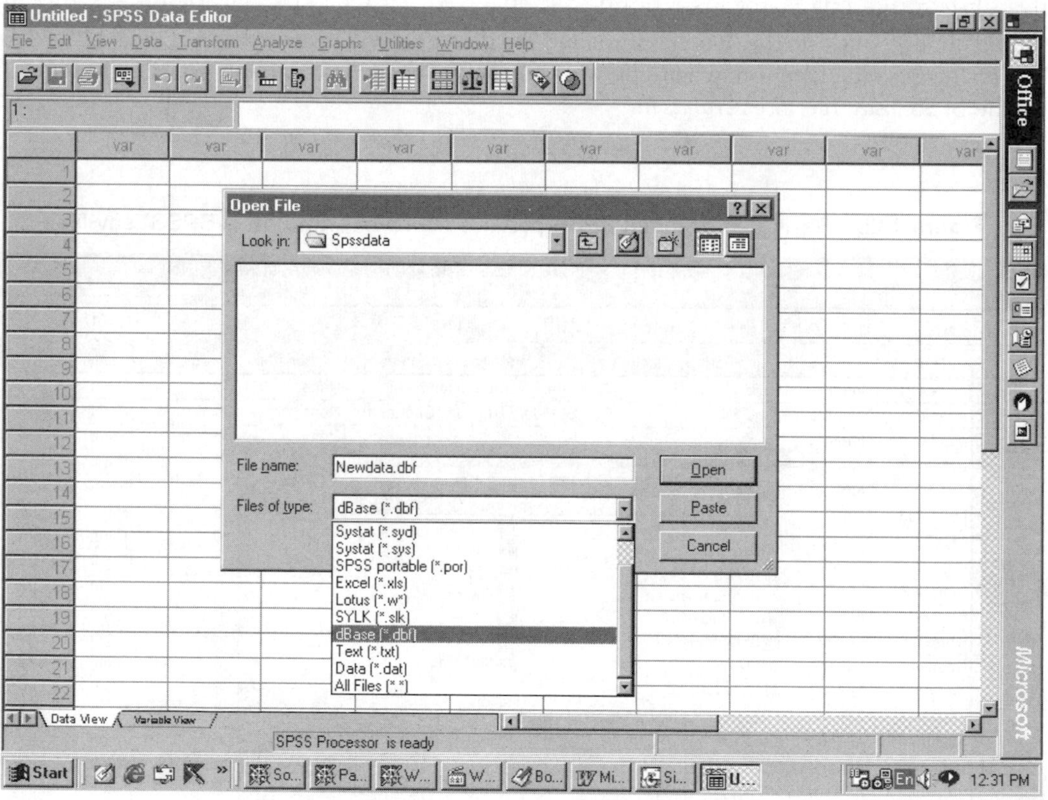

The default is a SPSS system data file *.**sav**. Scroll down to select file type (Here, a dBase File, **Newdata.dbf**, has been chosen).

Some caution is needed when importing files from different applications. Check if the SPSS version you are using can read the latest version of the database application you want to import. If SPSS cannot read the latest version, save the spreadsheet data using a version which can be read by the SPSS programme you are using.

SPSS also provides the option to import database files using the Capture Wizard using the pull-down menu. Click on the **File** menu as before, then on **Open Database** and then choose **New Query** to open the capture **Database Wizard**. A window like that in Figure 1.2d will appear. The **Database Wizard** provides a set of step-by-step instructions that can be followed to introduce a database file into SPSS.

Figure 1.2d   Importing spreadsheet files from other applications using **Database Wizard**

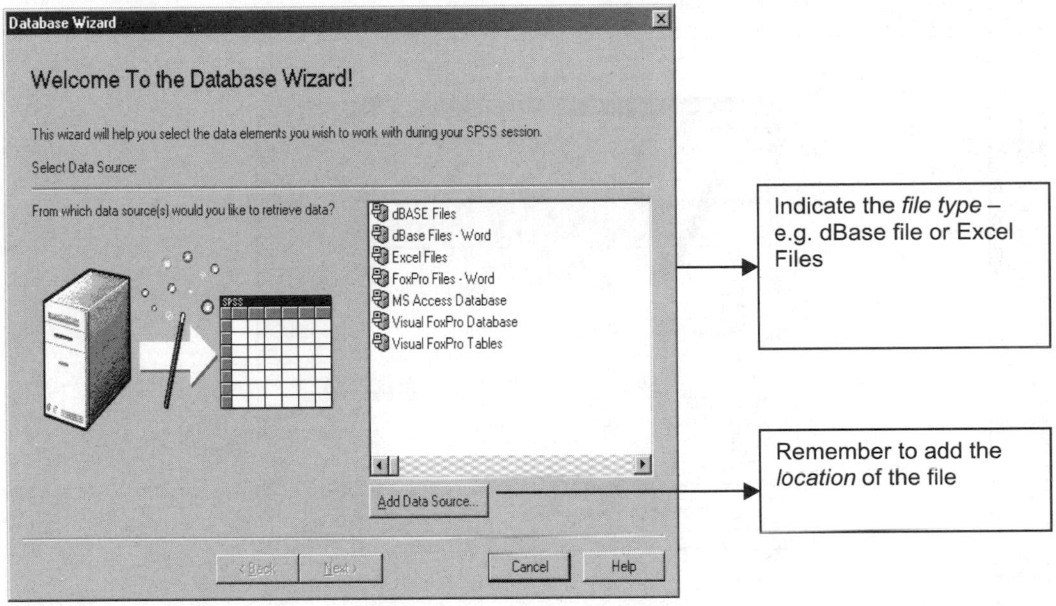

It is also possible to use **Copy** and **Paste** commands to import to and export from SPSS and other spreadsheet applications. To bring a distinct block of data from a spreadsheet into SPSS, simply open the spreadsheet application, and using the cursor highlight the data block (excluding any headings) and use **Copy** from the **Edit** menu to copy the data block. Once you have copied the data, go to the Data View window in SPSS (the SPSS data grid), 'drag' your mouse from the upper-left-hand corner of the data grid to highlight a block of cells in the grid and **Paste** the data onto the grid. **Note:** for this 'copy and paste' to work, the number of rows and columns highlighted on the data grid must *match* the number of rows and columns of data that are being taken from the spreadsheet. Once the data values are safely imported, the variables are labelled using **Variable View** (how to do this is explained below).

Option 3: importing text files

Others may have data coming from a non-spreadsheet source. These sources probably will be put into the form of an ASCII file. (Basically, here an ASCII file is a grid of rows and columns of raw numbers laid out in a similar manner to a spreadsheet, but without any of the labelling that a spreadsheet grid would have. ASCII files are a form of data that is basic to many different types of computer programmes and hence is used as a common means of transferring information between them.) SPSS can handle data from an ASCII file quite happily.

Open the main **File** menu and select **Read Text Data** in order to open a **Text Import Wizard** as shown in Figure 1.2e. The **Text Import Wizard** provides a set of step-by-step instructions that can be followed to introduce an ASCII file if data into SPSS.

Figure 1.2e   Text Import Wizard

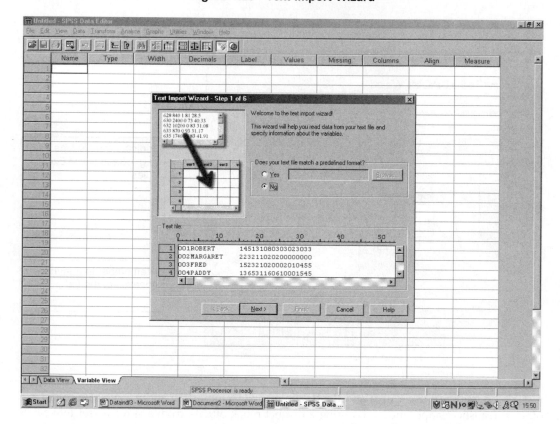

Option 4: creating a new SPSS data file

There are two stages to creating a new data file in SPSS. Enter the data into the Data View window, and specify the name, type and other characteristics of each variable. New data can be typed directly into the grid on the SPSS Data View window of the Data Editor.

When you first open SPSS the dialog box offers a range of options. A new file can be opened by selecting **Type in data** option from the dialog box and click on **OK** (Figure 1.2f). This will open the Data View window of the Data Editor.

Alternatively, a new data file can be opened using the pull-down **File** menu, choosing **New** and then **Data**.

Figure 1.2f Dialog box to create a new data file

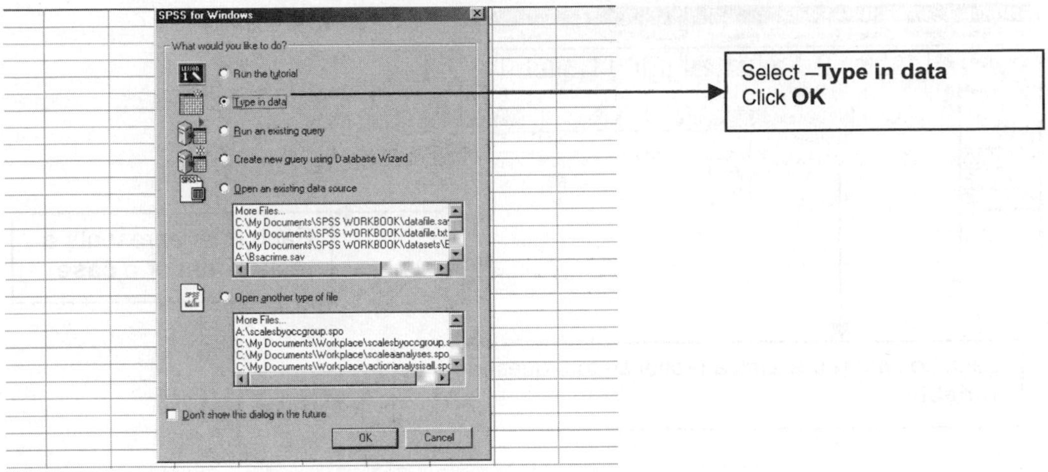

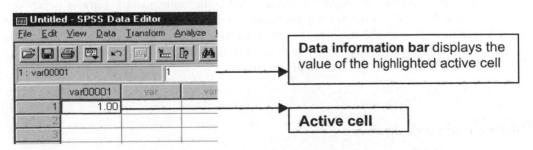

Select –**Type in data**
Click **OK**

Both procedures open an empty file on the Data Editor window. Remember that the Data Editor in SPSS V10 has two formats:

- **Data View**, which is the spreadsheet for *entering* the data (the default format)
- **Variable View**, for *naming* and *specifying* the *characteristics* of variables.

To change between the **Data View** and **Variable View** formats, click on the **tab label** on the bottom-left-hand side of the window.

To enter data using the **Data View** format on the Data Editor window, bring the cursor to the upper-left-hand corner of the grid (row 1, column 1). Click once, this will highlight the active cell where the data will be entered. Type in the first value. Once you have entered the data, press the **Enter** key (to move down the column) or the **Tab** key (to move across the row), and the next cell will be highlighted. As you enter data into the cells the value will appear in the data entry information bar above the column headings (Figure 1.2g).

Figure 1.2g Data entry directly to **Data View** window of the Data Editor

Data information bar displays the value of the highlighted active cell

Active cell

Remember data from an individual questionnaire (case) are entered in *rows*, and responses to a particular question are entered in *columns* (Figure 1.2h).

Figure 1.2h Questionnaire data entered directly to **Data View** window of the Data Editor

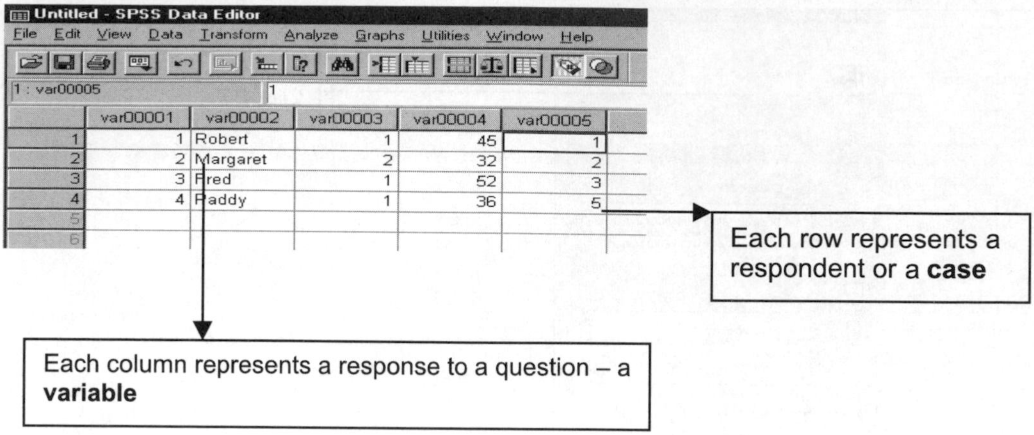

Each row represents a respondent or a **case**

Each column represents a response to a question – a **variable**

Editing data

It is possible to *edit* or *change* data in an existing data file by locating the data you wish to edit, clicking once on the cell, and replacing the old value in the cell by typing in a new value. You might want to edit data if you discover *errors* or *mistakes* in the existing data. Data editing can be done at any time, not just when a new dataset is first being created.

Entering new variables or cases

It is possible to enter new variables or cases to a data file. To insert a new case (for instance, a new respondent to a survey), simply select a cell in the row above which you want to insert the new row. Go to the **Data** main menu and click to open it. Click on **Insert Case** or click on the **Insert Case** button on the toolbar. This creates a new row, into which the data can be entered. Alternatively, go to the empty rows at the bottom of the grid and enter the data onto the first empty row.

To insert a new variable (or column), select any cell in the column to the right of which you want the new column. Open the **Data** main menu and click on **Insert Variable** or click on the **Insert Variable** button on the toolbar. This creates a new variable, into which new data can be entered. Again, alternatively you can go to the empty columns at the far-right-hand side of the grid and enter the data into the first empty column.

Deleting a variable or case

It is possible to delete a variable or case. To delete a case or row click on the case number on the shaded column in the left side of the file. This will highlight the entire row, then open the **Edit** main menu and click **Clear** or press the **Del** key. (In Figure 1.3a, we are deleting the variable **Margaret**.)

Figure 1.3a Deleting a case

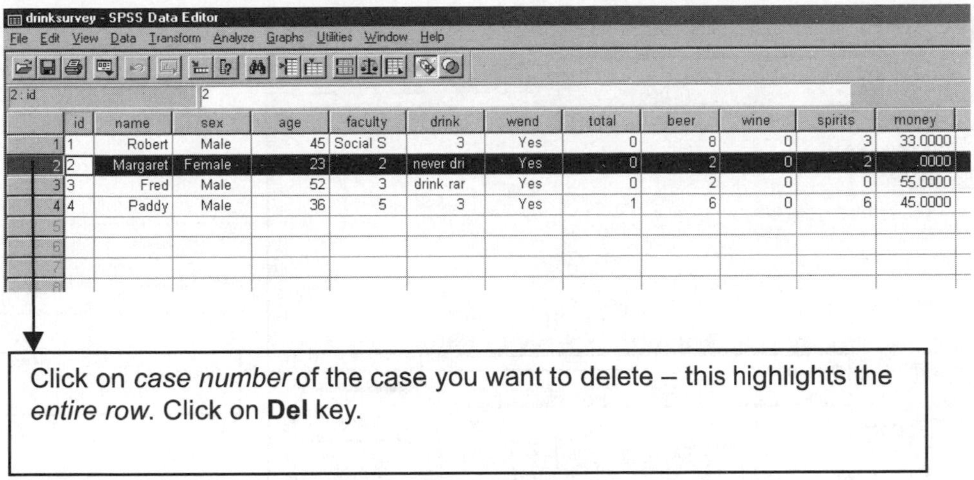

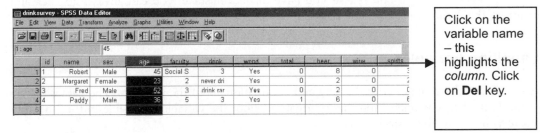

Click on *case number* of the case you want to delete – this highlights the *entire row*. Click on **Del** key.

To delete a variable or column click on the variable label on the shaded row (Figure 1.3b). This will highlight the entire variable, open the **Edit** main menu and delete the column by clicking **Clear** or press the **Del** key. (Here, we are deleting the variable **age**.)

Figure 1.3b Deleting a variable

Click on the variable name – this highlights the *column*. Click on **Del** key.

Saving new files

It is important to *name* and *save* the new datafile you have created. Do not wait until you have entered all the data, as computer malfunctions or power cuts can result in lost work. To save the file you must assign a *unique name* to the file which identifies the data which the file contains. For example, we might assign the name *drinksurvey* to the file which contains the data from the survey. Files can be saved using by opening the **File** main menu and selecting **Save As**. Then use the dialog box to select the directory or disk (floppy disk) in which you want to save the data. Enter the new name of the file in the **File Name Box** (In Figure 1.3c, *drinksurvey*), and click **OK**.

SPSS will save the data file as an SPSS data file (*.**sav**) as it is at the point in time when you save the data. Later on, if you make additional changes to the data file that you also want to be saved, you will want to save the newer version of the data file again. (See the Orientation chapter, p. 25, for more details about saving files.)

Figure 1.3c **Save Data** dialog box

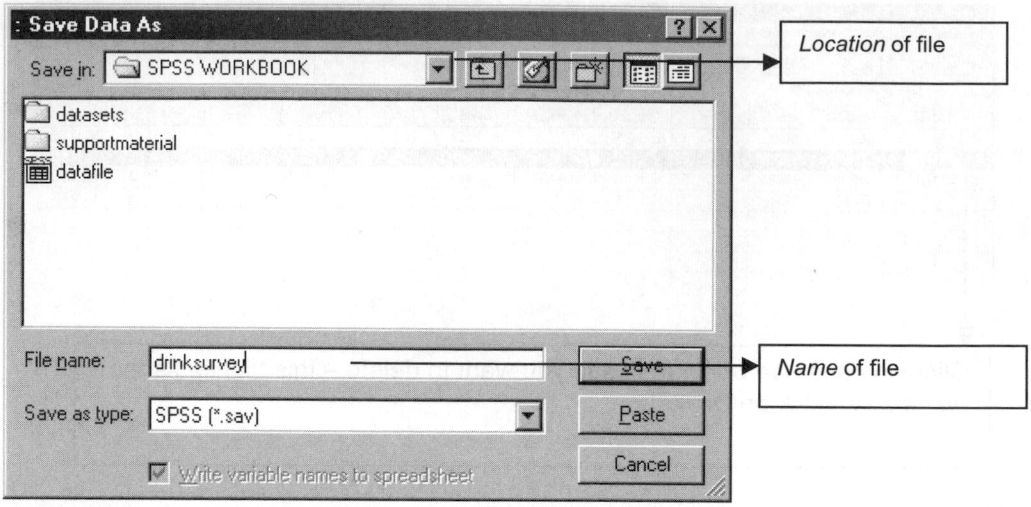

Be careful that the version of the data file you save is the version you want to *keep*! For instance, a common mistake students make is to select a subset of cases (say, only the males in the sample) and then save the datafile later on without 'turning off' the selection. The next time they come to analyse the data file, they discover to their consternation that only the selected cases are left! A 'safety net' is to save your later version under a slightly different file name; for example, **vers2**. Then, if you realise you have made a mistake, you can always go back and resurrect the earlier version of the data file: **vers1**.

Labelling variables

An SPSS data file requires both the data and information about the variables. The data is visible in the **Data View** window, and the information about the variables is visible in the **Variable View** window of the Data Editor.

When the SPSS Data Editor is in **Data View** format, each column in the grid represents a *variable*. SPSS requires each that each variable must have a unique 'name' that identifies that variable separately from any other variable. These variable names should be intelligible and adhere to the SPSS rules for naming variables. – SPSS requires that variable names should be short words (limited to a maximum of eight characters). It is good practice for these variable labels to be one of three types.

- *Self-explanatory* labels stating what information the variable signifies (for example, **sex**, **age**, **faculty**)
- An *acronym* that helps jog the researcher's memory about what the variable is (for example, **hoh** for 'Head Of Household' or **denom** for a religious denomination coding)
- Just a list of *letters and numbers in sequence* (for example, *V1, V2, V3, V4, ... Vn*).

Which is best depends largely upon personal preference and convenience. Some researchers use the question numbers as variable names, for example, **que1** as a variable name for the first question in a survey.

There are some conventions that must be followed when assigning variable names.

- A variable name must begin with a *letter* (not a number)
- A variable name cannot have a *blank space* within the name (for example **dog day** would not be acceptable but **dog_day** would be acceptable)
- A variable name cannot be more than *eight characters* (a character is a letter, number or the symbols **@**, **#**, **_**, **or $**)
- A variable name cannot have the *special characters* !, ? and * or other special characters except those listed in the previous bullet point
- A variable name cannot be one of the words SPSS uses as *keywords* (for example, AND, NOT, EQ, BY and ALL)
- A variable name cannot end with a *full stop*.

Coding

The data that one wishes to put into a computer package for analysis has to be transformed from its completely non-computerised form (which could be answers written onto a questionnaire, entries on a form or application, a personnel or student record file, etc.) into a shape that can be input into a computer. Usually, this means that the information is converted into number values – a process called *coding*. Coding operations can be carried out in several ways depending on the type of information you are dealing with. There are two types of data – *quantitative* and *qualitative*.

Quantitative data

If the information is already in number form, the coding is fairly simple; just the *direct* transfer of the numeric value. For instance, on the 'Drinking questionnaire', Robert is 45 years old, the code for **age** is simply __45__ . Similarly, the codes for pints of beer and cider, glasses of wine and measures of spirits are all coded directly on the 'Drinking questionnaire'.

Numbers with decimal points can be coded with or without the decimal point. For instance, Fred answered on the 'Drinking questionnaire' that he spent £4.55 on alcohol last weekend. This could be coded as **4.55** or **0455** (the first case is the version of coding we are using with the questionnaire). The default for SPSS is eight digits with two places to the right of the decimal point. If more digits or decimal places are required this can be changed in the **Variable View** window of the Data Editor (which is explained below).

These days, thanks to the power of modern computers and the ability to manipulate data after input into SPSS, one should always code in the most detail practicable. When coding numbers, this means that the number is the code – you should not amalgamate the number values together into larger categories at the coding stage. The reason for this is that, if the values are lumped together *before* input into SPSS, it will be impossible to get back to the detailed information of the real number. That is, you have unnecessarily thrown away some information that could prove vital at some future date. As you will see when you look at data manipulation in Module 3, it is a simple matter to aggregate numbers together after data has been input into SPSS.

For instance, as an example of bad coding procedure, some people would have coded people's ages on the 'Drinking questionnaire' *directly into categories.*

```
1 = Younger than 18
2 = 18 to 24
3 = 25 to 40
4 = 41 to 64
5 = 65 or older
```

We would advise that you avoid prematurely categorising quantitative data such as these. What if, later on, you discover that you really need to compare the drinking habits of those aged less than 21 with those aged between 21 and 29? It will be impossible because your age categories will not allow it. If you had coded age directly, you could easily amalgamate up into the categories required for your analysis. It is always possible to move from a *more* detailed coding to a *less* detailed coding: the reverse cannot be done! (If you are familiar with scaling or levels of measurement, you may have noted that so far we have been talking about the *quantitative* levels of measurement: interval and ratio scales. Levels of measurement will be discussed in more detail at the beginning of Module 2).

Qualitative data

Quite often, the information you want to code may not be number values, but instead in the form of *categories.*

- These can be *mutually exclusive*, binary 'black or white' categories where one category implies the absence or opposite of the other; for example, *YES* or *NO*
  or (from the 'Drinking questionnaire') *1 = Male, 2 = Female*
- There can also be *more than two* categories — a set of categories where each is a different type of a common characteristic:
  for example, Car Colours: *BLACK/RED/BLUE/GREEN/YELLOW*, etc.
  or (from the 'Drinking questionnaire')
  Faculty: *Social Sciences = 1; Arts = 2; Science = 3; Engineering = 4; Other = 5*

Here, of course, the number codes are only labels for the categories and do not have any arithmetic value in themselves (for example, *Engineering*, coded '4', is not twice as much a faculty such as *Arts*, coded '2'!). These sorts of categorial data can be described as being at the *nominal* level of measurement.

There is an in-between situation where you can have categories that fall into an *increasing* or *decreasing* order. The number codes used to represent the categories show the ordering effect but do not literally represent a true amount or quantity. For instance, people could be asked to rank a sensation by its pain:

tickles/uncomfortable/hurts/hurts a lot/excruciating!!!
  1   2   3   4   5

We could agree that 'only tickles' (1) is less pain than 'uncomfortable' (2), which is less pain than 'hurts' (3) and so on ($1 < 2 < 3 < 4 < 5$), but we would probably find it hard to agree that three 'tickles' and an 'uncomfortable' equals one 'excruciating!!!' ($1 + 1 + 1 + 2 = 5$)!

In the 'Drinking questionnaire' there is an example of this sort of **ordinal** measurement where the numbers imply a decreasing or increasing order, but the numbers themselves signify only less or more and not any definite amounts:

Do you

1 = 'Never drink alcohol', 2 = 'Drink rarely', 3 = 'Drink moderately',
4 = 'Drink frequently', 5 = 'Drink heavily'?

(The nominal and ordinal levels of measurement will be discussed in more detail at the beginning of Module 2.)

'String' data

While numbers are normally used to record information, it is possible to enter in letters − or, more exactly, *alphanumeric codes*. For instance, there could be good reasons to enter in people's own names; we have done this on the 'Drinking questionnaire' with the variable *name* which has respondents' names. Sometimes an interview schedule may contain 'open-ended' questions where you might want to record exactly what a person said in response to a question *verbatim* instead of converting what they said into a number code.

These alphanumeric codes are called *string* variables (technically, they are in 'A' format). Even if the codes of a variable declared as a string variable are numbers, they cannot have arithmetic operations performed on them as normal number-based codes unless they are specially altered.

Alphanumeric codes are fairly rare, especially in datasets designed for statistical analysis. They are more common in datasets which originate from a personnel file or the like. They have been mentioned here since you may encounter them, but we recommend that you avoid setting up variables as string variable if possible.

An important note: SPSS will permit alphanumeric codes (for example, words such as respondents' names) to be entered into the Data View window only if the variable has been defined as a *string variable*. To change the variable type, switch to the **Variable View** format of the Data Editor. Click on the **Type** cell of the variable you wish to change, and alter the setting to **String**. (The use of **Variable View** is covered in detail below in the section on SPSS operations to 'label' and 'refine' a dataset.)

Refining the data set

At this point after the data has been coded and input into SPSS, you could, in theory, move straight into a statistical analysis of some sort. In practice, however, the basic dataset is usually 'refined' before we can consider it to be completely ready for analysis. This 'refining' can consist of three types of operations.

- Attaching special descriptions or labels that help explain the *form* and *content* of the dataset
- Carrying out *validation or consistency checks* to remove or control errors and missing information in the dataset
- Tagging *missing* or *invalid codes* with special labels so that these incorrect codes aren't mixed in with valid values when analyses are being carried out.

Labelling the data

Attaching special descriptions or labels that help explain the form and content of the dataset is essential. While it makes no difference to the actual numerical analyses, it is a wise practice to document the structure of a dataset and to attach descriptions of the meanings of variable names and the codes of the variables. All of this may seem clear and straightforward to you – the person who set up the dataset – but this might not be the case for someone else who will have to try and analyse the data at some future date! Also, features of the data that seem straightforward to you *today*, might not be so obvious or straightforward to you *some weeks or months later*. Consequently, SPSS allows you to 'document' a dataset as you set it up. The information on each of the variables is presented in the **Variable View** window of the Data Editor.

Variable labels

A common feature for documenting a dataset is a provision that allows one to attach a 'descriptor' or 'label' to the short variable names. The variable names are restricted to eight characters, which may be obscure and require clarification. For instance, in the 'Drinking questionnaire' there is a variable named **fac**, which may be rather vague to someone not familiar with the dataset. But, if a descriptor/label is attached – for example, **fac** = *Faculty at university or college* – the meaning of the variable becomes much more clear. These details can be entered in column Label in the **Variable View** window.

Value labels

A similar problem exists for the individual codes of a variable. Again, a common feature of many data analysis packages is a provision for attaching a 'descriptor' or label to individual codes. For instance, the variable **fac** has six codes – 1, 2, 3, 4, 5 and 9 – that go with it. It would be easy to forget what these six codes mean. But, if descriptors/labels are attached, their meanings are much clearer:

1 = *Social sciences*, 2 = *Arts*, 3 = *Science*, 4 = *Engineering*,
5 = *Other*, 9 = *Not applicable*.

Once a variable and its values are 'labelled', these descriptors will appear on any printout where the variable name or the number codes would appear. For instance, without labelling, a tabulation of **fac** for 500 cases could look like this:

Variable: **fac**

1	57
2	186
3	98
4	132
5	4
9	23
Total	500

Unless one was very familiar with the dataset, this would be completely obscure. Now, with the descriptors, we obtain a much less vague tabulation:

Variable: **fac**, *Faculty*

1 *Social sciences*	57
2 *Arts*	186
3 *Science*	98
4 *Engineering*	132
5 *Other*	4
9 *Not applicable*	23
Total	500

These labels do not alter the mathematical calculations of the programme in any way. The effect they *do* have is to make the printout much easier to understand.

SPSS operations to 'label' and 'refine' a dataset

Now, let us go through the operations required to fully label new variables in a SPSS data file. There are a number of ways to set up variable labels and values in SPSS V10. (The procedures using SPSS V10 are slightly different to older versions of SPSS – see Appendix 2, p. 56, for examples using SPSS V9.)

As already described, the **Variable View** format of the Data Editor gives details of each of the variables whose values are entered in **Data View** format. While it is technically possible to complete some statistical procedures without details of each of the variables, it is good practice for the SPSS user to supply and complete the **Variable View** details. To change to **Variable View** format, click on the tab labelled **Variable View** at the bottom of the left-hand side of the Data Editor window (Figure 1.4a). Notice how the grid switches when you do this.

Figure 1.4a Opening **Variable View** in the Data Editor

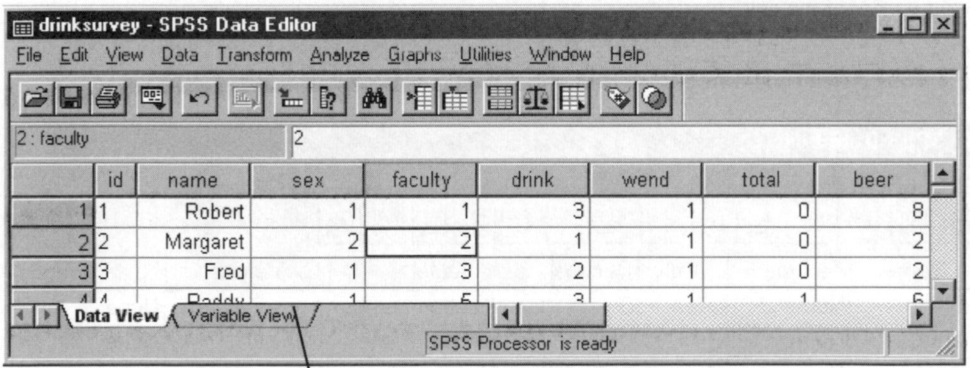

To open **Variable View** window click on the label on the bottom left-hand side of the **Data View** window in the Data Editor.

The *rows* in **Variable View** format contain details of each variable, beginning with the variable name (Figure 1.4b). Each *column* provides specific information about the variables. For example, the **Names** of the variables are presented in the first column, **Type** of each variable is in the second column, etc. Each *row* provides specific information of each variable, including **Name**, **Type of variable**, **Width**, **Decimals**, **Labels**, **Values** and so on.

Figure 1.4b **Variable View** window of the Data Editor

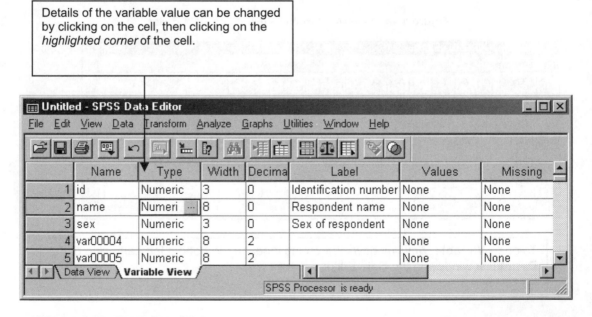

Each row provides specific information of a variable, e.g. **Id** is numeric, is three characters wide, has no decimal points.

Each *column* provides specific information about the variables, e.g. *Name* of each variable, *Type* of each variable, etc.

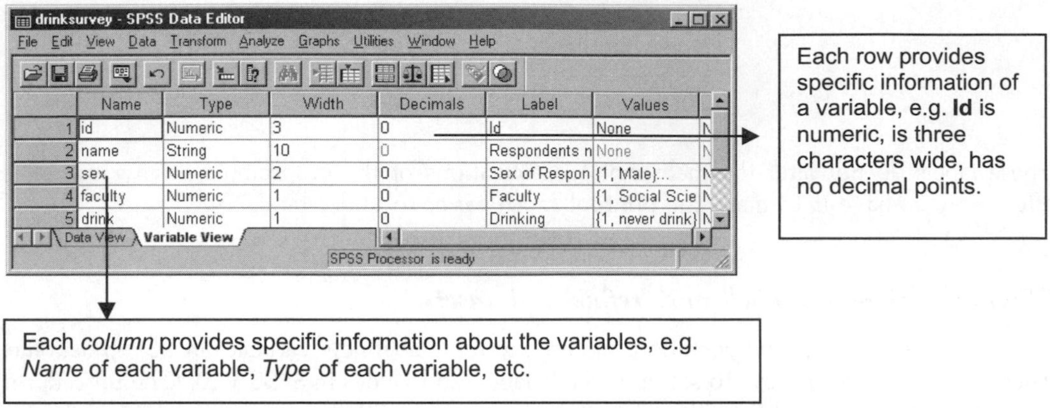

Until changed by the user, **Variable View** format presents the default aspects of the variable. For example, each variable will be **Type** 'Numeric' with a **Width** of '8' characters, '2' decimals, no specified **Labels** or missing data, etc. Any of these characteristics can be changed in the Data Editor window when it is in **Variable View** format (Figure 1.4c).

Figure 1.4c Editing/changing the **Variable View** window of the Data Editor

Details of the variable value can be changed by clicking on the cell, then clicking on the *highlighted corner* of the cell.

Variable names can be changed by *typing over* the default names.

Some of the default characteristics will be appropriate for each variable, but some may need to be changed. It is quite easy to change a characteristic by clicking on the cell containing the information. For example, the variable **id** is numeric, but the variable **name** is a *string* (person's name rather than number). To change the **Type**, move the cursor to the three dots in the shaded corner of the cell and click once. This will open the subwindow with eight variable types in Figure 1.4d. Click on 'string' variable, and change the width to 10 characters to accommodate longer names.

Figure 1.4d Changing **Variable Type**

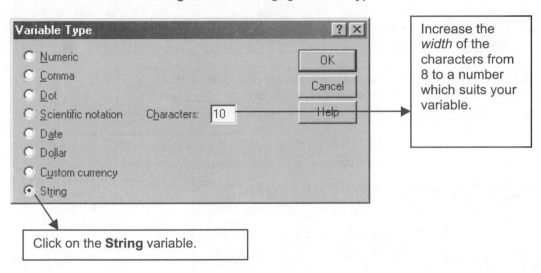

SPSS gives us the facility in **Variable View** for including fuller details for each variable name by attaching a longer label to it. For example, we might want to give the variable name **wend** (for the question in the survey *Did you drink last weekend between 12 noon on Friday and last Saturday Night?*) a longer label to help us remember what **wend** is. To *label the variable name*, simply type in the full label in the cell of that variable. For example, to give more details to the variable name **wend,** move the cursor along the row containing **wend** until you reach the **Label** column. Click on this cell, and type in the full details, as shown in Figure 1.4e.

It is important to *label each of the number codes* for categorical variables. To do so, click on the cell of the variable you wish to define. Move the cursor to the three dots in the shaded corner of the cell, and click once. This will open a dialog box which allows you to label each of the values, such as that in Figure 1.4f. In the example here, for the variable fac (*Faculty*), 1 = 'Social Science', 2 = 'Arts', 3 = 'Sciences', 4 = 'Engineering' and 5 = 'Other'. In the dialog box for this variable, type in the first number code (which is 1) in the **Value** box, then click on the **Value label** box and type in the label for the code (which is **Social Science**). Click on the **Add** button, and the value and its label are entered into the workbox. Repeat this for each value, and then click on **OK** to save the labels.

The longer labels attached to the short variable name or to the number codes of variables have no effect whatever on any analysis that SPSS will carry out. What the labels do is make the output resulting from an analysis *easier to interpret*. Once the variables have been labelled, SPSS automatically will print the longer labels next to variable names and values wherever these appear on the outprint, making the output much easier for you to read and understand.

Figure 1.4e Labelling a variable

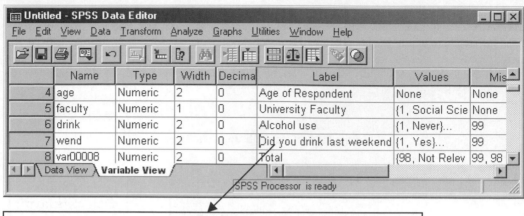

To insert additional information on the variable, click on the **Label** cell, type in the details, and press the **Enter** or **Tab key**.

Figure 1.4f Defining **Values**

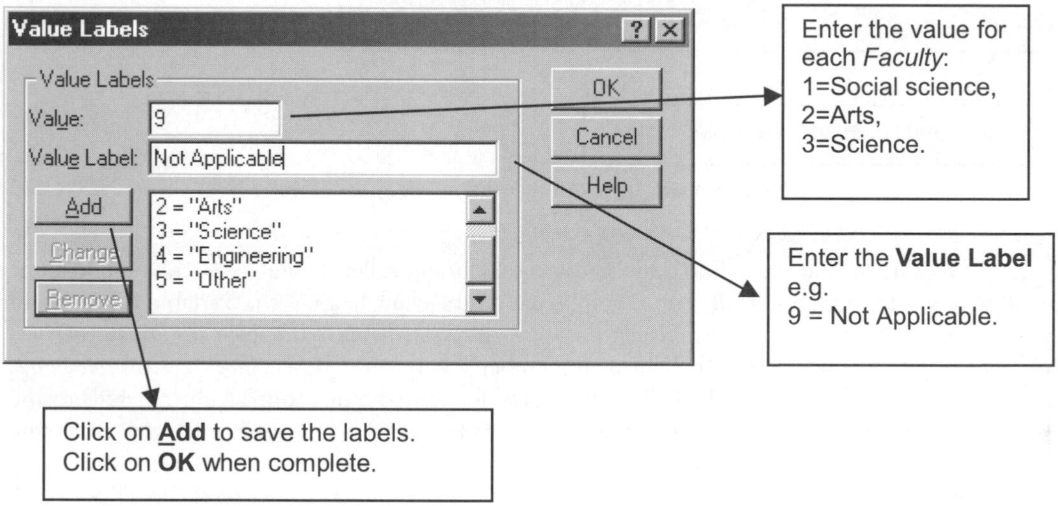

Enter the value for each *Faculty*:
1=Social science,
2=Arts,
3=Science.

Enter the **Value Label** e.g.
9 = Not Applicable.

Click on **Add** to save the labels.
Click on **OK** when complete.

It is also important to identify the *missing value* codes for SPSS (see the section below on missing values). Click on the **Missing Values** cell of the row of the required variable, move the cursor to the three dots in the shaded corner of the cell, and click once. A window like Figure 1.4g will come up. Enter the values which are consided missing, click on the **OK** button to go back to the Variable View window.

It is possible to change any of the characteristics (name, width, type, label, columns, measure (scale, ordinal or nominal)) in the Variable View window by clicking on the appropriate cell. It is also possible to copy a format from one variable to another using **Copy** and **Paste**. Highlight the cell which has been formatted, copy the format using **Edit Copy**. Move to the cell of the

Figure 1.4g Defining **Missing Values**

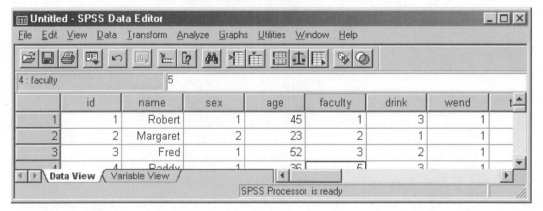

Missing Values

○ No missing values

● Discrete missing values

| 99 | 98 | |

○ Range plus one optional discrete missing value

Low: High:

Discrete value:

OK

Cancel

Help

For this variable – Total number of drinks last weekend – the value **99** is allocated for **missing** and **98** is allocated for **not relevant** (not a drinker).

variable you want to copy the format to, and paste the format using **Edit Paste**. This is particularly useful for entering labels from a questionnaire with the same values and labels such as Likert scales.

Once you have entered the data and defined the variables it is possible to view the data with the new labels instead of the numeric values. To view the value labels of the dataset, go to the **Data View** format in the Data Editor, open the pull-down menu **View**, and click on **Value Labels.** The appearance of the grid will change from that showing the numeric codes (as in Figure 1.5a) to a grid showing the alphanumeric labels (as in Figure 1.5b).

Figure 1.5a Drink survey data in **Value** format

Untitled - SPSS Data Editor

File Edit View Data Transform Analyze Graphs Utilities Window Help

4 : faculty   5

	id	name	sex	age	faculty	drink	wend	t
1	1	Robert	1	45	1	3	1	
2	2	Margaret	2	23	2	1	1	
3	3	Fred	1	52	3	2	1	
4	4	Paddy	1	36	5	3	1	

Data View / Variable View /

SPSS Processor is ready

Validating

Validation of a dataset is conducted using *consistency checks* to remove or control errors and missing information. It is easy for errors in codings to creep into a dataset from a variety of sources. Before commencing the first real analyses, it is good practice to try to remove as many errors as practicable. One efficient means of removing errors is to use the *computer package itself* to check for errors. Errors can be identified by checking for *invalid* or *inconsistent* codes.

Figure 1.5b   Drink survey data in **Label** format

	id	name	sex	age	faculty	drink	wend	t
1	1	Robert	1	45	Social S	Moderat ▼	Yes	
2	2	Margaret	2	23	Arts	Never	Yes	
3	3	Fred	1	52	Science	Rarely	Yes	
4	4	Paddy	1	36	Other	Moderat	Yes	

Untitled - SPSS Data Editor

File   Edit   View   Data   Transform   Analyze   Graphs   Utilities   Window   Help

1 : drink   3

Data View   Variable View

SPSS Processor is ready

Checking for invalid codes

The most obvious validation is to check for incorrect codes by seeking out impossible or invalid values. All possible *correct* code values for a variable are specified. Then, if any codes exist other than the possible values, they must be errors. For instance, in our **fac** example from the 'Drinking questionnaire', the only possible values are within the range 1 to 5 and 9. So, if you found a zero or a 6, 7 or 8 (or any other invalid value), it must be a coding error. These coding errors should be corrected before any analysis:

Variable: *fac, Faculty*

0	3	X
1 Social sciences	55	
2 Arts	186	
3 Science	97	
4 Engineering	131	
5 Other	4	
6	1	X
9 Not applicable	23	
Total	500	

Checking for inconsistent codes

Sometimes, a particular code or codes for one variable will mean that the codes for another variable must, or must not, fall within a certain range of values — that is, the codings of the two variables, while both are within the range of possible codes, may be *inconsistent* with each other.

For instance, you might do a consistency check with the 'Drinking questionnaire' data to see whether everyone coded as a 1 on the variable **drink** (that is, everyone who said they were a non-drinker) *also* has codings of zero for the variables **beer** (units of beer/cider drank over the weekend), **wine** (units of wine) and **spirit** (units of spirit). Non-drinkers should not have drunk any units of alcohol. If it appears that a claimed non-drinker does have some units of alcohol consumed, an inconsistency exists which should be resolved. (This might require going back to the original source of the information in order to trace the reason for the apparent error.) If the correct code can be established, the data grid can be edited to replace the error. If a correct code cannot be established, it may be necessary to declare the inconsistent or incorrect code as a *missing value*.

Software checks on invalid codes

You will note that tracking down the original sources of invalid codings or inconsistencies and then correcting them within the dataset can be a tedious and time-consuming operation, perhaps requiring going all the way back to the original source of the data. It is possible to get around this by using a specialist data entry package which is capable of performing checks for valid values and for inconsistencies between variables *at the point of coding the data*. The data is coded directly in and the package is continually checking for out-of-range and/or inconsistent values as they are keyed in. If an invalid or inconsistent value is entered, the error is highlighted on the spot. This allows the coder to check the error against the original source while that original source is in front of them and to repair the damage immediately.

Dealing with missing values

The expression 'missing values' may sound a bit odd to you, but there are many instances where, for only some variables for only some cases, data may be missing. For instance, our 'Drinking questionnaire' might have a second page where people are asked to tell us about the ill effects they suffer from drinking (hangovers). People who do not drink would not need to answer that section. That is, often a variable will not be coded for some cases because the variable *Does not apply* to those cases. Another example could be where only people who live in rented accommodation would answer the question about *'How much rent do you pay?'* or where questions about a person's children would not apply to people who have no children.

Information can of course be missing for other reasons. The information may not be available simply because it is *not known*. A person may *refuse* to answer some questions on a questionnaire or in an interview. Respondents sometimes write in illegible answers on a questionnaire or make simple mistakes like inadvertently skipping over some questions or even circling *two* answers when only one is required. *Errors* may have occurred in the coding or transcription of data so that you know the code is incorrect but you cannot find out the correct code.

Regardless of cause, all types of missing data are normally dealt with in the same manner; a special code or codes is applied to each instance of missing information. For example, with **fac** on the 'Drinking questionnaire', the code 9 was used to indicate those cases where the information on *'Faculty or division'* was not known or did not apply for some reason.

While any codes can be used to signify missing values, there are some rules of good practice with missing values which are advisable.

Strategies for coding missing values

It is tempting to avoid the problem of missing values by leaving blank the space where the code should go. After all, one does not know the code, so why not just put nothing? This, however, is not advisable. A blank space can easily end up being converted into a zero by accident ('__' → 0). If zero can be a genuine code for the variable, the result is an error in the dataset.

Secondly, blanks can occur for other reasons, such as someone accidentally skipping a space when typing in the data. Therefore, one can not be sure that the blank is a genuine missing value, or just a mistake.

Similarly, people often choose to use zeros as a *missing value code*. While better than blanks, this is still not advisable. As before, an accidentally entered blank space can end up being read as zero; introducing an error. Also, the value zero can often be a genuine code. For example, if people are asked to state how many children they have; many will legitimately say '0'.

The best practice is to use a value that is completely *out of the range of real possible values* as a missing value code. For instance, with **fac** above, the genuine code values were 1 to 5; 9 is used as a missing value code. It is completely out of the range of possible values and, being an actual number, has to be entered in as a deliberate code (so it cannot appear by accident as a zero or blank could).

Sometimes people use more than one missing value code so that they can keep track of *why* the value is missing. For instance, one might use different missing value codes to distinguish between: *'refused to answer'*; *'does not apply'*; *'answer unknown'*, etc. Whether one chooses to use more than one missing value code depends upon whether knowing the reason for data being missing is of importance. (For instance, it may be important to know if people refuse to answer a certain question.)

The convention many people follow with missing values is to use the highest possible values available.

For instance, with our example of **fac** where 1 to 5 are legitimate codes, one might use: 9 to mean *'Refused'*; 8 to mean *'Does not apply'*; and 7 to mean *'Missing for some other reason'*:

Variable: **fac**, *Faculty*

1 *Social* sciences	55
2 Arts	186
3 Science	97
4 Engineering	131
5 Other	4
7 *Missing, other reason*	3
8 *Does not apply*	1
9 *Refused*	23
Total	500

If the variable takes up two columns, say, 'Number of children', you could maintain this practice of using the highest values to signify missing values; for example, 97, 98 and 99 or 77, 88 and 99. People might have 0, 1, 2, 3, 4 ... maybe even some with 10, 11, 12+ children; but no one would have 77, 88, 97, 98 or 99 children!

For three-digit variables, one could use 777, 888, 997, 998 or 999; 7777, 8888, 9997, 9998, 9999 for four-digit variables; and so on for five digit variables, etc.

The importance of missing values

The importance of specifying missing value codes goes beyond just the cosmetic reasons of having them clearly displayed as missing values in tabulations. When certain codes for a variable are identified for SPSS as 'missing values', these codes will be excluded automatically from any mathematical calculations that are carried out on the variables. If this was not the case, completely misleading results would occur. For instance, taking the example of a code for 'Number of children' where the missing values codes of 97, 98 and 99 have been used. If the average number of children was calculated for the dataset with even a *small* proportion of missing value codes 97, 98 and 99 being averaged in with the true codes of 0, 1, 2, 3, etc. the overall average would be grossly inflated. Once these missing values have been specified to SPSS, however, they will play no part in the calculation and a misleading result will be avoided. A similar example of how SPSS would exclude missing values can be seen if we look at the tabulation of our variable **fac** with the numbers in each legitimate category being given as a percentage of the whole:

Variable: **fac**, *Faculty*

	N	%
1 Social sciences	55	11.6
2 Arts	186	39.3
3 Science	97	20.5
4 Engineering	131	27.7
5 Other	4	0.1
7 Missing, other reason	3	–
8 Does not apply	1	–
9 Refused	23	–
Total	500	100.0

27 cases are missing values

Conclusion

In the end, once:

- the data have been entered
- variables and their values have been 'labelled' and defined fully
- missing values are specified fully
- and the data have been 'cleaned' by checking for valid ranges of values and internal consistency

you have a *fully operational and self-supporting dataset*, ready for analysis.

Once the SPSS dataset has been created and data has been put into it, the resulting grid will look like Figure 1.5a, which shows the cases from our 'Drinking questionnaire'.

Some tips

- *Save your file frequently* as you enter the data. Do not wait until you have entered all of the data – save your file every 15 minutes. That way, you will have a permanent copy of most of your data even if something goes wrong while you're working.
- Make a *backup copy* (an extra copy) of the data to use in case your original data file is somehow lost or destroyed. Since disks can be damaged, put the backup copy on a *different physical disk*. If the data are important, be sure to label the backup floppy diskettes clearly and put them in a safe place
- Use the pull-down **Help** menu on the toolbar and the tutorial for *further advice and help*.

SPSS exercise

Now, as an SPSS exercise in inputting data into an SPSS file, try creating your own 'Drinker' SPSS datafile:

- Write *your* responses to the questionnaire onto the grid in Figure 1.1,
- Enter the data for the five cases into a new datafile in the Data View window. Remember you will need to define the variables in the Variable View window.
- Open the Variable View window, enter a short variable name for each question (variable), indicate the width and type of the variable, set up the variable labels and declare missing values where appropriate.
- Using **File Save**, name and save the resulting SPSS datafile to a floppy disk in drive **a:**.

Appendix 1
Student 'Drinking
Questionnaire'

Serial number: _____

1. What is your first name? (write in) _____

2. What is your sex?   1 Male
                       2 Female

3. What is your age in years? _____

4. What faculty/division are you in at your University/College
            1 Social Sciences
            2 Arts
            3 Science
            4 Engineering
            5 Other
            9 Not applicable

5. Do you: 1 never drink alcohol
             2 drink rarely
             3 drink moderately
             4 drink frequently
             5 drink heavily

6. Did you drink last weekend between 12 noon on Friday and last Sunday night?
            1. Yes   2. No
   If **YES** please answer question 7,
   If **NO** thank you for completing the questionnaire.

7. Please write down how many alcoholic drinks you had last weekend between 12 noon on Friday and late Sunday night.
      [*Write in the number*] _____
      How many pints of beer or cider in total did you have? _____
                  [*If none, write in 0*]
      How many glasses of wine in total did you have? _____
                  [*If none, write in 0*]
      How many measures of spirits/mixed cocktails did you have? _____
                  [*If none, write in 0*]

8. As close as possible, to the exact pound and pence, how much money did you spend on alcoholic drinks during the same time period?
      [*Write in the amount with the decimal point; for example, 5.25*]
      £_____ [*If you spent nothing, write in 0.00*]

Thank you for your cooperation.

Appendix 2
Labelling Using SPSS V9

SPSS V9 does not offer **Variable View** format on the Data Editor grid for defining variables. Instead, to define a 'new' variable with SPSS V9, go to the variable you want to label on the data grid and click on its column to select it (Figure A.1a). (Here, we have selected the column for the new variable, **fac**.)

Figure A.1a   D̲efine Variable window

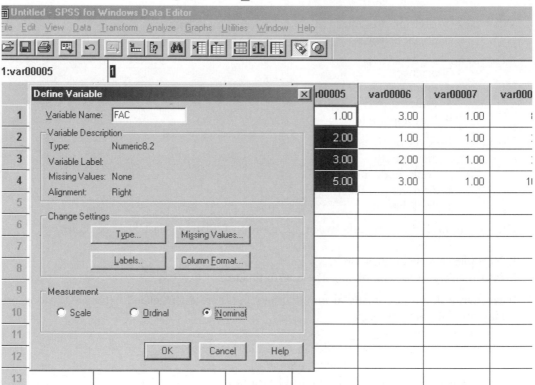

Pull down the **D̲ata menu** and select **Define Variable**. When the **Define Variable** window comes up (Figure A1a), click the **L̲abels** option to open the **Define Labels** window (Figure A1b). Type in the extended **V̲ariable Label** in its box (here, for the variable **fac**, the variable label is just *Faculty*).

It is important to label each of the number codes for the FAC variable. To do so, open the **Valu̲e** box under **Value Labels**, type in the first number code of the variable then go to the **Valu̲e Label** box and type in the extended label for that code, click on the **Add** button to enter

56

Figure A.1b   Define Labels Window

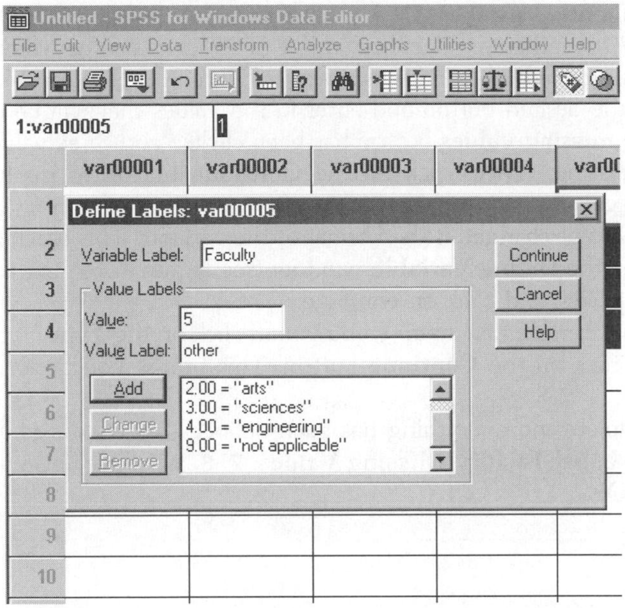

Figure A.1c   Defining Missing Values

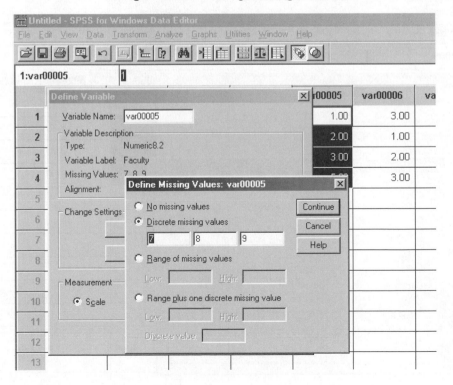

this into the 'work box'. Repeat this for each value of the variable. (The **Define Labels** window in Figure A.1b shows the end result after the five main values for **fac** have been labelled and a label for code 9, *Not applicable* is just about to be **Added**.) Then, click on the **Continue** button to go back to the **Define Variable** window (Figure A.1a).

Then, to identify the 'missing values' codes for SPSS, click on the **Missing Values** button under **Change Settings** and the window shown in Figure A.1c, **Define Missing Values:** will come up. Click on the desired button and enter in the values that will be considered missing. (Here, the **Discrete missing values** button has been clicked and three values, 7, 8 and 9, have been declared as missing.) Then, click on the **Continue** button to go back to the **Define Variable** window again.

The next settings to be changed is the Format of the variable. This is achieved by clicking on the **Type** Option on the **Define Variable** window (see Figure A.1d). Set the column width to 8 with no decimal places, and click on continue.

If you had a string variable (like **name**), you would click on the **Type** ... button and click the **String** button and click on the **Continue** button. This brings you back to the main **Define Variable** window.

Once this is complete and everything has been defined (**fac** is defined as: **Type**: **Numeric**; **Width**: 8; **Variable Label**: **Faculty**; **Missing Values**: **7, 8, 9**), so we finish defining the variable **fac** by clicking on **OK**.

Figure A.1d   Defining the variable **Type**

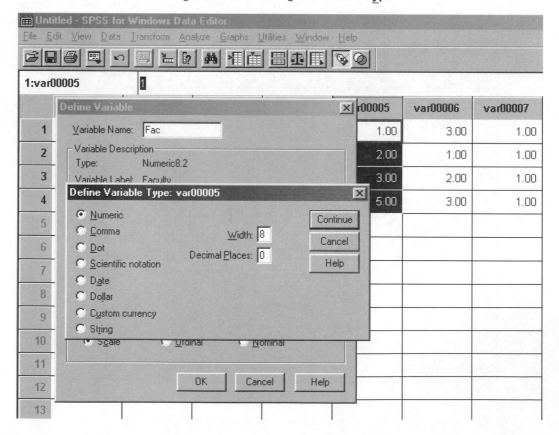

2 Listing and Exploring Data

Introduction

The process of data analysis should always begin with a *close examination of the data* you are working with. This is an important prerequisite to formal statistical testing and in this module we are going to examine some of the more common ways of exploring and summarising data. We have already looked at the SPSS menu system and identified the main features of each of the ten drop-down menus. The procedures we are going to focus on in this chapter can be accessed through either the **Analyze** or the **Graphs** menu. However, before we proceed to the practical application of SPSS we need to consider some important conceptual issues.

Levels of measurement

The concept of *levels of measurement* or *scales of measurement* is central to statistical analysis and helps to determine the types of procedure that may be carried out on particular variables. We can identify four broad levels of measurement according to the amount of information we have about a variable.

Nominal/Categorical

This is the lowest level of measurement and the most we can do with nominal variables is differentiate between the categories. We cannot place these categories in any meaningful order. Examples of variables measured on the nominal scale in the crime dataset include **religion** (respondent's religion), and **marstat2** (respondent's marital status). Although numbers have been assigned to the categories of these variables they are merely labels and have no intrinsic meaning. For instance, if we look at the frequency table for **marstat2** (Figure 2.3, p. 65) we can see the numbering of the categories from 1 to 6 is purely arbitrary as no meaningful order exists for them.

Ordinal

Ordinal variables differ from nominal variables in that here the different categories *can* be arranged into some kind of meaningful order (for example, from highest to lowest). In this respect assigning numbers to ordinal variables takes on a greater significance. However we cannot determine the degree of difference between the categories. For example, we can say that the response 'strongly disagree' is more extreme than 'disagree', but we cannot measure the difference between these two responses.

There are numerous examples of ordinal-level variables in the crime dataset, including **srinc** (self-rated income group) and **burglary** (incidence of burglary in this area). A frequency table for **burglary** is reproduced in Figure 2.4 (p. 65) and we can see there is a meaningful order to the categories (ranging from 'very common' to 'not common at all').

Interval

Variables measured at the interval level share all the qualities of nominal and ordinal variables and in addition it is possible to measure the precise distance between each of the categories. However the interval scale does not have an absolute zero point and it is therefore inappropriate to compute ratios between two values measured on this scale. True interval variables are extremely rare but one oft-cited example is temperature on the Fahrenheit scale.

Ratio

This is the highest level of measurement as it possesses all the features of the other three and, in addition, has an absolute zero. Ratio statements can be meaningfully made about such variables (for example, £20 is twice as much as £10). An obvious example of a ratio-level variable from the crime dataset is **rage** (respondent's age).

We should point out that for all practical purposes the distinction between interval and ratio scales has little significance in terms of the statistical procedures covered in this workbook and the two categories are generally grouped together as 'interval/ratio' or simply 'ratio'. You will also see these referred to as quantitative, scale or metric variables.

It is also important to be aware that a variable's scale of measurement can be altered, but generally only in a *downward* direction. So while a ratio variable such as income could be recoded into an ordinal scale by creating a series of income categories or income bands, it would not be possible to do this in reverse (see Module 3 for details on how to recode variables using SPSS).

An ability to distinguish between the different levels of measurement (nominal, ordinal and interval/ratio) is a fundamental prerequisite to even the most basic forms of statistical analysis. This issue will be examined in more detail later in the chapter when we consider the various descriptive statistics available in SPSS.

Frequency tables

Frequency tables allow you to summarise the data by counting the number of times each value or category of a particular variable occurs. For instance, if we wanted to find out how many of the respondents in the crime dataset were married, single, divorced and so on, we would ask SPSS to produce a frequency table for the variable **marstat2** (respondent's marital status). We can illustrate how this is done by requesting SPSS to produce frequency tables for **rmarstat** (respondent's marital status) and **burglary** (incidence of burglary in this area). Step-by-step instructions are as follows:

(a)   Access the **Analyze** menu (by clicking on **Analyze** in the menu bar) and click on **Descriptive Statistics** and then **Frequencies** . . . (see Figure 2.1).

Figure 2.1 **D̲**escriptive Statistics and **F̲**requencies

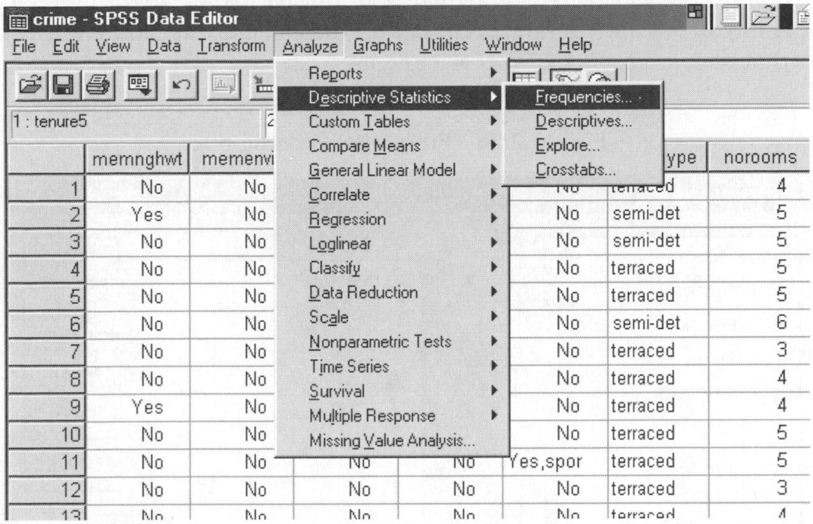

This will open up the **F̲requencies** dialog box shown in Figure 2.2a.

Figure 2.2a **F̲**requencies dialog box

Click here to transfer variables

Source variable list   Target variable list

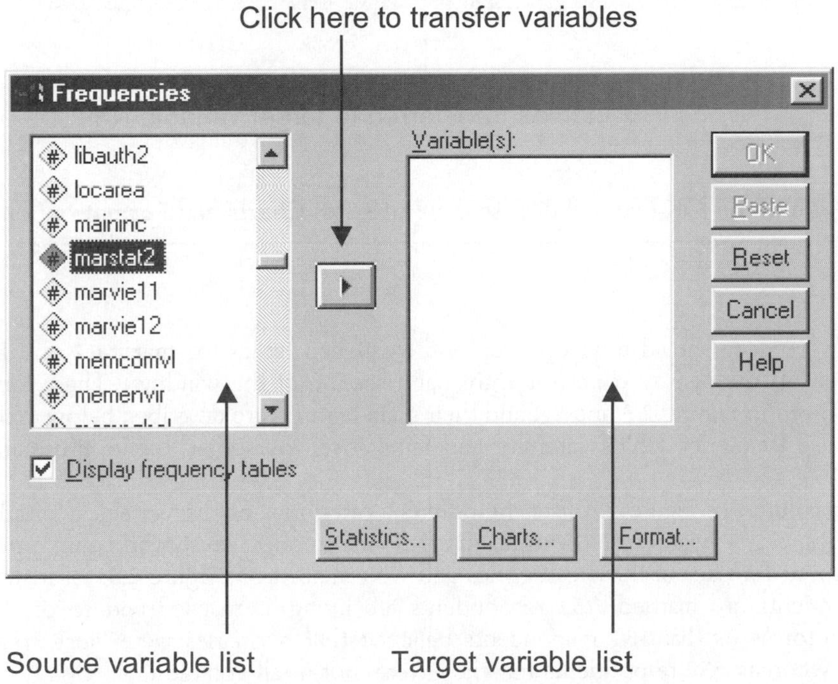

(b)   Then transfer the required variable(s) from the source variable list (the left-hand box) to the target variable list (the right-hand box).

So we need to highlight **marstat2** in the source variable list (see Figure 2.2a) by clicking on it and then transfer it to the target variable list by clicking on the right-pointing arrow in the centre of the dialog box. You can put as many variables into this target variable list as you wish. Simply scroll down through the source variable list until you come to the variable(s) you require and transfer them across to the target list the same way you did with **marstat2**. Do this for the variable **burglary** and you should end up with a dialog box similar to that in Figure 2.2b

Figure 2.2b   Frequencies dialog box

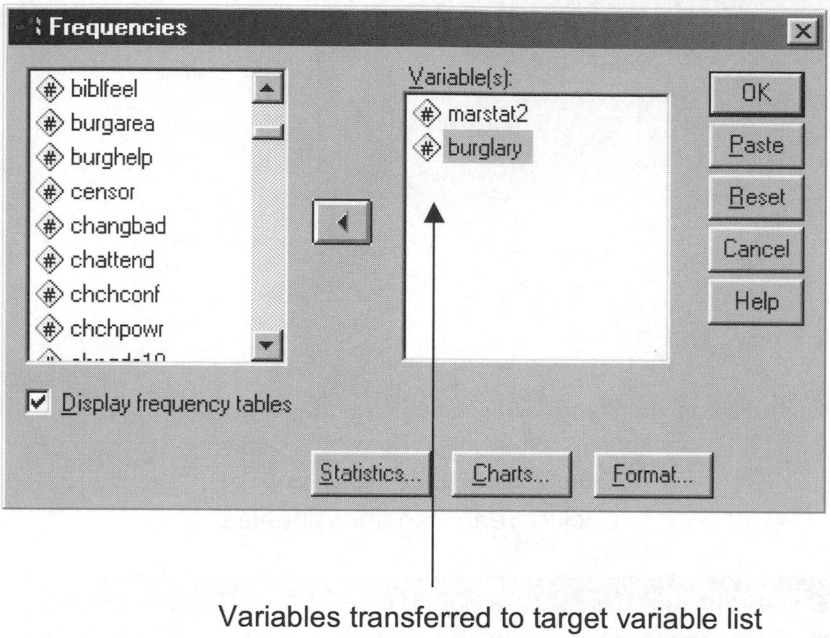

Variables transferred to target variable list

(c)   Finally click on **OK** (we will discuss the **Statistics**, **Charts** and **Format** options later).

The Viewer window should now open up and frequency tables for **marstat2** and **burglary** should appear in the display pane (the right-hand section of the window). These tables have been reproduced in Figures 2.3 and 2.4 and their main features are described below. You should examine these frequency tables carefully and familiarise yourself with the information they provide.

This first column of Figure 2.3 lists the different categories of the variables complete with number codes (e.g. 1 Married, 2 Living as married and so on). The second column provides a frequency count for each of these categories and we can see from Figure 2.3, for instance, that 1826 respondents are married, 252 respondents are living as married and so on. Similarly, Figure 2.4 informs us that 181 respondents believed that burglaries were 'very common' in their areas, whereas 659 respondents felt they were 'not at all common'.

The third column transfers these raw figures into percentages so we can say, for example, that in Figure 2.3 58 per cent of respondents are married, 5.5 per cent are divorced and 8.3 per cent are widowed.

The fourth column titled 'Valid Percent' excludes 'missing values' (if there are any) and provides a percentage breakdown of only those respondents who gave a valid answer to the question (see Module 1 for a more detailed discussion on missing values).

Figure 2.3   Frequency table for **marstat2**

MARSTAT2 Respondent's marital status[full]   Q109

		Frequency	Percent	Valid Percent	Cumulative Percent
Valid	1 Married	1826	58.0	58.1	58.1
	2 Living as married	252	8.0	8.0	66.1
	3 Separated(after married)	65	2.1	2.1	68.1
	4 Divorced	174	5.5	5.5	73.7
	5 Widowed	262	8.3	8.3	82.0
	6 Single(never married)	567	18.0	18.0	100.0
	Total	3145	100.0	100.0	
Missing	9 Not answered	1	.0		
Total		3146	100.0		

Figure 2.4   Frequency table for **burglary**

BURGLARY Incidence of burglary in this area Q142

		Frequency	Percent	Valid Percent	Cumulative Percent
Valid	1 Very common	181	5.8	5.9	5.9
	2 Fairly common	744	23.6	24.1	29.9
	3 Not very common	1506	47.9	48.7	78.7
	4 Not at all common	659	21.0	21.3	100.0
	Total	3090	98.2	100.0	
Missing	8 Don't know	56	1.8		
Total		3146	100.0		

The final column (Cumulative Percent) really becomes relevant only when the variables are ordinal or interval/ratio (in other words, where there is some sense of increase or decrease as we proceed through the categories). It totals the percentages cumulatively, so we can say, for example, that 29.9 per cent of respondents felt that burglaries were 'very common' or 'fairly common' in their area.

While frequency tables represent a useful first step in data analysis they are fairly limited in terms of the information they provide. To summarise the data further we would need to access some of the many descriptive or summary statistics available within SPSS. However, before showing you how to obtain these through SPSS it is necessary to consider briefly a number of important statistical concepts such as central tendency and dispersion.

Measures of central tendency

The concept of 'central tendency' refers to the 'average' or 'most typical' value of a distribution, and while the overall aim is to produce a figure that best represents the data there are a number of different ways of doing this. We will examine the three most common measures of central tendency — the mean, the median and the mode.

The mean

The *arithmetic mean* is the most familiar of all the measures of central tendency and corresponds with most people's notion of what an *average* is. The mean possesses a number of important mathematical properties and should be calculated only for *interval/ratio data*.

To calculate the mean you add together all the values in a batch and divide the total by the number of values. For example, if a tutorial group consisted of seven students with the following ages: 17, 18, 18, 19, 20, 20, 21 — the average age would be 19 (133 divided by 7). However, one of the main weaknesses of the mean as a measure of central tendency is that it is not 'resistant'. That is, it is disproportionately affected by *extreme values* in a distribution. So, if we replaced our 21-year-old student with a 56-year-old mature student the average age now becomes 24 (168 divided by 7). We can see, then, that one student has dragged up the average age of the class considerably, even though the other six students are all under 21. If there are extreme values in your batch, the mean could be misleading. In such circumstances it may be preferable to use an alternative measure of central tendency such as the trimmed mean or the median.

The *trimmed mean* is available in SPSS and involves removing the top and bottom 5 per cent of values before calculating the mean.

The median

The median is the most suitable measure of central tendency for ordinal data although it is also widely used with interval/ratio variables. It is simply the *middle value* in a distribution when the scores are ranked in order of size. To return to the tutorial group example above, the median age of our original seven students (17, 18, 18, 19, 20, 20, 21) would be 19. This is the value that splits the batch in two, with three scores above it and three scores below it. So the median is the same as the mean for these seven students.

However, unlike the mean, the median is resistant to extreme values and the introduction of our mature student in place of the 21-year-old does not have any effect on the result. 19 is still the middle value (17, 18, 18, 19, 20, 20, 56) in the batch.

(**Note** that if there is an even number of scores (for example: 17, 18, 18, 19, 20, 20, 56, 60) we will have two middle values (19 and 20). In this case, we simply calculate the *mean* of these two values (19 + 20 divided by 2 = 19.5)).

The mode

The mode is the simplest measure of central tendency to calculate and is the only measure that is appropriate for *nominal data*. The mode is the value that occurs *most frequently* in a distribution. So, for example, we can see clearly from Figure 2.3 that the modal value for the variable **marstat2** (marital status) is **1** (the code for married). In other words, more people (1826) fall into the married category than any of the other categories in variable **marstat2**. One of the drawbacks in using this as a measure of central tendency is that a distribution may have two or more modal values (these are referred to as *bimodal* and *multimodal* distributions, respectively).

Measures of dispersion

In the tutorial group example above we saw that both the mean and the median of our original seven students (aged 17, 18, 18, 19, 20, 20 and 21) was 19. If we consider the following seven family members (aged 2, 2, 8, 19, 20, 40 and 42) we see that the mean and median ages also turn out to be 19. However the first set of figures is tightly concentrated around the central value while the second set is much more dispersed. Clearly we need to measure more than just central tendency if we are to describe these two very different datasets adequately. Consequently this section will look at a number of measures which provide us with information on how *dispersed* or *spread out* the values in a distribution are. When dealing with ordinal data we are restricted to the range and interquartile range, while the variance and standard deviation are usually calculated only for interval/ratio variables. There are no appropriate measures of dispersion for nominal variables.

The range

The range is the most straightforward measure of dispersion and is calculated by subtracting the smallest value from the largest. However, this is a rather crude measure as it is totally dependent on the *two most extreme values* in the distribution. We need to treat the range with caution if either of these values differs substantially from the rest of the values in the batch.

The interquartile range

The interquartile range is designed to overcome the main flaw of the range by eliminating the most extreme scores in the distribution. It is obtained by ordering the batch from lowest to highest, then dividing the batch into four equal parts (*quartiles*) and concentrating on the middle 50 per cent of the distribution. The interquartile range is therefore the range of the middle half of observations, the difference between the first quartile and the third quartile. If you are using the median as a measure of central tendency then the interquartile range would be the appropriate measure of dispersion to accompany it.

The variance

The variance and standard deviation tell us how *widely dispersed* the values in a distribution are around the mean. Like the mean they require variables to be measured on the interval/ratio scale. If the values are closely concentrated around the mean the variance will be small, while a large variance suggests a batch of values which are much more dispersed.

There are three basic steps in calculating the variance:

(1) *Subtract the mean* from each of the scores
(2) *Square* each of these 'differences from the mean'
(3) *Add all the 'squared differences'* together and divide by the total number of observations minus 1.

In general terms, then, the variance represents the *average squared deviation* from the mean. (Precise instructions on how to calculate the variance, complete with examples, can be found in most introductory statistics books.)

However, the main problem with the variance is that because the individual differences from the mean have been squared it is not measured in the same units as the original variable (you should be aware that there are sound statistical reasons for squaring the deviations in the first place). To remove the effect of squaring we need to obtain the square root of the variance, more commonly referred to as the *standard deviation*.

The standard deviation

The standard deviation is the most widely used measure of dispersion and is obtained by simply calculating the *square root of the variance*. As this returns us to the original unit of measurement the standard deviation is much more meaningful than the variance. If the mean is being used as the measure of central tendency it is usually accompanied by the standard deviation. It is important to be aware that because the standard deviation, like the mean, is calculated using all the observations it is likely to be distorted by a small number of extreme values. As a general rule, therefore, it is advisable to check your data for any unusually high or low values before employing these kinds of statistics.

Descriptive statistics and charts in SPSS

Armed with an understanding of the concepts of central tendency, dispersion and levels of measurement and an appreciation of the relationship between them, you should now be in a position to select the appropriate descriptive statistics and charts for the different types of variables. These procedures can be accessed from within the **Frequencies** dialog box. To emphasise some of the points raised above we will select two variables at different levels of measurement (one nominal and one interval/ratio).

Example 1

We will begin with a variable you should be familiar with by now, **marstat2**. Descriptive statistics are located within the frequencies command, so proceed as before until you obtain the **Frequencies** dialog box shown in Figure 2.2a (p. 63). In other words, select **Analyze**, **Descriptive Statistics** and **Frequencies**. Then transfer **marstat2** into the target variable list. You will see the **Statistics**, **Charts** and **Format** options at the bottom of this dialog box (Figure 2.5).

Figure 2.5 Statistics, Charts and Format options

Figure 2.6 Frequencies: Statistics dialog box

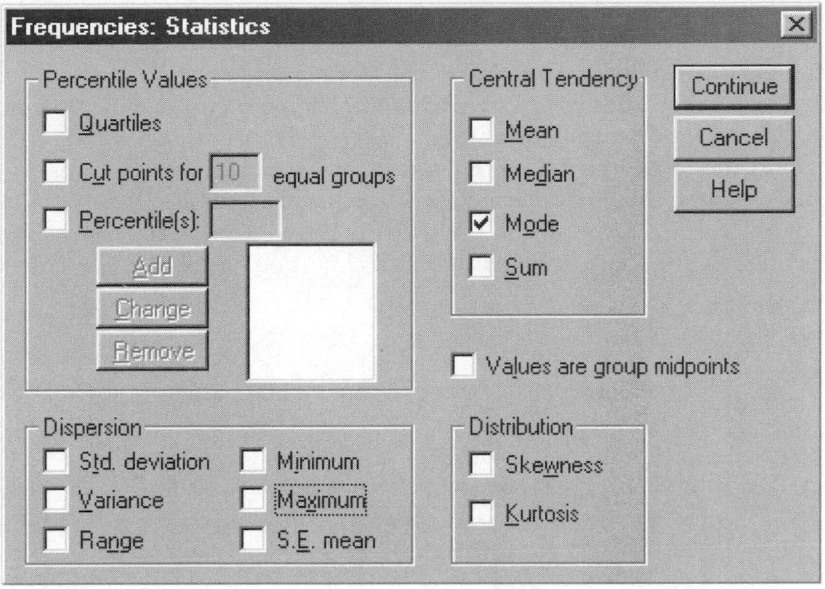

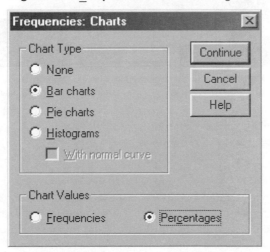

We will examine each of these options in turn:

If we click on the **Statistics** button, the **Frequencies: Statistics** dialog box (Figure 2.6) will open up.

This dialog box offers a number of different options including measures of central tendency, dispersion, distribution and percentiles. As **marstat2** is a nominal variable the most informative statistic available to us here is the mode. Select this by clicking in the **Mode** check box. Then click on **Continue**.

You will now be returned to the **Frequencies** dialog box. As we also want to select the appropriate chart for **rmarstat**, simply click on the **Charts** button.

Figure 2.7 Frequencies: Charts dialog box

This will open up the **Frequencies: Charts** dialog box (Figure 2.7). The options here include bar charts, pie charts and histograms (with bar charts you can choose whether to have frequencies or percentages displayed).

As a bar chart is an appropriate graphical display for nominal or ordinal level variables, click on the radio button next to **Bar** charts. If you want obtain percentages rather than frequencies you need to click on the **Percentages** button.

Click on **Continue** to return to the **Frequencies** dialog box and finally click on **OK**.

The resultant output is shown below and we can see from Figure 2.8a that the mode is 1 (the value code for 'Married'). However, the bar chart in Figure 2.8b highlights the modal value much more vividly and we can see immediately that almost 60 per cent of respondents fall into the 'Married' category.

Figure 2.8a   Statistics output for **marstat2**

Statistics

MARSTAT2 Respondent's marital status[full]   Q109

N	Valid	3145
	Missing	1
Mode		1

Figure 2.8b   Bar chart for **marstat2**

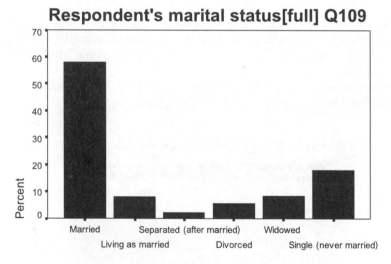

Respondent's marital status[full]   Q109

Cases weighted by WTFACTOR

The bar chart, then, provides a good visual representation of the data, as the height of each bar is proportional to the frequency or percentage (percentage in this example) of each category. However, bar charts are not always the most appropriate way to present data graphically and, as with descriptive statistics, our choice is largely determined by the variable's level of measurement.

Example 2

For our second example, we will use **rage** (respondent's age), one of the few true quantitative variables in the **Crime** dataset. As our earlier discussion showed, because interval/ratio variables are measured on a more sophisticated scale than nominal variables, it is appropriate to use a much broader range of summary statistics.

We access the **Frequencies** dialog box in the usual way (**Analyze**, **Descriptive Statistics** and **Frequencies**). Then transfer the variable **rage** over to the target variable list. With interval/ratio variables, however, we do not always want a frequency table to be produced, especially if the variable contains a large number of values. For instance, if the sample size is large, a frequency table for a variable like income may constitute several pages of output. To 'switch off' the frequency table, simply click on the **Display frequency tables** check box at the bottom of the **Frequencies** dialog box to remove the 'tick' (Figure 2.9).

Figure 2.9 Display frequency tables check box

Click here to block frequency tables (when the check box is blank, frequency tables will be suppressed).

An alternative method of curtailing lengthy frequency tables can be accessed via the **Format** option. Click on **Format** at the bottom of the **Frequencies** dialog box (see Figure 2.9) to open the **Format** dialog box (Figure 2.10).

Figure 2.10 Format dialog box

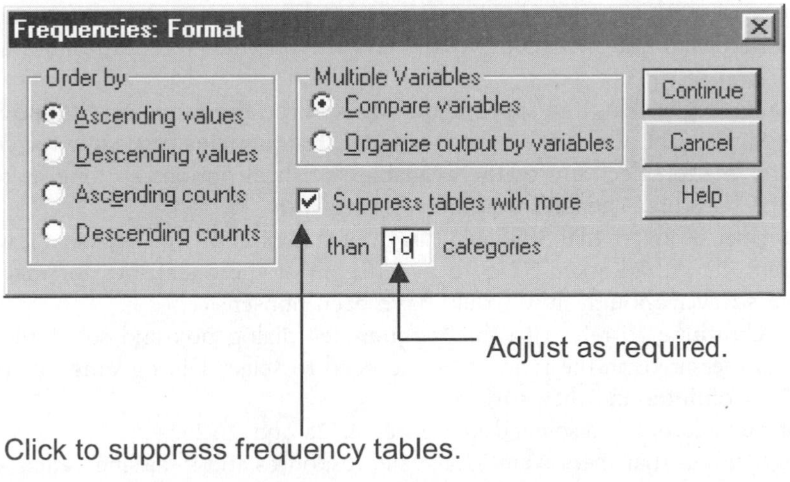

Adjust as required.

Click to suppress frequency tables.

Click on the **Suppress tables** check box and adjust the number of categories as required. This option is particularly useful if you are carrying out analysis on both quantitative and categorical variables simultaneously. However, you need to be careful not to set the number of categories too low, otherwise you will suppress frequency tables for some of the larger categorical variables.

For instance, the variable **religion** (religion of respondent) in the British Social Attitudes Survey contains seventeen different categories.

To access the statistics options click on the **Statistics** push button (at the bottom of the **Frequencies** dialog box).

As we have seen before, this will open the **Frequencies: Statistics** dialog box (Figure 2.11).

Figure 2.11 Frequencies: Statistics dialog box

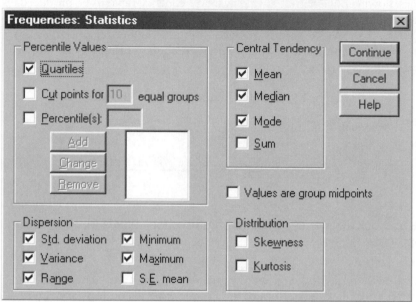

This time, however, we want to request a broader range of statistics: three measures of central tendency (mean, median and mode); three measures of dispersion (standard deviation, variance and range); minimum and maximum values; and the quartiles (the 25th, 50th and 75th percentiles).

These are obtained by clicking the appropriate boxes in the **Frequencies: Statistics** dialog box, as shown in Figure 2.11. Of course, when using the **Frequencies** procedure for your own examples, you are free to select any of the available statistical options so long as these are appropriate for the particular variables you are working with.

(**A note of caution**: Be aware that SPSS will carry out statistical procedures even if what you request is incorrect. If we had asked SPSS to produce all of these statistics for **marstat2**, it would have done so even though they would have been nonsensical.)

Next click on **Continue** to return to the **Frequencies** dialog box and select the **Charts** option. As **rage** is measured on the ratio scale, we need to select **Histograms** this time.

Finally click on **Continue** and then **OK**.

The results of our efforts are displayed in Figures 2.12a and 2.12b.

Figure 2.12a informs us that there were 3137 valid responses and 9 missing values and then reports the various summary statistics we requested. You should try to relate these results to our earlier discussion of central tendency and dispersion. For example, we can see that the mean (the average age) is 46.82. The median (the middle value in the batch) is quite close to mean at 45 years of age. However, the modal value (the one that occurs most frequently) is 32 and the disparity between this and the other two measures of central tendency suggests a *skewed*

Figure 2.12a: Descriptive statistics for **rage**

Statistics

RAGE Respondent's age in years YY   Q33

N	Valid	3137
	Missing	9
Mean		46.82
Median		45.00
Mode		32
Std. Deviation		17.89
Variance		320.15
Range		80
Minimum		17
Maximum		97
Percentiles	25	32.00
	50	45.00
	75	60.00

Figure 2.12b Histogram for **rage**

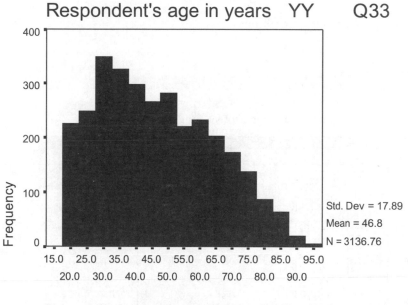

Respondent's age in years   YY   Q33

Std. Dev = 17.89
Mean = 46.8
N = 3136.76

Respondent's age in years   YY   Q33

Cases weighted by WTFACTOR

distribution. In terms of dispersion, we can see there is a standard deviation of approximately 18 years and a variance of 320 (remember that the standard deviation is the more meaningful of these two figures and represents the square root of the variance).

There is a range of 80 years of age (97 minus 17). The table in Figure 2.12a also reports the quartiles and, as we saw earlier, we can calculate the interquartile range by subtracting the lower quartile (or 25th percentile) from the upper quartile (75th percentile) (60 minus $32 = 28$). Finally, we also know from our earlier discussion that the 50th percentile represents the median value (45).

Figure 2.12b shows the histogram for **rage**. Each bar of the histogram covers a five-year age range. So, the first bar represents respondents between 17.5 and 22.5 years of age, the second those between 22.5 and 27.5 years of age and so on. We can determine how many respondents fall into each age category by looking at the vertical axis (frequency). As you can see from the graph the histogram also includes the mean and standard deviation of the distribution. Note that the chart starts abruptly with 17-year-olds since children were not sampled in this survey. Note also that there is an 'upward skew' to age – most respondents are young adults or middle-aged but there are decreasing proportions of respondents in the older age bands.

Explore

The facilities available under the **Explore** procedure in SPSS allow us to bring our exploration of the data a stage further. This section will focus on two techniques which fall under the rubric of Exploratory Data Analysis (see Tukey, 1977): the **boxplot** and the **stem and leaf display**. The **Explore** procedure is particularly useful because it provides a visual representation of some of the statistics we have just been considering. Locating these summary statistics within a graphical framework makes them more vivid and facilitates comparison between subgroups. In addition, **Explore** enables us to easily identify any values which are very different from the rest of the distribution.

To access the **Explore** option click on:

Analyze
    Descriptive Statistics
        Explore (see Figure 2.13).

Figure 2.13 Descriptive Statistics and **E**xplore

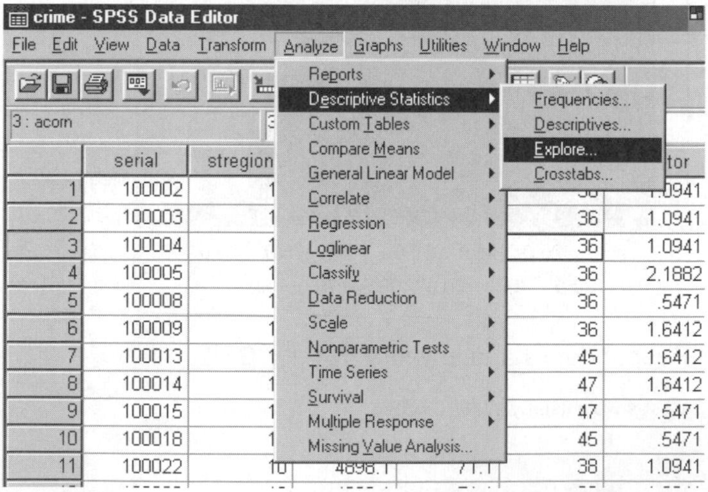

This will open the **Explore** dialog box shown in Figure 2.14.

Let us continue looking at age, only this time separately for men and women.

Transfer the variable **rage** (respondent's age) into the **D**ependent List box (**Explore** will calculate a variety of descriptive statistics including the mean and standard deviation for this

Figure 2.14 Explore dialog box

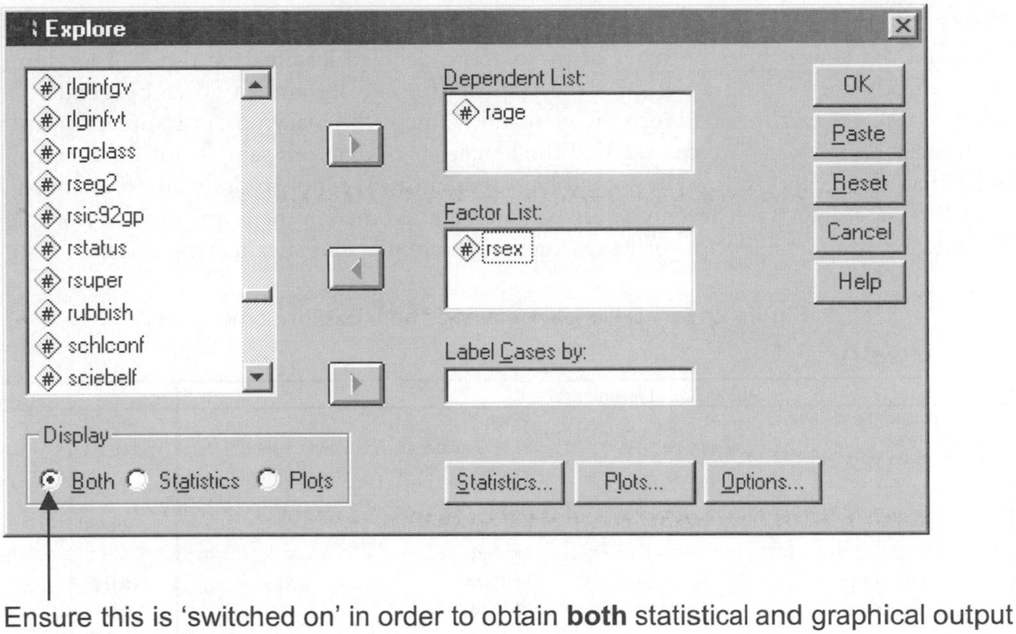

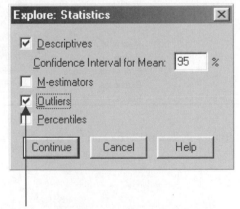

Ensure this is 'switched on' in order to obtain **both** statistical and graphical output

variable). As we want to calculate these statistics for males and females separately we need to put the variable **rsex** into the **Factor List** box.

Then Click on the **Statistics** button to open the **Explore: Statistics** dialog box (Figure 2.15). You will see that the **Descriptives** check box is already 'switched on' (the **Explore** procedure produces a variety of descriptive statistics by default). However, you also may want to identify the most extreme cases in the distribution and these can be obtained by clicking in the **Outliers** check box.

Figure 2.15 Explore: Statistics dialog box

Click here to obtain extreme values.

Then click on **Continue** to return to the **Explore** dialog box.

And finally click on **OK**.

The output from this procedure is shown in Figures 2.16a–2.16d and is discussed under four broad headings:

Descriptive statistics

Figure 2.16a includes a wide variety of descriptive statistics and while we have already discussed the key features of many of these, more detailed information can be found in most good introductory statistics texts. As the statistics for age are broken down by gender we are able to make comparisons between the men and women who make up our sample. For instance, if we focus on the mean we can see that the females (47.36) in our sample are, on average, a bit older than the males (46.16). We should be careful, however, not to draw any firm conclusions from this regarding the differences between men and women in the population as a whole (see Module 3 for a consideration of issues such as inferential statistics and significance testing).

Figure 2.16a Descriptive statistics from **Explore** procedure

Descriptives

RSEX Sex of respondent				Statistic	Std. Error
RAGE Respondent's age in years YY Q33	1 Male	Mean		46.16	.47
		95% Confidence Interval for Mean	Lower Bound	45.23	
			Upper Bound	47.09	
		5% Trimmed Mean		45.65	
		Median		44.00	
		Variance		318.042	
		Std. Deviation		17.83	
		Minimum		18	
		Maximum		97	
		Range		79	
		Interquartile Range		29.00	
		Skewness		.332	.065
		Kurtosis		-.823	.130
	2 Female	Mean		47.36	.43
		95% Confidence Interval for Mean	Lower Bound	46.51	
			Upper Bound	48.20	
		5% Trimmed Mean		46.85	
		Median		46.00	
		Variance		321.406	
		Std. Deviation		17.93	
		Minimum		17	
		Maximum		97	
		Range		80	
		Interquartile Range		28.00	
		Skewness		.387	.059
		Kurtosis		-.747	.118

Have a look at the other statistics in Figure 2.16a and try to get a grasp of what they are telling us about the data.

Extreme values

The second part of the output from **Explore** is shown in Figure 2.16b and relates to the **Outliers** option in the **Explore: Statistics** dialog box.

Selecting the **Outliers** option instructs SPSS to report the most extreme values in the distribution (that is, the five highest and five lowest values for each category of the **rsex** variable) and their respective case numbers. So we can see from Figure 2.16b that the five oldest males are 97, 94, 94, 91, and 91 and the five youngest males are all 18. The five oldest females are

Figure 2.16b Extreme values from **Explore** procedure

Extreme Values

	RSEX Sex of respondent				Case Number	Value
RAGE Respondent's age in years YY Q33	1 Male	Highest	1		2314	97
			2		3049	94
			3		2591	94
			4		173	91
			5		763	.a
		Lowest	1		2512	18
			2		651	18
			3		2711	18
			4		2027	18
			5		277	.b
	2 Female	Highest	1		57	97
			2		141	94
			3		540	94
			4		3120	93
			5		971	92
		Lowest	1		2678	17
			2		2445	18
			3		1337	18
			4		1250	18
			5		1394	.b

a. Only a partial list of cases with the value 91 are shown in the table of upper extremes.

b. Only a partial list of cases with the value 18 are shown in the table of lower extremes.

97, 94, 94, 93 and 92 and the five youngest are 17, 18, 18, 18 and 18. Identifying the most extreme values in this way helps us to become more familiar with the data and allows us to examine those cases to see if they are genuine values (and not due to an error at the data input stage, for example).

We should point out here that there is no way of telling from this table whether any of these values are 'outliers' or 'extreme values' in the technical sense. They are merely the most extreme values in the distribution, which may or may not be all that different from the other values in the batch (for a statistical definition of 'outliers' and 'extreme values' see the discussion on boxplots below).

Stem and leaf plots

Stem and leaf plots constitute the next section of the **Explore** output and, as you can see from Figure 2.16c, in graphical terms they resemble histograms quite closely. However, one of the main advantages of the stem and leaf plot is its ability to retain a considerable amount of information about the data. We can illustrate this by focusing on the main features of the plot shown in Figure 2.16c. (**Please note** that although SPSS did produce separate stem and leaf plots for males and females, the two plots are very similar and for reasons of space we have included only the plot for males here.)

The figures in the middle of the diagram represent the 'stem' and the figures to the right represent the 'leaves'. To transfer the information into actual values you need to multiply the 'stem' by 10 (stem width = 10) and add it to the 'leaf' (bearing in mind that each leaf represents four cases).

Figure 2.16c   Stem and leaf plots from **Explore** procedure

```
Respondent's age in years     YY          Q33 Stem-and-Leaf Plot for
RSEX= Male

    Frequency     Stem &   Leaf

       50.33        1 .   888889999999
      120.10        2 .   00000000001111222233333334444
      115.06        2 .   55555666667777788888889999999
      169.23        3 .   000000000011111112222222222223333333344444
      122.18        3 .   555555666666777777778888999999
      132.94        4 .   00000000011111112222222233333444444
      113.24        4 .   55555666666777778888899999
      118.08        5 .   00000001111112222222333334444
      108.32        5 .   55555666667778888889999999
       95.23        6 .   00000001111122223344444
       94.91        6 .   555556666677777888889999
       74.95        7 .   000011112222333444
       48.91        7 .   5555666778899
       27.35        8 .   0122334
       13.68        8 .   5679
        5.47        9 .   01&
         .55        9 .   &

Stem width:    10
Each leaf:      4 case(s)



& denotes fractional leaves.
```

So, for example, the first row of the table tells us that there are approximately 50 respondents (SPSS is overprecise in calculating frequencies here) in their teens. The first five values (the leaves) are 8, indicating that there are approximately twenty respondents (5 × 4) aged 18 (the stem [10] plus the leaf [8]) and the next seven values are 9, indicating that there are approximately twenty-eight respondents (7 × 4) aged 19.

Boxplots

The boxplot is an extremely efficient means of describing a number of important features of the data visually (Figure 2.16d). You can quickly identify the median, the range and the quartiles as well as any 'outliers' or 'extreme values' and the graphical nature of this information makes the impact all the more powerful. Moreover, by producing individual boxplots for each category of a particular variable, SPSS allows you to make quick comparisons between the different groups.

Figure 2.16d shows the boxplots for age by gender. As the top of the box represents the upper quartile (75th percentile) and the bottom of the box, the lower quartile (25th percentile) we can see the interquartile range at a glance (the length of the box). We know from our earlier discussion that 50 per cent of cases lie within this range. The median value can also be identified quite easily and is represented by the line inside the box.

Figure 2.16d Boxplots from **Explore** procedure

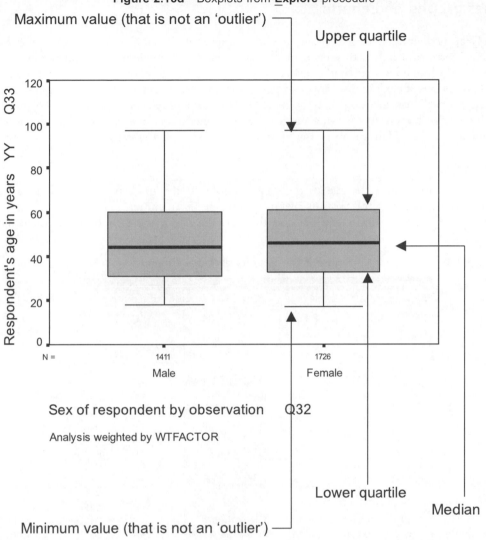

The outer lines of the boxplot represent the maximum and minimum values in the batch that don't qualify as *'outliers'* or *'extreme values'* (**Note**: in this example none of the cases qualifies as 'outliers' or 'extreme values'.)

- 'Outliers' are defined as those values that lie between 1.5 and 3 box lengths from the upper or lower quartiles; they are represented in SPSS by the symbol **O**.
- 'Extreme values' are cases which are more than 3 box lengths from the upper or lower quartiles; they are designated in SPSS by an asterisk (*).

The overall conclusion to be drawn from Figure 2.16d is that the boxplots for males and females are remarkably similar, reflecting the similar age distribution for male and female respondents (the only difference being that females are slightly older).

Other graphs and charts

The **Graphs** menu in SPSS contains a wide variety of techniques for presenting data in graphical form. Not only is this menu an alternative means of obtaining the charts and plots we have already looked at (bar charts, histograms, stem and leaf displays, boxplots), but a variety of other options including line, area and pie charts are also available. In the remainder of this module we will consider some of the most widely used graphical procedures. (To obtain a comprehensive picture of the wide range of graphs and charts available in SPSS you should consult the on-line **Help** menu or the SPSS Users' Guide, see References, p. 244).

Pie charts

While pie charts constitute one of the chart options in the frequencies procedure we will produce one here using the **Graphs** menu to illustrate its operation.

Click on **Graphs** in the menu bar and then on **Pie** ... in the **Graphs** drop-down menu (Figure 2.17).

Figure 2.17   Graphs drop-down menu

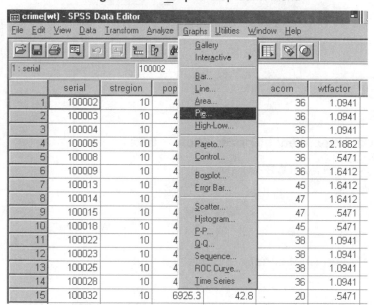

This will open up the **Pie Charts** dialog box (Figure 2.18).

Figure 2.18   Pie Charts dialog box

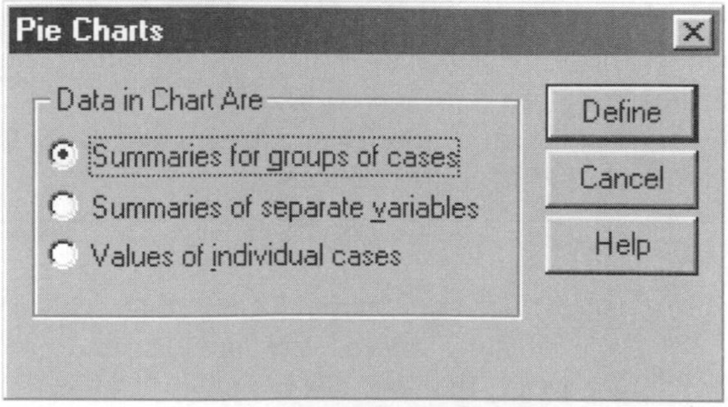

Click on **Define** to activate the default option and open the **Define Pie: Summaries for groups of cases** dialog box (shown in Figure 2.19).

To produce a simple pie chart, select the variable you want (in this case, **marstat2**) from the variable list and transfer it to the **Define Slices by**: box.

Figure 2.19 **Define Pie: Summaries** for **Groups of Cases** dialog box

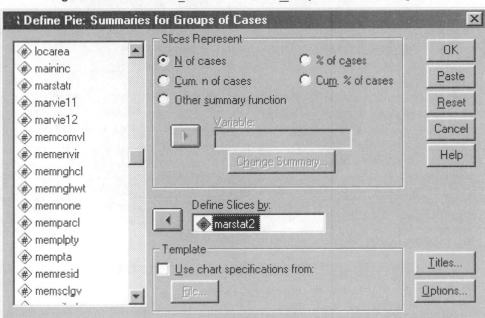

The default option in pie charts is to include missing values, so if you want these excluded you need to 'switch' the default off. To do this select **Options** (see Figure 2.19) and remove the tick from the '**Display groups defined by missing values**' check box (as shown in Figure 2.20) and click on **Continue**.

Figure 2.20 Pie chart: **Options** dialog box

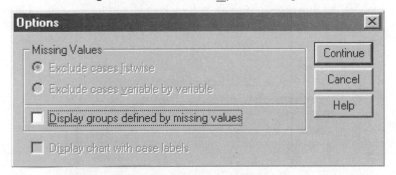

Finally, if you wish to include a title for the chart this can be done through the **Titles** option. Otherwise click on **OK** to obtain a pie chart for **rmarstat** (marital status).

Figure 2.21 Pie chart for **marstat2**

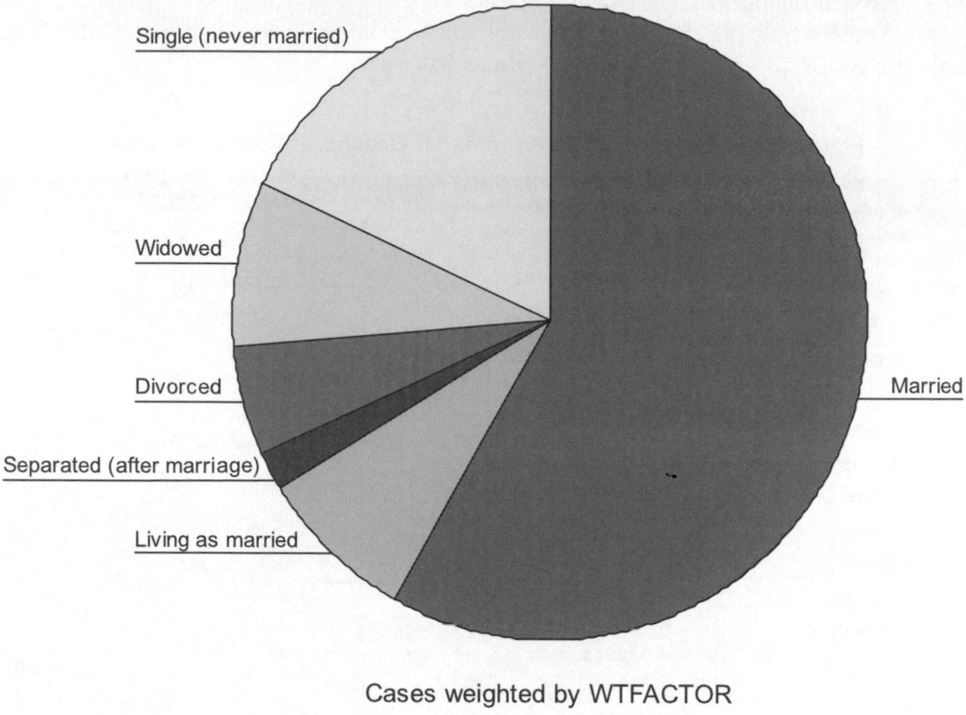

Cases weighted by WTFACTOR

A pie chart provides a pictorial display of the frequency distribution for nominal or ordinal variables and can be used as an alternative to a bar chart. Indeed you can compare the pie chart for marital status shown in Figure 2.21 with the bar chart for the same variable which was discussed earlier in this module (Figure 2.8b). From the pie chart we can see that that the married 'slice' is by far the largest, with more that 50 per cent falling into this category.

Scatterplots

While we have looked at pie charts, bar charts and histograms in the context of single variables, the scatterplot is a graphical display that allows us to examine the relationship between two quantitative variables. As this type of display will be considered in more detail in Module 7 on correlation and regression, we will confine ourselves here to the mechanics of obtaining the scatterplot in SPSS.

Figure 2.22 **Scatterplot** dialog box

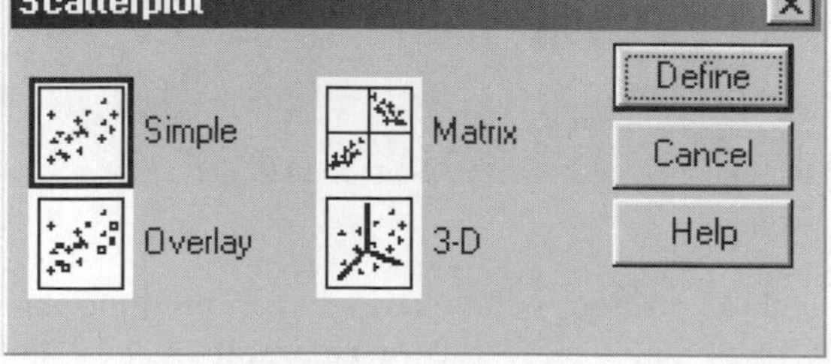

Figure 2.23   Simple Scatterplot dialog box

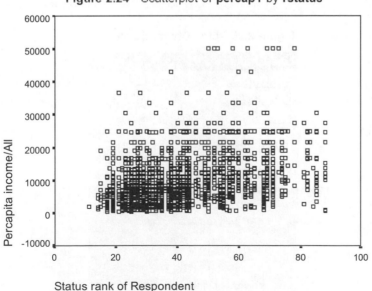

Simple Scatterplot

| abort1 |
| abort2 |
| abort3 |
| abort4 |
| abort5 |
| abort6 |
| abort7 |
| aborwrga |
| aborwrgb |
| accexpct |

Y Axis:
percap1

X Axis:
rstatus

Set Markers by:

Label Cases by:

OK
Paste
Reset
Cancel
Help

Template
☐ Use chart specifications from:
File...

Titles...   Options...

The scatterplot, like the pie chart, is accessed through the graphs menu (see Figure 2.17). Click on **Graphs** in the menu bar and then on **Scatter** ... in the **Graphs** drop-down menu. This will open the **Scatterplot** dialog box shown in Figure 2.22.

Click on **Define** to produce a simple scatterplot (as this is the default option) and this will open up the **Simple Scatterplot** dialog box (see Figure 2.23).

Figure 2.24   Scatterplot of percap1 by rstatus

Cases weighted by WTFACTOR

Select two quantitative variables from the variable list and transfer one to the **Y Axis** and one to the **X Axis**. In this example we have selected the variables **percap1** (per capita income) and **rstatus** (status rank of respondent) and we are expecting to find a positive relationship between them. In other words, the assumption is that those who are employed in low-status occupations will be located at the bottom end of the income scale and those in high-status occupations will receive high levels of income.

If you want to add titles to your scatterplot this can be achieved through the titles option, otherwise click on **OK**

The resulting scatterplot is shown in Figure 2.24 and the pattern, while not totally clear, seems to suggest a positive relationship between the two variables. In general, a low-status score tends to correspond with low incomes and a higher-status score with higher incomes. It is important to point out, however, that in order to determine whether this relationship is statistically significant we would need to carry out a *correlation* on these two variables. (A more detailed examination of scatterplots in the context of correlation and regression can be found in Module 7.)

Line charts

Line charts bear a much closer visual resemblance to bar charts and histograms than the pie chart we considered earlier. However, the use of a straight line to describe the data means that the line graph often has a much more immediate impact, particularly when comparing the distribution of a variable across two or more categories of a second variable. Line charts are particularly suitable for charting the distribution of quantitative variables that have been recoded into distinct ranked categories (see Module 3 for details on how to recode variables).

In the following examples we will use an income variable, **rearn** (respondent's gross earnings), and as this is already coded as income categories it is an ordinal rather than an interval/ratio variable. We will first produce a line chart for **rearn** on its own and then compare the distribution of this variable for males and females.

To obtain line graphs in SPSS, select **Line** from the **Graphs** drop-down menu (see Figure 2.17). This will open up the **Line Charts** dialog box, shown in Figure 2.25, where we have the option

Figure 2.25   **Line Charts** dialog box

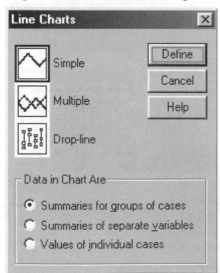

of choosing **Simple**, **Multiple** or **Drop-line** charts. We will begin with a **Simple Line Chart** for **rearn** and as 'Simple' and 'Summaries for groups of cases' are the default options we need only to click on **Define**.

This will open up the **Define Simple Line** dialog box shown in Figure 2.26. Place the variable **rearn** in the **Category Axis:** box in the usual way and then click on **% of cases** to obtain percentages rather than the number of cases.

Figure 2.26 Define Simple Line: Summaries for Groups of Cases dialog box

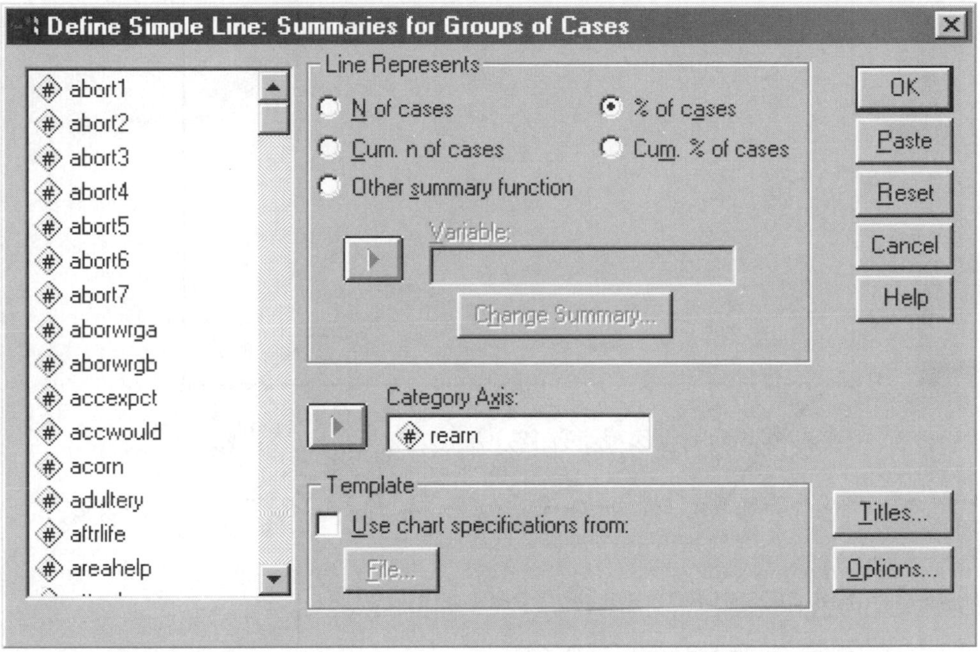

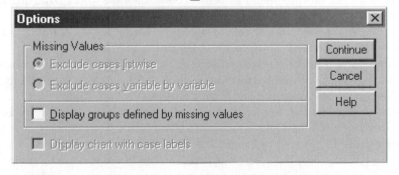

To exclude missing values from the chart, click on **Options** to open up the **Options** dialog box (Figure 2.27) and remove the tick from the '**Display groups defined by missing values**' check box. Then click on **Continue** and finally on **OK**.

Figure 2.27 Options dialog box

The results are displayed in Figure 2.28 and we can see from the line chart that there appears to be a clear pattern to the distribution. After the high point of 12 000 to 14 999 (the modal value), there is a steady decrease in the percentage of people who earn higher incomes (with the notable exception of the last two income groups; note that the last category of the **rearn** variables covers a wider range of values (£44 000 or above) than the other categories).

Figure 2.28 Simple line chart for **rearn**

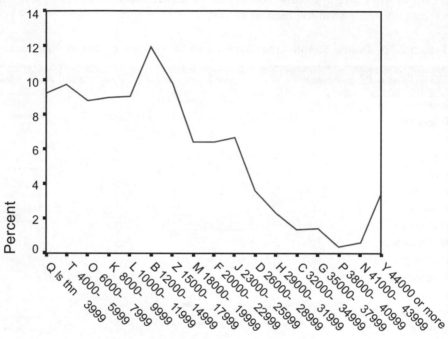

R's gross earnings [if in paid wrk]Q1190

Cases weighted by WTFACTOR

While this line graph provides a vivid picture of the income distribution of our sample, it would be interesting to break this down according to gender. To compare males and females we need to produce a *Multiple Line Chart*.

Choose **Line** from the **Graphs** menu as before, only this time select **Multiple** in the **Line Charts** dialog box (see Figure 2.25). This will open the **Define Multiple Line** dialog box shown in Figure 2.29. Transfer the variable **rearn** to the **Category Axis box** and **rsex** to the **Define Lines by** box and select **% of cases** as before.

Finally, ensure that missing values are excluded by selecting **Options** and removing the tick from the '**Display groups defined by missing values**' check box (see **Options** dialog box in Figure 2.27). Then click on **Continue** and finally on **OK**.

The results are reproduced in Figure 2.30 and clearly illustrate the disparity between the income distributions of males and females. The modal income category for females is 'less than £3999' (approximately 17 per cent of females fall into this income group) and the steep downward slope of the line indicates that decreasing proportions of women are found in the higher-income categories. In considerable contrast, a much smaller percentage of males are to be found in the lower income categories (approximately 2 per cent earn less than £3999) and the modal income category is £12 000–£14 999. We can also see clearly that a greater percentage of males falls into the highest income bracket (£44 000 or more).

Figure 2.29   Define Multiple Line: Summaries for **Groups of Cases** dialog box

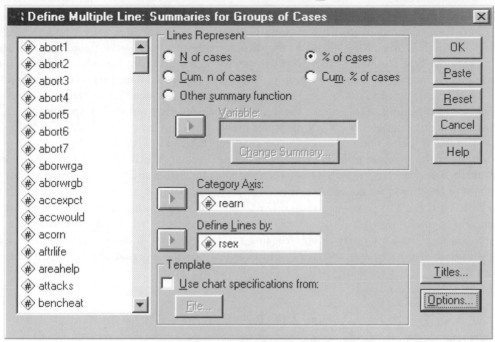

Figure 2.30   Multiple line chart for **rearn** by **rsex**

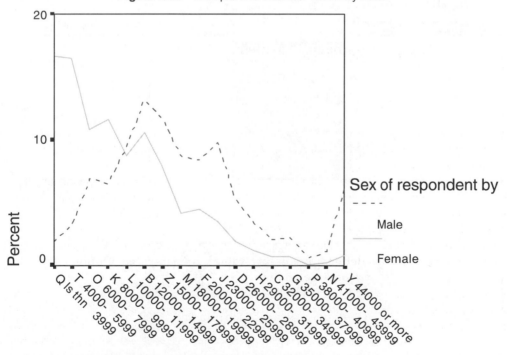

The Chart Editor

It is important to point out that SPSS allows you the freedom to *modify* your graphs and charts once you have created them. This is done through the Chart Editor which is activated by double-clicking on any of the charts in the display pane of your Viewer window. The Chart Editor window (see Figure 2.31) contains its own menu bar and tool bar which offer a variety of options for modifying charts and graphs. Most chart types contain their own unique set of options (the Scatterplot Chart Editor, for example, provides the facility for placing a regression line onto the plot) and details about these can be accessed through the **Help** menu.

While it is not possible to convey the full potential of the Chart Editor here, the following example, (which focuses on the multiple line chart reproduced in Figure 2.30), provides a good illustration of the practical utility of the Chart Editor. In the original SPSS output colours were used in the line chart to differentiate between the lines for males and females. However, for the purposes of this book, we needed the lines to be distinguishable in a black and white version of the chart. To solve this problem we used the Chart Editor to produce a discontinuous line for males. The steps involved in this process are quite straightforward and are outlined below.

Activate the Chart Editor by double-clicking on the line chart in the Viewer Window. Click on **Format** in the menu bar and select **Line Style** from the **Format** drop-down menu (see Figure 2.31).

Figure 2.31   Chart Editor window

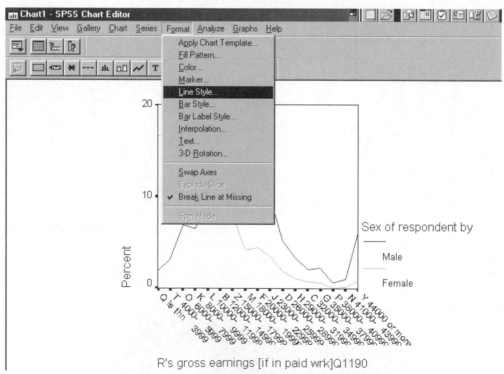

This will open the **Line Styles** dialog box as illustrated in Figure 2.32. Select the line in the chart you wish to modify by clicking on it (the line for 'males' in this instance). Then select the line **Style** and **Weight** (thickness) of your choice and click on **Apply** and finally on **Close**.

Figure 2.32   Chart Editor window with **Line Styles** dialog box

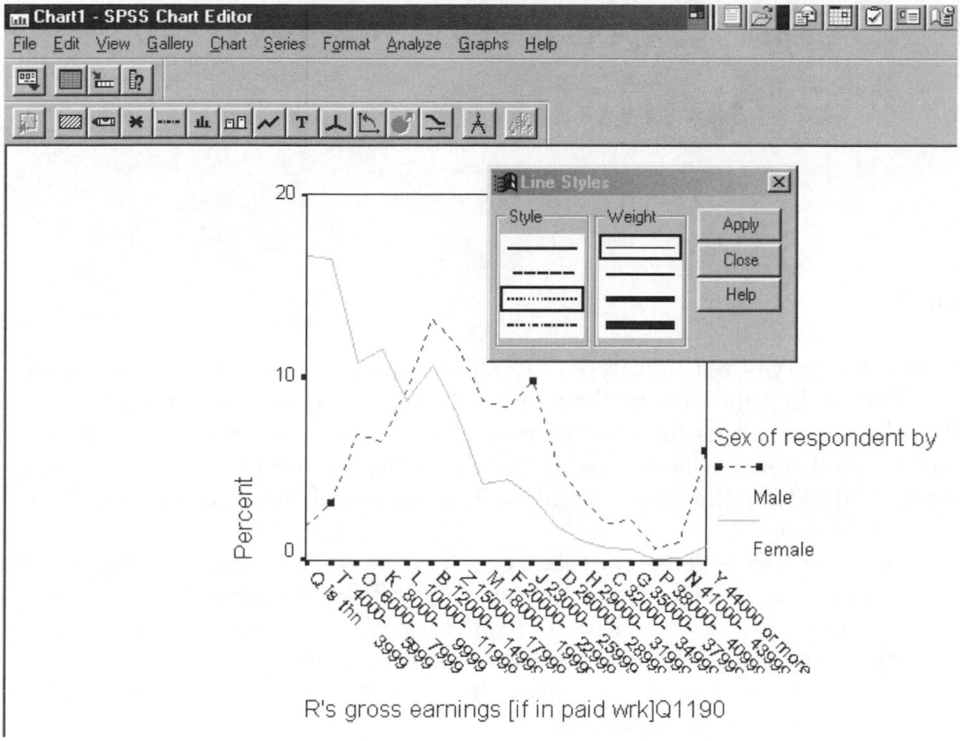

Finally, we should point out that while the graphical procedures covered in this module represent the most widely used techniques for visually presenting survey data, they account for only a small proportion of the data display options available within SPSS. You are encouraged to try out the procedures we have not covered and different variations on those we have.

SPSS exercise for Module 2

- Select a number of nominal, ordinal and interval/ratio variables from one of the datasets and produce appropriate statistics and charts using the **Frequencies** procedure in SPSS. Remember to take into account the level of measurement of each variable.
- Using the **Explore** procedure in SPSS, produce stem and leaf diagrams and box and dot plots in order to examine the distribution of an interval/ratio variable(s).
- Using the same interval/ratio variable(s), produce box and dot plots across the categories of a nominal or ordinal variable. Focus in particular on the median, interquartile range and the most extreme values for each category.

3 Data Selection and Manipulation

Introduction

Often a researcher carrying out an analysis of a dataset may want to alter or change its makeup in some way. This could particularly be the case if the researcher is analysing a dataset that was originally collected by others for other purposes. This is the situation here, where you are analysing datasets that were collected not for students to 'practice' on, but as part of the ongoing study of social attitudes in the United Kingdom. This analysis of an already-existing dataset is called *secondary analysis*.

Even if researchers have collected the data themselves, they may want to alter the form of the data in some way in order to carry out a particular analysis. These alterations to the 'core' dataset may even have been anticipated or planned from the outset of a project. The alterations are of two basic types: *data selection* or *data manipulation*. Practically all social science data analysis packages will have at least rudimentary facilities for data selection and data manipulation. The facilities that SPSS offers are quite advanced.

Since the goals of data selection and manipulation are similar — to 'recast' a dataset into a form more amenable to analysis — and much of the logic of the two processes is also similar, we will consider both processes in this module.

Data selection

Sometimes researchers know that they will not need all of the information contained within a dataset for a certain analysis or course of analyses that they intend to carry out. Hence, either the *cases* of interest or the *variables* of interest for the given analysis may be selected. This is done for two reasons.

- **Efficiency** If the analysis is restricted to less than the whole dataset, the *technical demands* on memory space, time to read the data and so forth will be lessened
- **Safety** By restricting the analysis to only the cases and variables of interest, one can ensure that *unwanted cases and variables* do not inadvertently get included in an analysis by mistake.

Researchers usually consider the gains in efficiency that can be made through wise data selection but often fail to recognise the *safety* aspect — the utility of data selection as an important safeguard for a valid analysis of only the cases of interest.

There are two generally recognised methods of data selection: *choosing subsets of cases*; and *choosing subsets of variables*. We will consider each in turn.

Subsets of cases

Often, the analyst may be interested in only a portion of the cases within the dataset. *Which* portion or portions will depend upon the dataset and the interests of the particular analysis in question.

A simple example

The British Social Attitudes datasets are made up of individuals drawn from the general population who are respondents to a sample survey. Let us say the researcher wishes to carry out a certain analysis on only the women in the sample. Since the survey respondents have their sex coded as a variable, the data selection procedure in SPSS can be employed to ensure than only the data from the females is used.

To select a subset of your sample you use the Select procedure. Ensure the Data Editor window is opened, using the **Data** pull-down menu, highlight **Select Cases**. The window that appears will look like Figure 3.1.

Figure 3.1 Select Cases window

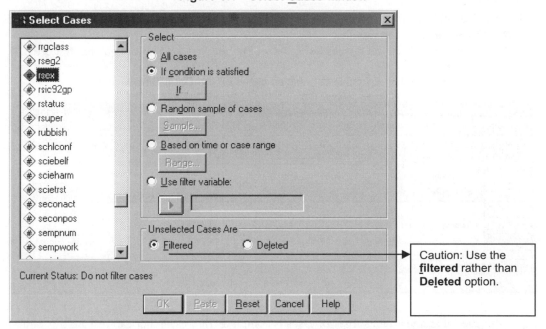

Caution: Use the **filtered** rather than **Deleted** option.

Click on the '**If condition is satisfied**' button, this opens the **Select Cases: If** subwindow (Figure 3.2).

Using the scroll bar on the side of the variable list, select **Sex of Respondent (rsex)** and click on the ▶ symbol to move it across to the '**work box**'. Then, select only cases on the variable **rsex** (the sex of the respondent) with the code **2** (female) by clicking on the = button and the number **2**. The resulting statement is: **rsex = 2**.

Click on the **Continue** button and you are back to the **Select Cases** subwindow (see Figure 3.2). Click on **OK** to have SPSS select only the female respondents. The goal of *efficiency* is met since the dataset actually being analysed, only women, is only about half as large as the original. The goal of *safety* is also met since, after selection, it is impossible for men to become

Figure 3.2   Select If subwindow

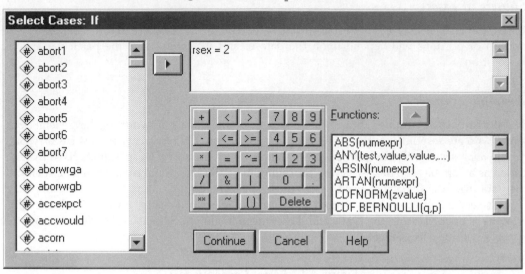

inadvertently mixed up in the analysis. The researcher will know for sure that any results obtained relate only to the women.

After this procedure, all the unselected cases will be marked with an oblique bar (Figure 3.3).

Figure 3.3   Example of selected cases on the **Data View** window

		stregion	popden	ownoccup	acorn	wtfactor	househld	rsex	
1		Greater	4898.1	71.1	Home o	1.0941	3	Male	
2		Greater	4898.1	71.1	Home o	1.0941	2	Female	
3		Greater	4898.1	71.1	Home o	1.0941	3	Male	
4		Greater	4898.1	71.1	Home o	2.1882	5	Male	

After the special analysis of a subset of cases is complete, the researcher can restore the dataset to its original full form if desired. The way to do this is to go back through **Data** to the **Select Cases** window and click on the '**All cases**' button and run it with **OK**.

(**A note of caution:** If you decide to save a new version of the dataset while only a subset of cases is selected, the new saved version will contain *only* the selected cases − all unselected cases would be lost to any subsequent analysis. This is a powerful reason to restore all cases once the analysis of a subset is completed.)

A more complex example

The selection of cases can be fairly straightforward and simple, as in our example of picking people of one sex, or the criteria used for selection of cases can be quite complex. A researcher might be interested in exploring 'a subset of a subset'. For example, we may be interested in analysing the attitudes to crime of females who live alone. The **Select If** procedure can be used to do this.

In order to carry out this procedure we must select on two variables. The first variable is **rsex** (Respondent's Sex), and the second variable is **Househld** (Number of people living in household). From the variable **rsex**, we want to select Females (value 2), and from the variable **Househld** we want to select Respondents Lives Alone (value 1). Thus for the subset we require, we need to select all cases where the value of **rsex** is 2, *and* the value of **househld** is 1.

To carry out this procedure use the **Data** pull-down menu to highlight **Select Cases**. Click in the **Select If** button. Click on the **If** button, this will open the **Select Cases: If** subwindow.

Transfer the variable **rsex** across to the work area. Click on the = button on the **keypad**. Return to the work area and type **2**. Click on the **&** on the keypad (or type in directly to the work area). Next, using the scroll bar on the left-hand side, highlight and transfer **househld**, to the work area. Click on the = button on the keypad. Return to the work area and type **1**.

Figure 3.4   Example of a more complex selection using **Select If**

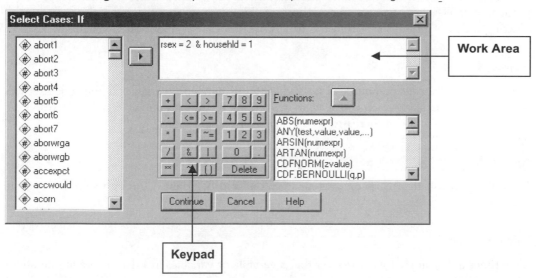

As in Figure 3.4, the work area should now have the following instruction: **rsex = 2 & househld = 1**. Click on **Continue**, this will bring you back to the first dialog box, and click on **OK**.

The keypad in SPSS

Before continuing, you may want to take a good look at the functions available on the 'keypad'.

- Some, like **+**, **−**, and **=** are obvious;
- ***** means *'multiply'*, **/** is *'divide'*, ****** is *'square'*
- Others include: **>** for *'greater than'*; **>=** for *'greater than or equal to'*; **&** for *'and'* | for *'or'*; and **[ ]** to enclose part of a statement in *brackets*
- **~=** means *'not equal to'*
- As you might guess, **<** means *'less than'* and **<=** is *'less than or equal to'*.

You can also scroll up and down to the right of the **keypad** to see some more obscure functions.

SPSS Exercises for selecting cases

Now, try out some 'selecting' cases for yourself:

● Choose a subset of the **Crime** dataset and select it yourself. Try a simple selection first and then perhaps a more complicated statement. (**Remember**, if you need the full dataset again — use the **Filtered** option rather than the **Deleted**. This way you can always get back to the original unselected dataset by 'pushing' the '**All cases**' button on the **Select Cases** dialog box.)

Subsets of variables

As well as choosing subsets of cases, the researcher can select a subset of *variables* from a complete dataset. As with case selection, this could be done either for reasons of efficiency or for reasons of safety. For example, the authors of this textbook created the **Crime** dataset by selecting a subset of variables from the total British Social Attitudes Survey dataset.

Efficiency

As with taking a smaller number of cases, reducing the number of variables within a dataset will decrease its gross size, which can lead to reductions in the amount of computing resources required and to significant increases in the speed of computations.

Safety reasons

While it is not as often realised, greater safety can also be attained through selecting subsets of variables.

Contamination

Sometimes a data analyst will discover that a variable or variables in a dataset are inaccurate or 'contaminated' in some way. For instance, there could have been an error in coding that cannot be fixed. If the 'contaminated' variable(s) was left in the dataset, it could cause problems for later analysts who might use it without realising that the variable was unreliable. Hence, the 'data manager' might conclude that the safest course is to 'purge' the variable from the dataset altogether.

Restrict access

The 'owner' or 'data manager' of a dataset may want to give access to the data to someone else so that person can carry out a specific analysis. The 'data manager', however, may not want to give the person *full* access to all the information in the dataset.

For instance, some variables may contain information that would make it possible to identify individual respondents. The 'data manager' may want to 'mask' these variables in order to preserve confidentiality. A way to do this is to release only a partial dataset that contains all of the variables they need to attain the goals of an analysis *but only* the variables sufficient for the stated goals of that analysis. Scrupulous secondary analysts are in no way inconvenienced by possessing only a partial dataset — for their purposes it is as if the data were complete.

The procedure for selecting a subset of variables is also quite simple. The 'data manager' uses the spreadsheet format of SPSS to choose the columns of the variables that are to be dropped, *cuts them* and then *saves a new version of the dataset* (which should have a *new file name*). One can of course combine selections of variables and selection of cases in order to produce a doubly truncated partial dataset.

Splitting files

It is sometimes helpful to split a file by the levels of a categorical variable so that data analysis is conducted automatically at each level separately – for example, by the sex of respondent whereby each analysis is carried out for males and females. To split a file use the Select procedure, ensure the Data Editor window is opened, using the **Data** pull-down menu, highlight **Split File**. The **Split File** dialog box should look like Figure 3.5. Select the variable you wish to split (Sex of Respondent **rsex**), click on the **Compare groups** or **Organize output by groups** button, and click on **OK**. Once the file has been split, any subsequent analysis will present a separate analysis for each group (male and female). Remember, the split can be cancelled by selecting the **Analyze all groups – do not create groups** option in the **Split File** dialog box.

Figure 3.5 Example of splitting a file by **rsex**

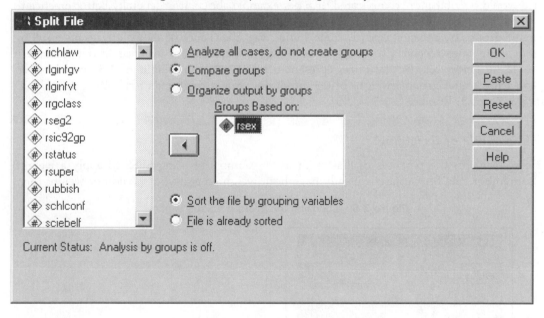

Weighting

(Note: The British Social Attitudes Datasets provided with this book are *already* *weighted* – students should read this section but not attempt to weight the dataset in the practice datasets.)

While not strictly *selection*, the procedure for *weighting* the cases in a dataset – that is, counting some cases more or less than others – does follow on from case selection.

The need to *weight* usually arises when a probability sample (as with the British Social Attitudes Survey) has been taken and the researcher knows or discovers that some categories of cases in the sample have been overselected or underselected. That is, some groups of cases have had a better chance of being selected in the sample than others. (Weighting is quite a normal procedure. Sample designs for surveys often are deliberately designed to oversample or under-sample some groups.) If researchers want to generalise from the sample results to the target population, they will want to equalise the representation of all the cases in their sample. *If the overrepresented or underrepresented groups can be identified in the dataset (that is, if there are variables in the dataset that allow the overrepresented or underrepresented groups to be identi-fied) and the researchers have an idea of how much the groups have been overrepresented or underrepresented, a corrective weight can be applied.*

For example, if the researchers know that their sample has underrepresented urban people in comparison to people in rural areas by a factor of three, they can correct this by counting each urban person three times (that is, weighting by 3).

Approaches to weighting

A normal convention is never to weight any individual case by more than a factor of 2. The reason for this is that, if individual cases are counted more than twice, the possibility of a distortion in the results due solely to weighting increases. If a case is weighted more than 2, and the case happens to be 'peculiar' in some way, the researcher may end up erroneously concluding that an odd characteristic is really quite common. Hence, the usual weighting prac-tice would be a bit more complicated than our example above. It is generally better practice to weight the *over*represented groups by a weight *less than* one and to weight the *under*repre-sented groups by a weight *more than* one. In this way, the chance of anomalous results resulting from some cases receiving too large a weight are minimised. For instance, in our example it would be better to give the underrepresented urban group a weight of 1.5 and the over-represented rural group a weight of 0.5, producing equal weightings for both at 1.5 (Urban: $1 \times 1.5 = 1.5$; Rural: $3 \times 0.5 = 1.5$).

An example of weighting

Here solely for the purposes of illustration is an example of using SPSS to apply a weight. (**Remember**, the BSA datasets already have been weighted and you should not weight them

Figure 3.6   Choosing the **Weight Cases** window

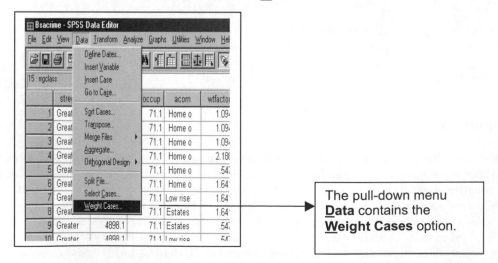

again.) Go to the **Data** list on the main Data View window of the Data Editor and select **Weight Case** ... (as in Figure 3.6) A **Weight Cases** window as in Figure 3.7 will open. The **Weight Cases** window displays a weight, **wtfactor**, being applied to a dataset. Once the weight has been applied a **Weight On** note appears on the bottom right-hand row of the Data Editor.

Figure 3.7   Example of a variable, **wtfactor**, being used to weight a dataset

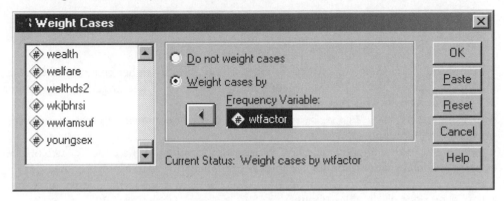

Data manipulation

As well as employing data selection to 'recast' a dataset into a smaller dataset made up of fewer cases or fewer variables or to weight the cases in a dataset, an analyst can also 'recast' a dataset by employing one or more techniques of *data manipulation*. In data manipulation, the number of cases usually remains the same and the number of variables is not reduced (in fact, the number of variables is often *increased*).

Data manipulation involves taking existing variables and either:

(1)   *Altering* the values/codes of the variables in some way;
       or
(2)   *Combining* the codes/values of two or more variables with some sort of logical statement to create a new variable.

Data manipulation is a powerful tool. No one, no matter how well organised they are or how clear a preconception they have of their analysis plans, can anticipate every eventuality in their analysis. At least some of the variables in a dataset will almost inevitably need to be modified or changed during the course of an analysis programme in order to satisfy the changing requirements of the analysis. (If for no other reason, because the researcher's own ideas and plans will (*should!*) change based upon early findings.)

These considerations of course will apply doubly to *secondary analysts* who are adapting a dataset collected by others to goals of their own.

In fact, data manipulation is so normal a practice that people setting up datasets will expect to do some data manipulation. In many cases data manipulation forms an essential preliminary step in the data analysis. Rather than trying to create every variable in exactly the form that will be needed for every analysis, they will set up the variables in a form that is *most readily amenable* for *later* data manipulation.

This means that those setting up a dataset will opt for the maximum practical amount of detail at the stages of coding and data input. Owing to the modern technologies of data input and the possibilities available with data manipulation, coding a set of information using codes based upon many detailed categories rather than codes made up of a few large, aggregate, categories is *always* a better practice in the long run.

SPSS V10 has excellent facilities for data manipulation.

There are some fairly esoteric data manipulation procedures but, thankfully, there are four main basic types of data manipulation techniques that are the most useful and that are employed 95 per cent of the time.

The four main data manipulation techniques are:

1. Altering individual codes or groups of codes of variables by either changing the actual individual values of the codes or combining blocks of codes together into larger aggregates (**Recode and Automatic Recode**)
2. Manipulating a variable's codes by carrying out simple or complex arithmetic operations on variables (**Compute**)
3. Carrying out logical manipulations on variables by combining the codes/values of two or more variables with some sort of logical statement to create a new variable (**If**)
4. Creating new variables by counting the occurrences of a value or a range of values across a number of variables (**Count**).

We will consider each of these in turn.

Altering individual codes or groups of codes (Recode)

Altering a variable's individual codes or groups of codes by changing either the individual values of the codes or combining blocks of codes together into larger aggregates is one form of data manipulation. Perhaps the best way to explain this is to provide some examples.

Combining codes

Combining blocks of codes together into larger aggregates

Often, a variable will have a large number of highly detailed codes. An analyst may wish to merge these detailed codes into a smaller number of aggregate categories.

Example 1

In the simplest cases, the original detailed codes are a series of numbers where the numbers represent real quantities (*integers*). For instance, the respondents to the British Social Attitudes survey all have their age recorded in years (the variable **rage**); the analyst may wish to lump these values into three categories:

   Young adults (those aged between 18 and 29)
   Adults (those aged between 30 and 64)
   Elderly (those aged 65 or more).

Visually, one wants to do something that would look like Figure 3.8.

Figure 3.8 Recoding age in years to age categories

Age-Years	Age-Category
18 19 ⇑ ⇓ 29	(1) Young adults
30 31 ⇑ ⇓ 65	(2) Young Adults
66 ⇑ ⇓ 97	(3) Elderly

There are two recode commands: **Recode into the Same Variable** and **Recode into Different Variables**. The first of these commands changes the code of the variable, whereas the second creates a new variable which contains the new codes. It is generally advisable to select the second option so that, as well as creating a new, recoded, variable, the original variable with its codes is retained.

To do a **RECODE** of Respondents Age (**rage**), open the **Transform** pull-down menu on the main window, choose **Recode** and the **Into Different Variables** option. This will open the 'Recode into **Different Values**' dialog window (see Figure 3.9a). From the variable list, select **rage** (Respondent's Age) and bring it across into the 'work box'. We choose the **Into Different Variables** option because we want to keep the original year-by-year age values as well as having the new age categories. Go to the **Output Variable** box and type in the name of the new variable, **agecats**. Label this new variable as **Recoded age categories**, and click on the **Change** button to replace the '?' for the new variable with its name, **agecats**.

To collapse of age in years into categories, we click on the **Old and New Values** box which opens a subwindow for us to create the categories (Figure 3.9b).

Here you work between the **Old Value** and **New Value** boxes to fill in the commands in the '**work box**' on the mid right-hand side of the window. There is a variety of ways you can specify the 'old values' that are to be converted into 'new values', it is possible to:

Figure 3.9a An example of **Recode: rage** into a new variable, **agecats**

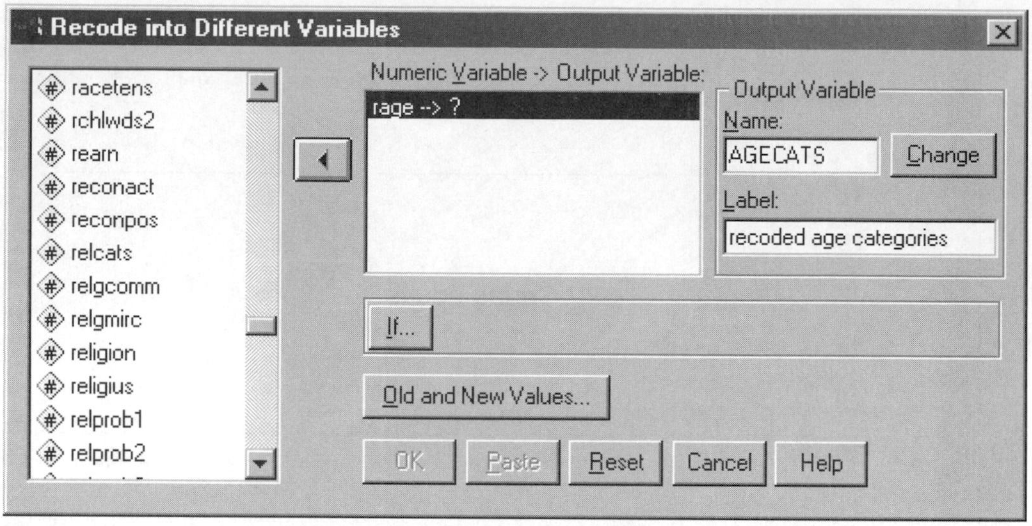

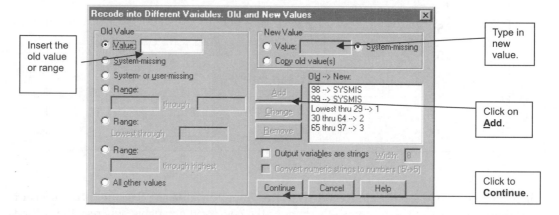

Figure 3.9b Identifying old and new values for **agecats**

- Specify individual values
- Specify a range of values (for example, **30 thru 64**)
- Specify the lowest value up to a limit (for example, **Lowest thru 29**)
- Specify a value up to the highest value (for example, **65 thru highest**)
- Ensure that the missing values in the 'old' variable remain missing values in the 'new' variable (for example, **99 → SYSMIS**).

The keywords **lowest** and **highest** are used to avoid the problem of our not being sure of the exact code of the lowest or highest value. Here, **Lowest thru 29** includes everyone aged 29 or younger, even if we do not know the age of the youngest person.

Note how since the values '98' and '99' in the original variable, **rage**, were missing values ('Don't know' and 'Not answered', respectively) and not actual ages, we had to use **65 thru 97 → 3** instead of **65 thru highest** to create the **Old** category in **agecats**.

In all instances, after the range of old values have been specified, the new value for each category must be entered. For example, the age range from 30 to 64, inclusive, is recoded into age category '2': **30 thru 64 → 2**.

After each recode has been entered, it is added to the 'work box' by clicking the **Add** button. When all the recode from 'old' to 'new' values are set, click on the **Continue** button, and **OK** to run the re-code. A new variable, **agecats**, will come into existence. You can verify this by scanning to the far right-hand side of the Data Editor grid. There you will find a new column in the data grid which contains the values for the variable **agecats**.

The next stage is to label each of the values of the new variable. To label AGECATS, open the **Variable View** window of the Data Editor and label the new recoded variable in the same way as you would label variables when you are creating a new dataset (see the section on Labelling in Module 1).

Example 2

A similar, though slightly more complex, aggregation arises when we have a variable with a series of detailed codes, but the detailed codes do *not* represent any steadily increasing or decreasing 'run' of quantities. For example, in the British Social Attitudes dataset the variable called **religion** has a detailed list of categories of religious denominations to which the survey respondents belong.

For the purpose of the survey, it is important to have this level of detail but in many cases a religious denomination may constitute only a small proportion of the group (for example, 11 per cent of the respondents in the survey are members of the Baptist church). But we may want to conduct comparative analysis on the main religious groups. To do so, we must aggregate the data from the eighteen categories in the original **religion** variable into a smaller number of

Figure 3.10 Recoding religion into a new variable. **Old Categories** (from **religion** variable) and **New Categories** (**relcats** variable)

Old CODE	Current Categories	New Categories	New CODE
3	Catholic	CATHOLIC	1
4	Church of England/Anglican		
5	Baptist		
6	Methodist		
7	Presbyterian/Church of Scotland	PROTESTANT	2
21	Free Presbyterian		
22	Brethren		
23	URC/Congregational		
27	Other Protestant		
8	Other Christian		
14	Christian – No denomination		
1	No religion		
9	Hindu	OTHER	3
10	Jewish		
11	Islam/Muslim		
12	Sikh		
13	Buddhist		
14	Other non-Christian		

larger categories – for example: Catholic; Protestant; and Others. The old and new categories with codes are presented in Figure 3.10.

The procedures for recoding the variable **religion** into a new variable **religcat** are outlined in Figures 3.11a and 3.11b. As before, use the **Transform** pulldown menu, then select the **Recode into Different Variables** option. This opens the **Recode into a Different Variable** window for aggregating the variable into a new variable called **relcats** (Figure 3.11a). While the technique of aggregating is the same as before, we have to be more careful to make sure that each detailed category gets put into the right 'pigeonhole' and also that we do not forget any of the detailed categories (Figure 3.11b). Note how we again we had to make sure that those respondents coded as a missing value on the original **religion** variable still have a

Figure 3.11a Collapsing the **religion** categories into a new variable, **relcats**

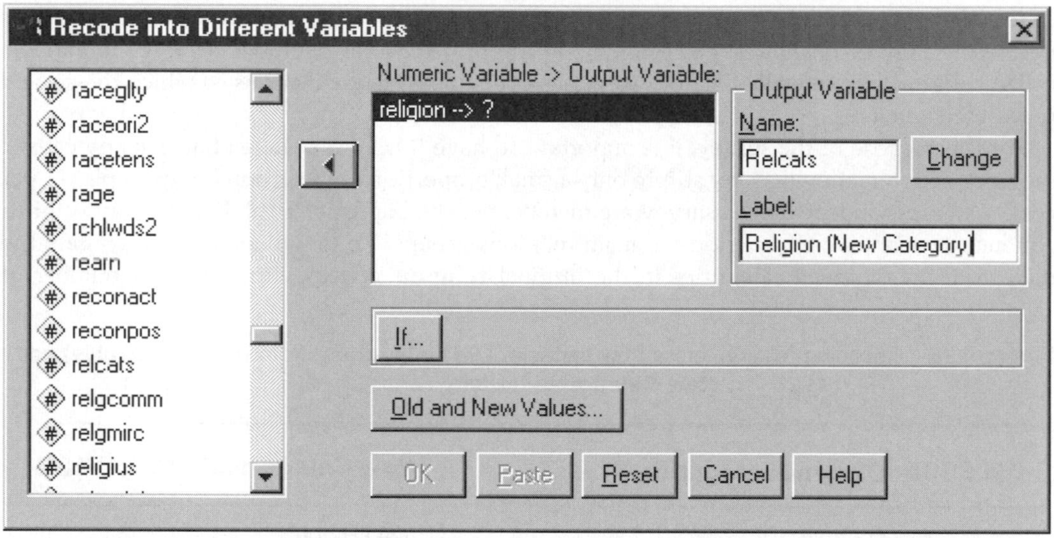

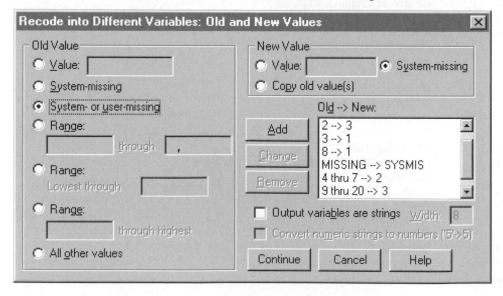

Figure 3.11b Identifying old and new variables for the new **religion** variable, **relcats**

missing value code for the new variable. Here, we have done this by telling SPSS to set all '**System or user-missing**' values on the old variable equal to '**System-missing**' values on the new variable, '**MISSING → SYSMIS**'.

Once you have recoded all the original values, click on **Continue** to go back to the first window of the **Recode into Different Variables** window. Click on **Change** (output variable), and **OK**. This will create a new variable **relcats** which will appear in the last column of your data set.

The final stage is to label each of the values of the new variable. To label **relcats**, open the **Variable View** window of the Data Editor and label the new recoded variable in the same way as you would label variables when you are creating a new dataset (see the section on Labelling in Module 1 and Figure 3.12).

Figure 3.12 Defining labels for the new variable **relcats** in the **Variable View** window

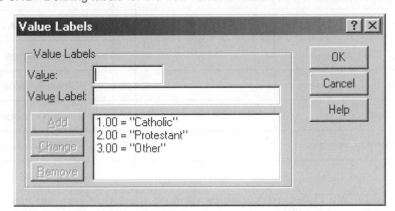

Altering variable codes

Sometimes, we might want to alter the codes of a variable *without aggregating*. For instance, we might want to change the numerical order of a series of codes for a variable in order to improve its presentation (for example, altering the detailed codes of the **religion** variable so that all of the Protestant denominations would automatically appear next to each other in a **Frequencies** output).

We may also want to alter a variable's codes for more mundane reasons. For instance, when cleaning data, we might discover some invalid codes in a variable. We might want to simplify matters by 'sweeping' all these invalid code values together into a single 'missing value' code — or, if we check back and establish what the correct code should be, we will want to change the invalid code to its correct value. For example, if we might find that some error has been made in entering information into the **rsex** variable (which should have only two values, **1 = Male** and **2 = Female**), and that some codes **6** and **7** have been entered erroneously. Using **Transform → Recode → Into the Same Variable**, the codes 6 and 7 can be recoded to a third category 3 = Don't Know.

Recoding a list of variables

SPSS provides a way of specifying a range of variables without having to put in the recoding commands for each variable separately. For instance, in the original British Social Attitudes dataset there are two questions on respondents' views on the advisability of religious leaders having influence on voting and government (**rlginfvt** and **rlginfgv**). These are ordinal-level questions with 7 categories (1 = Strongly agree, 2 = Agree, 3 = Neither agree or disagree, 4 = Disagree, 5 = Strongly disagree, 8 = Can't choose, 9 = Not answered). For the purpose of future analysis using these variables in our practice datasets it was useful to change the 'Can't choose' value from 8 to 3 (representing a neutral/middle value, Figure 3.13a).

Figure 3.13a   Chart of recoding values: **rlginfvt** and **rlginfgv**

Catagories – Original Values   New Categories and values

1	Strongly Agree		1	Strongly Agree
2	Agree		2	Agree
3	Neither Agree or Disagree		3	Neither Agree or Disagree
4	Disagree		4	Disagree
5	Strongly Disagree		5	Strongly Disagree
8	Can't choose	⟶	3	Can't choose
9	Not Answered		9	Not Answered

Within the **Recode into Different Variables** window, more than one 'old' variable can be selected, with each 'old' variable having a different 'new' variable name specified (see Figure 3.13b). The same **Recode into Different Variable: Old and New Values** window applies to all the selected variables.

Figure 3.13b   Recoding two variables into new variables: **rlginfvt** and **rlginfgv**

Give each new variable a new name and label.

Click on **Old and New Values**.

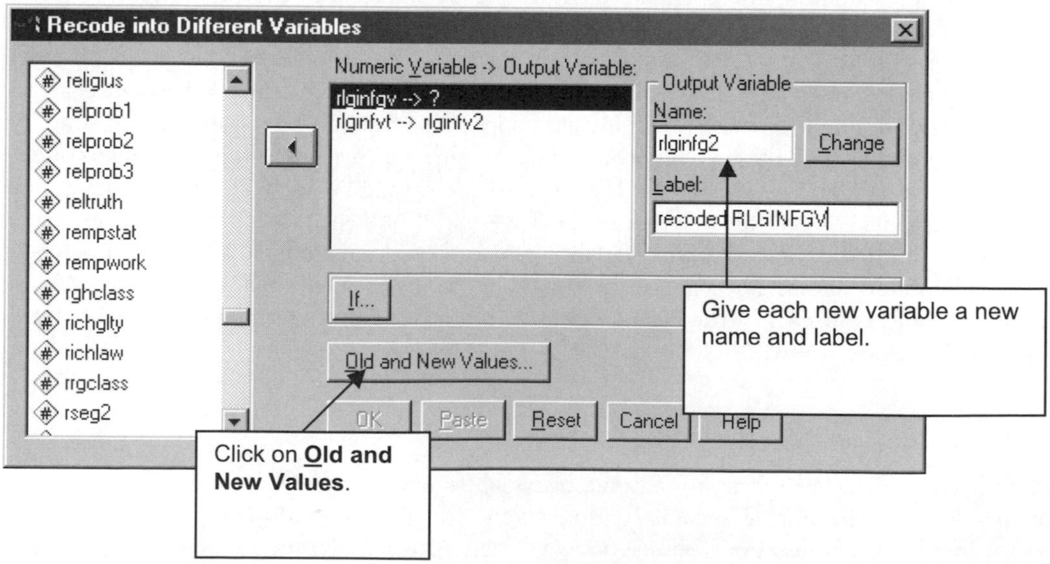

Change the old code 8 to 3 by typing 8 in the **Old Value** section **Value** box and 3 in the **New Value** section **Value** box, and click on **Add**. To keep the remaining codes click on **All other values** in the old value section, and click on **Copy old value** and **Add**. Once all changes have been completed click on the **Continue** button (Figure 3.13c).

Figure 3.13c Recoding new variables — **relinfv2** and **relinfg2**

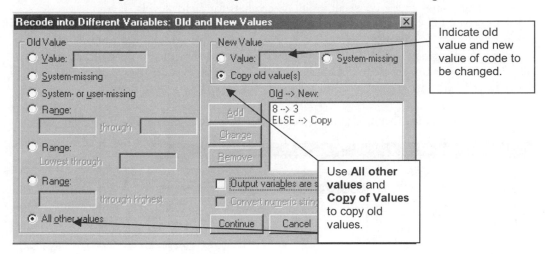

Good practice

From these examples of 'recodes', it should be clearer now why it is good practice to code variables initially into the maximum amount of detail that is feasible. One can always go from a *more* detailed to a *less* detailed coding, but not vice versa. Note how SPSS is set up so that when you use the **Recode into Different Variables window, you create a new variable that is the** *exact duplicate* of the variable that you want to alter. The codes of the new 'mirror' variable are altered, leaving the original variable untouched. SPSS provides this 'mirroring'

Figure 3.14 Recoding chart

rage	→	agecats
religion	→	religcat
relinfvt relinfgv	→	relinfv2 relinfg2

automatically when you enter in the name of the new (recoded) variable into the **Output Variable** box. So, if you discover sometime later on that you need the original, more detailed, codes, you still have them. (*In effect, you can have your cake and eat it too!*)

Automatic Recode converts string and numeric values into consecutive integers. When category codes are not sequential, the resulting empty cells reduce performance and increase memory requirements for many procedures. Additionally, some procedures cannot use string variables, and some require consecutive integer values for factor levels.

Take for example the variable **rlginfvt** used in the previous section. This variable is ordinal with 7 categories (1 = Strongly agree, 2 = Agree, 3 = Neither agree or disagree, 4 = Disagree, 5 = Strongly disagree, 8 = Can't choose, 9 = Not answered). For the purpose of future analysis using this variable it might be useful to change the '*Can't choose*' value from 8 to 6. Figure 3.15a shows how to do this.

Figure 3.15a   Example of using **Automatic Recode** to create a new variable

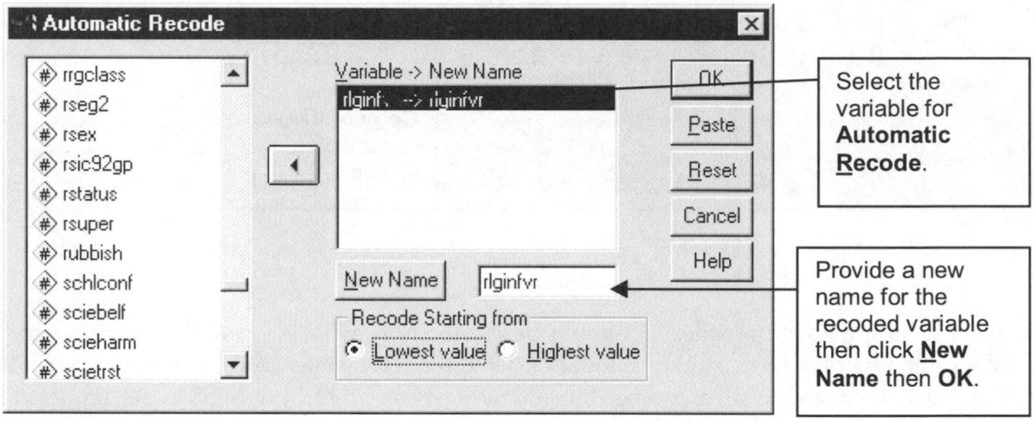

The new variable **rlginvr** created by **Automatic Recode** retains the defined variable and value labels from the old variable. For any values without a defined value label, the original value is used as the label for the recoded value. A table (Figure 3.15b) displays the old and new values and value labels.

Figure 3.15b   Table displaying new and old values of the recoded variable

```
RLGINFVT    RLGINFVR   Relg leaders shd notinfluenc vote B2

Old Value   New Value  Value Label

    1           1   Strongly agree
    2           2   Agree
    3           3   Neither
    4           4   Disagree
    5           5   Strongly disagree
    8           6   Can't    choose
   -2M          7M  Skp,A+C versions
   -1M          8M  No self-completn
    9M          9M  Not      answered
```

String values are recoded in alphabetical order, with uppercase letters preceding their lowercase counterparts. Missing values are recoded into missing values higher than any nonmissing values, with their order preserved. For example, if the original variable has 10 nonmissing values, the lowest missing value would be recoded to 11, and the value 11 would be a missing value for the new variable.

SPSS exercises for recoding variables

Now, try some recodes yourself:

- As was done in the example of age categories, choose a 'quantitative' variable and amalgamate it into some categories
- As was done with the example of religion, amalgamate a variable with a large number of categories into a new variable with fewer categories.

Arithmetical operations on a variable's codes (Compute)

Carrying out simple or complex arithmetical operations on a variable's codes is a second basic form of data manipulation. If the number codes of one or more variables truly represent quantities and not just labels of categories, these codes can be subjected to arithmetical operations.

These arithmetical commands are algebraic in form and can be quite simple. For example, we have two variables in the BSA dataset representing:

- The *number of adults including respondent* (**househld**); and
- The *number of children in the household* (**kids**)

but there is no variable with the *number of adults in each household*. A new variable, **numadult**, representing the total number of adults could be easily **computed** by subtracting the number of children (**kids**) from the household size (**househld**).

Figure 3.16a shows how to do this. Select **Compute Variable** from the **Transform** menu. The new 'Target Variable' is entered in the upper-left-hand corner of the box. Using the variable list, select the first variable (**househld**), and move it across to the **Numeric Expression** box. Next, using the **keypad** of functions, select the function (−). Go back to variable list, and select the second variable (**kids**), and move it across to the **Numeric Expression** box. Once the command **househld − kids** has been entered, click on **OK**, the computation is carried out and the result of the calculation, a new variable called **numadult** will appear as a new column at the right-hand end of the Data View window.

Compute can of course be used to perform more complex arithmetical operations. Figure 3.16b gives an illustration of a more complex operation. Here, a new variable, **sqrtavbn**, is constructed which is the square root of the average number of benefits per adult in the household (**numben** divided by the number of adults in the household).

The construction of this variable requires a number of distinct steps which must be carried out in the correct order. **sqrtavbn** is entered into the **Target Variable:** box. The function **sqrt** (for square root) is selected from the list of **Functions** on the lower right-hand side of the window and entered into the **Numeric Expression:** box with the upper arrow ▲ **Sqrt [ ]** appears in the **Numeric Expression** box with the cursor blinking inside the brackets. Enter the variable **numben** inside the brackets by choosing it from the variable list. Then, enter in the division symbol (/) from the **keypad**, followed by a second set of brackets, **[ ]**, from the

Figure 3.16a Example of using **Compute** to create a new variable

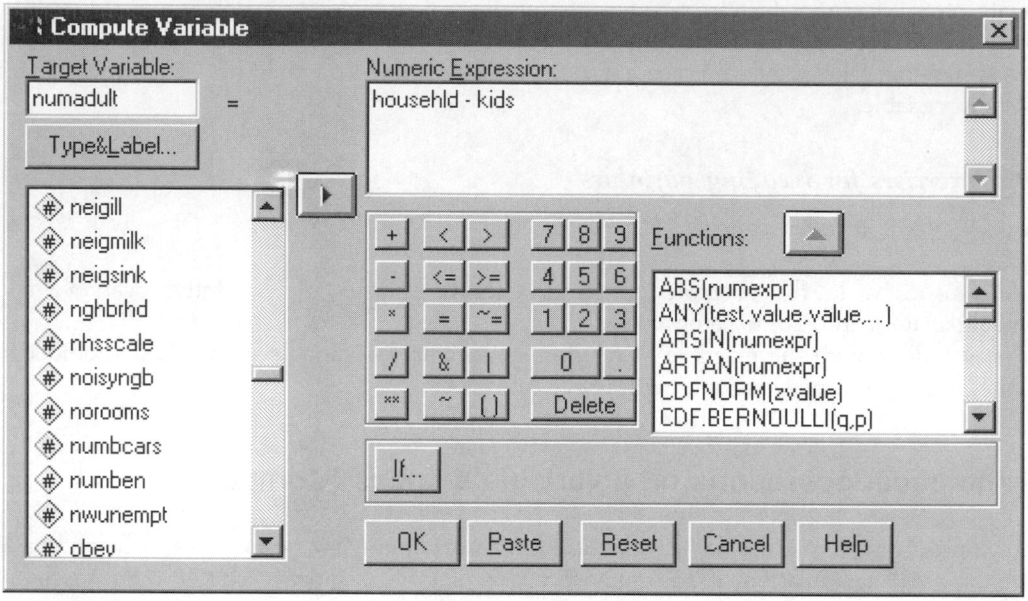

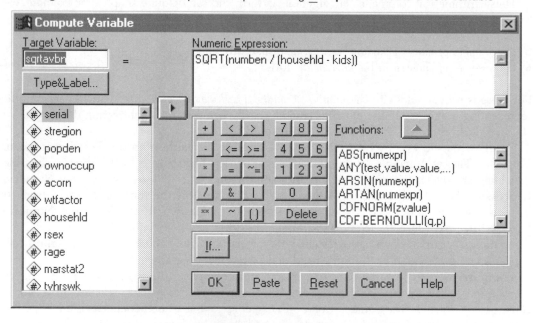

Figure 3.16b A more complex example of using **Compute** to create a new variable

keypad. Insert the expression **househld − kids** inside the second pair of brackets. The expression is now complete and is run by clicking on **OK**.

Note that it is important when constructing more complex arithmetical expressions to use *brackets* to ensure that the steps of the computation are carried out in the *correct order*. SPSS will carry out the expression inside the innermost brackets first, and then work its way out to the outermost brackets. For instance, in the above example, the arithmetical operations will take place in the *opposite* order from the sequence in which they are typed. The innermost expression is **household — kids**, which gives the number of adults in a household. Then, the number of adults is divided into **numben**, the number of benefits the household receives. Finally, as the outermost and final step, SPSS takes the square root (**sqrt**) of the resulting figure in order to produce the values for the variable **sqrtavbn**.

SPSS exercises for *C*OMPUTE

Now, try to do some computing yourself:

● Using quantitative variables in the dataset (variables whose codes represent true numerical values), carry out some arithmetical computations. Start with a simple computation and work your way up to more complex operations.

If: using logical statements to create a new variable

So far, we have demonstrated the use of **Recode** to manipulate data by altering or combining the codes of a variable and the use of **Compute** to carry out the arithmetical manipulation of variables.

Using a *logical statement* to create a new variable by combining the codes/values of two or more variables is the third basic sort of data manipulation that one can do with SPSS. Again, we will use examples drawn from the data to explain the use of this sort of data manipulation.

An example of using logical statements

In the British Social Attitudes survey the level of educational qualification of respondents was coded in the variable called **hedqual**. Respondents could be coded into seven levels of educational qualification, with the highest level being Code 1 *'Degree level or higher'*. Respondents also were given a number of social class codes, including **rghclass**, for which the highest level is Code 1 *'Service class, higher'*. Let us say you want to create a new variable that creates an 'elite' category, those who have *both* the highest level of educational qualification *and* the highest social class code. We use logical combinations of **hedqual** and **rghclass** to create a new variable, **elite**, which will have the codes:

Code **1:** Possessing both the highest educational qualification and having the highest social class code (**hedqual = 1 & rghclass = 1**)
Code **2**: *Either* not possessing the highest educational qualification *and/or* not having the highest social class code (**hedqual ~= 1 OR rghclass ~= 1**).

We create the new variable **elite** by going through **Transform** to **Compute**. In the **Compute Variable** dialog window type in **elite** as the **Target** variable. Type the first numeric value you want the **Target variable** to take in the **Numeric Expression** box, (in this example code '**1**' (see Figure 3.17a).

Once the target variable and code have been entered click on the **If** button to bring up the **Compute Variable If: Cases** window (Figure 3.17b), click on the **Include if case satisfies condition** button and type the 'condition' into the work box (**hedqual = 1 & rghclass = 1**). Then, click on **Continue** to go back to the **Compute Variable** window and run it by clicking on **OK**. The new variable **elite** will appear on the far right-hand side of the Data Editor grid with a code '**1**' for every case in which the condition in the **If** statement is satisfied.

Figure 3.17a Example of creating a new variable using **Compute** and **If**, first code

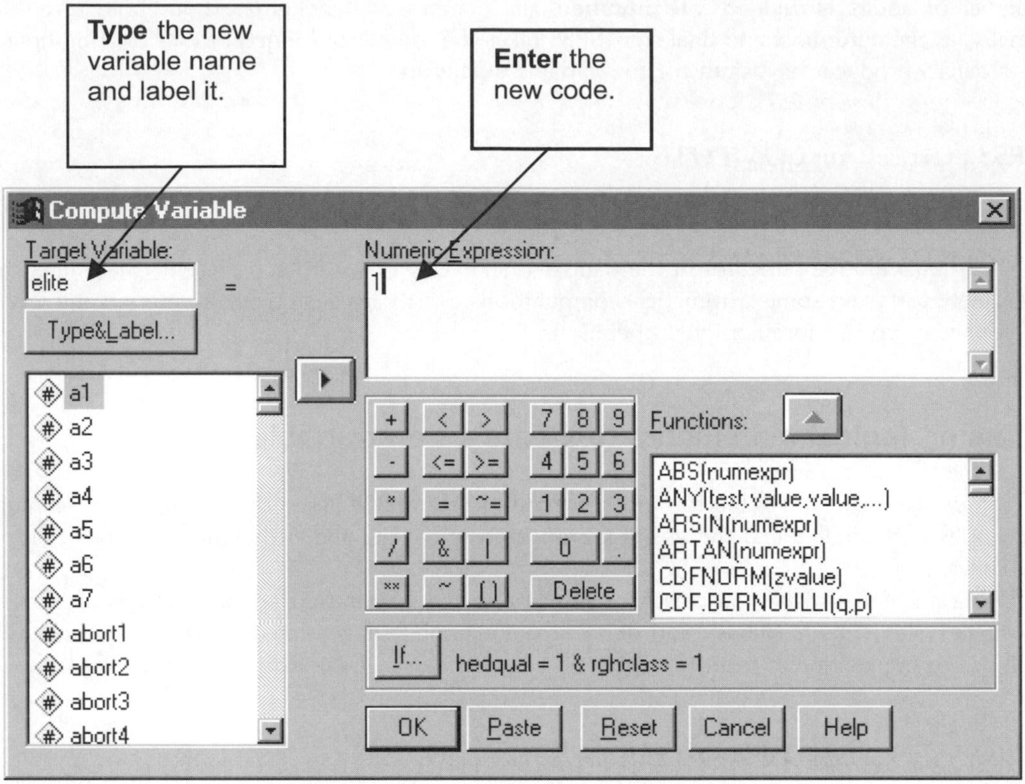

Type the new variable name and label it.

Enter the new code.

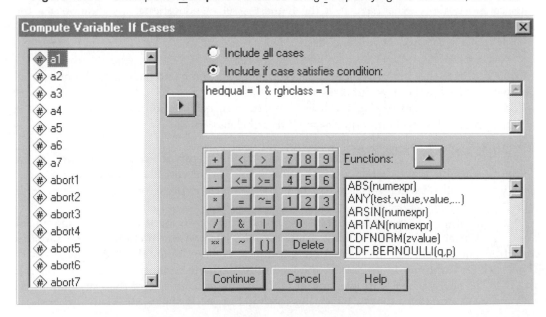

Figure 3.17b Example of **Compute Variables** using **If**: specifying the condition, first code

Since in this example there are two logical possibilities (being in the top 'elite' category or not) the two possibilities need to be set up individually in order to get the codes 1 and 2 for the new variable, **elite**. This means repeating the above process for code 2. In the **Compute Variable** dialog window, change the '1' to a '2'. As before, click on the **If** button to bring up the **Compute Variable If: Cases** window (Figure 3.17c), click on the **Include if case satisfies condition** button and type the 'condition' into the work box (only this time the condition will be **hedqual $\sim= 1$ | rghclass $\sim= 1$**). Then, click on **Continue** to go back to the **Compute Variable** window and run it by clicking on **OK** (Figure 3.17d). When you make the second

Figure 3.17c Example of creating a new variable using **Compute** and **If**, second code

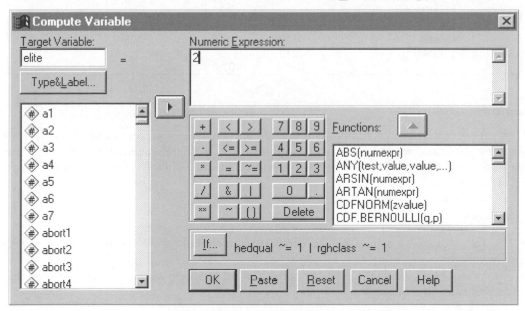

Figure 3.17d Example of **Compute Variables** using **If**: specifying the condition, second code

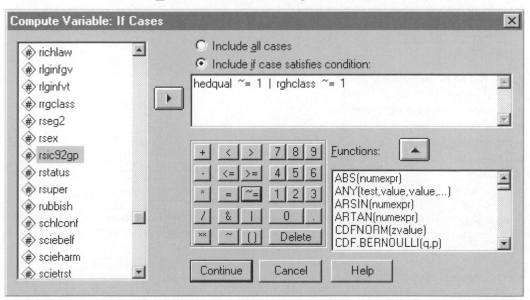

change, SPSS will advise you that this procedure will change the variable, don't worry, just click **OK**. The new variable **elite** will now have values 1 *and* 2 (in fact, since most respondents do not fall into the 'elite' combination, most values of **elite** will be 2). Note that the creation of **elite** was not complete until you went through the procedure of using **If** to create new categories *twice* (Figure 3.17e).

Figure 3.17e Frequency count of the new variable, elite

		Frequency	Percent	Valid Percent	Cumulative Percent
Valid	1.00 Highest ed AND Class	**143**	4.6	4.6	4.6
	2.00 All others	2989	95.0	95.4	100.0
	Total	3132	99.6	100.0	
Missing	9.00	14	.4		
Total		3146	100.0		

Logical operators

There are a number of conventional operators appearing on the **key pads** of the **Recode Variable: If Cases** and the **Compute Variable: If Cases** windows that are used to make up these logical statements. These have been mentioned before, but each is now presented in more detail below.

Comparisons

- The codes of two variables can be compared to see if they are the same (equal ($=$)) or different (*not* equal $\sim=$)
- The codes of two variables can be compared to see if the codes of one variable are more than (greater than ($>$)) or less than ($<$) another variable.

And the 'equals to' and the 'greater than'/'less than' operators are often combined to give:

- Greater than *or* equal to ($=>$) and
- Less than *or* equal to ($<=$)

Summarising:

- For the same (equal ($=$))
- for different (not equal) ($\sim=$)
- for more than (greater than) ($>$)
- for less than ($<$)
- for greater than *or* equal to ($>=$)
- for less than *or* equal to ($<=$).

Booleans

A second type of operator, the so-called 'Boolean' operators, are used to link different portions of a logical statement together. There are two 'Boolean' operators, 'AND' (&) and 'OR' (|) where:

- AND means that a statement holds *only* if *both* 'halves' of the statement are 'true'; and
- OR means that a statement holds if *either* 'half' of the statement is 'true'.

For instance, going back to our example, respondents fell into the 'elite' category only if they had *both* the highest educational qualification code *and* the highest social class code:

hedqual = 1 & rghclass = 1

In contrast, the **IF** statement:

hedqual = 1 | rghclass = 1

would hold if respondent had *either* the highest educational qualification code *and/or* the highest social class code. Note that using **OR** (|) instead of **AND** (&) requires much less strict conditions for the statement to be 'true'.

Complex statements

All of these operators for logical statements can, as you would expect, be combined to produce quite involved, complex statements. For instance, let us expand our example to demonstrate a more complicated **IF** statement:

The dataset also has two other variables:

- **rage**, which is the respondent's age in years
- **rsex**, which is the respondent's gender: (1) male; (2) female.

Figure 3.18 Crosstabulation of **rghclass** by **hedqual** as a check on **If** statements

RGHCLASS Respondent:Goldthorpe-Heath cl 1990 Q549 *

HEDQUAL Highest educational qual.obtained? Q1078 Crosstabulation

Count

		HEDQUAL Highest educational qualification obtained?							
		1 Degree	2 Higher educ below degree	3 A level or equiv	4 O level or equiv	5 CSE or equiv	6 Foreigh or other	7 No qualificat ion	Total
RGHCL ASS Respond ent Goldthor e-heath cl 1990 Q549	1 Service class, higher	**143**	150	39	39	5	0	24	400
	2 Service class, lower	94	229	75	92	20	4	67	581
	3 Routine non-manual	19	52	67	127	45	4	77	391
	4 Personal service	3	37	35	71	28	3	94	271
	5 Small proprietors, with empl	4	8	14	24	13	1	24	88
	6 Small proprietors, no empl	4	14	20	33	24	1	48	144
	7 Farmers & smallholders	0	0	0	0	1	0	7	8
	8 Foremen & technicians	0	37	14	52	27	4	109	243
	9 Skilled manual workers	0	22	33	59	33	0	83	230
	Semi & unskilled manual	7	45	45	128	59	5	347	636
	Agricultural workers	0	1	0	4	1	0	7	13
Total		274	595	342	629	256	22	887	3005

Now, let's look at the kind of logical statement that would hold only **if** the respondent is male, **and** falls into the 'elite' categories of top educational qualification and social class, **and** is aged between 45 and 64. (Note how the brackets have to be 'nested' to keep the logic of the statement clear):

[rsex = 1] & [hedqual = 1 & rghclass = 1] & [rage >= 45 & rage <= 65]

(**HINT:** If you know how to use the SPSS CROSSTABS statistical procedure (see Module 5), you can produce a crosstabulation table of two variables that you want to combine in a series of **IF** statements. Looking at the crosstabulation table will help you remember all of the possible combinations of categories of two variables and will show you how many cases you can expect to fall into each combination of categories For example, Figure 3.18 shows the crosstabulation of **hedqual** and **rghclass**. Note that there are 143 cases in the upper left-hand cell of the crosstabulation table, the same number as appear in category 1 of the variable **elite**.)

SPSS exercises for If

Now, look over the variables in the dataset and think up some interesting logical manipulations that can be performed on them:

- As before, start out with something fairly simple – say, a logical manipulation involving only two variables where neither of them has too many *codes*.
- Then, try moving on to something more complicated, perhaps using more variables and/or an imaginative combination
- Try to have some statements that make (sensible) use of both the 'Boolean' operatives, **AND** and **OR**. Remember that you must go through the procedure of setting up a logical **IF** statement for *each* category of the new variable you are creating.

Transformations using count

Sometimes you may want to find out how often a certain code or range of codes occurs across a number of different variables. SPSS has a special procedure called **Count** that allows this to be done easily.

In the British Social Attitude dataset, there are ten questions on membership in community organisations and associations (**memcomvl** to **memsikvl**). In each of these variables, the code 1, indicates that the respondent is a member of the organisation. **count** will scan across the ten variables, and count the number of code 1s a person has given to the question. A score of 10 would indicate a membership in all of the ten groups, and a score of 0 would indicate that the respondent is not a member of any of the organisations.

To carry out the count procedure, go to the **Transform** menu and click on **Count**. This opens the **Count** window (Figure 3.19a), where the new **Target Variable** and **Target Label** must be specified, and the variables to be counted must be selected and entered in the **Numeric Variables** box. Here, our new variable will be called **cominv** with the label *community involvement* and the variables **memcomvl** to **memsikvl** go into the **Numeric Variables** box. Once the variables have been selected and moved across, click on the **Define Values** box to bring up Figure 3.19b. To define the **Value** (or values) to be counted (here, the value is '1'), click on the **Add** button so that the value '1' appears in the **Values to Count** box, and then on **Continue** to return to the main **Count** window. Click on **OK** to create the new variable, **cominv**.

Figure 3.19a Main window for **Count**

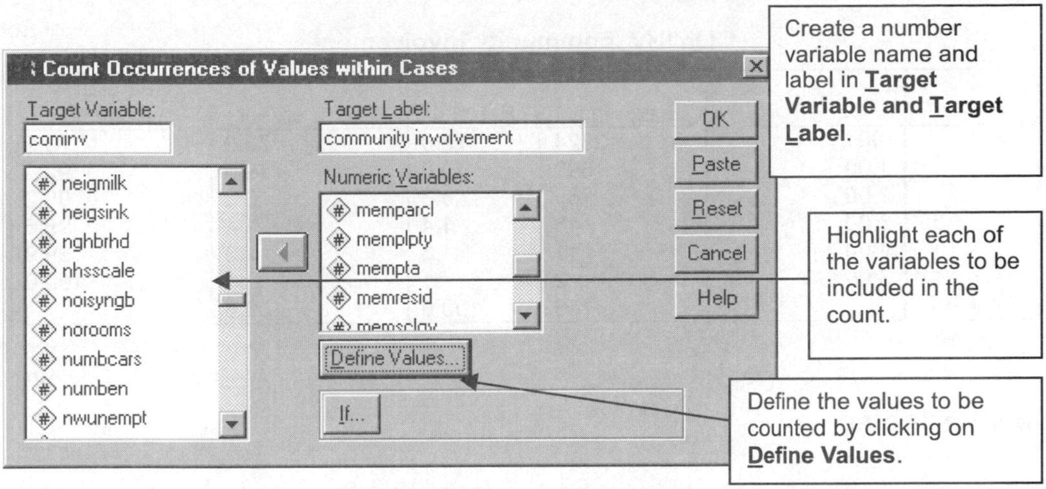

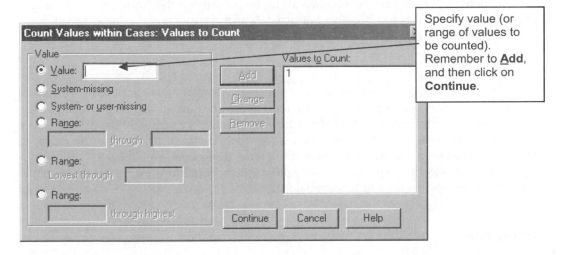

Figure 3.19b Example of setting values to **Count**

Looking at a table of frequencies of the new variable (**cominv**) we can see that approximately 74 per cent of respondents are not members of any of the associations/ organisations, only 19 per cent indicated their membership of one of the associations with six being the maximum number of organisations that any respondents belonged to (Figure 3.19c).

SPSS exercise for Count

- Choose a range of variables in the dataset where it would be sensible to sum up one or more of the values across the whole range. Carry out a **Count** procedure of your own, producing a new variable that is the sum of the codes.

Figure 3.19c   Frequency table of the newly created variable

COMINV community involvement

		Frequency	Percent	Valid Percent	Cumulative Percent
Valid	.00	2324	73.9	73.9	73.9
	1.00	599	19.0	19.0	92.9
	2.00	165	5.3	5.3	98.2
	3.00	45	1.4	1.4	99.6
	4.00	11	.3	.3	99.9
	6.00	2	.1	.1	100.0
Total		3146	100.0	100.0	

New variables

By now you will have noted that, data manipulation, unlike data selection, does not reduce the total number of variables held in a dataset. In fact, the opposite is likely to happen; after data manipulation it is quite possible that there will be some 'new' variables existing in the dataset (like **agecats**, **religat**, **numadult**, **elite**, **cominv**).

These 'new' variables can be considered to be similar to the variables in a dataset immediately after the data has been 'read into' a data analysis package. The 'new' variables are part of the dataset – they are formatted and possess 'variable names'.

Labelling

As with the variables in a completely 'brand new' dataset, however, what they do *not* possess are *labels*. So, in order to document the dataset correctly and to avoid potentially serious errors in interpretation, these 'new' variables must have labels declared. You define the labels of a variable created by a data transformation in the same way as you would label variables in a newly created dataset, by going to the Data Editor grid in **Variable View** format (See Module 1 for the instructions on how to label variables.)

Missing values

You may also remember from Module 1 that care must be taken to declare as 'missing values' any codings that have been used to represent invalid responses. This is necessary in order to avoid these invalid codes being inadvertently included into any statistical analyses.

As you might guess, this is also a potential problem with any 'new' variables created by data manipulation. Being 'new', it is possible that one or more codes may exist in the 'new' variable that in fact represent invalid cases. As before, these invalid codes must be kept out of any analyses that will assume that all codings are genuine. Hence, care must be taken to ensure that missing values are established for the 'new' variables that result from data manipulation just as for the variables in a completely new dataset.

SPSS does have a convention that acts as a partial 'fail safe' to ensure the correct declaration of missing values for 'new' variables arising from data manipulation. During data manipulation, if SPSS encounters a missing value code for the variables that go into making up a 'new' variable *and* the analyst has not used that variable in his or her recoding, that case's coding for the 'new' variable will be set to a 'system missing' code.

Note, however, that this is only a partial 'fail safe'; the safest practice is for the analyst to declare missing values for a new variable. (Module 1 explains how to declare missing values by going to the **Missing** column in the Variable View window of the Data Editor.)

A final bit of advice about data manipulation

Whenever you have created new variables with data manipulation, you are *strongly* advised to 'check' them with a quick **Frequencies** run to ensure that the data manipulation actually did what you intended. Often you discover that you have fooled yourself and the manipulation did not turn out quite as you expected! While data manipulation requires care on the part of the analyst, the ability to 'customise' datasets and create or modify variables to suit the needs of your own analysis is one of the most useful features of SPSS.

4 Hypothesis-testing and *t*-tests

Confirmatory statistics

This module covers hypothesis testing using *t*-tests. Modules 1–3 have covered the preliminary stages in data entry and analysis. Module 2 has provided examples of data exploration and description. Exploring and describing the data using descriptive statistics (means, medians, frequency counts, etc.) and charts provides us with the opportunity to become more familiar with the data, and may generate questions for further analysis and testing.

Such questions may be concerned with the testing of *relationships* between variables in the data – for example, the age of the respondent and their perceptions of crime in the local area or respondents' social class and their assessment of the National Health Service (NHS). You may have ideas (called *hypotheses*) about the relationships between variables, and may want to *test* these ideas to see if they really hold true. To do so you need to use confirmatory statistics. Confirmatory statistics allow you to test or evaluate the validity of results. Hence, confirmatory statistics are sometimes called *hypothesis-testing statistics*.

Let's take an example from the British Social Attitudes dataset. The dataset contains a variable called **smokday** (number of cigarettes smoked per day). It might be interesting to explore whether, for those who smoke, males' smoking habits differ in comparison to females. We could start exploring by using *descriptive statistics* such as the mean number of cigarettes each gender smokes or generating boxplots of their smoking (see Module 2 for details about how to generate these and other descriptive statistics). Figure 4.1a and Figure 4.1b present the descriptive statistics and boxplots of number of cigarettes smoked per day by gender (**rsex**) for all those who smoke at least some.

Inspection of Figure 4.1a and 4.1b *suggests* a gender differences in the smoking habits, as the mean number of cigarettes smoked by males is higher than the mean for females. However, we must test this observation using confirmatory statistics. In this case our research question might be: '*Among those who smoke, do the two sexes differ in the number of cigarettes smoked per day?*

Hypothesis-testing

Before proceeding with our research question, we must specify the comparisons to be completed by translating our research question into a *hypothesis*. A hypothesis is a statement of a relationship between population parameters or variables – a statement or prediction of what

Figure 4.1a Descriptive statistics for number of cigarettes smoked per day (**smokday**) by sex (**rsex**)

Gender	Mean	N	Std. deviation
1 Male	15.57	398	9.95
2 Female	13.16	461	7.26

Figure 4.1b   Boxplot of number of cigarettes smoked per day (**smokday**) by sex (**rsex**)

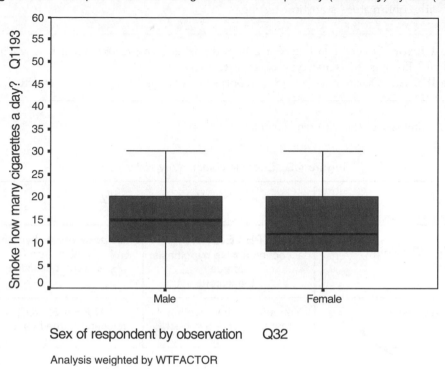

Analysis weighted by WTFACTOR

you expect to find. This statement typically takes the form of predicting *differences* between groups or of *relationships* between variables.

Using our example, the hypothesis might be: *Among smokers, males smoke more cigarettes per day than females*. (Thus we are hypothesising a difference, and giving a direction to the difference − male smokers differ from female smokers by smoking more cigarettes per day.)

For every hypothesis in research, there is a *Null hypothesis*, which is a statement of *no* or an *opposite* relationship between the two variables. The Null hypothesis is the logical opposite of the hypothesis. Once we have generated the hypothesis, we must prove it by *disproving* its logical opposite. Using our example, the Null hypothesis would be: *Among smokers, females smoke* the same or more *cigarettes than males*.

However, it is also important to remember that these data come from a survey and it is possible that, by chance, we might have sampled respondents who are not typical of the population. If this is the case, any observed difference may be a product of chance and may not be a real reflection of the two sexes' smoking behaviour. That is, even with a correctly designed sample survey, it is possible that we may have been unlucky and just happened to have picked up a set of males in the sample who smoke more than the rest of the male population and a set of females who smoke less than the rest of the female population. To put it in jargon, our *sample estimates* might not match our *population parameters*.

In our example here, in order to test if the difference between the sexes in their smoking is real, we must conduct a confirmatory statistical test on the data. The *t*-test, which we will introduce below, is just such a confirmatory statistic. The *t*-test is explicitly designed to test whether the differences between the means of two groups are real, or *statistically significant*.

Before we can look directly at how to use SPSS to carry out a *t*-test, however, we need to consider more closely the logic that underlies confirmatory statistical testing.

Statistical tests are not infallible and we can make mistakes. There are two types of errors possible with confirmatory statistical testing.

> • **Type I Error**: Occurs if you accept a hypothesis as being *correct* when it is *really false*. A Type I Error is the worst type of error to make.
> • **Type II Error**: Occurs if you *reject* a hypothesis as being wrong when it is actually *true*.

Figure 4.2 summarises the different errors.

Figure 4.2 Errors in confirmatory statistics

Researcher decides to	Hypothesis is really . . .	
	False	True
Accept hypothesis	**TYPE I ERROR –** accepting a false hypothesis as true (the worst!)	You *accepted* an hypothesis that is True – a correct decision
Reject hypothesis	You *rejected* an hypothesis that is False – a correct decision	**TYPE II ERROR –** rejecting a true hypothesis

Statistical significance

The results of all statistical tests are expressed in these terms of probability or risk (for example, $p < 0.001$). This is the odds that a Type I Error has been made. So, the *smaller* the size of the level of significance, the *less likely* it is that a Type I Error has been made and the *more likely* it is that our hypothesis really is true. There are 'standard' cut-off points for accepting hypotheses.

> • $p < 0.05$ means a 5 in 100 (1 in 20) chance of a Type I Error
> • $p < 0.01$ means a 1 in 100 chance of a Type I Error
> • $p < 0.001$ means less than a 1 in 1000 chance of a Type I Error.

To test the significance, you need to set a *risk level* (called the *alpha level*). In most social research, the 'rule of thumb' is to set the alpha level at 0.05 (which means that five times out of every 100 you would find a statistically significant difference even if there was none). Usually, levels of significance (or risk) greater than 0.05 are not considered good enough to reject the Null hypothesis. For instance, even though $p < 0.10$ means only a 1 in 10 chance of a Type I Error, we usually would not accept the hypothesis. The reason for this is that it is much less of a calamity to make a Type II Error (rejecting a true hypothesis) than it is to make a Type I Error (accepting a false hypothesis). So, the odds of probability testing are highly skewed against making Type I Errors.

It is worth saying a bit more about this important point. One can make an analogy between a traveller trying to make his or her way down an unfamiliar road. The traveller may come to a fork in the road where he or she has an idea (a hypothesis!) that the left-hand fork is the correct way. In fact, however, the right-hand fork is the way they should go. If they decide that the left-hand way is the correct way and proceed down that road, they have made what amounts to a Type I Error. As they go further and further down the wrong way, they will become more and more confused and ever more hopelessly lost. Eventually, they will realise that a mistake must have been made some time ago and then will have to painfully retrace their steps back to the point of the original mistake. On the other hand, if they stay at the fork, unable to establish which is the correct way, they are making what amounts to a Type II Error. They are stuck at a crossroads, but at least they know they are stuck and are not rushing down the wrong route. In our smoking example, a researcher could make a Type I Error and wrongly conclude that one gender smokes more than the other. If the researcher then acts on their wrong conclusion and implements a large-scale anti-smoking campaign directed at the wrong sex of smoker, a considerable amount of money would be wasted and possibly even lives would be lost unnecessarily. Because a Type I Error means that a researcher will act on erroneous premises, it is more serious than a Type II Error.

Hence, 'really important research' (for instance, research in which the consequences of reaching a wrong decision would entail high financial costs or perhaps the loss of life) often adopts a stricter level of confidence cut-off than the 0.05 level, usually the 0.01 or 0.001 level.

Confirmatory statistics: *t*-tests

The descriptive statistics in Figures 4.1a and 4.1b reveal that the mean number of cigarettes smoked by females is 13.40, and by males is 15.19. There appears to be a difference between the two, with males smoking more. However, we must remember that there is a chance of a Type I Error. The mean (average) is calculated by dividing the sum of the total score by the number of respondents. The mean score provides an average score for this variable, but does not provide details of the range of scores – the variability. Extreme values at either end of the scale can distort the overall mean. Thus, relying solely on the observed differences in mean scores between two groups can be misleading. When comparing the scores of the two groups, it is important to examine the difference between their mean scores relative to the *spread* or *variability* of their scores. The *t*-test statistic does this.

t-tests are most commonly used to examine whether the means of *two* groups of data are significantly different from one another. Hence with a *t*-test the independent variable is nominal or categorical and the dependent variable is measured at *interval* or *ratio* scale of measurement. The populations from which the two groups are drawn can be independent (or unrelated) or matched (related). *t*-tests indicate the sample differences by using means and the distribution of sample scores around the mean.

There are two main *t*-tests. The first type of *t*-test is used with unmatched data and is known under a number of names including 'Independent-Samples *t*-test', '*t*-test for two independent means', 'independent *t*-test' and '*t*-test for unrelated samples'. Regardless of the exact title, with this type of *t*-test there are *two distinct categories* for the independent variable (such as males and females) and one dependent variable measured at the interval or ratio level (such as number of cigarettes smoked per day). The 'independent samples *t*-test' will be testing whether the means of the dependent variable for each group defined by the independent variable are significantly different.

The second *t*-test is used with matched data and is also known under a number of names, these include 'Paired-Samples *t*-test', '*t*-test for related measures', 'related *t*-test', or 'correlated *t*-test'. This test can be used in a number of circumstances where the question calls for the repeated measurement of responses from the *same respondent*. Data might be collected on a single occasion where individuals are asked to respond to the same or similar questions twice (for example, where a researcher decides to repeat a question later on in an interview in order to see if respondents will give the same answer if asked a second time). The same or similar data may also be collected on more than one occasion (where individuals are followed over a period of time – for example, repeated measures). Longitudinal surveys and 'before and after' studies or experiments are examples of designs where respondents may be required to provide an answer to the same question on different occasions. The 'paired-samples *t*-test' will be testing whether the means of each of the 'paired' or 'before/after' variables are significantly different or not.

Independent-Samples t-test: example 1

We will now test the hypothesis in our 'smokers' example. Remember the hypothesis is: *Among smokers, males smoke more cigarettes per day than females.* In order to disprove the Null hypothesis, we must carry out an *Independent-Samples t-test*. It will tell us the odds (or probability) that the difference we see in the raw figures really *is* genuine. If it is real (or statistically significant), we accept our hypothesis and reject the Null hypothesis. (Remember the variable **rsex** (independent variable) is categorical with two categories Male and Female. **smokday** (the dependent variable) is a ratio variable.)

The Independent-Samples *t*-test establishes whether the means of two unrelated samples differ by comparing the difference between the two means with the standard error in the means of the different samples:

$$t = \frac{\text{Sample one mean} - \text{sample two mean}}{\text{Standard error of the difference in mean}}$$

Figure 4.3a Example of Independent *t*-test procedures

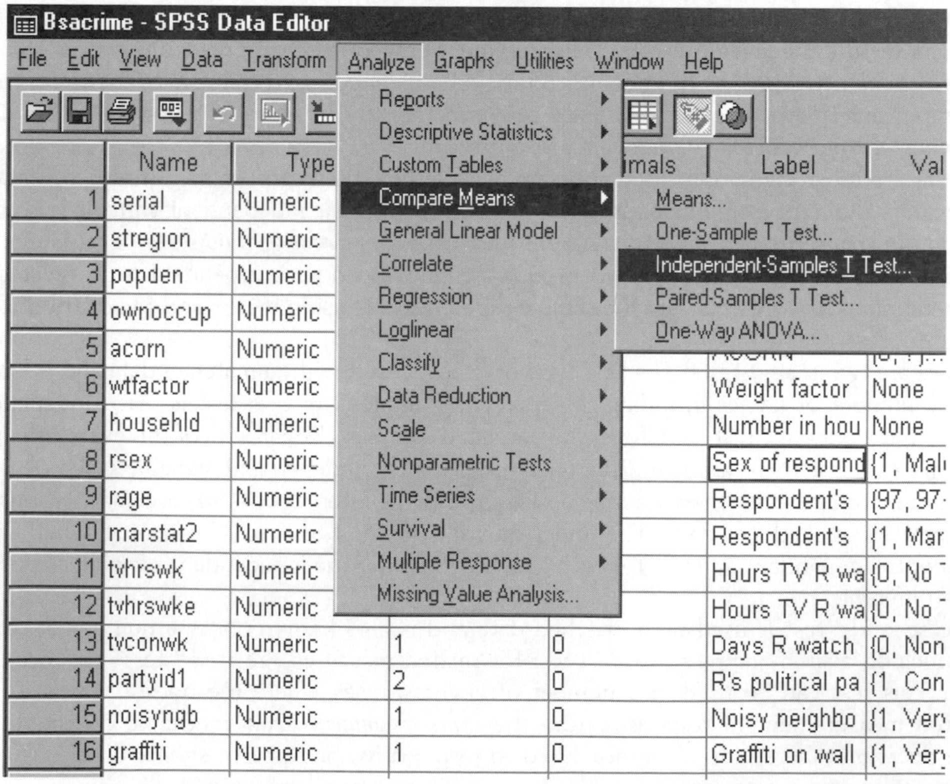

Figure 4.3a indicates the steps required to run the Independent-Samples *t*-test. Pull down the **Analyze** main menu, point to **Compare Means** and click on **Independent-Samples T Test**.

The window in Figure 4.3b will appear. Transfer the variable **smokday** to the **Test Variable box** by using the cursor to highlight it, and clicking on the > button to move the required dependent variable to the **Test Variable box**. Similarly, highlight the grouping variable **rsex** and transfer it to the **Grouping Variable box**.

Figure 4.3b   Running the independent *t*-test

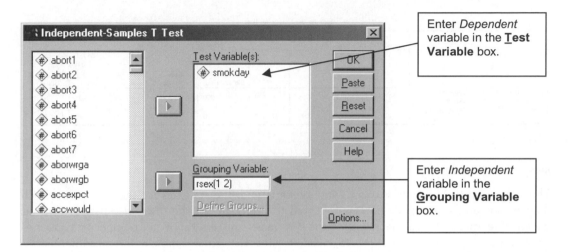

You have to define the two values of the grouping variable. Define the values of the groups by clicking on **Define Groups button**. The subwindow in Figure 4.3c will appear.

It is possible to define groups by using specified values or by selecting *cut-points* (to split a variable into two categories). In the example used here we wish to compare males and females. The **rsex** variable has two values: 1 = Male, 2 = Female. We specify males as Group 1 by typing the value '**1**' in the **Group 1** box and similarly '**2**' for females in the **Group 2** box; then click on **Continue** to return to the main window. The values 1,2 will appear in the brackets after **rsex**. Now click on **OK** to run the *t*-test.

Once SPSS has completed running the *t*-test procedure the viewer window opens displaying the output. Figure 4.4 provides an example of the output from an Independent-Sample *t*-test.

Figure 4.3c   Defining Values of Grouping Variable

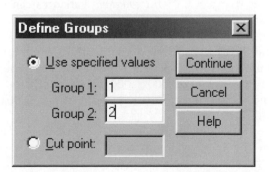

Figure 4.4   Independent *t*-test output: cigarettes smoked per day (**smokday**) by gender (**rsex**)

Group Statistics

	RSEX Sex of respondent by observation Q32	N	Mean	Std Deviation	Std. Error Mean
SMOKDAY Smoke how many cigarettes a day? Q1193	1 Male	398	15.57	9.95	.50
	2 Female	461	13.16	7.26	.34

Independent Samples Test

		Levene's Test for Equality of Variances		t-test for Equality of Means						95% Confidence Interval of the Difference	
		F	Sig.	t	df	Sig. (2-tailed)	Mean Difference	Std. Error Difference	Lower	Upper
SMOKDAY Smoke how many cigarettes a day? Q1193	Equal variances assumed	10.136	.002	4.087	858	.000	2.41	.59	1.25	3.56
	Equal variances not assumed			3.997	716.297	.000	2.41	.60	1.22	3.59

Interpreting the output

The output on the **Output Viewer** window starts with the statistics for the two groups with their means and standard deviations followed by the value of the difference between means (mean difference). We can see that for the 398 male smokers the mean number of cigarettes smoked per day was 15.57 (sd = 9.95), while for the 461 female smokers the mean number of cigarettes smoked per day was 13.16 (sd = 7.26). The mean difference is 2.41. We now want to see if there is a significant difference between the mean scores for the two independent groups.

Interpretation of the Independent *t*-test output is a two-stage process. The first stage involves examining the *homogeneity of the variance* between the two groups. In order to test your hypotheses, a number of assumptions about the populations being compared must be made. First, the researcher assumes that the variance in the populations being compared is the same. The Independent-Samples *t*-test analysis tests this assumption using *Levene's Test for Equality of Variances*. This test is based on the *F*-statistic (which will be discussed in Module 6, 'Analysis of Variance'). SPSS computes both the *F*-statistic and *p*-value (Sig.). If 'Sig.' is less than 0.05 ($p < 0.05$), the Levene's test indicates that the variances between the two populations are not equal. If is 'Sig.' is greater than 0.05 ($p > 0.05$), the Levene's test indicates that equal variances can be assumed.

To return to the example above, the first stage of the interpretation is to examine the output for the Levene's Test for Equality of Variances. In this instance $F = 10.136$ and Sig. $(p) = 0.002$ which indicates that $p > 0.05$ thus *unequal* variances can be assumed.

Since Levene's test indicated that homogeneity of variances cannot be assumed, we test the hypothesis using the *t*-test row of results labelled *Equal variances not assumed*. This gives us the *t*-value ($t = 3.997$) and the degrees of freedom (df = 716). SPSS calculates a Sig. (2-tailed) value, which is the actual probability of making a Type I error. From the table in Figure 4.4, we find a two-tailed significance (*p*-value) of .000. ('.000' means a *p* that is 'off the scale', *less than 0.001*). Hence the difference between means is significant at $p < 0.001$. This is expressed as $t = 3.997$, df = 716, $p < 0.001$.

Therefore, we can reject the Null hypothesis and conclude that a *statistically significant* difference exists between the two groups in terms of the number of cigarettes smoked. The research hypothesis that men smoke more cigarettes per day than women is upheld, and the Null hypothesis is rejected. The odds of a Type I Error is less than 1 in one thousand ($p < 0.001$).

Independent-Samples t-test: example 2

Let us take another example from the British Social Attitudes dataset. There is a variable called **Perception of Crime** in the Local area (**Crime**), which is a *scale* based on responses to six questions on crime in the local area. Low scores (minimum score is 0) indicate a perception of a low level of crime, whereas high scores (maximum score is 19) indicate that the respondent believes that there is much crime in their local area. It may be interesting to explore if males differ from females in their perception of crime in their local area. In this case our research question might be: *'Do the two sexes differ in their perceptions of the crime in the local area?*

Similar to the last example, we must specify the comparisons to be completed by translating our research question into a *hypothesis*. For this example the hypothesis might be: *Females mean score* on the *Perception of Crime in Local Area scale is higher than males mean score* on the *Perception of Crime in Local Area scale*. The Null hypothesis would be: *Females' mean score on* the *Perception of Crime in Local Area scale is* **the same or lower** *than males' mean score on* the *Perception of Crime in Local Area scale*.

For this example, we follow the same procedures as carried out in Example 1. **Analyze > Compare Means > Independent-Samples T Test**. Transfer the variable **Crime** to the **Test Variable box** by using the cursor to highlight it, and clicking on the > button. Similarly, highlight the grouping variable **rsex** and transfer it to the **Grouping Variable** box, clicking on the **Define Groups** button to define its values as before.

Once SPSS has completed running the *t*-test procedure the Viewer Window opens displaying the output. Figure 4.5 provides our second example of output from an Independent-Sample *t*-Test.

Figure 4.5 Independent *t*-test output: perceived crime (crime) by gender (**rsex**)

Group Statistics

	RSEX Sex of respondent by observation Q32	N	Mean	Std. Deviation	Std. Error Mean
CRIME Perception of crime in local area	1 Male	1288	5.9702	3.5327	9.843E-02
	2 Female	1522	6.0862	3.5498	9.098E-02

Independent Samples Test

		Levene's Test for Equality of Variances		t-test for Equality of Means						95% Confidence Interval of the Difference	
		F	Sig.	t	df	Sig. (2-tailed)	Mean Difference	Std. Error Difference	Lower	Upper
CRIME Perception of crime in local area	Equal variances assumed	.026	.872	-.865	2809	.387	-.1160	.1341	-.3789	.1470
	Equal variances not assumed			-.865	2736.349	.387	-.1160	.1340	-.3788	.1469

Interpreting the output

The output on the Output Viewer window starts with the statistics for the two groups with their means and standard deviations followed by the value of the difference between means (mean difference). We can see that for the 1288 males the mean score is 5.97 (sd = 3.53), while for the 1522 females the mean score is 6.09 (sd = 3.55). The difference between the means for the two groups is 0.1160. There appears to be very little difference between the two, but we can confirm this using the Independent *t*-test.

As with Example 1, interpretation of the Independent *t*-test output is a two-stage process. This time when we examine the homogeneity of the variance between the two groups using *Levene's Test for Equality of Variances*, the F-value is 0.026, and the 'Sig.' (*p*-value) is 0.872, This is considerably greater than 0.05 (thus not significant), indicating that equal variances can be assumed. It is now possible to test the hypothesis using the *t*-test row of results labelled *Equal variances assumed*. This provides the *t*-value (*t* = 0.865), the degrees of freedom (df = 2809). From the table in Figure 4.5, we find that 'Sig. (2-tailed)' is .387, greater than the 5per cent cut-off level (*p* > 0.05). Thus, the result is not significant. Therefore, we reject the hypothesis, and accept the null hypothesis.

This is expressed *t* = 0.865, df = 2809, *p* = .387 *ns*.

Women do not perceive a significantly higher level of crime in their local area in comparison to men.

Paired-samples t-test (for dependent/matched groups)

The second *t*-test, the *paired-samples* t-*test*, is used with matched pair data, or is used in circumstances where the research question calls for the repeated measurement of the responses from the same individual. Data might be collected on one occasion where individuals are asked to respond to similar questions two or more times. (For example, a paired-sample *t*-test might be used to compare responses to the same question administered by means of a self-completion questionnaire and interview.) Alternatively, data may have been collected on more than one occasion where individuals are followed over a period of time and asked the same or similar questions at different times; for example, comparing 'before and after' values). This test is also used when a researcher wants to ensure that two subjects who had been allocated to matched groups are evenly matched before beginning an experiment or study.

Running the paired-sample t-test: an example

While the BSA survey is repeated annually, a different sample is drawn each year, so the same people do not appear in subsequent years of the survey. Also, the BSA datasets do not have any examples of paired variables where the same people have been asked the same question twice during their interview. In order to provide an example of running the *paired-sample* t-*test* procedure, we have decided to use the two ratio-level questions on income. The first variable, **percap1**, has details of *per capita* income based upon the total household income averaged out over all members of the household. The second variable, **percap2**, has *per capita* income details averaged out for only the adults in the household. The same respondents have provided the responses to the two questions. Note that, technically, it is not appropriate to use the paired–sample *t*-test to examine the differences between these two variables, as the questions are slightly different and measure different *per capita* incomes. We are using these variables because the BSA datasets do not contain any appropriate variables and it is important that we cover the use of this version of *t*-test.

Our hypothesis is: *The average per capita income based upon all household members is significantly different than the average per capita income based upon adults only*
Our Null hypothesis is: *The average per capita income based upon all household members is not significantly different than the average per capita income based upon adults only.*

Figure 4.6a   Running the paired-samples *t*-test

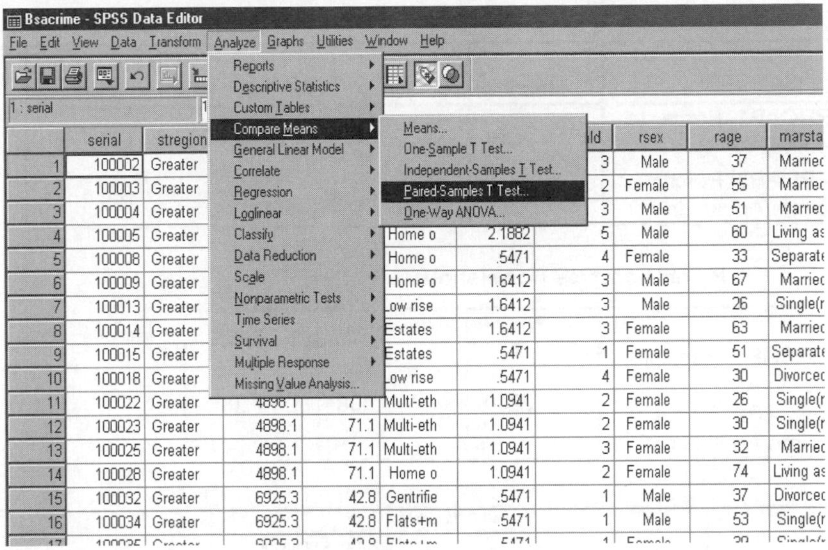

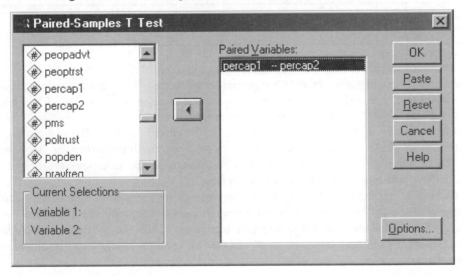

Figure 4.6b   Selecting the variables for the paired-samples *t*-test

The paired samples *t*-test is selected by opening the **Analyze** menu, selecting **Compare Means** and then **Paired-Sample T test** (Figure 4.6a).

In order to select two variables for comparison, use the **Paired *t*-test** dialog box to highlight the required variables, and click on **>** to transfer to the paired variables box. Here, we have chosen **percap1** and **percap2** to produce the **Paired Samples T Test** window in Figure 4.6b. Click on **OK** to run the procedure.

Interpreting the output of a paired-samples t-*test*

Once SPSS has completed running the *t*-test procedure the viewer window opens displaying the output. Figure 4.7 provides an example of the output from the paired-samples *t*-test.

Figure 4.7 Output from the paired-samples *t*-test

Paired Samples Statistics

		Mean	N	Std. Deviation	Std. Error Mean
Pair 1	PERCAP1 Percapita income/All	8643.5692	2700	6764.6690	130.1799
	PERCAP2 Percapita income/Adults only	10295.49	2700	7285.5425	140.2036

Paired Samples Correlations

		N	Correlation	Sig.
Pair 1	PERCAP1 Percapita income/All & PERCAP2 Percapita income/Adults only	2700	.900	.000

		Paired Differences					t	df	Sig. (2-tailed)
		Mean	Std. Deviation	Std. Error Mean	95% Confidence Interval of the Difference				
					Lower	Upper			
Pair 1	PERCAP1 Percapita income/All - PERCAP2 Percapita income/Adults only	-1651.92	3186.6533	61.3242	-1772.17	-1531.67	-26.937	2699	.000

The first box in Figure 4.7 presents the paired-samples statistics (mean, standard deviation and standard error) for both variables. For instance, the mean value of **percap1** is £8643.57 with a standard deviation of 6764.67 for 2700 respondents.

The second box in Figure 4.7 presents the data on the extent to which the two variables are similar or correlated. As one might expect there is a high correlation between the two variables ($r = 0.900$, significant at $p < 0.001$). This is not surprising as the questions are very similar, both concerned with a household's *per capita* income.

The third box in Figure 4.7 present the findings from the paired *t*-test: $t = -26.937$, $df = 2699$, $p < 0.001$. The mean difference between **percap1** and **percap2** is £1651.91 and the *t*-test indicates that this difference is highly significant. Thus our hypothesis is confirmed: the average *per capita* income based upon all household members is significantly different (it is less) than the average *per capita* income based upon adults only.

SPSS *t-test exercise*

• Using one of the datasets, test hypotheses using the independent samples *t*-test.

To complete the task you need to: (1) state your research question; (2) generate your research hypothesis and the Null hypothesis; (3) select the appropriate variables, and (4) describe and interpret the output.

(For practice, you may also want to try out the paired samples *t*-test, but recognise that since the BSA datasets do not contain appropriate variables for a paired samples *t*-test that you will have to choose two interval/ratio variables that do not strictly meet the 'repeated measurements' assumption of the test.)

5 Crosstabulation

Introduction

Crosstabulation tables, or contingency tables, are frequently employed to examine the relationship between two variables (usually nominal or ordinal) that have a small number of categories. Although, as we saw in Module 3, quantitative variables such as age can be transformed in broad categories using the **Recode** procedure. Displaying the distribution of two or more variables jointly in the form of a crosstabulation table allows us to make some important observations about the relationship between them.

A simple example, the crosstabulation of **soctrust** by **rsex**, should help to illustrate this. Before looking at the crosstabulation table itself it is worth considering the frequency table for **soctrust** (the associated question for this variable is 'Would you say that most people can be trusted, or that you can't be too careful in dealing with people'). As we can see from Figure 5.1, 910 respondents (44.7 per cent) believed that people could be trusted, whereas 1123 respondents (55.3 per cent) felt that people were not trustworthy.

Figure 5.1 Frequency table of **soctrust**

SOCTRUST R say most people can be trusted?   Q790

		Frequency	Percent	Valid Percent	Cumulative Percent
Valid	1 Most people can be trusted	910	28.9	44.7	44.7
	2 Can t be too careful in dealing with peo	1123	35.7	55.3	100.0
	Total	2033	64.6	100.0	
Missing	-2 Skp, C version	1079	34.3		
	8 Don't know	16	.5		
	9 Not answered	17	.5		
	Total	1113	35.4		
Total		3146	100.0		

In order to examine this issue further we may want to look at the relationship between **soctrust** and **rsex**. In other words, is there any difference between men and women in terms of how much trust they place in people? A crosstabulation table of **soctrust** by **rsex** will help us to address this question.

Crosstabs in SPSS

To access Crosstabs in SPSS, click on **Analyze**, **Descriptive Statistics** and then **Crosstabs** (Figure 5.2).

Figure 5.2 Accessing the **Crosstabs** procedure

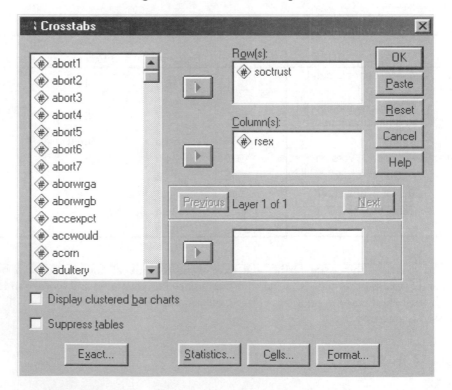

This will open up the **Crosstabs** dialog box (Figure 5.3). As we want to examine the relationship between **soctrust** and **rsex**, we simply transfer these variables from the variable list to the row and column boxes. If it is possible to identify an independent or causal variable this, by convention, should be our column variable. In this example **rsex** is the column variable because we are hypothesising that the respondent's sex (gender) is an important factor in determining whether or not they trust people.

Figure 5.3 **Crosstabs** dialog box

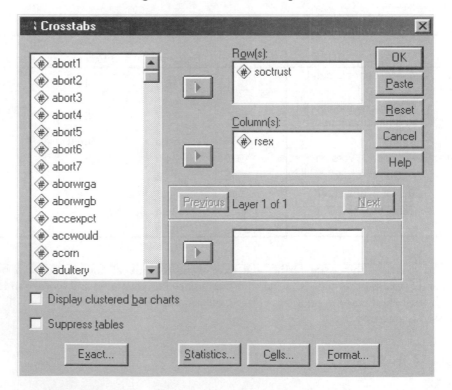

Then Click on **Cells** to open up the **Cell Display** dialog box (Figure 5.4).

Figure 5.4   Crosstabs: Cell Display dialog box

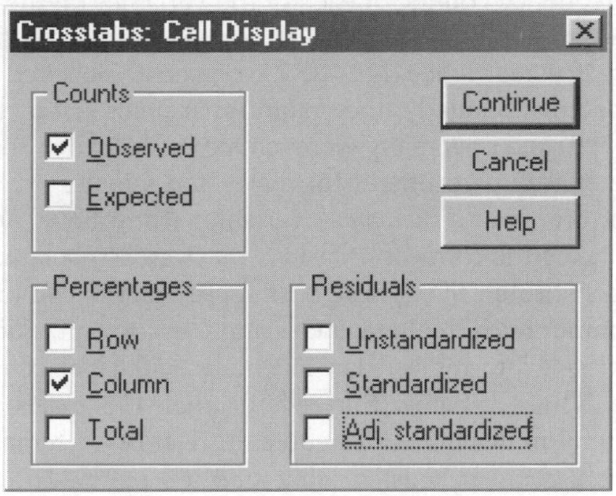

We will look at the **Cell Display** dialog box in more detail a little later, but for the moment simply click in the **Observed Counts** and **Column Percentages** check boxes.

Finally, click on **Continue** and then **OK**.

The resultant SPSS output is shown in Figure 5.5. While this crosstabulation table is quite basic in that it includes only frequency counts and column percentages, it nevertheless provides us with some very important information and is worth looking at more closely.

Figure 5.5   Crosstabulation of **soctrust** by **rsex**

SOCTRUST R say most people can be trusted?   Q790 * RSEX Sex of respondent by observation Q32 Crosstabulation

| | | | RSEX Sex of respondent by observation Q32 | | Total |
			1 Male	2 Female	
SOCTRUST R say most people can be trusted? Q790	1 Most people can be trusted	Count	452	458	910
		% within RSEX Sex of respondent by observation Q32	50.8%	40.0%	44.7%
	2 Can t be too careful in dealing with peo	Count	438	686	1124
		% within RSEX Sex of respondent by observation Q32	49.2%	60.0%	55.3%
Total		Count	890	1144	2034
		% within RSEX Sex of respondent by observation Q32	100.0%	100.0%	100.0%

Column Marginals ——————

Row Marginals ——————

Grand Total ——————

We will begin with the number in the bottom right-hand corner of the table in Figure 5.5, which is known as the *grand total*. This figure (2034) simply represents the total number of people who provided valid responses for both variables (that is, excluding missing values).

The numbers around the edge of the table represent the individual row and column totals (or marginals) and provide frequency counts for each of the variables on their own. So, for example, if we look at the row marginals we can see that 910 of our 2034 respondents (44.7 per cent) felt that 'most people can be trusted' while 1124 (55.3 per cent) believed that you 'can't be too careful in dealing with people'. Similarly, the column marginals tell us how many of the 2034 respondents were male (890) and how many were female (1144). Note that as we only requested column percentages, the overall percentages for males and females are not provided.

As **soctrust** and **rsex** are both *dichotomous* variables (they have only *two* categories) the main body of the table takes the form of a basic 2 by 2 crosstabulation, containing just four cells (marginals do not constitute cells). These cells represent the combination of categories of the two variables and contain both the frequencies and the corresponding column percentages. So, for example, the first cell informs us that 452 males (50.8 per cent of all males) felt that people could be trusted. The cell below this tells us that 438 males (49.2 per cent) believe that you can't be too careful in dealing with people. In relation to females, 458 (40 per cent of all females) thought people could be trusted while 686 (60 per cent) took the opposing view.

When column percentages are used the percentages in each column will add up to 100 per cent and we therefore need to compare across the categories of the column variable (**rsex** in this example). If we do this we can see that a greater percentage of males than females are willing to put their trust in people (51 per cent as opposed to 40 per cent). We can conclude that for this particular sample of 2034 people there is an association between gender and willingness to trust people (if there was no association we would expect to find the same percentages of males and females in our sample willing to trust people).

However, as we discussed in Module 4, with inferential statistics we are more interested in drawing conclusions about the 'population' that the sample was drawn from than in the sample itself. In other words, we want to find out whether the difference between males and females that we observed in the crosstabulation above actually represents a *real difference in the population as a whole*. The Chi-square test enables us to make such a judgement.

The Chi-square test

The Chi-square test allows us to determine whether or not there is a *statistically significant association* between two variables. If the variables are not associated they are said to be *statistically independent* (hence Chi-square is often referred to as the 'Chi-square test of independence'). As an inferential statistic it allows us to draw conclusions about the population on the basis of our sample results. So, for example, we can calculate the probability that the differences between males and females observed in the crosstabulation above (in relation to the **soctrust** variable) are the result of a real association between **rsex** and **soctrust** in the population as a whole. This can be put into more formal language by framing the Null (H_0) and alternative (H_1) hypotheses:

H_0: **soctrust** and **rsex** are *independent* (any observed association has occurred by chance).
H_1: **soctrust** and **rsex** are *dependent* (any observed association is the result of a real association).

As with the *t*-test (see Module 4), the Chi-square test allows us to choose between H_0 and H_1 and determine whether or not there is a statistical association between the two variables.

In order to illustrate the logic behind the Chi-square statistic it is necessary to elaborate on the crosstabulation table of **rsex** and **soctrust** outlined above. To facilitate this, we will ask SPSS to produce additional cell displays and statistics.

CROSSTABULATION **131**

Open the **Crosstabs** dialog box as before (click on **Analyze**, **Descriptive Statistics** and then **Crosstabs**). Next, transfer the **soctrust** and **rsex** variables to the appropriate locations (**rsex** to the column box and **soctrust** to the row box as shown in Figure 5.3). Then click on **Cells** to open the **Cell Display** dialog box (see Figure 5.6).

Figure 5.6   Cell Display dialog box

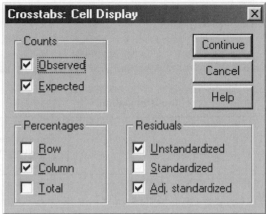

Select **Column** percentages as before, but this time in addition to **Observed** counts, select **Expected** counts also. Finally, select **Unstandardized** and **Adj. standardized** Residuals and click on **Continue**.

This will return you to the **Crosstabs** dialog box (Figure 5.3).

This time, however, we also want some inferential statistics for the crosstabulation table. Click on **Statistics** to open the statistics dialog box (Figure 5.7) and then click on **Chi-square** and **Phi and Cramér's V** (all of these selections will be explained in the context of the SPSS crosstabulation output).

Figure 5.7   Crosstabs: Statistics dialog box

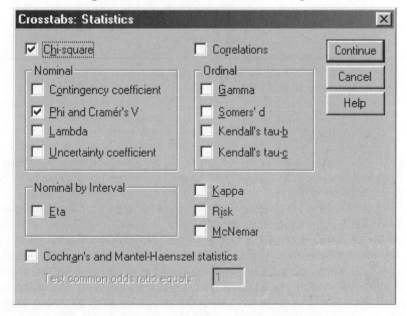

Then click on **Continue** and finally on **OK**.

The resultant output is shown in Figures 5.8a, 5.8b and 5.8c, and in order to gain an understanding of how Chi-square operates it is necessary to examine the various elements of these tables.

Figure 5.8a displays a more detailed version of the table shown in Figure 5.5. We have already looked at the frequency counts and column percentages and can see that these have not changed. In the first cell, for example, it is still the case that 452 males (50.8 per cent of all males) feel that people can be trusted.

Figure 5.8a   Crosstabulation table for **soctrust** by **rsex**

SOCTRUST R say most people can be trusted?   Q790 * RSEX Sex of respondent by observation   Q32
Crosstabulation

| | | | RSEX Sex of respondent by observation Q32 | | |
			1 Male	2 Female	Total
SOCTRUST R say most people can be trusted? Q790	1 Most people can be trusted	Count	452	458	910
		Expected Count	398.2	511.8	910.0
		% within RSEX Sex of respondent by observation Q32	50.8%	40.0%	44.7%
		Residual	53.8	-53.8	
		Adjusted Residual	4.8	-4.8	
	2 Can't be too careful in dealing with people	Count	438	686	1124
		Expected Count	491.8	632.2	1124.0
		% within RSEX Sex of respondent by observation Q32	49.2%	60.0%	55.3%
		Residual	-53.8	53.8	
		Adjusted Residual	-4.8	4.8	
Total		Count	890	1144	2034
		Expected Count	890.0	1144.0	2034.0
		% within RSEX Sex of respondent by observation Q32	100.0%	100.0%	100.0%

Figure 5.8a, however, also includes expected counts for each of the cells. The expected counts provide us with the frequencies we would expect in each cell if there was no association between the two variables (that is, if the Null hypothesis was true). For example, if the two variables were totally independent we would expect to find that the same percentage of males and females (44.7 per cent, or 398 males and 512 females) believed people could be trusted (see **Expected Count** in Figure 5.8a).

The fourth figure in each cell in Figure 5.8a is referred to as a *residual* (an unstandardised residual) and represents the difference between the *expected* frequencies and the *observed* frequencies (observed minus expected value). For example, in the first cell we have residual of 53.8 (452 − 398.2) which informs us that approximately 54 more males than we would expect (if there were no association between the variables), felt that people could be trusted.

The final value in each cell is the adjusted standardised residual and, although derived from the unstandardised residual, it is of much more practical benefit in terms of our analysis. When we obtain a significant Chi-square result this figure helps us to identify the form that the association takes and is particularly useful in larger tables. The general guideline is that those cells with adjusted residual values greater than 2 or less than −2 should be given special attention.

While it is not appropriate in a book of this nature to examine how the final Chi-square result is calculated (most statistics textbooks cover this quite well), it is important to have a general awareness of what this figure represents. In broad terms the value of Chi-square provides a measure of the *overall difference* between the observed frequencies and the expected frequencies. The greater the overall difference, the larger the value of Chi-square and the more confident we can be that there is a real association between these two variables in the population. Of course, as we saw in Module 4, we need to decide just how confident we want to be (95 per cent, 99 per cent or 99.9 per cent).

From Figure 5.8b we can see that the Chi-square value (Pearson Chi-Square) for **soctrust** by **rsex** is 23.405 with a significance level of .000. It is important to point out that when SPSS records a significance level of .000 this should be read as .0005 or less, rather than zero. As this significance level is less than .001 we can be at least 99.9 per cent certain that there is an association between **soctrust** and **rsex** in the population. To put it another way, if the Null hypothesis were true we would only expect to find a Chi-square as large as 23.405 in less than five out of every 10 000 samples. Therefore we can reject our Null hypothesis.

Figure 5.8b   Chi-square results for **soctrust** by **rsex**

Chi-Square Tests

	Value	df	Asymp. Sig. (2-sided)	Exact Sig. (2-sided)	Exact Sig. (1-sided)
Pearson Chi-Square	23.405[b]	1	.000		
Continuity Correction[a]	22.972	1	.000		
Likelihood Ratio	23.410	1	.000		
Fisher's Exact Test				.000	.000
Linear-by-Linear Association	23.393	1	.000		
N of Valid Cases	2034				

a. Computed only for a 2x2 table

b. 0 cells (.0%) have expected count less than 5. The minimum expected count is 398.18.

In order to determine the form that this significant association takes we need to return to the original table and examine the individual cells. This is quite straightforward in the current example as we are dealing with a simple 2 by 2 table. We can see clearly from Figure 5.8a that males are more likely to put their trust in people than females (50.8 per cent as opposed to 40 per cent). The adjusted residuals are not particularly useful here as all of the cells have identical values (their utility is more evident in larger tables as will become clear when we consider the second Chi-square example on p. 135).

Measures of association

While our Chi-square result confirmed the existence of a significant association between **soctrust** and **rsex** we are also interested in finding out the *strength* of that association.

However, because Chi-square is heavily dependent upon the size of the sample (for example, if you multiply the sample size by 10, the Chi-square result will increase by a factor of 10 also), it cannot provide us with such information. Fortunately, a number of statistics are available for the purposes of measuring the strength of an association and, as usual, our choice will be influenced by the level of measurement of the variables we are working with. Two such measures, Phi and Cramer's V, are frequently used if one or more of the variables is nominal (Phi for 2 by 2 tables and Cramer's V for tables larger than 2 by 2).

Absolute values of Phi and Cramer's V range between 0 and 1, with 0 representing no association and 1 a perfect association. So, while Figure 5.8c confirms that there is a significant association between **soctrust** and **rsex**, the Phi value of .107 informs us that this association is relatively weak (.107 is quite close to zero).

Figure 5.8c Measures of association for **soctrust** by **rsex**

Symmetric Measures

		Value	Approx. Sig.
Nominal by Nominal	Phi	.107	.000
	Cramer's V	.107	.000
N of Valid Cases		2034	

a. Not assuming the null hypothesis.

b. Using the asymptotic standard error assuming the null hypothesis.

So far, we have focused only on Phi and Cramer's V but, as we can see from the dialog box in Figure 5.7, the **Crosstabs** procedure in SPSS provides a variety of alternative measures of association. A number of these options are discussed briefly in the Appendix at the end of this module, although for more detailed information regarding the appropriate measures of association to use with crosstabulations it is recommended that you consult a specialised statistics text.

A note of caution

Before moving on to a second Chi-square example and a consideration of the concept of a 'control' variable, it is necessary to draw attention to some of the restrictions that apply when using Chi-square.

(a)	For a 2 by 2 table (2 rows and 2 columns) Chi-square should not be used if any of the expected frequencies is *less than 5*.
(b)	For tables larger than 2 by 2, Chi-square should not be used if any of the expected frequencies is *less than 1* or more than 20% of the expected frequencies are *less than 5*.

It is not necessary to request expected frequencies in order to check this when running the **Crosstabs** procedure as SPSS automatically includes the relevant information in the output (see the bottom of Figure 5.8b).

In certain circumstances it may be possible to overcome the problem of low expected frequencies by combining together some of the categories of the variables you are using. This will have the effect of reducing the number of categories and increasing the number of cases in the cells. (See Module 3 for details on how to combine categories using the **Recode** procedure.)

Chi-square: a second example

As a precursor to a discussion of control variables we will carry out a second Chi-square test, this time using the variables **rsex** (Sex of respondent) and **homosex** (Is sex between same sex adults wrong?). We can see from the frequency table of **homosex** (Figure 5.9) that respondents are quite divided on this issue, with 43 per cent of people expressing the view that homosexuality is 'Always wrong' and 29 per cent believing that it is 'Not wrong at all'.

Figure 5.9   Frequency table for **homosex**

Homosex Is sex between samesex adults wrong?Q966

		Frequency	Percent	Valid Percent	Cumulative Percent
Valid	1 Always wrong	726	23.1	42.8	42.8
	2 Mostly wrong	181	5.8	10.7	53.4
	3 Sometimes wrong	211	6.7	12.4	65.8
	4 Rarely wrong	84	2.7	5.0	70.8
	5 Not wrong at all	496	15.8	29.2	100.0
	Total	1697	54.0	100.0	
Missing	-2 Skp,A+B versions	1267	40.3		
	6 (Depends/ varies)	139	4.4		
	8 Don't know	31	1.0		
	9 Not answered	13	.4		
	Total	1449	46.0		
Total		3146	100.0		

However, it would be interesting to carry out a crosstabulation of **homosex** by **rsex** to see what effect, if any, gender has on people's attitudes to homosexuality. In this example, then, we want to see whether or not there is a significant association between **homosex** and **rsex**:

H_0: **homosex** and **rsex** are *independent* (any observed association has occurred by chance).
H_1: **homosex** and **rsex** are *dependent* (any observed association is the result of a real association).

Open the **Crosstabs** dialog box as before (click on **Analyze**, **Descriptive Statistics** and then **Crosstabs**). This time transfer the variable **homosex** over to the row box and **rsex** to the column box (**rsex** is the independent or causal variable in this instance because we are hypothesising that a person's gender has a determining influence on their attitudes to homosexuality).

Then click on **Cells** to open the **Cell Display** dialog box. This time we will select only the **Observed** frequencies, **Column** percentages and **Adj. standardized** residuals, as shown in Figure 5.10.

Figure 5.10 Crosstabs: Cell Display dialog box

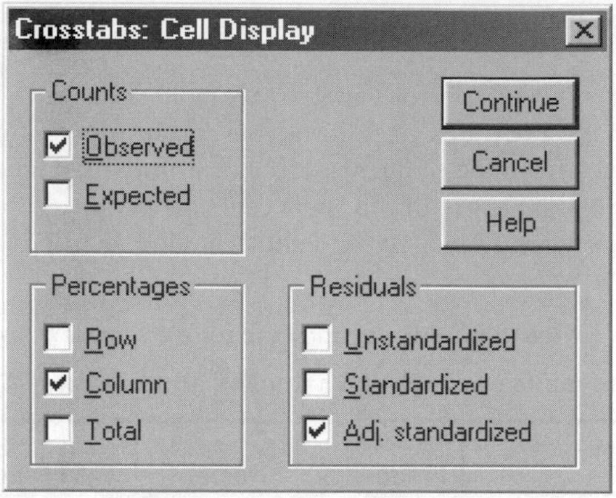

Click on **Continue** to return you to the **Crosstabs** dialog box and click on **Statistics** to open the **Crosstabs: Statistics** dialog box. Select **Chi-square** and **Phi and Cramér's V** (as we did in the previous example) and then click on **Continue** and finally on **OK**.

The output is shown in Figures 5.11a, 5.11b and 5.11c. We will consider these tables briefly before examining the impact of the introduction of a 'control' variable on the relationship between the two variables.

Figure 5.11a shows the crosstabulation table for **homosex** by **rsex**. Although it is much larger than the 2 by 2 table in our first example, the decision to select only frequency counts, column percentages and adjusted residuals ensures that it is still relatively easy to interpret. Before commenting on the individual cells of the table, however, we need to consult our Chi-square results in Figure 5.11b.

We can see from Figure 5.11b that the Chi-square result of 17.059 has a significance level of .002. So if the Null hypothesis were true we would only expect to find a Chi-square as large as 17.059 in two out of every thousand samples. Consequently, we can safely reject the Null hypothesis and conclude that there is a significant association between **homosex** and **rsex**.

(**Note** that Figure 5.11b also informs us that there are no cells with an expected count lower than 5 and indeed that the minimum expected count is 37.47. Consequently, we can be sure that the prerequisites referred to earlier in relation to low expected frequencies have been met.)

As the crosstabulation table for **homosex** by **rsex** is larger than 2 by 2 we need to consult Cramer's V rather than Phi for our measure of association. We have already determined that there is an extremely significant association (.002) between these two variables and the Cramer's V value of .100 indicates that this association is relatively weak (Figure 5.11c).

The final stage in our analysis of these tables involves an examination of the form that this significant association takes. As it is possible for the same Chi-square value to be produced by *completely different* patterns of association we need to look closely at the adjusted residuals. By focusing on the cells with the most extreme adjusted residuals (those that have an absolute value greater than 2) we can identify the pattern of association that has produced a significant result. So, for example, the first cell in Figure 5.11a contains an adjusted residual of 3. This informs us that a proportionately much larger number of males (than we would expect if the

Figure 5.11a Crosstabulation table for **homosex** by **rsex**

Homosex Is sex between samesex adults wrong?Q966 *
Rsex Sex of respondent by observation   Q32 Crosstabulation

			RSEX Sex of respondent by observation Q32		Total
			1 Male	2 Female	
Homosex Is sex between samesex adults wrong?Q966	1 Always wrong	Count	354	372	726
		% within RSEX Sex of respondent by observation Q32	46.8%	39.6%	42.8%
		Adjusted Residual	3.0	-3.0	
	2 Mostly wrong	Count	91	90	181
		% within RSEX Sex of respondent by observation Q32	12.0%	9.6%	10.7%
		Adjusted Residual	1.6	-1.6	
	3 Sometimes wrong	Count	81	130	211
		% within RSEX Sex of respondent by observation Q32	10.7%	13.8%	12.4%
		Adjusted Residual	-1.9	1.9	
	4 Rarely wrong	Count	38	46	84
		% within RSEX Sex of respondent by observation Q32	5.0%	4.9%	4.9%
		Adjusted Residual	.1	-.1	
	5 Not wrong at all	Count	193	302	495
		% within RSEX Sex of respondent by observation Q32	25.5%	32.1%	29.2%
		Adjusted Residual	-3.0	3.0	
Total		Count	757	940	1697
		% within RSEX Sex of respondent by observation Q32	100.0%	100.0%	100.0%

Figure 5.11b Chi-square results for **homosex** by **rsex**

Chi-Square Tests

	Value	df	Asymp. Sig. (2-sided)
Pearson Chi-Square	17.059[a]	4	.002
Likelihood Ratio	17.126	4	.002
Linear-by-Linear Association	12.860	1	.000
N of Valid Cases	1697		

a. 0 cells (.0%) have expected count less than 5. The minimum expected count is 37.47.

Figure 5.11c Measures of association for **homosex** by **rsex**

Symmetric Measures

		Value	Approx. Sig.
Nominal by Nominal	Phi	.100	.002
	Cramer's V	.100	.002
N of Valid Cases		1697	

a. Not assuming the null hypothesis.

b. Using the asymptotic standard error assuming the null hypothesis.

variables were independent) believe that homosexuality is 'Always wrong' (46.8 per cent of males compared to 42.8 per cent of all respondents). By contrast, the adjusted residual of −3 in the adjacent cell suggests that females are more tolerant of same-sex relationships as only 39.6 per cent of this group felt that homosexuality was 'always wrong'.

The only other noteworthy adjusted residuals are located in the bottom two cells of the table in Figure 5.11a (−3 and 3, respectively). These confirm our earlier assertion that females appear to be more tolerant than males (32.1 per cent of females feel that homosexuality is 'Not wrong at all' compared to only 25.5 per cent of males).

From these results, then, we can conclude that there is a significant association between gender and attitudes towards homosexuality, to the extent that females are more tolerant of same-sex relationships than males.

Introducing a control variable

Very often we will want to develop our crosstabulation analysis further and examine the relationship between two variables for each category of a third variable. Introducing a second independent or 'control' variable in this way represents a shift from bivariate to multivariate analysis. SPSS allows us to carry this out quite easily. We may suspect, for example, that the relationship between **homosex** and **rsex** that we observed above is somehow mediated by age. It may be that the relationship is different, or even non-existent, for certain age groups.

(**Note** that before introducing age into a crosstabulation we need to recode it into distinct categories or age groups – see Module 3 for details on how to recode variables). For this

Figure 5.12 Frequency table for **newage**

NEWAGE rage recoded

		Frequency	Percent	Valid Percent	Cumulative Percent
Valid	1.00 Young (under 35)	969	30.8	30.9	30.9
	2.00 Middle-aged (35 to 54)	1125	35.8	35.9	66.8
	3.00 Old (55 or above)	1042	33.1	33.2	100.0
	Total	3137	99.7	100.0	
Missing	98.00	3	.1		
	99.00	7	.2		
	Total	9	.3		
Total		3146	100.0		

example, we have created a new variable **newage** (see frequency table in Figure 5.12) by recoding **rage** into three distinct categories (under 35; 35 to 54; and 55 or older).)

The introduction of **newage** (**rage** recoded) as a control variable effectively holds age constant (that is, we are *controlling* for the effects of age). In practical terms, we are asking SPSS to produce three separate tables of **homosex** by **rsex** (one for 'young', one for 'middle-aged' and one for 'old' respondents).

To obtain these tables simply open up the **Crosstabs** dialog box (Figure 5.13) as we did for the bivariate analysis (click on **Analyze**, **Descriptive Statistics** and then **Crosstabs**).

Figure 5.13 Crosstabs dialog box

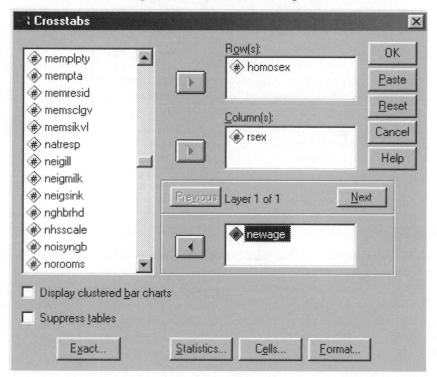

This time, however, in addition to the row and column variables we need to select our control variable (**newage**) and transfer it to the box labeled 'Layer 1 of 1' at the bottom of the dialog box (as shown in Figure 5.13).

Select the same **Cells** (**Observed** frequencies, **Column** percentages and **Adj. standardized** residuals) and **Statistics** (**Chi-square** and **Phi and Cramér's V**) as before, and then click on **OK** to run the procedure.

The output from this multivariate analysis is shown in Figure 5.14a, 5.14b and 5.14c. If we look at the Chi-square results in Figure 5.14b, we can see that there is a significant association between **homosex** by **rsex** for 'Young' people. The Chi-square statistic is 22.916 with a significance level of .0005 (remember that we read .000 as .0005). However, if we look at the Chi-square results for 'Middle-aged' respondents we can see that there is not a significant association between **homosex** and **rsex** for this age group (Chi-square = 3.498, significance level = .478). Finally, the bottom section of Figure 5.14b informs us that there is not a

Figure 5.14a Crosstabulation table for **homosex** by **rsex** by **newage**

Homosex Is sex between samesex adults wrong?Q966 * Rsex   Sex of respondent by observation   Q32 * Newage rage recoded Crosstabulation

NEWAGE rage recoded					RSEX Sex of respondent by observation Q32		Total
					1 Male	2 Female	
1.00 Young (under 35)	HOMOSEX Is sex between samesex adults wrong?Q966	1 Always wrong		Count	78	44	122
				% within RSEX Sex of respondent by observation Q32	32.2%	16.1%	23.7%
				Adjusted Residual	4.3	-4.3	
		2 Mostly wrong		Count	26	21	47
				% within RSEX Sex of respondent by observation Q32	10.7%	7.7%	9.1%
				Adjusted Residual	1.2	-1.2	
		3 Sometimes wrong		Count	34	47	81
				% within RSEX Sex of respondent by observation Q32	14.0%	17.2%	15.7%
				Adjusted Residual	-1.0	1.0	
		4 Rarely wrong		Count	17	22	39
				% within RSEX Sex of respondent by observation Q32	7.0%	8.1%	7.6%
				Adjusted Residual	-.4	.4	
		5 Not wrong at all		Count	87	139	226
				% within RSEX Sex of respondent by observation Q32	36.0%	50.9%	43.9%
				Adjusted Residual	-3.4	3.4	
	Total			Count	242	273	515
				% within RSEX Sex of respondent by observation Q32	100.0%	100.0%	100.0%
2.00 Middle-aged (35 to 54)	HOMOSEX Is sex between samesex adults wrong?Q966	1 Always wrong		Count	106	135	241
				% within RSEX Sex of respondent by observation Q32	40.3%	36.4%	38.0%
				Adjusted Residual	1.0	-1.0	
		2 Mostly wrong		Count	35	41	76
				% within RSEX Sex of respondent by observation Q32	13.3%	11.1%	12.0%
				Adjusted Residual	.9	-.9	
		3 Sometimes wrong		Count	30	56	86
				% within RSEX Sex of respondent by observation Q32	11.4%	15.1%	13.6%
				Adjusted Residual	-1.3	1.3	
		4 Rarely wrong		Count	14	17	31
				% within RSEX Sex of respondent by observation Q32	5.3%	4.6%	4.9%
				Adjusted Residual	.4	-.4	
		5 Not wrong at all		Count	78	122	200
				% within RSEX Sex of respondent by observation Q32	29.7%	32.9%	31.5%
				Adjusted Residual	-.9	.9	
	Total			Count	263	371	634
				% within RSEX Sex of respondent by observation Q32	100.0%	100.0%	100.0%
3.00 Old (55 or above)	HOMOSEX Is sex between samesex adults wrong?Q966	1 Always wrong		Count	169	191	360
				% within RSEX Sex of respondent by observation Q32	67.1%	65.4%	66.2%
				Adjusted Residual	.4	-.4	
		2 Mostly wrong		Count	30	28	58
				% within RSEX Sex of respondent by observation Q32	11.9%	9.6%	10.7%
				Adjusted Residual	.9	-.9	
		3 Sometimes wrong		Count	18	27	45
				% within RSEX Sex of respondent by observation Q32	7.1%	9.2%	8.3%
				Adjusted Residual	-.9	.9	
		4 Rarely wrong		Count	7	7	14
				% within RSEX Sex of respondent by observation Q32	2.8%	2.4%	2.6%
				Adjusted Residual	.3	-.3	
		5 Not wrong at all		Count	28	39	67
				% within RSEX Sex of respondent by observation Q32	11.1%	13.4%	12.3%
				Adjusted Residual	-.8	.8	
	Total			Count	252	292	544
				% within RSEX Sex of respondent by observation Q32	100.0%	100.0%	100.0%

Figure 5.14b   Chi-square results for **homosex** by **rsex** by **newage**

Chi-Square Tests

NEWAGE rage recoded		Value	df	Asymp. Sig. (2_sided)
1.00 Young (under 35)	Pearson Chi-Square	22.916[a]	4	.000
	Likelihood Ratio	23.079	4	.000
	Linear-by-Linear Association	20.663	1	.000
	N of Valid Cases	515		
2.00 Middle-aged (35 to 54)	Pearson Chi-Square	3.498[b]	4	.478
	Likelihood Ratio	3.520	4	.475
	Linear-by-Linear Association	1.318	1	.251
	N of Valid Cases	634		
3.00 Old (55 or above)	Pearson Chi-Square	2.090[c]	4	.719
	Likelihood Ratio	2.097	4	.718
	Linear-by-Linear Association	.662	1	.416
	N of Valid Cases	544		

a. 0 cells (.0%) have expected count less than 5. The minimum expected count is 18.33.

b. 0 cells (.0%) have expected count less than 5. The minimum expected count is 12.86.

c. 0 cells (.0%) have expected count less than 5. The minimum expected count is 6.49.

significant association between **homosex** and **rsex** for 'Old' people either (Chi-square = 2.090, significance level = .719).

A closer examination of the individual cells in the crosstabulation table (Figure 5.14a) will provide us with more detailed information on these results. We will begin with the table for 'Young' people and focus on the important adjusted residuals (those with an absolute value greater than 2). We can see that males and females have very different opinions on homosexuality and that these differences are most apparent at the extreme end of the attitude scale. For example, the top two cells of the table have adjusted residuals of 4.3 and −4.3, respectively. Whereas over 32 per cent of males felt that homosexuality was 'Always wrong', only 16 per cent of females held this belief. Turning to the opposite end of the attitude scale we can see that over 50 per cent of women stated that homosexuality was 'Not wrong at all', in contrast to only 36 per cent of men (adjusted residuals of 3.4 and −3.4, respectively).

As the Chi-square results for the two older age groups ('Middle-aged' and 'Old') are not significant we would not expect to find any noteworthy adjusted residuals (they all lie between 2 and −2). Indeed if we look at the column percentages we can see that there is very little difference in the attitudes of males and females towards homosexuality for these two age groups.

Finally, Figure 5.14c provides information on the strength of the association between **homosex** and **rsex** for each of the categories of the control variable (**newage**). We can see from the table that the value of Cramer's V for the 'Young' age category is .211, indicating a slightly stronger association than our previous example (as we already know, the results are not significant for the other two age groups).

Figure 5.14c Measures of association for **homosex** by **rsex** by **newage**

Symmetric Measures

NEWAGE rage recoded			Value	Approx. Sig.
1.00 Young (under 35)	Nominal by Nominal	Phi	.211	.000
		Cramer's V	.211	.000
	N of Valid Cases		515	
2.00 Middle-aged (35 to 54)	Nominal by Nominal	Phi	.074	.478
		Cramer's V	.074	.478
	N of Valid Cases		634	
3.00 Old (55 or above)	Nominal by Nominal	Phi	.062	.719
		Cramer's V	.062	.719
	N of Valid Cases		544	

a. Not assuming the null hypothesis.

b. Using the asymptotic standard error assuming the null hypothesis.

From these results, then, we can conclude that there is a significant association between gender and attitudes towards homosexuality for 'Young' people only, to the extent that 'Young' women are more tolerant of same-sex relationships than 'Young' men.

Appendix
Measures of Association

When selecting an appropriate measure of association to accompany a crosstabulation our choice is influenced by a variety of factors and, as with most of the statistics covered in this book, the level of measurement of the variables we are using is a key determinant. In this Appendix we will consider some of the most commonly used measures.

Measures of association for nominal variables

As we have already seen, **Phi** is an appropriate measure of association when the variables in a crosstabulation table are categorical. It is closely related to Chi-square and is easily calculated by dividing the Chi-square result by the sample size and obtaining the square root of the result. Values are bounded between 0 and 1, with 0 representing no association and 1 signifying a perfect association. Phi is suitable for 2 by 2 tables only, as with larger tables it may produce values greater than 1. (The variables in our first example, **soctrust** by **rsex**, were both nominal with only two categories; so Phi was appropriate). *Cramér's V* should be used for tables exceeding 2 rows and 2 columns.

An alternative measure of association for nominal variables is *Lambda*. This is one of a family of measures based upon the principle of *proportional reduction in error* (PRE). In basic terms, PRE measures calculate the degree to which you can predict values of the dependent variable when you know the values of the independent variable (you will need to consult a statistics textbook in order to fully appreciate the principle of PRE). Where the independent variable allows you to accurately predict all values of the dependent variable, Lambda will achieve a value of 1 (a perfect association). On the other hand, where our knowledge of the independent variable provides no help in predicting the dependent variable Lambda will equal zero. SPSS produces both symmetric and asymmetric versions of Lambda and you should use the symmetric value if you are unable to make a decision as to which of your variables is dependent/independent. Finally, we should point out that *Goodman and Kruskall's tau*, another PRE-based measure for nominal variables, is automatically produced by SPSS when Lambda is requested.

Measures of association for ordinal variables

Gamma is the most popular measure of association when both variables are ordinal. Like Lambda, it is a PRE measure, although Gamma takes advantage of the fact that ordinal data can be ranked. The calculation of Gamma is based upon the difference between the number of concordant pairs (two cases that are ranked the same on both variables) and the number of discordant pairs (two cases that are ranked differently on both variables). Moreover, because we are dealing with ordinal data it is possible to achieve negative values for Gamma. A negative Gamma score indicates that there are more discordant than concordant pairs, whereas a greater proportion of concordant pairs will produce a positive result (-1 represents a perfect negative association, whereas $+1$ indicates a perfect positive association). Finally, as Gamma is a symmetric measure of association the result will be the same regardless of which variable you deem to be dependent/independent.

One of the problems with Gamma is that it ignores all pairs that are tied so it may overestimate the strength of an association if there is a high percentage of tied cases.

Somer's d is an alternative measure of association for ordinal variables and differs from Gamma in that it is asymmetric and also takes into account cases tied on the dependent variable. As with Gamma, SPSS also calculates a symmetric version of this statistic.

Kendall's tau-b takes account of tied pairs on both variables (separately) and is therefore a good alternative to Gamma when there is a high proportion of tied ranks. One limitation of Kendall's tau-b is that it can obtain the values of $+1$ or -1 only if the crosstabulation table has the same number of rows and columns. Kendall's tau-b is also a symmetric measure of association.

Making a decision regarding the most appropriate measure of association to use can sometimes be a complex process and many of the issues involved are beyond the remit of this text. There are a variety of additional measures that have not been considered here, some of which are specifically designed for tables that have combinations of levels of measurement. For further details on these procedures, including discussions on when and under what conditions they should be employed, you should consult a dedicated statistical text.

SPSS exercises on crosstabulation

You should now produce some crosstabulation tables yourself:

- Select some pairs of nominal or ordinal variables and produce crosstabulation tables for these.

  Get SPSS to carry out Chi-square tests for these tables and determine whether or not a statistically significant association exists between the variables.

  If a significant association does exist, look at the adjusted residuals in the cells of the table to see which cells have produced the significant association by having significantly more or significantly fewer cases in them than would be expected by chance.
- Choose one or more of the pairs of variables that produced interesting results and carry out the exercise again, only this time introducing a third variable as a 'control' variable. Is the relationship between the two variables in the tables different for different layers of the control variable? What information can we glean from the adjusted residuals?
- **Note** that the total number of cells in a crosstabulation table is the product of the number of rows times the number of columns times the number of 'layers'. For this reason you should take care that you do not request a table with so many cells that it becomes nonsensical. For instance, if you had three variables with nine categories, crosstabulating two of these with a third as a control would produce 729 cells (9 multiplied by 9 multiplied by 9)! Even if all of the more than 3000 cases in the British Social Attitudes dataset appear in the tables, there would only be four people, on average, in each cell.

6 Analysis of Variance (ANOVA)

Introduction

ANalysis Of VAriance (ANOVA), or *F*-test, is an extension of the independent groups *t*-test. Analysis of variance is a more general statistical procedure than the groups *t*-test. You will remember that the *t*-test was used when we had two levels of the independent variable (males and females) and we wanted to see how the groups differed on a interval/ratio variable. However, often there are categorical variables which have more than two levels. In the **Crime** dataset, for instance, these include social class (**rrgclass**), religion (**religion**) and educational qualifications (**hedqual**). Analysis of Variance is similar to the independent groups *t*-test; only it is when there are more than two levels of an independent variable.

ANOVA compares whether the average values or levels of one variable (the means of the dependent variable) differ significantly across the categories of another variable or variables (the independent variable). The way in which ANOVA calculates this is to see how the values that go into making up the means in each category are dispersed. If the variance in each category is very high (each category has cases both with high values and people with low values), the chances of a person with a high or low value being in any one particular category is not large and therefore there probably is not a significant difference between groups. However, if the variance in each category is relatively low, some categories will have almost all of the high values, and other categories will have almost all the low values. That is, whether or not a case has a high value or a low value will be likely to be determined by the category and there probably is a significance difference between groups. To put it another way, what an ANOVA does is to compare the variance *between* groups (or categories) with the variance *within* groups (or categories). If there is more difference between groups than there is within individuals in groups, it must be the groups that make the difference and the result is statistically significant.

What does a significant result with an ANOVA mean? Figure 6.1 is a pictorial example of a *significant* result (on the left) and *non-significant* result (on the right), where we have 3 groups (A, B, C) and an interval/ratio variable called X. In the diagram in Figure 6.1, the vertical 'box and dot' plots represent the distributions of scores on Variable X. The boxes indicate the middle 50 per cent of values on Variable X and the lines above and below the boxes each represent, respectively, the upper and lower 25 per cent of values on Variable X. There are three 'box and dot' plots on each side of the diagram to represent the distribution for each of the three groups, A, B and C.

On the left is a diagram of a significant result. Here, as depicted by the relatively 'short fat' boxes and short lines, the range of scores for each of the three groups are closely bunched together. Once we know a person's group (A, B, C), we would be close to knowing their score on Variable X. The diagram on the right of the figure is an example of a non-significant result. The range of scores for each of the groups is quite wide, as depicted by the 'long thin' boxes and the relatively long lines. There is a little variance *between* groups, but a lot of variance *within* groups for scores on Variable X — therefore even when we know the group, we would not necessarily know what the level of an individual's score on Variable X is going to be.

Figure 6.1 Diagram depicting a significant and nonsignificant ANOVA result

A significant result

A nonsignificant result

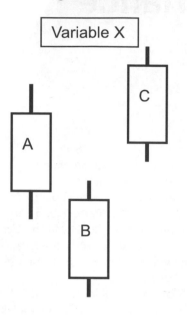 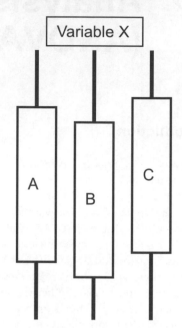

This is precisely what ANOVA does. It compares the variance *between* groups with the variance *within* groups to arrive at a number called the **F-ratio**. The larger value of the F-ratio, the larger the variance between groups. Hence, we use the F-ratio statistic to see whether the difference between groups is significant.

How to do a simple ANOVA using SPSS

Let us take an example from the **Crime** dataset: We want to find out whether there is a significant difference between the categories of people's self-rated income group (**srinc**) in their responses for the scalar variable **locarea** (the higher respondents' scores are on **locarea**, the more satisfied they are with their local area). Therefore, the ANOVA used here will examine whether the three categories of High Income, Medium Income and Low Income differ *significantly* from each other on the mean values of their view of the local area.

Pull down the **Analyze** menu and click on **Compare Means**, and then **One-Way ANOVA**. You should now get a screen that looks like Figure 6.2.

To put the dependent variable (**locarea**) into the procedure, click on **locarea** in the variable box and then click on the > to transfer it into the **Dependent** box. To put the independent variable (**srinc**) into the computation, click on the variable **srinc** in the **Variable menu** box, and then click on the > next to the **Factor:** box.

We could now run the ANOVA at this point. However, there are a number of options we can choose. As the ANOVA compares the means scores of certain groups, it might be handy to ask the computer what the means are. If we click on the **Options** box here, the box in Figure 6.3 should come up.

Figure 6.2 One-Way ANOVA window

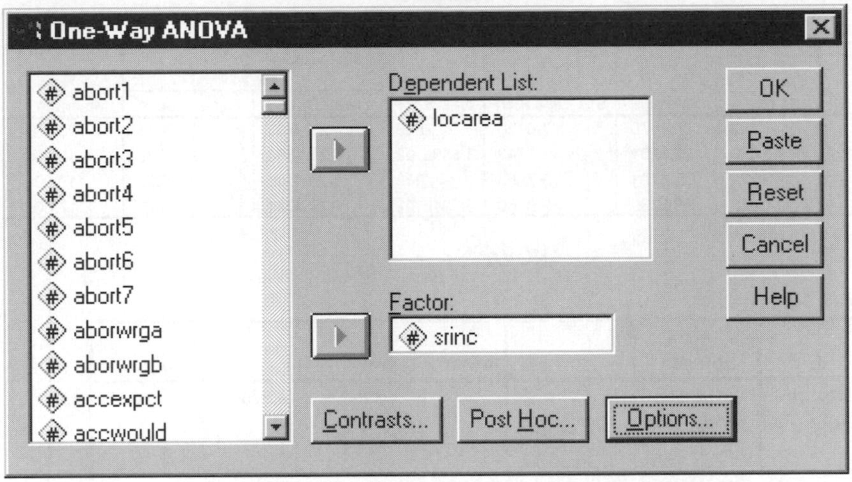

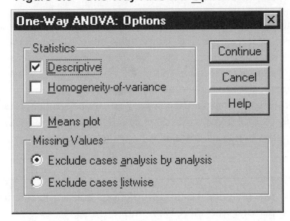

Figure 6.3 One-Way ANOVA: Options window

As we want the means for each group, it is necessary to tick the **Descriptives** box. Then click on **Continue** to return to the main ANOVA window. We are now ready to run the ANOVA, so click on **OK**. Your **Output** window should look like that in Figure 6.4.

To interpret these results we examine the mean scores on level of satisfaction with the local area for the three income groups. For satisfaction levels of the local area, high-income individuals score a mean of 30.48 (standard deviation = 3.0), middle-income individuals score a mean of 29.63 (standard deviation = 3.6) and low-income group individuals score a mean of 29.32 (standard deviation = 3.8). The ANOVA box results inform us whether the difference between the means is significant. Here F is 7.392 (always report the value of F). The Significance of F is .001 As this level of significance means that there is less than a one in 1000 chance that the difference between income groups came about by chance, we accept there genuinely is a significant overall difference between income groups in their level of satisfaction with their local area.

However, at present the findings provide an unclear interpretation of where the differences lie. Looking at the gross differences between the mean levels of satisfaction with local area

Figure 6.4   One-Way ANOVA output
Descriptives

Eval of local area

	N	Mean	Std. Deviation	Std. Error	95% Confidence Interval for Mean		Minimum	Maximum
					Lower Bound	Upper Bound		
high income	133	30.4870	3.0126	.2609	29.9709	31.0031	20.00	38.00
middle income	1628	29.6291	3.5743	8.859E-02	29.4553	29.8029	18.00	40.00
low income	1324	29.3191	3.7953	.1043	29.1145	29.5238	17.00	39.00
Total	3085	29.5332	3.6566	6.584E-02	29.4041	29.6622	17.00	40.00

ANOVA

Eval of local area

	Sum of Squares	df	Mean Square	F	Sig.
Between Groups	196.905	2	98.453	7.392	.001
Within Groups	41036.259	3081	13.319		
Total	41233.165	3083			

above we can see that the *high-income* people score higher on level of satisfaction with their local area than *middle-income* people and *low-income* people, and *middle-income* people score higher than *low-income* people on satisfaction with local area. Yet we are really unable to say which of these noted differences are the source of the significant *F*-value: that is, are all the differences we note significant, or just some of them?

SPSS gives us facilities for locating the patterns of any significant differences found in an ANOVA. We are able to make contrasts that break down the differences between groups. Within SPSS there are two types of comparisons using ANOVA.

- **Contrasts** – used when you are making predictions about the relationships between the variable before you perform the ANOVA; and
- **Post-hoc comparisons** – used when you have *not* made any predictions about the relationships between the variables before you perform the ANOVA.

(**Note**, of course, that there is no need to make comparisons when you find no significant overall difference in the ANOVA.)

Let us consider the last example. Here we may have decided that it would be difficult for us to make any strong *a priori* statements about self-rated income affecting satisfaction with local area (we do not believe that just because people are richer means that they should be more satisfied with their local area). Therefore we use post-hoc comparisons to compare the means.

As for the previous example, repeat the steps for the one-way ANOVA (**Analyze, Compare Means, One-way ANOVA**). (The variables should still be in their boxes.) This time, however, click on **Post Hoc** ... and click on the **Scheffe** test (a commonly used comparison) as in Figure 6.5. There are many post-hoc comparisons you can use but the Scheffe is a common one.

You will get the same output as before, but you also get some additional information in the **Multiple Comparisons** table. This is shown in Figure 6.6

Figure 6.5   One-Way ANOVA: Post Hoc Multiple Comparisons window

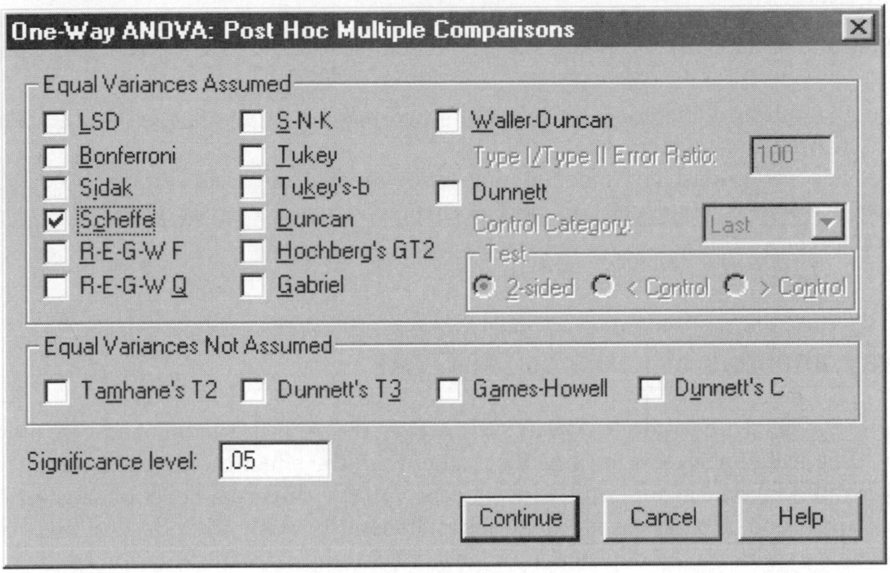

Figure 6.6   Post-Hoc comparison using **Scheffe**
Multiple Comparisons

Dependent Variable: Eval of local area
Scheffe

(I) Self-rated income group Q448	(J) Self-rated income group Q448	Mean Difference (I-J)	Std. Error	Sig.	95% Confidence Interval	
					Lower Bound	Upper Bound
high income	middle income	.8579*	.3288	.033	5.273E-02	1.6631
	low income	1.1679*	.3316	.002	.3557	1.9800
middle income	high income	-.8579*	.3288	.033	-1.6631	-5.2726E-02
	low income	.3100	.1351	.072	-2.0801E-02	.6408
low income	high income	-1.1679*	.3316	.002	-1.9800	-.3557
	middle income	-.3100	.1351	.072	-.6408	2.080E-02

*· The mean difference is significant at the .05 level.

Here in each row are the comparisons for each group's mean with each of the others: (1) high-income, with middle-income and then low-income; (2) middle-income, with high-income and low-income; and (3) low-income with high-income and middle-income. For interpreting these statistics we are interested in the Sig. Column. Any figure less than .05 is deemed significant. So, using the first row, the high-income group is significantly different from the middle- and low-income groups. In the second row, the middle-income is significantly different from the high-income but not significantly different from the low-income group. The third row is somewhat redundant, but shows that low-income is significantly different from high-income. Together these findings show that, though there is a significant difference between high-income individuals and the middle- and low-income groups, the middle- and low-income groups do *not* significantly differ in levels of satisfaction with the local area. As higher scores on satisfaction with the local area indicate more satisfaction with the local area, we conclude that high-income individuals are significantly more satisfied with their local area than middle- and low-income individuals.

ANOVA exercise

Now try some ANOVAs by yourself:

- Is there a significant difference between Self-rated income group (**srinc**) and the perception of crime (**crime**) in the local area?
- Choose one categorical and one interval/ratio variable, and perform an ANOVA. If a significant result is obtained, use post-hoc comparisons to break down the pattern of significant relationships.

Two-way analysis of variance (ANOVA)

We have just dealt with a simple ANOVA; however the ANOVA command can allow us to do more complicated analyses. Imagine that rather than the effect of one independent variable (**srinc**: Self-rated income group) on the dependent variable (**locarea**: Level of satisfaction with the local area), you actually want to deal simultaneously with the effect of two or more independent variables on the dependent variable. For example, in an extension to the one-way ANOVA that we covered above, you might want to look how Self-rated income group *plus* the effect of whether respondents are male or female (**rsex**) both affect respondents' levels of satisfaction with their local area (**locarea**).

Two-way ANOVA allows this type of examination. Two-way ANOVA takes the effect of both independent variables into account at the same time. Therefore we can establish the *simultaneous effects* of both of the independent variables on the dependent variable – and, furthermore, whether the effect of one of the independent variables is actually being caused or modified in some way by the other independent variable.

The two-way ANOVA give us an overall picture of the difference between the variables and also shows whether there is an *interaction* between two independent variables (here, self-rated income group and sex of respondent). Knowing what the term 'interaction' means will help us interpret the results of ANOVAs. Interaction is the expression of the linkage or association between two or more independent variables. This linkage or association is beyond what would be expected by chance. If one does have a statistical interaction, this means that one cannot just add together the effects of each independent variable upon a dependent variable; the effect of each independent variable varies depending on the other independent variable.

Or, to put it more simply, it may be, for example, that Males in the low-income group may hold a significantly different view about the Local area than the rest of the rest of the sample, with this difference not just being a simple addition of the effect of being Male and the effect of being in the low-income group.

A two-way ANOVA for SPSS

In this case we will use an example from the **Health** dataset. We will examine the interaction of two independent variables – (1)**rsex** (respondent's sex) and (2)**privmed** (whether the respondent has private health insurance or not) – on a dependent variable, **nhsscale** (dissatisfaction with the National Health Service (higher scores mean that respondents are more dissatisfied with the NHS)).

Pull down the <u>**A**</u>**nalyze** menu and click on **General Linear Model** and then on **<u>U</u>nivariate**. A window like that in Figure 6.7 will appear.

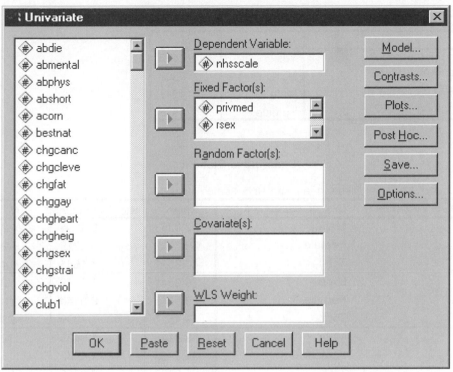

Figure 6.7 Univariate window

Transfer the variables to the boxes in the usual way, by clicking on the variables in the variable menu list and moving them into the boxes using the > sign. So, in this case we place the variable **nhsscale** in the **Dependent Variable** box. This time, however, we have two independent variables, **rsex** and **privmed**. Transfer these into the **Fixed Factor[s]:** box.

We again want means and other descriptive statistics. To obtain them, click on the **Options** ... button, and tick the **Descriptives** box in the subwindow. Press **Continue** to return to the main box. Then press **OK** (bottom left-hand corner of this box) to run the procedure. You should get an output that looks like Figure 6.8.

The output from the two-way ANOVA provides us with the means and standard deviation for each group (**Descriptive Statistics** box) and the *F*-values and their associated significance levels for the main effects and the two-way interaction (**Tests of Between-Subjects Effects** box). In the **Descriptive Statistics** box we are able to determine how mean scores in level of satisfaction with the NHS vary between the categories of each group *and* between each combination of categories for both groups. For example, females who have private health insurance have a mean of 39.73 (standard deviation = 7.2).

The *F*-values given in the **Tests of Between-Subjects Effects** box shows that the contribution of sex (**rsex**) to the ANOVA is significant (F = 7.70, Sig = .006) and the contribution of whether the respondents has private medical insurance (**privmed**) to the ANOVA is significant (F = 14.15, Sig = .000). Males generally have a higher mean dissatisfaction score (39.87) than females (39.56), and those with private health insurance have a higher mean score (40.86) than those without private health insurance (39.45).

In addition to the main effects of both variables, there is a significant interaction. The interaction between the two independent variables **rsex** * **privmed** on satisfaction with the National

Figure 6.8 Univariate Analysis of Variance

Between-Subjects Factors

		Value Label	N
R has private health insurance? Q459	1	Yes	483
	2	No	2309
Sex of respondent by observation Q32	1	Male	1217
	2	Female	1575

Descriptive Statistics

Dependent Variable: Dissatisfied with NHS scale

R has private health	Sex of respondent by	Mean	Std. Deviation	N
Yes	Male	42.0253	6.9104	237
	Female	39.7317	7.2219	246
	Total	40.8571	7.1561	483
No	Male	39.3541	7.3539	980
	Female	39.5245	8.0146	1329
	Total	39.4521	7.7399	2309
Total	Male	39.8743	7.3435	1217
	Female	39.5568	7.8943	1575
	Total	39.6952	7.6593	2792

Tests of Between-Subjects Effects

Dependent Variable: Dissatisfied with NHS scale

Source	Type III Sum of Squares	df	Mean Square	F	Sig.
Corrected Model	1439.886[a]	3	479.962	8.245	.000
Intercept	2565676.077	1	2565676.077	44074.511	.000
PRIVMED	823.848	1	823.848	14.152	.000
RSEX	448.245	1	448.245	7.700	.006
PRIVMED * RSEX	603.662	1	603.662	10.370	.001
Error	162295.730	2788	58.212		
Total	4563115.000	2792			
Corrected Total	163735.616	2791			

a. R Squared = .009 (Adjusted R Squared = .008)

Health Service (**nhsscale**) is significant (F = 10.37, Sig = .001). By examining the means carefully we can begin to interpret the source of the significant interaction. As we might expect, males who own private health insurance score higher on dissatisfaction with the National Health Service than all the other combination of categories but, surprisingly, it is *males* who do not have private health insurance (with a mean of 39.35) rather than females who do not have private health insurance (with a mean of 39.52) who are the least dissatisfied with the NHS. That is, there is an *interaction* – the effect of the two independent variables are linked in some way once the effects of gender and having private health insurance are considered in tandem.

As well as identifying the interaction by carefully inspecting the means for all the combinations of the groups, one can also take advantage of a graphical display provided by SPSS. SPSS can plot the means of the dependent variable for each combination of categories of two independent variables in a graphical representation of an interaction. To do this, run the two-way ANOVA again as before, but before clicking **OK**, click on **Plots** ... The **Univariate: Profile Plots** subwindow as in Figure 6.9 will come up. Transfer **rsex** into the **Horizontal Axis** box, and **privmed** into the **Separate Lines** box (if one of the variables has more categories than the other, put the one with the most categories into the **Separate Lines** box). Then press the **Add** button and **Continue** to return to the main **Univariate** window.

Figure 6.9   Univariate: Profile Plots

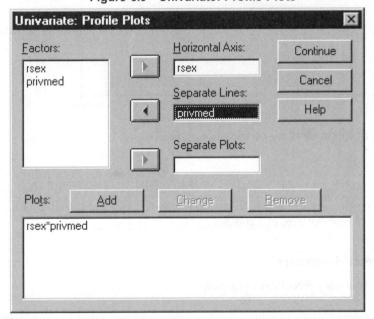

When you rerun the analysis, Figure 6.10 should result.

In this graph, the Male and Female categories are plotted on the horizontal X axis. The vertical Y axis is the mean value of the dependent variable (Dissatisfaction with the NHS). The lower line connects the mean values for Males and Females who do not have private health insurance. The means for Males and Female who *do* have private health insurance are plotted on the higher line (these lines will be in colour on your computer screen).

The differences between the groups and the form of the statistical interaction can be clearly seen. For three of the combinations of categories, Males without private health insurance and Females both with and without private health insurance, the means are very similar, around 39.5. However, for males who have private health insurance, the plot clearly shows that their mean level of dissatisfaction is higher. So, the source of the significant statistical interaction is that Males who own private health insurance exhibit a dramatically higher level of dissatisfaction with the NHS than do others.

So in our final interpretation on the results, we would note that sex and ownership of medical health insurance, when considered together, are each having an independent significant effect on individual perceptions of the NHS. Furthermore, while using sex of respondents and

Figure 6.10 Profile Plots

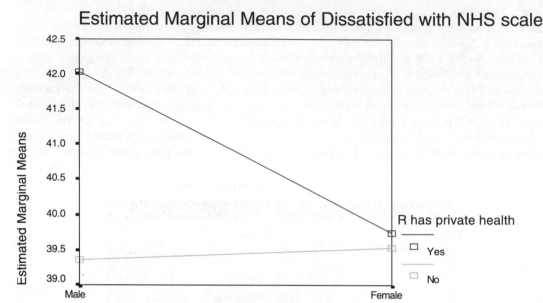

ownership of health insurance separately reveals differences in dissatisfaction with the NHS, a more complete analysis that takes account of statistical interaction shows that males who own private health service are the most dissatisfied with the NHS and that this dissatisfaction is more than just a combinations of variables.

Two-way ANOVA exercises

Now try some two-way ANOVAS yourself:

- Is there a significant interaction between Sex (**rsex**) and Self-rated income (**srinc**) concerning how happy the respondent is with the local area (**locarea**)? Remember to produce means and try using a plot to help you intepret your findings if necessary.
- Choose two categorical variables and one interval/ratio variable, and perform a two-way ANOVA. Remember to produce means and try using a plot to help you intepret your findings if necessary.

7 Correlation and Regression

Before considering the correlation and regression statistics, we will look at some of the 'logic' behind what is generally known as 'general linear modelling'. The basic idea behind general linear modelling, which includes both correlation and regression, is that you can depict the relationship between two quantitative variables (whose codes are numbers representing true numeric values; interval or ratio variables) by *'drawing' straight lines*.

Scattergrams

Figure 7.1a is an example of a positive relationship between two variables. Here SPSS has plotted the relationship between two variables:

(1) **revision**: How much revision an individual did for an exam (scored from 0 to 30 hours)

by

(2) **score**: Exam Score (marked out of 30).

on to a chart called a *scattergram*.

These two variables are not identical, but you would expect a strong *positive relationship* between them. When you have a 'positive relationship', the *low* values on one variable tend to go with *low* values on the other variable and *high* values on one variable tend to go with *high* values on the other. Here, we would expect that people doing only a small amount of revision for an exam should tend to score low on the exam, and people doing a lot of revision should tend to score high. Therefore a positive relationship on a scattergram plot of points will look like that in Figure 7.1a, the plotted points moving from the lower left-hand corner upwards to the upper right-hand corner of the chart.

With a *negative relationship* you would find the opposite. Below, SPSS has plotted the negative relationship between two variables:

(1) **out**: How many hours individuals spent socialising the week before the exam (scored from 0 to 30 hours)

by

(2) **score**: Exam Score (marked out of 30)

on to a scattergram.

When you have a 'negative relationship', the *low* values on one variable tend to go with *high* values on the other variable and *high* values on one variable tend to go with *low* values on the other. Here, people socialising a lot in the week before an exam should tend to score low on the exam, and people not going out (and presumably doing a lot of revision) before an exam

155

Figure 7.1a A positive relationship between two variables

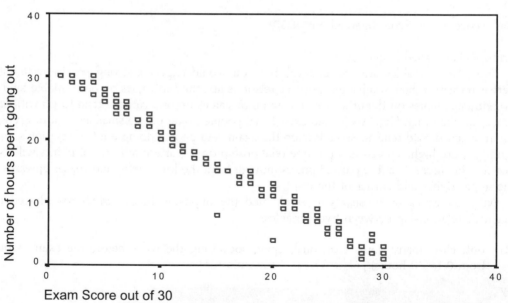

Exam Score out of 30

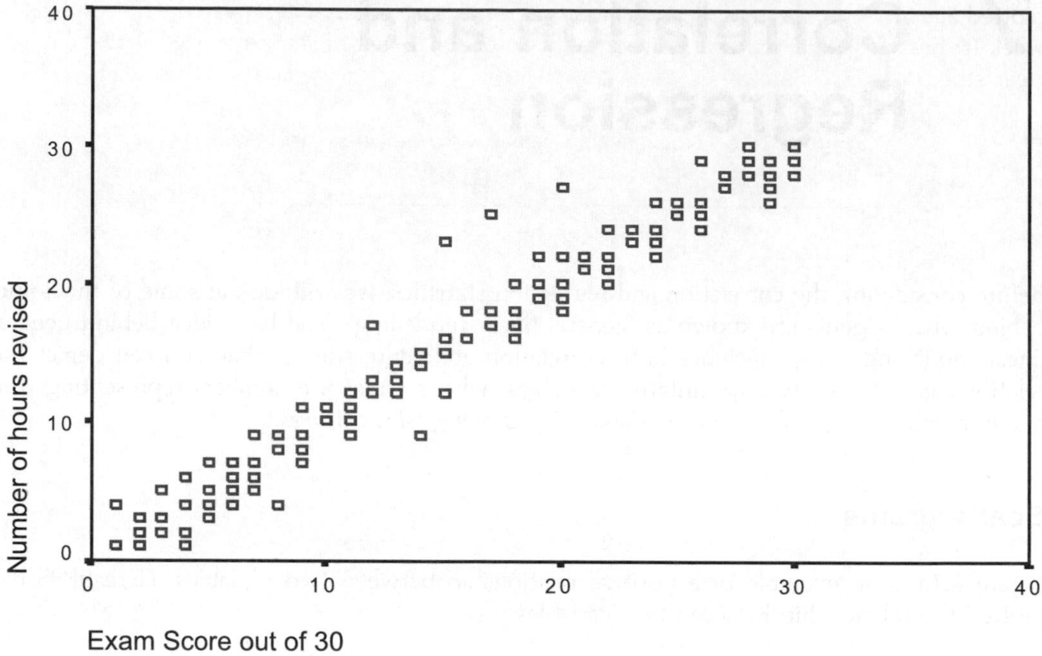

Figure 7.1b A negative relationship between two variables

Exam Score out of 30

tend to score high on the exam. Therefore a negative relationship on a scattergram plot of points will look like that in Figure 7.1b, the plotted points moving from the upper left-hand corner downwards to the lower right-hand corner of the chart.

However, with most data the relationships are not this clear, and it is quite possible that two variables will not be strongly related in either a positive or a negative sense. We can see an example of a scattergram of two variables that are not related in Figure 7.1c. Here we have plotted age scores (**rage**) against the number of hours that a respondent watches TV during the week (**tvhrswk**). Note that the scattergram is more or less a *random scatter of points*, with no clear straight lines going either up or down.

Figure 7.1c   No significant relationship between two variables

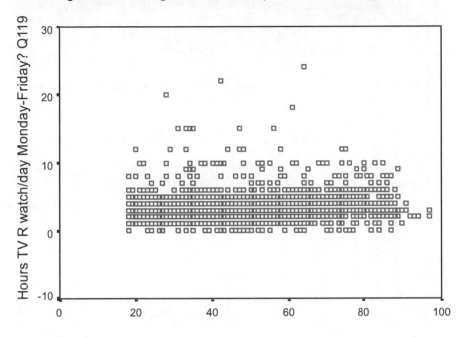

Producing scattergrams with SPSS

Now, let us produce that last Scattergram with SPSS. Respondent's age (**rage**) and the number of hours spend watching TV a week (**tvhrswk**) are the interval/ratio variables that will be used for this example of a scattergram. Bring down the **Graphs** menu and click on **Scatter**. The window shown in Figure 7.2a will come up.

Click on the **Simple** scatterplot and click the **Define** button; a **Simple Scatterplot** window like Figure 7.2b will appear. Then use the arrows to select the **tvhrswk** variable for the **Y Axis** and **rage** for the **X Axis**. (The 'Y axis' is the *vertical* axis on a scattergram and the 'X axis' is the *horizontal* axis on a scattergram. As a general convention, if one variable can be thought of as

Figure 7.2a   Scatterplot Define window

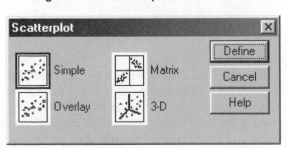

preceding the other in time or as being the cause of the other, the usual practice is to place the *preceding/causal* variable on the X axis and the *following/caused* variable on the Y axis.)

Figure 7.2b   Simple Scatterplot window

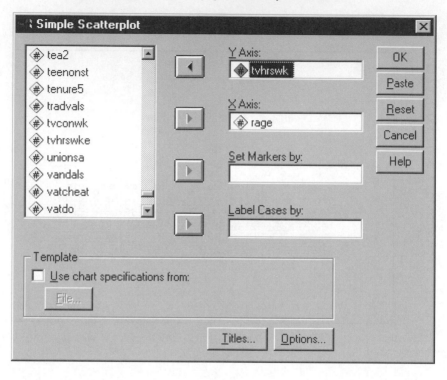

Run the procedure by clicking on **OK**. A scattergram like the one we have already seen in Figure 7.1c will be the result.

Points about scattergrams

A scattergram can be thought of as a exploratory data analysis-type technique since it provides a *visual depiction* of the relationship between two quantitative variables. Note that the scattergram alone is not a confirmatory statistical procedure. The scattergram allows you to check visually the validity of a general linear confirmatory procedure that you are using (such as correlation or regression). There are instances where a quick inspection of the scattergram can alert you to problems with the data that could invalidate the use of a statistical procedure based upon linear assumptions. Two problems are worth mentioning specifically:

Outliers

Correlation and regression statistics can be inordinately affected by the presence of a few extremely *low* or *high values* in the data. That is, the presence of cases with outliers can lead to a misleading or inaccurate result. For example, in our earlier description of a strong positive relationship between revision spent and exam score, it might be that one individual could have spent hours and hours revising, but may have felt ill on the day and received a very low mark. This score then might be viewed as an outlier. One way of spotting these extreme 'outliers' is to look at a scattergram: one or two points located out on their own way away from the rest indicate outliers. An analyst may then decide to exclude this small number of outlier cases from the analysis. (Occasionally, outliers may simply be due to coding errors. Another common cause of outliers is forgetting to declare a missing value code. For instance, respondents given a missing value code of '999' for their age would appear as a confusing group of extremely elderly Methuselahs if the analyst forgot to put down '999' as a missing value for age. Inspecting the scattergram can alert the analyst to outliers of these types, which can then be fixed or removed.)

Curvilinear trends

General linear statistics initially assume that relationships between variables can be depicted by *straight lines*. It is possible, however, to have a strong linear relationship where the line is not straight. Sometimes these curvilinear relationships become apparent when one inspects the scattergram. Figure 7.3, a graph of 'Age of woman' by 'Likelihood of having a child in the next year', shows an example of a curvilinear relationship – the odds of a young teenage girl having a child are quite low, this rises steeply to a peak for women in their mid-late twenties and then gradually tails off through the thirties into the forties. The value of a simple correlation or regression coefficient for the data depicted in this graph (which assumes a straight-line relationship) would be quite low – hence, underestimating what is in fact a very strong, but curvilinear, relationship.

Figure 7.3   Example of a strong curvilinear relationship

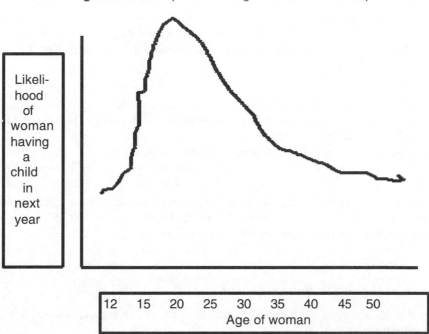

Scattergram exercise

Select some pairs of variables from one of the datasets and have SPSS produce scattergrams of the relationships between them. Remember to choose quantitative variables where the codings are *genuine numbers* in order to produce meaningful scattergrams.

Hints:
- Choose pairs of variables where you think the likely relationships will be either *strongly positive* or *strongly negative*.
- The scattergrams will look better and be more informative if you select quantitative variables where there are a *large number of numeric codes* for both variables in a pair rather than just a few codes.

Pearson's product-moment correlation coefficient (*r*)

The usefulness of the scattergram for examining the relationship between two quantitative variables, however, is rather limited. You may have noted while doing your own scattergrams that, though the apparent presence of a pattern in the scattergram plot gave a feeling of the direction of the relationship between the two variables, you are unable to determine whether there actually is a genuine relationship or not.

The aim of the correlation coefficient is to determine:

(1)   whether there is a *real relationship* between two interval/ratio variables
(2)   the *direction* of the relationship, and
(3)   the *strength* of the relationship.

Pearson's product-moment correlation coefficient is a parametric test. We use hypothesis testing criteria and confidence levels in order to determine whether a significant correlation occurs between two variables, and the direction of this correlation (positive or negative).

The correlation coefficient can take values ranging from +1.00 through 0.00 to −1.00.

- A correlation of +1.00 would be a *'perfect' positive relationship*
- A correlation of 0.00 would indicate *no relationship* (no single straight line can sum up the almost random distribution of points)
- A correlation of −1.00 would be a *'perfect' negative relationship*.

Since the correlation coefficient digests all of the information contained in a scatterplot into a single number, it is a statistic that is very efficient at describing the data. (Statistics that are 'efficient' in this manner are sometimes called *powerful* statistics.)

Assumptions of the correlation coefficient

The data used in correlations (and regressions and *all* versions of the general linear model) must meet some assumptions.

- The data should be *interval/ratio* data. (But correlation is *robust*. 'Robust' means that the assumption does not have to be strictly met for the statistic still to perform reasonably well; so this condition can be 'bent' to some degree; for example, by correlating variables that are ordinal variables.)

- *Homoscedasticity* (that is, if the intersection points between variables are plotted around the correlation 'line', they will be 'normally' distributed around the line – some will be above the line, some will be below it and more points will be close to the 'line' than far away).
- The relationship between the variables in question can be adequately portrayed by *straight lines*.

Correlating with SPSS

Pull down the **Analyze** menu, choose **Correlate** and then **Bivariate** .... A window as shown in Figure 7.4 will come up. We are going to examine people's fear of crime in this example. Within the area of the fear of crime, sociological findings have demonstrated that the more TV people watch the more they tend to perceive crime around them. The reason given for this is that TV is usually full of crime stories: through the news, documentaries and detective dramas. To examine this idea using the present data, we are going to correlate three variables from the dataset.

Figure 7.4 Bivariate Correlations window

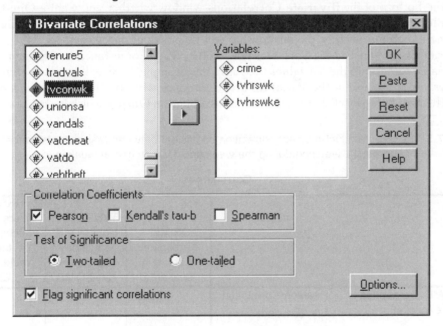

1. **crime** – an interval scale variable, designed to measure individual's perception of crime of their area compared to elsewhere; higher scores on this variable indicate a perception of *more* crime in the respondent's area compared to elsewhere
2. **tvhrswk** – the amount of television (in hours) watched during Monday to Friday
3. **tvhrswke** – the amount of television (in hours) watched during the weekend.

Use the right-hand arrow to bring the three variables into the central **Variables** box. Don't press **OK** yet. You need to adapt the correlation window to suit your needs. Tick the box next to the type of **Correlation Coefficient** you want to obtain. Here click on the **Pearson** box.

Also, you need to decide here whether to carry out a 'two-tailed' or 'one-tailed' test of significance. There are two types of 'tailed' test (the rather peculiar use of the word 'tailed' refers to either one or both ends, or 'tails', of a normal distribution of possible correlations).

- With a *two-tailed test*, SPSS assumes that you do not have any idea before you begin whether the correlation will be positive or negative (2 possibilities, hence 'two-tailed').
- With a *one-tailed test*, SPSS assumes that you anticipate beforehand whether the correlation is going to be a positive or negative, what you are testing, then, is not whether the correlation will be positive or negative, but whether the correlation will be statistically significant or not (only one possible 'direction' to the correlation, hence 'one-tailed'). Because you 'have gone further out on a limb' (when you predicted beforehand the direction of the correlation) the size of the correlation coefficient needed to reach statistical significance for a one-tailed test is not as large (or, to put it another way, the criteria for a one-tailed test to be significant is more lenient).

To select a one-tailed or a two-tailed test of significance, specify in the **Test of Significance** box at the bottom of the **Bivariate Correlations** window whether you want a **One-tailed** or **Two-tailed** test of significance. This time we will use a two-tailed test − that is, we are making no prediction about whether the relationship will be positive or negative.

You can also manipulate the **Variables** box in other ways. For instance, by pasting more than two variable names into the **Variables** box, as in this example, SPSS will correlate each variable with *every other* variable in the **Variables** box to produce what is called a *correlation matrix*.

Run the correlation by clicking on **OK**. You will obtain an **Output** which looks like Figure 7.5.

Figure 7.5 Pearson product-moment correlation coefficient between respondents' perception of crime, TV watched during the week and TV watched at weekends

Correlations

		CRIME Perception of crime in local area	TVHRSWK Hours TV R watch/day Monday-Friday? Q119	TVHRSWKE Hours TV R watch/day at the weekend?Q 120
CRIME Perception of crime in local area	Pearson Correlation	1.000	.068**	.084**
	Sig. (2-tailed)	.	.004	.000
	N	2811	1842	1842
TVHRSWK Hours TV R watch/day Monday-Friday? Q119	Pearson Correlation	.068**	1.000	.715**
	Sig. (2-tailed)	.004	.	.000
	N	1842	2065	2065
TVHRSWKE Hours TV R watch/day at the weekend?Q120	Pearson Correlation	.084**	.715**	1.000
	Sig. (2-tailed)	.000	.000	.
	N	1842	2065	2065

** Correlation is significant at the 0.01 level (2-tailed).

In Figure 7.5, each 'box' contains:

- The correlation coefficient: **Pearson Correlation**
- The statistical significance, Sig (2-tailed) = **.xxx**
- The number of cases: **N**
- ' **.** ' is printed if a coefficient cannot be computed.

Interpretation of the correlation coefficient (r)

You will see nine boxes with numbers in them in Figure 7.5. A lot of this information is redundant, as the three boxes on the diagonal running from the top left to the bottom right are only reporting the relationship between each variable and itself (so the correlation in all of those boxes is 1.000 and N is the number of valid cases for the variable). We are really interested in the boxes off the diagonal that report the correlations between the different variables. Remember that we use each of the Pearson correlations to inform us of three things: (1) the direction of the correlation; (2) whether the relationship is significant); and (3) the strength of the relationship. For instance, all the boxes above the diagonal in the upper right-hand part of the table, report the following.

(1) For the first box in the 'Perception of crime in local area' row, where the variable is correlated with 'Hours TV R watch/day Monday-Friday', the Pearson Correlation (r) is .068, the Sig (2-tailed) is .004 and N = 1842. The correlation is positive and a significance level of .004 means that the probability of the correlation not being statistically significant is below the 0.01 confidence level.

(2) In the next column, using the same row, 'Perception of crime in area' with 'Hours TV R watch/day at the weekend', the Pearson Correlation (r) is .084, the Sig (2-tailed) is .000 and N = 1842.

(3) Using the second row for 'Hours TV R watch/day Monday-Friday' with the final column 'Hours TV R watch/day at the weekend', the Pearson Correlation (r) is .715, the Sig (2-tailed) is .000 and N = 2065.

(**Note** that the boxes in the *lower left-hand* corner of the table mirror those on the *upper right-hand* corner.)

Interpreting results

(1) **crime** ('Perception of crime in area') correlated with **tvhrswk** ('Hours TV R watch/day Monday-Friday') − The correlation is .068, $p < 0.01$. Therefore, we conclude that there is a significant relationship between the two variables. What is important in interpreting this relationship is to remember what higher scores on each of the variables mean. That is, the higher respondent's scores are on **crime**, the *more* crime they perceive, and the higher respondent's scores are on **tvhrswk**, the more TV they watch. People who watch a lot of television during the week tend to perceive that there is more crime in their area. This finding is consistent with what we expected to discover.

(2) **crime** ('Perception of crime in area') correlated with **twhrswke** ('Hours TV R watch/day at the weekend') − We find a similar relationship when examining the relationship between perception of crime and the amount of television watched by respondents during the week. There is a highly significant ($p < 0.001$) positive correlation of .084 so we

conclude that there is a positive relationship between perception of crime and the amount of TV that respondents watched at the weekend. What is important in interpreting this relationship is to remember what higher scores on each of the variables mean. That is, the higher respondent's scores are on **crime**, the *more* crime they perceive, and the higher respondent's scores are on **tvhrswke**, the more TV they watch. Hence, since there is a significant *positive* relationship between the two variables, people who watch more TV at the weekend tend to perceive there being *more* crime in their area (a positive relationship). This finding is consistent with what we expected to discover.

(3)   **tvhrswke** correlated with **tvhrswk** − The correlation in the third relationship, between the amount of television that respondents watched at the weekend and during the week is +.715 ($p < 0.001$). People who watch a lot of TV during the week tend to watch a lot of TV at the weekend, and this is a very strong positive relationship.

It is important to take account the *strength* of relationships as well as their statistical significance. Remember correlations can range from highly negative (-1.00) to highly positive ($+1.00$). Within this range, we use the actual value of r to determine the strength of relationship. Therefore a correlation of 0.50 (regardless of whether it is either positive or negative) is stronger than one of only 0.10. Note here that the correlation between television viewing at the weekend and during the week is very high, close to 1.000 ($r = +.715$) while the other relationships, while *statistically* significant, are relatively low, .068 and .084 (close to 0). Clearly the relationship between the two 'amount of TV watched' variables is strong, while both their relationships to perception of crime is weaker. This often happens when samples are very large, as with this dataset.

   (While the conventions for deciding when a result is statistically significant are clear, with $p < 0.05$, $p < 0.01$ and $p < 0.001$ being the commonly accepted 'cut-off' points, there are no such agreed conventions for statistica*lly significant weak* relationships. Deciding when a statistically significant correlation is so weak that it should considered to have little substantive importance is a matter of judgement. One helpful indicator may be that the square of the correlation coefficient (r^2) provides an indication of the amount of variance in one variable that may be considered to be linked to the values of the other variable in a correlation pair. So, with our correlations above, the correlation of .715 means that over half (51.1 per cent) of the variance in weekday television viewing can be linked to the amount weekend television viewing and vice versa − quite a respectable amount. While, in contrast, the weak correlation of **crime** with weekday television viewing ($r = .068$) implies that only one-half of 1 per cent of the variance between **crime** and weekday viewing is linked and the amount of variance accounted for between **crime** and weekend viewing is not much better, just over one-half a per cent. Hence, these weak correlations are statistically significant results which are of doubtful substantive importance. It might help to note that a correlation must be above .30 in order to account for at least 10 per cent of variance.)

Exercises in producing correlations with SPSS

- Select a pair of quantitative variables from the dataset and correlate them using SPSS.
- Then, choose a list of variables and produce a correlation matrix.
- Try doing the correlation matrix with a one-tailed test and then a two-tailed test and note how the levels of significance change.

Hint:
Use the same variables that you used for the scattergrams and you will be able to compare the correlation coefficients with the plots of the variables that produced the coefficients.

A final point on the correlation coefficient

With Pearson's product-moment correlation, you have examined the *association* between variables. However, it is important to remember that you have not shown that one *causes* another. The example above suggested a significant relationship between the perception of crime and the amount of television viewing. It does not follow from the significant correlation results, however, that you can assert that one causes the other, rather we use terms such as 'this view is accompanied by that view'.

Sometimes you may have variables where you feel that you are predicting causation. For instance, in the last example, we began by noting that sociological literature had suggested reasons for a hypothetical causal link between television viewing and a heightened perception of crime. If you wish to examine such a causal relationship, you could use regression statistics.

Regression

The assumptions for regression are the same as for correlation.

---

(1) interval/ratio data (but, like correlation, regression is *robust* and can tolerate violations of its assumptions with ordinal variables).
(2) Homoscedasticity.
(3) The relationships between variables can be portrayed by straight lines.

What makes regression different from correlation is that regression assumes that the *independent* (X) variable is, at least in part, a *cause* or a *predictor* of the *dependent* (y) variable. For instance, we could have a hypothesis that more years of education will *cause* people to have higher monthly incomes. So, Years of education will be the independent/causal 'X' variable and Monthly income will be the dependent/caused 'y' variable.

Hence, regression is a version of the general linear model that allows us to test hypotheses in which *causality* is asserted. Regression assumes that an *independent* (x) variable is, at least in part, a cause of a *dependent* (y) variable.

Using SPSS to carry out a simple regression

For this example we will stick to the variables used in the correlation example (perception of crime and the amount of television watched). Here the argument is that the amount of television individuals watch affects their perception of crime in their local area (**crime**). For this example will use only one of the television variables, **tvhrswk**, amount of TV watched during the week. So, **crime** is the dependent variable and **tvhrswk** is the independent variable.

Pull down the **Analyze** menu and select **Regression** and then **Linear** .... A **Linear Regression** window like that in Figure 7.6 will come up.

Here, in order to have SPSS carry out a simple regression of the effect of television viewing upon the perception of crime, the variable **crime** has been placed in the **Dependent** box and the variable **tvhrswk** (hours of TV watched during the week) into the **Independent[s]:** box. When you click on **OK**, SPSS will carry out the regression and produce the output in Figure 7.7.

When reporting the regression it is good practice that you note and write the following statistics in any report. Though some may not seem relevant now it is common practice to provide information on all the following.

Figure 7.6 **Linear Regression** window

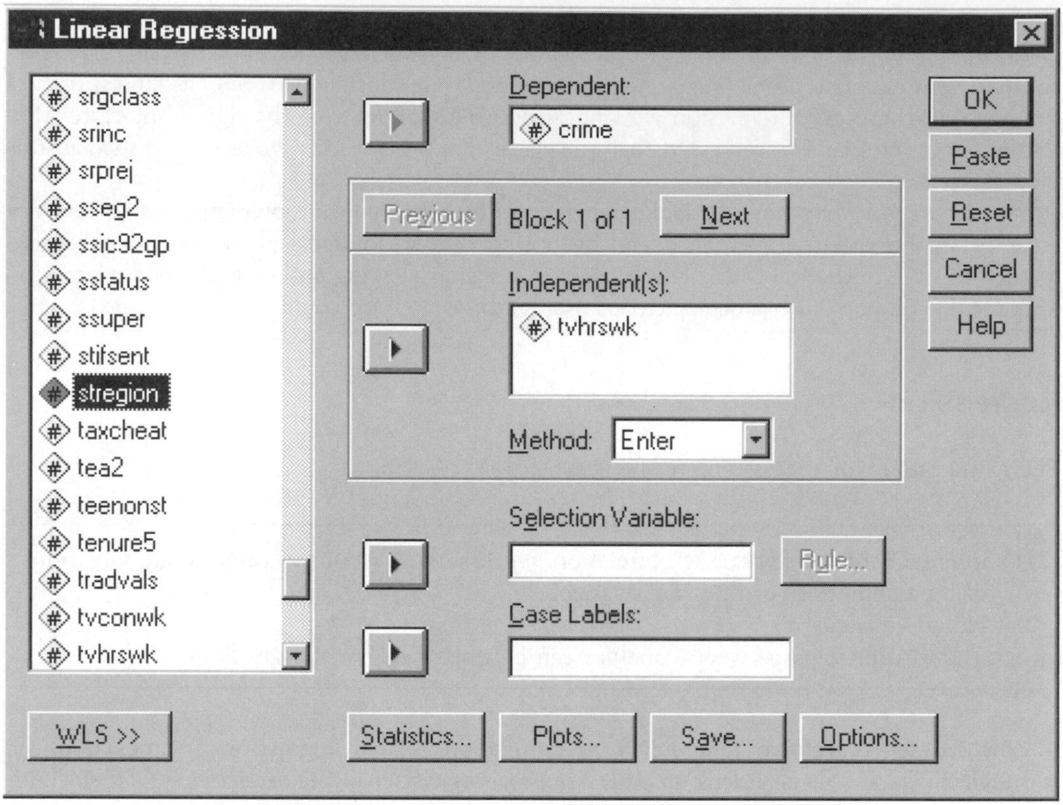

Figure 7.7 Regression results

Model Summary

Model	R	R Square	Adjusted R Square	Std. Error of the Estimate
1	.068[a]	.005	.004	3.5473

a. Predictors: (Constant), TVHRSWK Hours TV R watch/day Monday-Friday? Q119

ANOVA[b]

Model		Sum of Squares	df	Mean Square	F	Sig.
1	Regression	107.025	1	107.025	8.505	.004[a]
	Residual	23147.090	1840	12.583		
	Total	23254.115	1841			

a. Predictors: (Constant), TVHRSWK Hours TV R watch/day Monday-Friday? Q119

b. Dependent Variable: CRIME Perception of crime in local area

Figure 7.7 (*continued*)

Coefficients[a]

Model		Unstandardized Coefficients		Standardized Coefficients	t	Sig.
		B	Std. Error	Beta		
1	(Constant)	5.686	.145		39.284	.000
	TVHRSWK Hours TV R watch/day Monday-Friday? Q119	.107	.037	.068	2.916	.004

a. Dependent Variable: CRIME Perception of crime in local area

---

1. Look in the **Model Summary** box. R(r) (Pearson product-moment correlation): here .068 in the model summary box.
2. Look in the **Model Summary** box. R square (r^2): the percentage variance that the two variables share (out of possible 100 per cent if the same variable was correlated with itself) is calculated by squaring the r figure. In this example, this figure, .005, can be found in the **Model Summary** box representing 0.5 per cent of shared variance.
3. Look in the **Model Summary** box. Adjusted R square: The r^2 figure may not be reliable, and instead the Adjusted r^2 figure is used. Here it is .004, in the **Model Summary** box.
3. Look in the **ANOVA**[b] box. ANOVA is used to establish whether our findings might have arisen from a sampling error. Here we establish whether our regression line is different from zero. If it is, then we can claim that our findings have not arisen simply from a sampling error. In the present table (ANOVA) we look at the F and Sig columns. Here the F value = 8.505 and the confidence value = .004 (very significant). The result is not due to sampling error.
5. Look in the **Coefficients** box. B written as b is the slope of the regression line. For the present example it is .107.
6. Also in the coefficients box is a *t*-value (2.916) and its confidence value (Sig. = .004). This shows you the statistical significance of the predictor value.

The standard regression formula is: $y = a + bx$.

This can be translated into English as: *The value of the dependent variable (y) is predicted to be a constant (a) plus a coefficient (b) times the independent variable (x)*.

We can take the values from the table in Figure 7.7 and insert their values in the standard regression formula to produce: $y = 5.686 + .107x$

In terms of interpreting Figure 7.7, we first note the statistic found for the slope, B = .107. This means that every rise of one unit for the independent variable **tvhrswk** predicts a rise on the dependent variable **crime** of 0.107 unit. (The Constant of 5.686 is the predicted score on **crime** if a respondent watches no television (if **tvhrswk** = 0).) The Analysis of Variance shows that the regression result is significantly different from zero (F = 8.505, $p < 0.01$). Hence, our result did not occur by chance and, consistent with our research hypothesis, the amount of TV watched significantly raises the respondents' perceived view of crime in their area.

Multiple regression

Regression is a *multivariate* statistical technique. The regression equation can be extended to take in more than one independent causal 'X' variable.

Each independent variable, 'X', will explain some of the variance in the dependent variable, 'y'. To put it another way, multiple regression is testing the extent to which each independent 'X' variable will play a part in predicting what the most likely value of the dependent variable 'y' will be.

This is a great advantage because true models of social relationships can be tested by quantitative statistical estimation. However, there are two cautions:

1. The result produced by a multivariate computer programme, such as a multiple regression result, will be *reliable* (since SPSS goes through a set mathematical routine in order to produce its results).
2. *But* it may not necessarily be *valid*. A change in the mathematical procedure *or* the independent, causal variables in the model could produce a different, equally reliable result. And, more significantly, like any statistical calculation programme, SPSS cannot provide any information on the conceptual validity of the variables being included in a model. A poorly specified or just stupidly conceived model may produce a mathematically elegant solution.

Figure 7.8 attempts to depict visually the amount of variance in a single dependent variable 'y' that three independent 'X' variables could explain. Each 'x' explains a unique part of the variance in 'y' (the part of each circle that does not overlap with any other circle). The problem, however, is that, as indicated by the overlap of the circles, some of the explained variance in 'y' can be attributed to a combination of two or even all three of the 'x' variables.

Figure 7.8   How variables may overlap

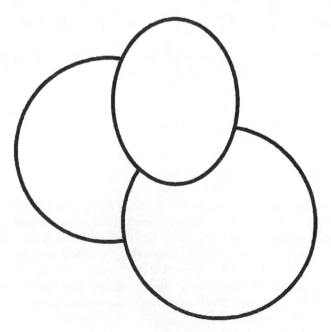

SPSS will apportion this 'shared' variance between the three independent 'x' variables; *but* the proportion of the variance that it 'gives' to each is no more than an 'educated guess' of how it should be divided up. A slight change in the mathematical (iterative) routine that apportions the shared variance can result in a radically different result if a large amount of the total variance is shared.

Aside from trying to produce the best 'educated guess' (the best mathematical routine) and exercising caution when interpreting results, there really is no perfect solution to this problem. Those that claim there is, are, to put it diplomatically, 'being economical with the truth'!

In addition, independent, causal variables can *interact* so that the effect of two or more independent variables working *in concert* upon the dependent variable may be different from the simple additive effect of each independent variable on its own. (For a discussion of *interaction effects* see 'Two-way analysis of variance' in Module 6.)

An SPSS example of multiple regression

These ideas can be applied to our example using respondents' television viewing habits (**tvhrswk**) and their perception of crime (**crime**). So far we have speculated that television influences respondents' perceptions of crime in their area compared to the rest of Britain. However there may be other variables that also influence their perception. For example, age may be a causal factor: older respondents may perceive crime in their area to have become worse over the years. Similarly, the number of people who live in a respondent's household might affect his or her view of crime levels in their neighbourhood (perhaps because their chances of hearing more stories about local crime rise as a consequence of seeing more people everyday). Furthermore, a respondent's age and the number of people in their household may be related with each other: for instance, elderly people often live alone or only with their spouse.

A multiple regression allows you work through these speculations. The multiple regressions allow you to establish which of the variables are most important by stating which of the variables explain variance in the dependent variable that is *unique* (that is, variance that is not shared with one of the other independent variables). In summary, using multiple regression, you could establish which of the independent factors (TV watching, age, or the number of people living in the household) might be important influences upon the respondents' perceptions of crime.

Producing a multiple regression with SPSS is basically the same as producing a simple regression. Pull down the **Analyze** menu and select **Regression** and then **Linear** .... A **Linear Regression** window like that in Figure 7.9 will come up.

As before, the variable **crime** is the **Dependent** 'y' variable. Here, however, instead of testing to establish the effect of a single independent variable, a number of other independent variables have been included in the regression:

- **tvhrswk**: TV watched during the week
- **rage**, respondent's age
- **househld**: number of people in respondent's household.

To carry out this multiple regression, you put all three of the variables into the Independent[s]: box. Click on **OK** and SPSS will carry out the multiple regression. The result can be seen in Figure 7.10.

All the columns of statistics are the same as with the simple linear regression. The Analysis of Variance (**ANOVA**[b] box) shows that the regression statistic was significantly different from zero ($F = 23.817$, $p < 0.001$). This shows us that we can be confident that our results did not

Figure 7.9 Linear Regression window

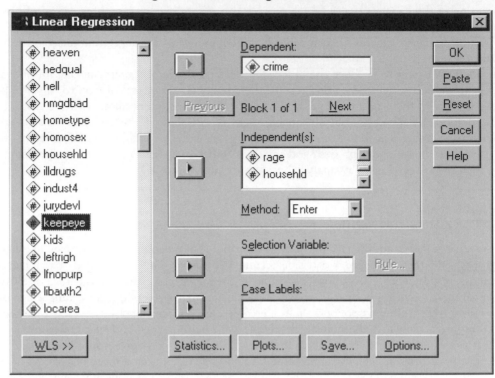

occur by chance. Within the **Coefficients** box we are able to determine the relative importance (by using the statistics in the Sig. column) of each of the independent variables in accounting for variance in respondents' perception of crime levels in their area. We discover the following three things regarding our independent variables.

(1) Look in the **Coefficients** box. Consistent with our earlier findings, we find that the respondents' TV watching explains a significant amount of variance in respondents' view of crime levels in their area (Sig. = .000, $p < 0.001$). The direction of the effect is as before, more television viewing predicts the respondents will perceive there is more crime in their area.

(2) Look in the **Coefficients** box. We also find that the age of respondents also explains significance variance in respondents' view of crime levels in their area as compared to the rest of Britain (Sig = .000, $p < 0.001$). Perhaps surprisingly, note that the coefficient for **rage** is negative. Hence, the *older* they are, the more respondents view their area as having *less* crime than other areas. It is noteworthy that this effect of age holds in this multiple regression where the amount of television has been taken into effect, and vice versa;

(3) Look in the **Coefficients** box. The number of people in the respondent's household does not explain any unique variance in the perception of crime levels in the local area *once the effects of the other two variables of television viewing and age have been taken into account* (Sig. = .223, $p > 0.05$).

Figure 7.10   Multiple Regression results

Model Summary

Model	R	R Square	Adjusted R Square	Std. Error of the Estimate
1	.194[a]	.037	.036	3.4918

a. Predictors: (Constant), HOUSEHLD Number in household including R?   Q30, TVHRSWK Hours TV R watch/day Monday-Friday? Q119, RAGE Respondent's age in years   YY   Q33

ANOVA[b]

Model		Sum of Squares	df	Mean Square	F	Sig.
1	Regression	871.141	3	290.380	23.817	.000[a]
	Residual	22377.282	1835	12.192		
	Total	23248.423	1838			

a. Predictors: (Constant), HOUSEHLD Number in household including R?   Q30, TVHRSWK Hours TV R watch/day Monday-Friday? Q119, RAGE Respondent's age in years YY   Q33

b. Dependent Variable: CRIME Perception of crime in local area

Coefficients[a]

Model		Unstandardized Coefficients		Standardized Coefficients	t	Sig.
		B	Std. Error	Beta		
1	(Constant)	6.913	.377		18.323	.000
	TVHRSWK Hours TV R watch/day Monday-Friday? Q119	.144	.036	.091	3.940	.000
	RAGE Respondent's age in years YY Q33	-3.38E-02	.005	-.168	-6.622	.000
	HOUSEHLD Number in household including R? Q30	8.502E-02	.070	.031	1.219	.223

a. Dependent Variable: CRIME Perception of crime in local area

Therefore, in summary, both age (**rage**) and amount of television watched (**tvhrswk**) are independent variables that account for unique variance in the dependent variable **crime**, but the independent variable **househld** has no statistically significant effect.

Other considerations

Standardised coefficients

In multiple regression, the **Standardized Coefficients** (Beta) column in the output can become important. Remember that the literal interpretation of B is the amount of change in y caused by a change of one unit in X. If an 'x' variable has values that are much higher or lower than the dependent 'y' variable or the other independent 'x' variables, the values taken by 'B' for different independent variables in a multiple regression solution can be wildly different. This can make direct comparison between different independent variables quite difficult. (Our above example illustrates this, where the 'B' for **tvhrswk** (television watched during the week) is .144 but the 'beta' for **rage** (respondent's age) is $-3.38E-02$ (or $-.0338$). Even though both variables are significant, it is difficult to compare their B coefficients directly because their scales are so different.) Regression coefficients for the independent variables in a regression equation can be standardised so that each independent variable has a mean of zero and a standard deviation of one. The effect of this is to place the 'betas' for different variables onto basically the same scale and make comparison between the 'betas' for different variables much more direct and easier. 'Standardised' regression coefficients (normally) will range between $+1.00$ and -1.00 like correlation coefficients.

Note how the standardised 'betas' in our example are much more directly comparable than their unstandardised counterparts. The largest standardised 'beta' is $-.168$ for **rage**, the most statistically significant independent variable. This is followed by **tvhrswk** at .091, which is still statistically significant (though the effect upon **crime** is less strong); and finally by **househld**, the smallest at .031, which is not statistically significant.

Also, you should be aware of two options with the regression procedure that become relevant when you are doing multiple regression.

Method

The default method of carrying out a regression is to have SPSS enter all of the variables into the regression equation simultaneously. This default is called **Enter** and is the one used here.

There are other ways of introducing independent 'X' variables into a regression equation. The one you might want to consider is called **Stepwise**, where the 'X' variables that have a significant effect upon the dependent 'y' variable are put in one at a time (that is, 'step by step') until none is left. The result is a lengthy printout where you can see the effect that each variable has upon the overall result as it is added in. This is handy if you think there may be a lot of variance being shared between the independent 'X' variables and you want to see how the relative strengths of the effects of the independent 'X' variables change as each new independent variable is entered into the equation. The final result of this 'stepwise' procedure will be the inclusion of all independent variables in the regression equation that SPSS finds to have a statistically significant effect upon the dependent variable.

'Listwise' versus 'Pairwise' deletion of missing cases

In simple regression, if either variable has a missing value, the case in question is excluded from the analysis. The default for multiple regression, however, is 'listwise' deletion of cases: if *any* of the variables used in the multiple regression has a missing value, the case is deleted. Problems can arise if different cases all have only a small proportion of missing values *but* each case has its values being missing on *different* variables.

For example, let us say you have six variables in your multiple regression and each of these six variables has 10 per cent missing values. If it is the same 10 per cent of cases that have the 10 per cent missing values for all six variables, you lose only about 10 per cent of the cases from the analysis – no big problem. But, if *different* cases have missing values on *different* variables, you could find SPSS deleting up to 60 per cent of the cases from the analysis:

10 per cent + 10 per cent + 10 per cent + 10 per cent + 10 per cent + 10 per cent
= 60 per cent – a big problem!

One way around this is to use 'pairwise' deletion of cases: basically, SPSS computes a correlation matrix on the way to producing a multiple regression result. With 'pairwise' deletion, SPSS is told to use the correlations in the matrix with only those cases being excluded from calculating the correlations when one or the other variable in each individual correlation is missing. So, with 10 per cent missing values in each of six variables, the maximum loss of cases from any single correlation would be 20 per cent (10 per cent + 10 per cent).

You can obtain 'pairwise' deletion by clicking on the **Options** ... button in the **Linear Regression** window. A **Linear Regression: Options** window, like that in Figure 7.11 will come up. As has been done here, click the **Exclude cases pairwise** button in the **Missing Values** box, then on the **Continue** button to get back to the **Linear Regression** window.

Figure 7.11 Linear Regression: Options subwindow

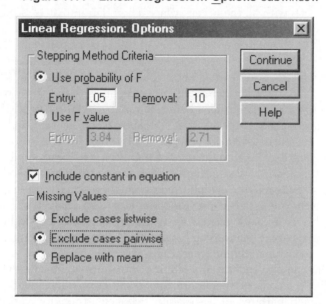

Regression exercises

Think of a causal hypothesis that can be tested using some of the quantitative variables in the dataset you have chosen. You need a dependent (y) variable and at least three independent (X) variables that could conceivably be a 'cause of' or have an effect upon the y variable:

- Do simple regressions of each independent 'X' variable in turn upon the dependent 'y' variable. Note whether or not each independent variable has a significant effect (the significance level) and the extent of the effect (the regression coefficient (*b*) and the 'constant' (*a*)).
- Then run a multiple regression upon the dependent variable of all the independent variables at the same time. Note the overall significance of this multiple regression and the extent of the effect of each independent variable when it must 'compete' with other independent variables in a multiple regression. Since all the independent variables are 'competing' with each other in the multiple regression, what probably will happen is that each independent 'X' variable in the multiple regression will show a smaller effect on the dependent 'y' variable than it did on its own in a simple regression. It is quite possible that some independent variables that were shown as having significant effects upon the dependent variable in the simple regressions may lose out to other independent variables in the multiple regression to the extent that they are no longer significant. If this happens, their previous significant effect can be considered to have been spurious.

8 Factor Analysis

Introduction

Factor Analysis is a 'data reduction' statistical technique that allows us to simplify the *correlational relationships* between a number of *continuous variables*. As demonstrated in Module 7, the correlation procedure can be used to generate a *correlation matrix* – the correlations of a large number of variables, each with all the others. Once a correlation matrix is produced, however, it can be difficult systematically to identify reliable patterns of correlation between the variables. Factor analytic techniques are a solution to this type of problem, allowing us to look at the *patterns that underlie the correlations* between a number of variables.

Why would you wish to do so? Imagine if you wanted to look at all of the patterns of association, or correlation, between ten quantitative variables (Variables 1 to 10). This would imply having to interpret 52 relationships between variables. (For example, Variable 1 can be correlated with Variables 2 through 10; and, Variable 2 can be separately associated with Variables 3 through 10, Variable 3 with Variables 4 through 10 and so on.) Identifying real patterns is complicated further because the relationship between, for example, Variables 1 and 2 may be affected by the separate relationships each of these variables has with Variable 3, with Variable 4 and so on. This leads to a complicated explanation of 52 relationships, similar to the shared variance problem discussed in previous modules. The analyst will find it difficult to explain which variable is actually related to which other variables, as he or she may be uncertain whether the apparent relationship between two variables is genuine, or simply a facet of both variables' relationships with another, third, variable.

Indeed, even writing an explanation of multiple correlations is difficult. What factor analysis does is provide reliable means of simplifying the relationships and identifying within them what *factors*, or common patterns of association between groups of variables, underlie the relationships.

A simple way of explaining the process of factor analysis is depicted in Figure 8.1.

Figure 8.1   Simple example of what Factor Analysis does

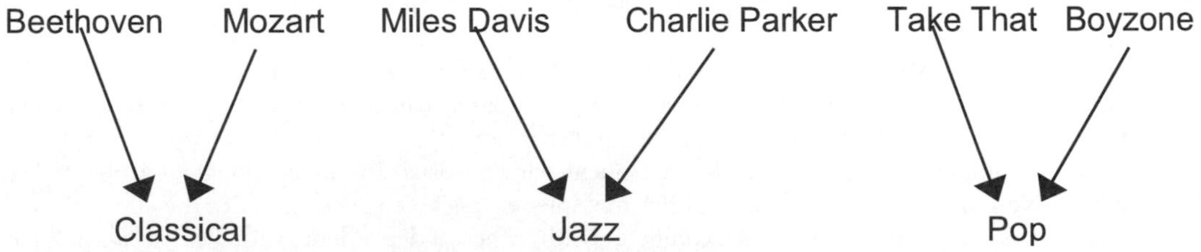

We use the main principle of factor analysis all the time. Imagine that the top line of Figure 8.1 represents all the musicians and music groups in the world. What we do is group certain types of music into categories. So, Beethoven, Mozart and others fall under a category of Classical Music, Miles Davis, Charlie Parker and others fall into a Jazz category and so on ... In the same way that themes such as Classical Music, Jazz, Pop, Rap, Dance, Indie and so on can be used to identify underlying groupings that categorise all musicians and music groups, factor analysis will work to establish *common features* underlying the relationships between the variables in a dataset.

Using factor analysis in SPSS

The main aim of this chapter is to present the main two features of factor analytic techniques.

1. **Extraction** – The process by which we determine the factors underlying a collection of variables
2. **Rotation** – A second step, used in order to simplify structure when the Extraction techniques have identified more than one factor underlying the relationships between a number of variables.

Extraction

Extraction techniques allow you to determine the factors underlying the relationship between a number of variables. There are many extraction procedures, but the most common one is called 'Principal Component Analysis'.

Let us use an example from the **Crime** dataset. There are seven questions in the **Crime** dataset in which the respondents are asked to express their view of how common certain types of nuisance are in their area. In the survey, these variables are all prefixed with the question 'How common?' and then a list of nuisances and problems follows.

(1) **noisyngb**: noisy neighbours and loud parties
(2) **graffiti**: Graffiti on walls/buildings
(3) **teenonst**: Teenagers hanging round the street
(4) **drunks**: Drunks and tramps on the street
(5) **rubbish**: Rubbish or litter lying around
(6) **hmgdbad**: Home and gardens in bad condition
(7) **vandals**: Vandalism and deliberate damage.

Figure 8.2 shows the Pearson product-moment correlations coefficients statistics for correlations between all seven variables.

You will notice that the correlations are very high. High correlations between a number of variables suggest that they may represent a single factor. Therefore, to test for this, we will perform a factor analysis on these variables.

Pull down the **Analyze** menu and then click on **Data Reduction** and then **Factor** ... You should obtain a screen that looks like Figure 8.3 (Factor Analysis is found under the general heading termed 'Data Reduction' because, by condensing the information ina large number of variables into a smaller number of factors, it can be considered to be *reducing* the complexity of the raw data). Transfer the variables **noisyngb**, **graffiti**, **teenonst**, **drunks**, **rubbish**, **hmgdbad** and **vandals** into the **Variables** box.

There are two types of criteria that are most commonly used to determine the number of factors to extract. The first is *Eigenvalues*. SPSS calculates the potential factors, and assigns each,

Figure 8.2   Correlation matrix between all the variables

Correlations

		Noisy neighbours/loud parties? Q134	Graffiti on walls/buildings? Q135	Teenagers hanging round street Q136	Drunks/tramps on the streets? Q137	Rubbish or litter lying about? Q138	Homes+gardens in bad condition? Q139	Vandalism+deliberate damage? Q140
Noisy neighbours/loud parties? Q134	Pearson Correlation	1.000	.398**	.395**	.351**	.318**	.366**	.365**
	Sig. (2-tailed)	.	.000	.000	.000	.000	.000	.000
	N	3142	3137	3133	3136	3139	3125	3136
Graffiti on walls/buildings? Q135	Pearson Correlation	.398**	1.000	.514**	.426**	.488**	.408**	.512**
	Sig. (2-tailed)	.000	.	.000	.000	.000	.000	.000
	N	3137	3139	3130	3132	3137	3123	3133
Teenagers hanging round street Q136	Pearson Correlation	.395**	.514**	1.000	.471**	.475**	.391**	.524**
	Sig. (2-tailed)	.000	.000	.	.000	.000	.000	.000
	N	3133	3130	3135	3130	3132	3121	3131
Drunks/tramps on the streets ? Q137	Pearson Correlation	.351**	.426**	.471**	1.000	.433**	.364**	.472**
	Sig. (2-tailed)	.000	.000	.000	.	.000	.000	.000
	N	3136	3132	3130	3137	3136	3122	3133
Rubbish or litter lying about? Q138	Pearson Correlation	.318**	.488**	.475**	.433**	1.000	.497**	.536**
	Sig. (2-tailed)	.000	.000	.000	.000	.	.000	.000
	N	3139	3137	3132	3136	3141	3126	3136
Homes+gardens in bad condition? Q139	Pearson Correlation	.366**	.408**	.391**	.364**	.497**	1.000	.521**
	Sig. (2-tailed)	.000	.000	.000	.000	.000	.	.000
	N	3125	3123	3121	3122	3126	3127	3124
Vandalism+deliberate damage? Q140	Pearson Correlation	.365**	.512**	.524**	.472**	.536**	.521**	1.000
	Sig. (2-tailed)	.000	.000	.000	.000	.000	.000	.
	N	3136	3133	3131	3133	3136	3124	3138

**. Correlation is significant at the 0.01 level (2-tailed).

Figure 8.3   Factor Analysis main window

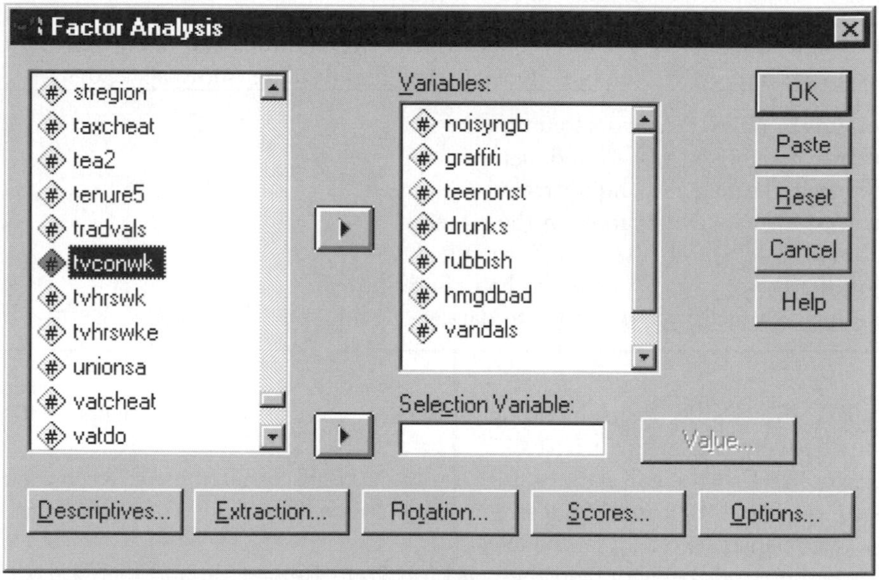

in descending order, an 'Eigenvalue'. Traditionally factors with Eigenvalues above 1 are seen as significant factors and SPSS will extract that number of factors. However, some statisticians prefer to use the Scree Test. What the Scree Test does is plot the Eigenvalues in order to provide a visual assessment that allows the analyst to see which factors should be accepted. We will use both in this example.

Figure 8.4 Factor Analysis: Extraction

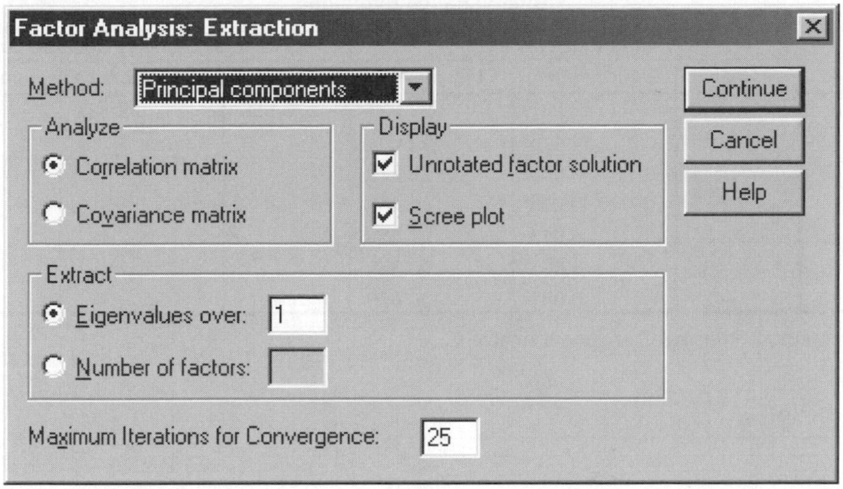

Click on **Extraction** in the main **Factor Analysis** window and you should obtain Figure 8.4.

Note that the default setting on SPSS is to extract all factors with Eigenvalues over 1. However, we also want to plot a Scree plot so tick the **Scree plot** box. Press on **Continue** in order to go back to the main window and then press **OK** to run the procedure. You should then get an **Output** like Figure 8.5.

Look in the **Total Variance Explained** box. This is where you obtain information on the number of factors to extract. Here, you will notice two sets of three columns ('Total', 'per cent of variance' and 'Cumulative per cent') under **Initial Eigenvalues** and under **Extraction sums of squared loading**. Those columns under **Initial Eigenvalues** show all values of Eigen and those under **Extraction sums of squared loading** show what SPSS has selected. In each case, the column **Total** is the Eigenvalue, the 'per cent of the variance' is the amount of variance (up

Figure 8.5 Factor Analysis output

Communalities

	Initial	Extraction
Noisy neighbours/loud parties? Q134	1.000	.374
Graffiti on walls/buildings? Q135	1.000	.557
Teenagers hanging round street Q136	1.000	.565
Drunks/tramps on the streets ? Q137	1.000	.482
Rubbish or litter lying about? Q138	1.000	.563
Homes+gardens in bad condition? Q139	1.000	.493
Vandalism+deliberate damage? Q140	1.000	.622

Extraction Method: Principal Component Analysis.

Figure 8.5   (*continued*)

Total Variance Explained

Component	Initial Eigenvalues			Extraction Sums of Squared Loadings		
	Total	% of Variance	Cumulative %	Total	% of Variance	Cumulative %
1	3.656	52.227	52.227	3.656	52.227	52.227
2	.729	10.416	62.643			
3	.671	9.585	72.229			
4	.575	8.215	80.443			
5	.484	6.913	87.356			
6	.462	6.603	93.959			
7	.423	6.041	100.000			

Extraction Method: Principal Component Analysis.

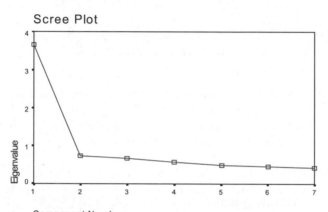

Scree Plot

Component Number

Analysis weighted by WTFACTOR

Component Matrix[a]

	Component
	1
Noisy neighbours/loud parties? Q134	.611
Graffiti on walls/buildings? Q135	.746
Teenagers hanging round street Q136	.752
Drunks/tramps on the streets ? Q137	.695
Rubbish or litter lying about? Q138	.750
Homes+gardens in bad condition? Q139	.702
Vandalism+deliberate damage? Q140	.789

Extraction Method: Principal Component Analysis.

a. 1 components extracted.

to a maximum of 100 per cent explanation of the relationship between the variables) each factor takes up and 'Cumulative per cent' is the amount of variance for each factor added together in ascending order. Here, we can see that only the first factor has an Eigenvalue over 1. Therefore SPSS is suggesting we extract one factor that accounts for 52.227 per cent of the variance of the relationship between variables.

The number of factors the method of using Eigenvalues chooses can be slightly inaccurate — sometimes selecting too many factors when the number of variables used is below 20. Therefore another way of determining factors through the use of the Scree plot. What the Scree plot does is plot the Eigenvalues in order to provide visual criteria which we use to determine the number of factors. The Scree plot is named after the debris, or scree, that collects at the bottom of a rocky slope on a mountain. As we can see, the Scree plot does resemble the side of a mountain. We determine the number of factors to retain by selecting those whose Eigenvalues occur before the plot straightens outs (or roughly straightens out). Here we choose only the first factor, as the plot starts to straighten out at point 2 on the axis. Another way is to imagine the plot as an 'arm' with a 'bend' in the elbow. You would select all points above the elbow.

As we must acknowledge from the above, using Scree plots to choose the best number of factors is hardly an exact science, however many suggest the Scree test is a more reliable way of determining factors. We suggest that you use both Eigenvalues and the Scree plot to come to a decision about the number of factors to retain.

Finally, look at the figures contained in the **Component Matrix** in Figure 8.5. This table contains the 'Factor Loadings' of each of the variables on the factor. *Loadings* are the strength of each variable in defining the factor. The reason we used the word 'defining' is that factor analysis does not tell you the conceptual meaning of the factor — you must decide that for yourself. That is, you look at what variables 'load' on a factor. Hopefully, these variables have some meanings or features in common which you can use as clues to the common conceptual feature of the factor. Based upon your assessment of what this common conceptual feature may be, the practice is for the analyst to give that factor a name. What you call the factor is up to you, it is usually a general term representing the factor.

(**Caution:** Note that all SPSS has done is identify which variables have codings that appear to 'hang together' in a numerical sense. It is the judgement of the human analyst that decides what the meaning of the factor may be. Since a characteristic of humans is to see patterns where there may be none, or just to make a mistake, you must be cautious when attributing meaning to a factor. Once a factor is given a name, that name may begin to take on a spurious reality.)

Loadings on factors can be positive or negative. (All the loadings in the present example are positive.) A negative loading indicates that this variable has an *inverse relationship* with the rest of the factor. The higher the loading (positive or negative) the more important it is to that factor. Opinions are fairly arbitrary about at which point loadings become important to a factor. However, Comrey (1973: 1346) suggests that anything above 0.44 can be considered salient, with increased loadings becoming more vital in determining the factor.

On our present example the loadings on all the variables are high. Hence this factor can be considered to be representative of all the variables. The 'logic' behind the factor is fairly clear in this example — all questions have to do with the prevalence of various types of nuisance or anti-social behaviour in the respondent's own area.

Rotation

'Rotation' is necessary when extraction techniques suggest there are two or more factors. The rotation of factors is designed to give us an idea of how the factors we initially extracted differ from each other and to provide a clear picture of which items load on which factor.

There are two basic types of rotation techniques.

1. **Orthogonal Rotations**: These are rotations that assume that the extracted factors *share no association* and are unique to each other. This is often used when the analyst is applying a theoretical model to factor analysis in which the model predicts that the factors are independent. The goal is to produce factors that are as distinct from each other as possible.
2. **Oblique Rotations**: These tend to be used more often. Oblique rotations allow for the possibility that factors *are related* one to another.

Each of these categories have a number of different types of rotation within it. We will take you through an example which uses the most popular approach: 'direct oblimin'.

We will have to start from the beginning. This time we will do a Principal Components Analysis with Direct Oblimin Rotation of extracted factors.

For this example we will continue to use the same basic set of questions that ask respondents to give their view on how common a number of types of 'nuisance' incidents are in their area – **noisyngb graffiti teenonst drunks rubbish hmgdbad vandals** – but we will add four additional variables:

(1) **burglary**: Incidence of burglary in the area
(2) **vehtheft**: Cares broken into/stolen in this area
(3) **attacks**: People attacked in the street
(4) **illdrugs**: People dealing in illegal drugs.

Pull down the **Analyze** menu, click on **Data Reduction** and then **Factor** ... Transfer **noisyngh, graffiti, teenonst, drunk, rubbish, hmgdnbad, vandals, burglary, vehtheft,**

Figure 8.6a Factor Analysis main window: 'rotation example'

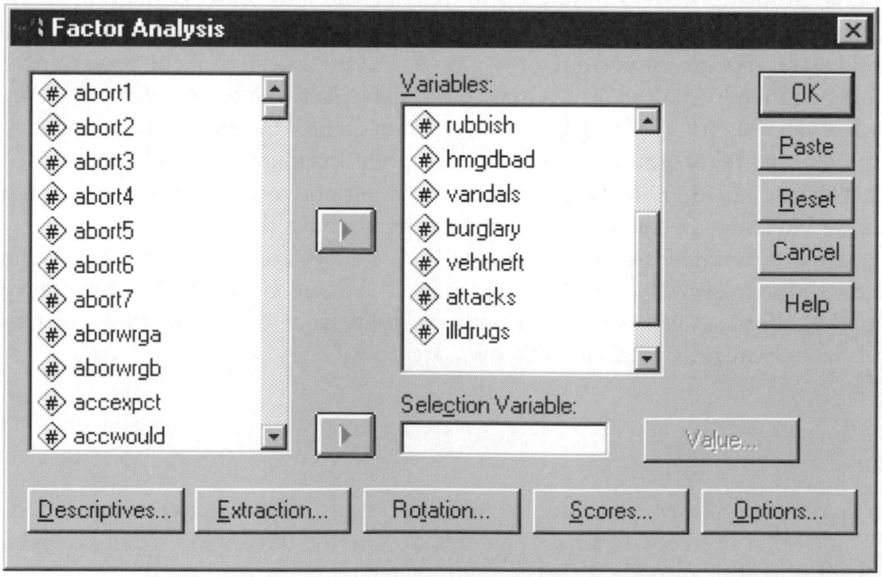

Figure 8.6b   Factor Analysis: Rotation subwindow

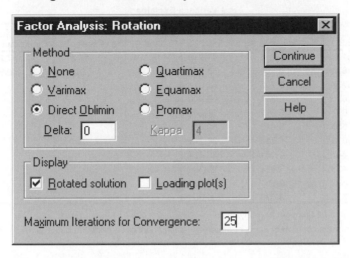

attacks and **illdrugs**. Select **Scree plot** as before from the **Extraction** box, and then select **Rotation**. When the submenu comes up, click on the circle next to **direct Oblimin**.

You should then get an **Output** that looks like Figure 8.7.

Figure 8.7   Factor Analysis

Communalities

	Initial	Extraction
Noisy neighbours/loud parties? Q134	1.000	.474
Graffiti on walls/buildings? Q135	1.000	.568
Teenagers hanging round street Q136	1.000	.579
Drunks/tramps on the streets ? Q137	1.000	.505
Rubbish or litter lying about? Q138	1.000	.529
Homes+gardens in bad condition? Q139	1.000	.474
Vandalism+deliberate damage? Q140	1.000	.635
Incidence of burglary in this area Q142	1.000	.747
Cars broken into/stolen in this areaQ143	1.000	.743
People attacked in the street? Q144	1.000	.470
People dealing in illegal drugs? Q145	1.000	.503

Extraction Method: Principal Component Analysis.

Figure 8.7 (*continued*)

Total Variance Explained

Component	Initial Eigenvalues			Extraction Sums of Squared Loadings			Rotation
	Total	% of Variance	Cumulative %	Total	% of Variance	Cumulative %	Total
1	5.194	47.218	47.218	5.194	47.218	47.218	4.654
2	1.034	9.400	56.618	1.034	9.400	56.618	3.652
3	.737	6.703	63.321				
4	.695	6.318	69.640				
5	.657	5.972	75.611				
6	.555	5.049	80.660				
7	.518	4.712	85.373				
8	.447	4.061	89.434				
9	.433	3.932	93.366				
10	.392	3.561	96.927				
11	.338	3.073	100.000				

Extraction Method: Principal Component Analysis.

a. When components are correlated, sums of squared loadings cannot be added to obtain a total variance.

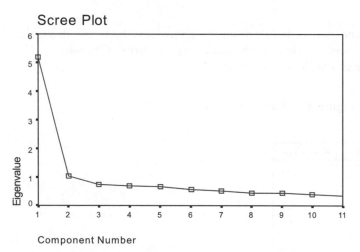

Scree Plot

Analysis weighted by WTFACTOR

From both the **Eigenvalues (Total Variance Explained** box) and the Scree test (**Scree plot** – note that factors start to straighten out between points 2 and 3), we would argue that two factors should be extracted. The following boxes (**Component Matrix, Pattern Matrix, Structure Matrix**) all relate to the rotation. For interpretation, however, we should concentrate upon the **Pattern Matrix**. Note the two columns, these refer to the loadings on each of the two factors. (Remember that the numbers with E in them are just a means for the notation of very small numbers (for instance, −4.36E-03 = − 0.00436).) Now we interpret these factors.

To define each factor, we will decide to include those variables with salient loading on the factors (above .44). On factors 1, the variables: **noisyngb** (.772); **graffiti** (.747); **teenonst** (.759); **drunks** (.672); **rubbish** (.662); **hmgdbad** (.601); and **vandals** (.569) load above .44. On factor 2 **burglary** (-.901); **vehtheft** (-.849); and **attacks** (-.497) load above .44.

Now we must *name each factor*. Looking at the items, those variables loading on factor 1 all represent nuisances in the neighbourhood, while those variables on factor 2 all represent illegal activities. Therefore we would argue that these variables together represent two conceptually

Figure 8.7 (*continued*)

Component Matrix[a]

	Component	
	1	2
Noisy neighbours/loud parties? Q134	.559	.402
Graffiti on walls/buildings? Q135	.707	.262
Teenagers hanging round street Q136	.711	.271
Drunks/tramps on the streets ? Q137	.682	.199
Rubbish or litter lying about? Q138	.707	.170
Homes+gardens in bad condition? Q139	.677	.127
Vandalism+deliberate damage? Q140	.797	6.883E-04
Incidence of burglary in this area Q142	.646	-.575
Cars broken into/stolen in this areaQ143	.696	-.509
People attacked in the street? Q144	.656	-.202
People dealing in illegal drugs? Q145	.698	-.125

Extraction Method: Principal Component Analysis.

a. 2 components extracted.

distinct factors. Factor 1 seems to describe variables asking about nuisance activities in respondents' neighbourhoods, and hence could be labelled '*Nuisance*'. Factor 2 contains variables which ask respondents to comment on illegal activities in the neighbourhood and hence could be labelled '*Illegal*'.

illdrugs, the one variable that does not load sufficiently on either factor, is an interesting case. While it does not quite reach .44 on either factor, **illdrugs** comes close for both; .382 on Factor 1 and -.432 on Factor 2. This is what is sometimes referred to a *crossloading* (where variables are pulled onto two factors). For the present example, illegal drug dealing in the area seems to be a somewhat ambiguous area for the respondents, more 'criminal' than nuisance behaviour but not seen as destructive as the other types of criminal behaviour which comprise breaking into houses, stealing cars or attacking people.

Other considerations

Remember that factor analysis is a very descriptive procedure. It requires us to describe things and to attach conceptual ideas to its statistical results; this is not always an exact science.

Your goal with factor analysis is a clear interpretation. What we mean by a 'clear interpretation' is that the variables that make up each factor on the one hand ideally should load highly on that one factor, and low on all other factors and on the other hand, the variables that go to make up each factor form a group that goes together conceptually as well as statistically.

Figure 8.7 *(continued)*

Pattern Matrix[a]

	Component	
	1	2
Noisy neighbours/loud parties? Q134	.772	.204
Graffiti on walls/buildings? Q135	.747	-1.20E-02
Teenagers hanging round street Q136	.759	-4.36E-03
Drunks/tramps on the streets ? Q137	.672	-7.05E-02
Rubbish or litter lying about? Q138	.662	-.113
Homes+gardens in bad condition? Q139	.601	-.147
Vandalism+deliberate damage? Q140	.569	-.335
Incidence of burglary in this area Q142	-7.38E-02	-.901
Cars broken into/stolen in this areaQ143	2.362E-02	-.849
People attacked in the street? Q144	.280	-.497
People dealing in illegal drugs? Q145	.382	-.432

Extraction Method: Principal Component Analysis.
Rotation Method: Oblimin with Kaiser Normalization.
a. Rotation converged in 7 iterations.

If you have a number of variables which load on several factors, or variables that load on none of the factors, then there is something wrong with your extraction techniques. The loading of a number of variables across different factors suggests you have not extracted enough factors, while if a number of variables do not load on any factor then you have extracted too many. (However, don't concern yourself overly if you have a result like the one above where only a single variable loads on two factors. The crossloading of a single variable may be due to that variable being ambiguous, or genuinely applicable to both factors.)

It is usually expected that you might wish to perform a number of extractions and different rotation techniques during the same analysis. Therefore revisiting extraction techniques and extracting more or fewer factors in order to see whether this has a substantial effect on the final results is perfectly acceptable and useful.

So how, then, do you know you have made a good analysis? There are some generally accepted criteria. The first was mentioned immediately above – all variables loading on only one factor and low on all other factors. Other criteria are less certain: if you have an interpretation that is consistent with theory, or just makes common sense, then it is useful. Having said that, the reason why Principal Components Analysis and Direct Oblimin Rotation are popular is that experience has shown statisticians that these procedures usually provide a reasonably good picture of the relationships between the variables.

Figure 8.7   (*continued*)

Structure Matrix

	Component	
	1	2
Noisy neighbours/loud parties? Q134	.666	-.198
Graffiti on walls/buildings? Q135	.754	-.401
Teenagers hanging round street Q136	.761	-.399
Drunks/tramps on the streets ? Q137	.708	-.420
Rubbish or litter lying about? Q138	.721	-.457
Homes+gardens in bad condition? Q139	.677	-.459
Vandalism+deliberate damage? Q140	.743	-.631
Incidence of burglary in this area Q142	.395	-.862
Cars broken into/stolen in this area Q143	.466	-.862
People attacked in the street? Q144	.539	-.643
People dealing in illegal drugs? Q145	.606	-.630

Extraction Method: Principal Component Analysis.
Rotation Method: Oblimin with Kaiser Normalization.

Component Correlation Matrix

Component	1	2
1	1.000	-.521
2	-.521	1.000

Extraction Method: Principal Component Analysis.
Rotation Method: Oblimin with Kaiser Normalization.

Factor Analysis exercises

- Continuing with the variables used in the last example (**noisyngb**, **graffiti**, **teenonst**, **drunks**, **rubbish**, **hmgdbad**, **vandals**, **burglary**, **vehtheft**, **attacks** and **illdrugs**), add some variables of your choice (between three and four). How does this change the results of the analysis?
  - How many factors now emerge from the analysis?
  - What names can you give to the rotated factors?
- Using a different selection of variables taken from one of the datasets, carry out a completely new factor analysis of your own.

9 Loglinear Analysis

Introduction

Loglinear analysis is a prime example of necessity being the mother of invention. By the early 1970s, the development of multivariate techniques for the analysis of quantitative or interval/ratio data in the social sciences was well in hand. Analysis of variance, multiple regression and factor analysis, all techniques covered in Modules 6–8 in this text, were firmly established and made up part of the statistical techniques available in SPSS at that time. Most of the variables available in a typical set of social science data, however, are categorical or ordinal variables with a limited number of distinct levels and hence are not suitable for parametric techniques. Social scientists had learned to think about data analysis in terms of multivariate problems but often were frustrated from carrying out multivariate analyses owing to the lack of a technique suitable for nominal or ordinal data. Loglinear analysis was created expressly to fill this gap.

We will present the loglinear analysis technique in the following manner. First, the types of problem that loglinear analysis can answer will be discussed in a general manner. Second, the 'logic' underlying the loglinear analysis procedure will be presented in non-statistical terms. Third, to illustrate the general discussions, specific examples will be given of loglinear analyses carried out on the Crime dataset.

Problems that loglinear analysis can answer

The loglinear analysis technique makes possible the multivariate analysis of data in which all the variables in the analysis are made up of categories – either *nominal* data in which the categories do not fall into any particular order or *ordinal* data in which they do. The technique can address two basic types of issues.

On the one hand, loglinear analysis can be thought of as an extension of contingency table or crosstabulation analysis in which there are several control variables. Let us take a very basic and general example in order to illustrate this first type of problem. Assume that we have four categorical or ordinal variables, which we call: A, B, C and D. Each of these four variables can take three distinct values or levels: 1, 2 or 3. We can indicate a variable and level by a subscript. For instance, the three values that variable A can take would be indicated by: A_1, A_2 and A_3; and the three values that variable B can take would be: B_1, B_2 and B_3 and so on. If we think there may be an association between variables A and B, we could put them into a crosstabulation table of A by B and test for an association using the techniques presented in the crosstabulation analysis module – applying a statistical test of association like Chi-square and, if a significant association is found, working out which cells in the table cause the association by using adjusted residuals. If we think the form of the association between A and B might be different depending upon the level of variable C, we could produce three crosstabulation tables of A by B, one for each level of variable C (that is, variable C would be a *control variable*). Each table could be checked in turn for whether it had a significant association and what the pattern of association in the table's cells might be.

So far so good. The problems begin to arise if we also suspect that the pattern of associations we find in the A by B tables with C as a control *also* might vary depending upon the value that D takes. If we use both C and D as control variables, we will end up with *nine* separate A by B tables, one for each of the combinations of the variables C and D. Each table could have a different pattern of association, with some of these tables having statistically significant associations while others did not. Also, there may be no real reason why we should not present the data in the form of *C by D* tables with A and B as control variables (or *A by C* tables with B and D as controls ... or *B by D* tables with A and C as control variables and so on ...). This is a *multivariate problem* – we require a means of deciding which of the many possible associations between these four categorical variables are important so we can concentrate on them and ignore the many other insignificant associations. Loglinear analysis can provide an answer to this problem.

A second version of loglinear analysis can be thought of as a categorical parallel to multiple regression analysis. Staying with our 'A to D variables' format, let us say that variable A can be considered possibly affected or caused by variables B to D. (For example, A could be whether a person had decided to take early retirement. B could be a person's sex, C whether the person's health had been good, average or poor, and D whether the person had a pension plan or not. B, C and D could be thought of as existing prior to the decision about early retirement and possibly to have affected the decision.) We could produce individual crosstabulation tables of A by B, A by C and A by D with the association in each table *considered on its own* apparently statistically significant. But if we also suspect or know that B, C and D are strongly associated with each other, the apparent significant links of one or more of these variables with A could in fact be illusory. Again, this is a *multivariate* problem – we require a means of deciding which of the three associations are important and which are statistical artefacts. A special case of loglinear analysis called *logit analysis* can provide an answer to this problem.

The 'logic' of loglinear analysis

Continuing with the format that has been followed in the previous modules, we will now give a non-statistical presentation of the 'logic' that underlies loglinear analysis. The basic idea of loglinear analysis is in fact a simple extension of the reasoning behind Chi-square. Let us take another example using four variables – A, B, C and D – only simplify the example even further and have only two levels for each of the four variables so that, for instance, variable A will have two values: A_1 and A_2. So, taking all four of the variables together, there will be 16 possible combinations (or possible cells) of the variables ($2 \times 2 \times 2 \times 2 = 16$). Also, let us say we have a small dataset with 144 people.

Loglinear analysis builds up a model based upon the effects of distribution. These effects can be broken down in the following manner.

1. **Cell frequency/Gross effect**
   First, we would expect to find on average nine people in each of the sixteen cells ($144/16 = 9$). That is, holding everything else equal, if the 144 people are scattered completely at random across the sixteen cells, by chance each cell should have nine people in it.
2. **Marginal effects**
   For the sake of argument, let us assume that for each of our variables A, B, C and D, level 2 has twice as many people as level 1. So, for example, level A_1 will have 48 people and level A_2 will have 96 people (a $1:2$ ratio), variable B will be the same ($B_1 = 48$ people and $B_2 = 96$ people) as will C_1 and C_2 and D_1 and D_2. Holding everything else equal,

you would expect to find that any cell associated with level A_2 should have twice as many cases as any equivalent cell associated with level A_1. The same should hold for B_1 cells contrasted with B_2 cells, C_1 cells contrasted with C_2 cells and D_1 contrasted with D_2 cells. These are called *marginal effects*.

3. **Two-way interactions**

If any two variables are crosstabulated together, say A by B, the actual, observed distribution of cases in the cells of the crosstabulation may differ significantly from that which would be expected by chance. If this is the case, we have a *two-way interaction* between the two variables. Look at Figure 9.1.

Figure 9.1   A by B, 'chance' and 'actual' distributions

Expected ratio of cases if A and B are not associated			A hypothetical ratio of cases If A and B are associated		
	B_1	B_2		B_1	B_2
A_1	1	2	A_1	3	1
A_2	2	4	A_2	2	2

On the left-hand side, you can see the ratio of how the cases would be distributed by chance in the table A by B, if there was no association between the two variables. If there is an association, the actual distribution would differ significantly from that expected by chance, yielding a different distribution across the cells of the crosstabulation table. The right-hand table illustrates one such possible different form that this distribution could take.

You will note that the logic of loglinear modelling parallels that which underlies Chi-square: the actual distribution of cases in cells is contrasted with that which you would expect to find by chance.

4. **Three-way interactions**

It is also possible that the distribution of cases in the A by B crosstabulation can be different depending upon the level taken by a third variable. If this is the case, that the A by B association varies for different values of a third variable, C, we have a *three-way interaction*. Figures 9.2a and 9.2b illustrate the possible appearance that the absence and presence of a three-way interaction could have.

Figure 9.2a   A by B for two levels of C, 'three-way' interaction absent

C_1			C_2		
	B_1	B_2		B_1	B_2
A_1	3	1	A_1	3	1
A_2	2	2	A_2	2	2

Figure 9.2b   A by B for two levels of C, 'three-way' interaction present

C_1			C_2		
	B_1	B_2		B_1	B_2
A_1	2	3	A_1	3	1
A_2	2	7	A_2	2	2

Note that the ratio of cell numbers in Figure 9.2a are exactly the same regardless of which value is taken by the third variable, C. In contrast, note that the ratio of cell numbers in Figure 9.2b differ depending upon the value taken by the third variable, C. That is, when the pattern of association between A and B varies depending upon the value taken by C, there is a three-way interaction between A, B and C.

5. **Four- or N-way interactions**
   The distribution of cases in the A by B crosstabulation tables that are different for each value of C could also vary for each value of a fourth variable, D, yielding *four-way interactions*. This pattern of increasingly complex interactions can be extended for an additional number of N extra variables.

All this ends up in a linear equation that can be expressed like this:

Any cell's frequency = Gross effect × Marginal effects × Interaction effects

To make the computation easier, the effects are put into terms of logs so they can be added rather than multiplied; hence, the name of the procedure: *Loglinear analysis*.

The goal of a loglinear analysis usually is *parsimony* – to establish the simplest possible loglinear equation that manages to produce predicted frequencies for each cell that do not vary significantly from the actual cell frequencies. This is accomplished by eliminating the most complex interactions in turn. If the cell frequencies predicted after the most complex interaction is removed do not diverge significantly from the actual cell frequencies, the next most complex interaction term is removed and again the predicted frequencies are compared with those that actually occur. This process is repeated until eventually no more interaction terms can be removed without producing a model whose predicted values do not 'fit' the actual cell frequencies well. For instance, taking our $A \times B \times C \times D$ example, it may be possible to remove the most complex four-way interaction term ($A \times B \times C \times D$) and all of the three-way interactions before arriving at the simplest model that still gives a good 'fit' – a model that includes only two-way interactions. If such a result can be obtained, the interpretation of associations is comparatively easy. You would not need to worry about complex tables with one or more control variables and instead would need to describe what is going only on in a series of two-way, relatively simple crosstabulation tables.

We will now demonstrate this procedure through the use of specific examples drawn from the Crime dataset.

Loglinear analysis: specific examples with SPSS

Three examples of loglinear analysis will be given to illustrate the procedure.

1. First, 'Model Selection' will be used to show the steps involved in gradually eliminating more complex interactions from a model until the simplest possible model is found that still gives predictions of the expected frequencies in the individual cells that do not diverge significantly from the actual observed cell frequencies.
2. Second, a 'General' loglinear analysis will be used to show how a too-simple set of interactions produces a model whose predicted cell frequencies match the actual frequencies poorly.
3. Third, a 'Logit' model will be given in order to illustrate a 'regression-style' predictive analysis in which one variable can be considered dependent upon several other variables.

The same set of variables will be used in all three analyses.

> • **rsex**. A variable in the Crime dataset where code '1' is 'Male' and '2' is 'Female'
> • **edqual**. A variable based upon a collapsing together of the seven categories of educational qualification in '**hedqual**' into four larger categories, where code '1' is 'Degree level or higher', '2' is 'A-level or third level equivalent', '3' is 'O-level or CSE equivalent' and '4' is 'No qualification'
> • **clsgrps**. A collapsing together of the eleven categories of '**rhgclass**' into three categories — '1' 'Service' or upper middle class, '2' 'Intermediates' and '3' 'Working class'
> • **majors**. A variable based upon **partyid1**, consisting of the three major parties — '1' 'Conservative', '2' 'Labour' and '3' 'Liberal Democrat'.

This recoding of original variables in the Crime dataset in order to produce fewer, larger categories is advisable owing to the multiplication of cells in a multivariate crosstabulation. For instance, the number of categories in these four recoded variables in combination imply 72 cells ($2 \times 4 \times 3 \times 3 = 72$). If the original variables had been used, 1386 cells would have been implied ($2 \times 7 \times 11 \times 9 = 1386$). If the people in the Crime dataset were scattered equally across all categories, just over two people on average would be found in each cell. (And, since people will be clustered rather than scattered at random across the cells, many cells would have no one at all.) In a multivariate loglinear analysis which involves a number of variables with a large number of categories, it is quite possible to generate more potential cells than there are cases — even for datasets with a very large number of cases. In general, if the number of categories of variables can be collapsed without losing much information, it is advisable to do so. (Deciding how much, and where, to combine categories without losing information is, however, more of an art than a science; that is, a matter of judgement and familiarity with the data. Generally, the analyst wishes to keep the number of empty cells or cells with almost no cases to a minimum, but this must be balanced against the need to retain the substantive discrimination between categories.)

'Model selection'

In the first example, 'Model Selection' will be used to show the steps involved in gradually eliminating more complex interactions from a model. Here the goal is *parsimony* — to find the simplest possible model that still gives predictions of the expected frequencies in the individual cells that do not diverge significantly from the cell frequencies actually observed. Before beginning, we can anticipate that the four variables — sex, education, class and party identification — will be associated with each other and, furthermore, that the patterns of association may be quite complex. For instance, educational level and social class are almost surely associated so that people with higher educational qualifications are more likely to be found in the service class category and it is quite possible that the exact form or strength of this link between education and class could vary depending upon which sex people are. By starting with a set of complex patterns of associations (here, all three-way interactions between the four variables) and gradually simplifying the model by removing the most complex associations in turn, a solution will be reached — the model that posits the smallest number of least complex associations (interactions) between the four variables (Figure 9.3).

You begin by opening the **Analyze** menu, clicking on **Loglinear** and selecting the **Model Selection** window (Figure 9.4a).

Figure 9.3 Selecting **Loglinear**

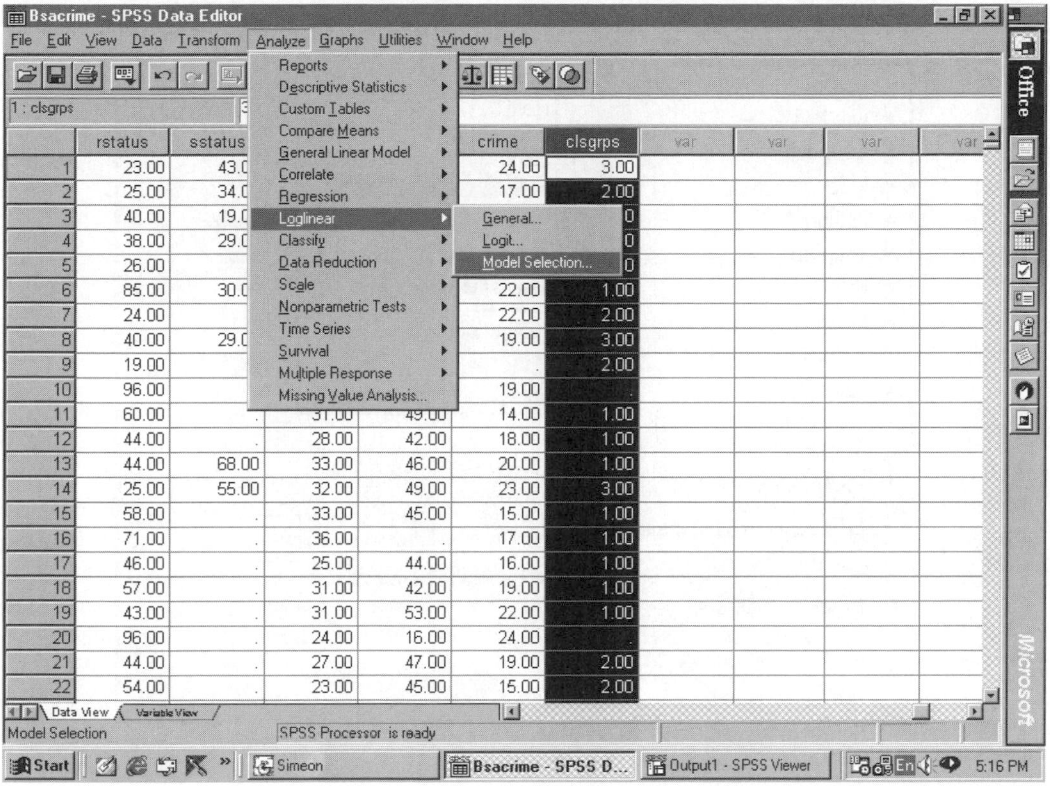

Your first step with the **Model Selection** window is to choose the variables for the analysis from the list on the left-hand side and use the arrow to insert them into the list of **Factor[s]** in the middle of the window. Here, **rsex**, **edqual**, **clsgrps** and **majors** have all been inserted.

Next, you need to define the range of values for each variable that will be used in the analysis. The range of values for **rsex [1 2]**, **equal [1 4]** and **clsgrps [1 3]** have been set and **majors [? ?]** shows this range needs to be defined. To do that, click on the **Define Range'** button to bring up the subwindow shown in Figure 9.4b.

Type in 1 and 3 as the **Minimum** and **Maximum** values for the variable **majors** and then click on the **Continue** button to return to the main window.

Note that the range of values should not have any gaps. For instance, a variable with three codes, 1, 3 and 5 would pose problems. The range would be 1 to 5 and SPSS would assume that the variable had five levels, **1, 2, 3, 4 and 5** and would seek cell combinations for the nonexistent levels **2** and **4** (and consequently would find many empty cells). All of the codes implied by a range must have genuine values. (The gaps could be rectified by recoding the codes 1, 3 and 5 into three consecutive numbers.)

Next, you have to specify a loglinear model. Click on the **Model** button in the **Model Selection** window (Figure 9.4a) to bring up the subwindow in Figure 9.4c. The default is the **Saturated** model − all possible associations between all variables. You do not want this, but rather the simplest possible model. Click on the **Custom** button. Next, you need to give SPSS a starting point from which to work backwards to reach the simplest possible model. You do this by bringing down the small submenu in the middle of the window that is initially set on **Interaction**. Here, we decide to begin with **All 3-way** interactions (that is, all possible

Figure 9.4a The **Model Selection** window

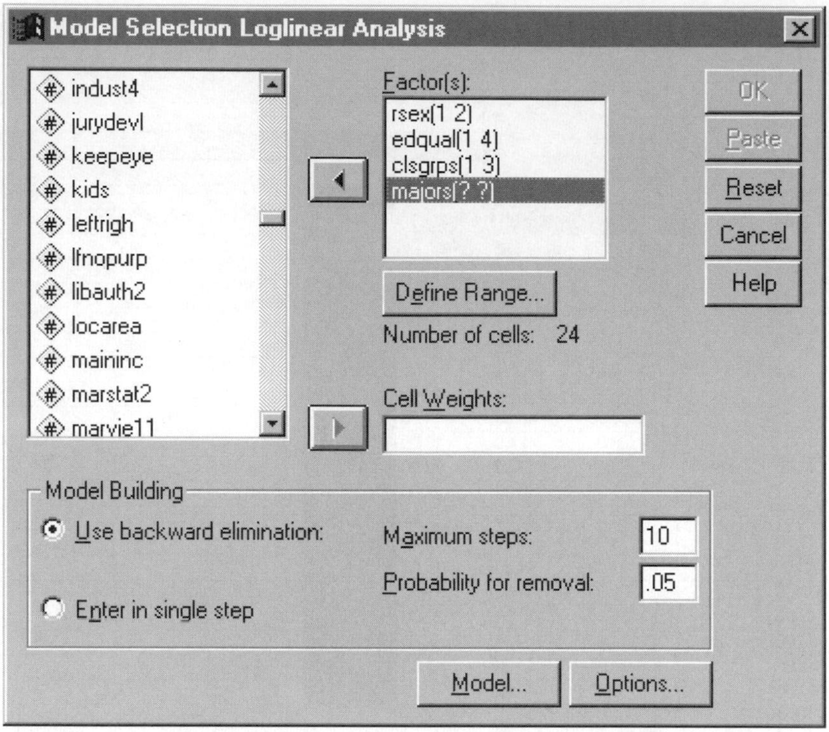

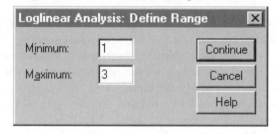

Figure 9.4b The **Define Range** subwindow

combinations of three of the variables). You do this by selecting *All 3-way*, then highlighting all four of the variables and clicking the right-hand arrow button under **Build Term[s]**. All possible 3-way interaction combinations appear in the right-hand box, **Generating Class**. There are four possible 3-way interaction combinations:

- **clsgrps*edqual*majors**
- **clsgrps*edqual*rsex**
- **clsgrps*majors*rsex**
- **edqual*majors*rsex**

Now, click on **Continue** to go back to the main window.

Sometimes you may want to change the default settings. To do this, click on the **Options** button to bring up the subwindow in Figure 9.4d. Here, the default is to include cell frequencies

Figure 9.4c The **Model** subwindow

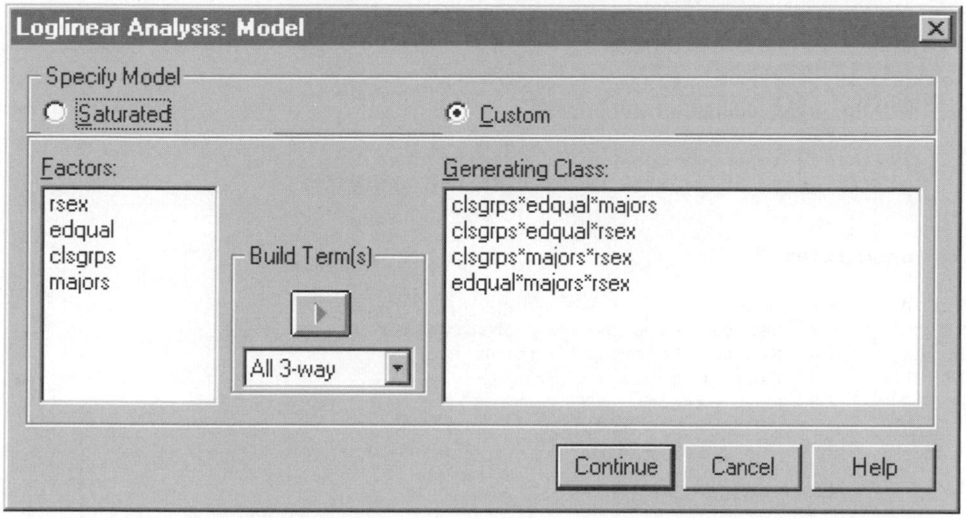

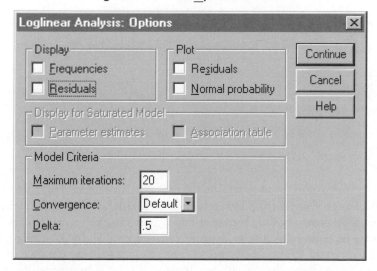

and residuals in the output. We want to simplify the output for this illustration by removing these. This is accomplished by removing the ticks in the **Frequencies** and **Residuals** boxes under **Display**. Click on **Continue** to return to the main window.

Figure 9.4d The **Options** subwindow

You are now prepared to run the loglinear model selection. Note that the Model Building button for **Use backward selection** is switched on. As usual, run the procedure by clicking **OK**.

The output begins by reporting that 2437 cases were accepted and 709 cases were rejected (owing to the values for one or more of the variables in a case falling outside the ranges we stated – in this example, these 'out-of-range' cases are in fact missing values plus anyone who did not state that they supported one of the three major parties). The variables in the analysis and the number of levels in each variable's range is given.

Figure 9.5 Results for a 'backward elimination' loglinear analysis

```
* * * * * * * *  H I E R A R C H I C A L   L O G   L I N E A R  * * * * * * * *

DATA   Information

      2437 unweighted cases accepted.
         0 cases rejected because of out-of-range factor values.
       709 cases rejected because of missing data.
      2448 weighted cases will be used in the analysis.


FACTOR Information

     Factor  Level  Label
     RSEX       2   Sex of respondent by observation
     EDQUAL     4   Recoded Ed qualification
     CLSGRPS    3   Class groupings
     MAJORS     3   Main parties
```

- -

The analysis begins with the most complex model that we specified, all three-way interactions of the variables.

This complex model produces a reasonably good 'fit' to the data. 'P = .234' can be interpreted as meaning that there is at least a 23.4% chance that any difference between the cell frequencies predicted by the model and the actual observed cell frequencies could be due to chance only, well within the conventional 0.05 cutoff level for a significance test.

```
* * * * * * * *  H I E R A R C H I C A L   L O G   L I N E A R  * * * * * * * * *

Backward Elimination (p = .050) for DESIGN 1 with generating class

   CLSGRPS*EDQUAL*MAJORS
   CLSGRPS*EDQUAL*RSEX
   CLSGRPS*MAJORS*RSEX
   EDQUAL*MAJORS*RSEX

Likelihood ratio chi square =     15.14257    DF = 12  P = .234
```

- -

SPSS then looks to see if any of the interactions could be taken out while still retaining a good fit to the cell frequencies. the three-way interaction 'clsgrps*edqual*majors' is the best candidate because its removal will raise degrees of freedom [DF] by 12 while producing a relatively small increase in Chi-square of 8.336. The chances that the removal of this three-way interaction will produce a loss in 'fit' is a long way from significance (Prob = 0.7583). The new, simpler model in fact produces a much *better* 'fit' to the data; 'P = .492'.

If Deleted Simple Effect is	DF	L.R. Chisq Change	Prob	Iter
CLSGRPS*EDQUAL*MAJORS	12	**8.336**	**.7583**	**6**
CLSGRPS*EDQUAL*RSEX	6	13.632	.0340	5
CLSGRPS*MAJORS*RSEX	4	11.891	.0182	4
EDQUAL*MAJORS*RSEX	6	12.211	.0574	3

Figure 9.5 (*continued*)

```
CLSGRPS*EDQUAL*RSEX                        4            11.891   .0182    4
CLSGRPS*MAJORS*RSEX                        4            11.891   .0182    4
EDQUAL*MAJORS*RSEX                         6            12.211   .0574    3
```

Step 1

  The best model has generating class

  Likelihood ratio chi square =   23.47864   DF = 24 **P =   .492**

- -

SPSS then checks for the best candidate for the next interaction that can be taken out with little deterioration in 'fit'. 'edqual*majors*rsex' (Prob = .0662) is just eligible.

(Note that its removal means that the two-way interaction of edqual*majors is no longer implied, so that two-way interaction must now appear as a separate term.)

The 'fit' deteriorates but, at p = .232, is still within acceptable levels.

```
If Deleted Simple Effect is            DF   L.R. Chisq Change    Prob   Iter

CLSGRPS*EDQUAL*RSEX                     6            13.687   .0333    7
CLSGRPS*MAJORS*RSEX                     4            12.549   .0137    6
EDQUAL*MAJORS*RSEX                      6            11.817   .0662    6
```

Step 2

  The best model has generating class

        CLSGRPS*EDQUAL*RSEX
        CLSGRPS*MAJORS*RSEX
        EDQUAL*MAJORS

  Likelihood ratio chi square =   35.29530   DF = 30 **P =   .232**

- -

```
If Deleted Simple Effect is            DF   L.R. Chisq Change    Prob   Iter

CLSGRPS*EDQUAL*RSEX                     6            12.604   .0498    7
CLSGRPS*MAJORS*RSEX                     4            18.388   .0010    6
EDQUAL*MAJORS                           6            41.085   .0000    2
```

Step 3

  The best model has generating class

        CLSGRPS*EDQUAL*RSEX
        CLSGRPS*MAJORS*RSEX
        EDQUAL*MAJORS

  Likelihood ratio chi square =   35.29530   DF = 30 P =   .232

- -

SPSS then checks whether there are any more interactions that can be taken out. **'clsgrps*edqual*rsex'** is close to a possibility, but the probability that its removal will result in a significant deterioration in 'fit' is just too high (Prob = 0.0498). Since there are no other interaction terms that can be removed without producing a significant loss in 'fit', this model becomes the 'best' model and the final solution to the loglinear analysis.

Figure 9.5 (*continued*)

```
The final model has generating class

    CLSGRPS*EDQUAL*RSEX
    CLSGRPS*MAJORS*RSEX
    EDQUAL*MAJORS


The Iterative Proportional Fit algorithm converged at iteration 0.
The maximum difference between observed and fitted marginal totals is      .097
and the convergence criterion is      .250

- - - - - - - - - - - - - - - - - - - - - - - - - - - - - - - - - - - - - - -


  Goodness-of-fit test statistics

      Likelihood ratio chi square =      35.29530     DF = 30   P =   .232
                Pearson chi square =      34.45233     DF = 30   P =   .263


- - - - - - - - - - - - - - - - - - - - - - - - - - - - - - - - - - - - - - -
```

The final model is the simplest set of interactions that can accurately depict the pattern of associations (the cell frequencies) between the four variables in the analysis: **rsex**; **edqual**; **class**; and **party**:

---

1. Class and level of educational qualification are significantly associated and this pattern of association is different depending upon whether the respondent is male or female (**clsgrps*edqual*rsex**)
2. Class and the political party supported are significantly associated and this pattern of association is different depending upon gender (**clsgrps*majors*rsex**)
3. There is a significant assocation between educational qualification and party identification (**edqual*majors**).

The procedure concludes with two versions of 'Goodness-of-fit test statistics'. The gist of each is the same: the final model is the simplest possible set of associations that will yield predicted cell frequencies that are not significantly different from those actually observed (P = .232 and P = .263).

The above output demonstrates the usual procedure that you would follow in a loglinear analysis, using the changes in Chi-square and degrees of freedom to indicate the goodness of fit of successively simpler models. There are instances, however, where you may wish to try out a specific loglinear model; for example, instead of seeking the most simple model, you may want to compare the 'fit' of two contrasting model specifications. In these instances, you would conduct a general loglinear analysis.

'General loglinear analysis'

In the next example, we will carry out a general loglinear analysis using the same four variables – **rsex**, **edqual**, **clsgrps** and **majors**. We will produce a loglinear analysis restricted to two-way interactions only in order to see how much worse the fit is than the previous 'final/best' solution we found above.

For a general loglinear analysis, you select **General** from the types of loglinear analysis shown in Figure 9.3. The window shown in Figure 9.6a will appear.

As in our previous example, the four variables **rsex**, **edqual**, **clsgrps** and **majors** have been brought as **Factor[s]** into the model by selecting them from the list of variables in the left-hand column and clicking on the right-pointing arrow.

Figure 9.6a   General loglinear analysis

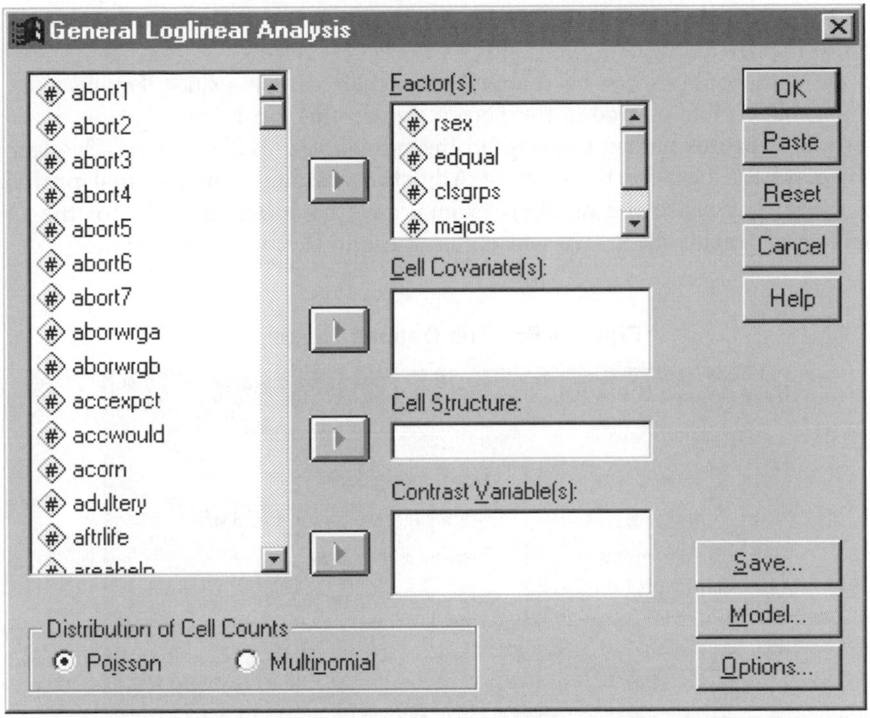

Figure 9.6b   Geneal loglinear analysis model of two-way interactions

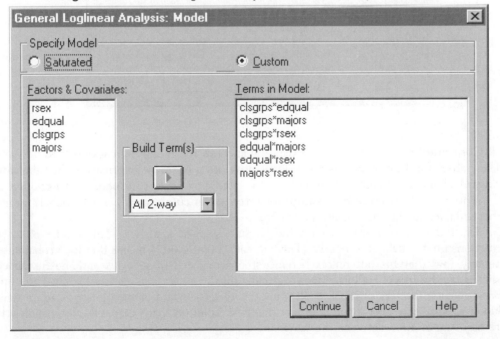

We want to produce a general loglinear model of all two-way interactions. To do so, click on the **Model** button to bring up the window in Figure 9.6b. Click the **Custom** button.

To produce the model of all two-way interactions, select **All 2-way** from the drop-down menu under **Build Term[s]**, then highlight all the variables in the **Factors & Covariates** list on the left and click on the right-hand **Build Term[s]** button. All of the 2-way interactions will appear on the right-hand **Terms in Model** list. Then click the **Continue** button in order to return to the main window.

If you wish, the options can be changed from their default values. For instance, here we decide not to have plots printed in the output. To do this, go to the **Option** subwindow by clicking on the **Options** button to bring up the subwindow in Figure 9.6c. Deselect the plots by switching off the ticks for the plots of **Adjusted residuals** and **Normal probability for adjusted**. Note that unlike the previous example, we have left the ticks for the **Display** of **Frequencies** and **Residuals**, so we will obtain these in the output this time.

Figure 9.6c The **Options** subwindow

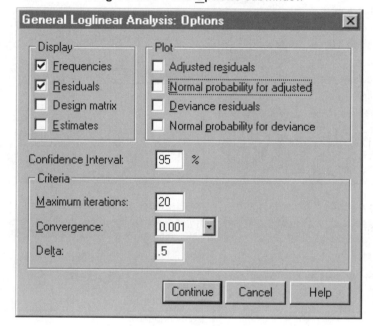

Click **Continue** to return to the main window and run the model by clicking **OK**.

The output for a general loglinear analysis provides a bit more information than that for a 'backward elimination' analysis. As before, the number of cases included and excluded are given. Three cells have no cases (**3 sampling zeros are encountered**). Here, the labels for each of the variables in the analysis are given (Figure 9.7).

Finally, the output concludes with the 'Goodness-of-fit statistics'. This model of 2-way interactions fits the data very poorly. (The 'Sig.' of 0.0069/0.0074 means that the probability is extremely low that the differences between the actual cell frequencies and the frequencies predicted by the model could be due to chance only.)

We conclude that the original result found by the 'backward elimination' procedure which included a three-way interaction is in fact the 'best' solution that is capable of explaining the patterns of association between the variables.

Figure 9.7 Results for a general loglinear analysis

```
                    GENERAL LOGLINEAR ANALYSIS
- - - - - - - - - - - - - - - - - - - - - - - - - - - - - - - - - - - - - -


Data Information

     2437 cases are accepted.
      709 cases are rejected because of missing data.
  2448.26 weighted cases will be used in the analysis.
       72 cells are defined.
        0 structural zeros are imposed by design.
        3 sampling zeros are encountered.


- - - - - - - - - - - - - - - - - - - - - - - - - - - - - - - - - - - - - -


Variable Information

Factor     Levels    Value

RSEX         2                 Sex of respondent by observation     Q32
                        1 Male
                        2 Female

EDQUAL       4                 Recoded Ed qualification
                     1.00 Degree
                     2.00 A-level & 3rd level
                     3.00 O-level & CSE
                     4.00 No qualifcation

CLSGRPS      3                 Class groupings
                     1.00 Service
                     2.00 Intermediates
                     3.00 Working class

MAJORS       3                 Main parties
                     1.00 Conservative
                     2.00 Labour
                     3.00 Liberal Democrat

- - - - - - - - - - - - - - - - - - - - - - - - - - - - - - - - - - - - - -


Model and Design Information

 Model: Poisson
Design: Constant + EDQUAL*CLSGRPS + CLSGRPS*MAJORS + RSEX*CLSGRPS + EDQUAL
       *MAJORS + RSEX*EDQUAL + RSEX*MAJORS
```

The interaction terms that are in the model are given (above) ...

... and the parameters in the design are numbered and linked to terms in the model (below):

```
- - - - - - - - - - - - - - - - - - - - - - - - - - - - - - - - - - - - - -
                    GENERAL LOGLINEAR ANALYSIS
- - - - - - - - - - - - - - - - - - - - - - - - - - - - - - - - - - - - - -

Correspondence Between Parameters and Terms of the Design

Parameter   Aliased  Term

        1            Constant
        2            [EDQUAL = 1.00]*[CLSGRPS = 1.00]
        3            [EDQUAL = 1.00]*[CLSGRPS = 2.00]
```

Figure 9.7 (*continued*)

```
 4              [EDQUAL = 1.00]*[CLSGRPS = 3.00]
 5              [EDQUAL = 2.00]*[CLSGRPS = 1.00]
 6              [EDQUAL = 2.00]*[CLSGRPS = 2.00]
 7              [EDQUAL = 2.00]*[CLSGRPS = 3.00]
 8              [EDQUAL = 3.00]*[CLSGRPS = 1.00]
 9              [EDQUAL = 3.00]*[CLSGRPS = 2.00]
10              [EDQUAL = 3.00]*[CLSGRPS = 3.00]
11              [EDQUAL = 4.00]*[CLSGRPS = 1.00]
12              [EDQUAL = 4.00]*[CLSGRPS = 2.00]
13       x      [EDQUAL = 4.00]*[CLSGRPS = 3.00]
14              [CLSGRPS = 1.00]*[MAJORS = 1.00]
15              [CLSGRPS = 1.00]*[MAJORS = 2.00]
16       x      [CLSGRPS = 1.00]*[MAJORS = 3.00]
17              [CLSGRPS = 2.00]*[MAJORS = 1.00]
18              [CLSGRPS = 2.00]*[MAJORS = 2.00]
19       x      [CLSGRPS = 2.00]*[MAJORS = 3.00]
20              [CLSGRPS = 3.00]*[MAJORS = 1.00]
21              [CLSGRPS = 3.00]*[MAJORS = 2.00]
22       x      [CLSGRPS = 3.00]*[MAJORS = 3.00]
23              [RSEX = 1]*[CLSGRPS = 1.00]
24              [RSEX = 1]*[CLSGRPS = 2.00]
25              [RSEX = 1]*[CLSGRPS = 3.00]
26       x      [RSEX = 2]*[CLSGRPS = 1.00]
27       x      [RSEX = 2]*[CLSGRPS = 2.00]
28       x      [RSEX = 2]*[CLSGRPS = 3.00]
29              [EDQUAL = 1.00]*[MAJORS = 1.00]
30              [EDQUAL = 1.00]*[MAJORS = 2.00]
31       x      [EDQUAL = 1.00]*[MAJORS = 3.00]
32              [EDQUAL = 2.00]*[MAJORS = 1.00]
33              [EDQUAL = 2.00]*[MAJORS = 2.00]
34       x      [EDQUAL = 2.00]*[MAJORS = 3.00]
35              [EDQUAL = 3.00]*[MAJORS = 1.00]
36              [EDQUAL = 3.00]*[MAJORS = 2.00]
37       x      [EDQUAL = 3.00]*[MAJORS = 3.00]
38       x      [EDQUAL = 4.00]*[MAJORS = 1.00]
39       x      [EDQUAL = 4.00]*[MAJORS = 2.00]
40       x      [EDQUAL = 4.00]*[MAJORS = 3.00]
41              [RSEX = 1]*[EDQUAL = 1.00]
42              [RSEX = 1]*[EDQUAL = 2.00]
43              [RSEX = 1]*[EDQUAL = 3.00]
44       x      [RSEX = 1]*[EDQUAL = 4.00]
45       x      [RSEX = 2]*[EDQUAL = 1.00]
46       x      [RSEX = 2]*[EDQUAL = 2.00]
47       x      [RSEX = 2]*[EDQUAL = 3.00]
48       x      [RSEX = 2]*[EDQUAL = 4.00]
49              [RSEX = 1]*[MAJORS = 1.00]
50              [RSEX = 1]*[MAJORS = 2.00]
51       x      [RSEX = 1]*[MAJORS = 3.00]
52       x      [RSEX = 2]*[MAJORS = 1.00]
53       x      [RSEX = 2]*[MAJORS = 2.00]
54       x      [RSEX = 2]*[MAJORS = 3.00]
```

Note: 'x' indicates an aliased (or a redundant) parameter.
      These parameters are set to zero.

- -

Convergence Information

```
Maximum number of iterations:          20
Relative difference tolerance:        .001
Final relative difference:      2.20748E-05
```

Maximum likelihood estimation converged at iteration 4.

Figure 9.7 (*continued*)

Since we ticked '**Frequencies**' in the '**Options**' subwindow, a table of the observed (actual) and expected (predicted by the model) frequencies for each possible combination of values of the four variables in the model are given. (The middle of this lengthy table has been abbreviated.

- -
GENERAL LOGLINEAR ANALYSIS
- -

Table Information

Factor	Value	Observed Count	%	Expected Count	%
RSEX	Male				
EDQUAL	Degree				
CLSGRPS	Service				
MAJORS	**Conservative**	**30.64** (	**1.25)**	**24.84** (	**1.01)**
MAJORS	Labour	54.20 (	2.21)	58.21 (	2.38)
MAJORS	Liberal Democrat	17.51 (	.72)	15.94 (	.65)
CLSGRPS	Intermediates				
MAJORS	Conservative	2.19 (	.09)	1.74 (	.07)
MAJORS	Labour	3.83 (	.16)	7.07 (	.29)
MAJORS	Liberal Democrat	1.09 (	.04)	1.66 (	.07)
CLSGRPS	Working class				
MAJORS	Conservative	.00 (	.00)	.24 (	.01)
MAJORS	Labour	2.19 (	.09)	1.65 (	.07)
MAJORS	Liberal Democrat	.00 (	.00)	.29 (	.01)
EDQUAL	A-level & 3rd level				
CLSGRPS	Service				
MAJORS	Conservative	100.99 (	4.12)	94.73 (	3.87)
MAJORS	Labour	89.17 (	3.64)	97.30 (	3.97)
MAJORS	Liberal Democrat	30.82 (	1.26)	32.36 (	1.32)

⋮

[The middle of this lengthy table has been abbreviated.]
⋮
⇓

EDQUAL	No qualifcation			
CLSGRPS	Service			
MAJORS	Conservative	1.90	.59	.46
MAJORS	Labour	−1.95	−.60	−.49
MAJORS	Liberal Democrat	.90	.57	.50
CLSGRPS	Intermediates			
MAJORS	Conservative	−3.19	−.67	−.46
MAJORS	Labour	13.56	2.45	1.43
MAJORS	Liberal Democrat	3.11	1.10	.84
CLSGRPS	Working class			
MAJORS	Conservative	−12.37	−3.19	−2.74
MAJORS	Labour	−.12	−.02	−.01
MAJORS	Liberal Democrat	−1.86	−.76	−.67

- -

Similarly, because we ticked '**Residuals**' in the '**Options**' window, a table of the 'residuals' (the differences between the observed and expected frequencies for each possible combination of values of the four variables in the model are given. (If you wish, you can check this: for instance, in the top row in **bold** above [resex = Male, edqual = Degree, clsgrps = Service, majors = Conservative], the 'observed' minus the 'expected' value [30.64 − 24.84]

Figure 9.7 (*continued*)

yields a residual of 5.80. the value 5.80 can be found in **bold** in the top row of the residual portion of the table below.)

The residual table can be useful for identifying which cells in a poorly fitting model are causes of the bad 'fit' (those cells for which the residual is large). There may be something 'special' about the offending cell(s) that explains why their fit is poor.

Three figures are given in the residual table:

(1) 'Resid.' − the actual difference
(2) 'Adj. Resid' − a figure adjusted for the number in the cells and the effects of other variables, including the covariate (the adjusted residual is a better indicator of the true amount of divergence between the observed and expected values)
(3) 'Dev. Resid.' − a measure of the variance (or potential error) around the residual.

```
Table Information


                                         Adj.      Dev.
Factor                    Value    Resid. Resid.   Resid.

RSEX                      Male
 EDQUAL                   Degree
  CLSGRPS                 Service
   MAJORS                 Conservative     5.80    1.84    1.12
   MAJORS                 Labour          -4.01   -1.06    -.53
   MAJORS        Liberal Democrat          1.56     .58     .39
  CLSGRPS                 Intermediates
   MAJORS                 Conservative      .44     .36     .32
   MAJORS                 Labour          -3.24   -1.59   -1.34
   MAJORS        Liberal Democrat          -.56    -.48    -.47
  CLSGRPS                 Working class
   MAJORS                 Conservative     -.24    -.50    -.69
   MAJORS                 Labour            .54     .49     .40
   MAJORS        Liberal Democrat          -.29    -.56    -.77
 EDQUAL   A-level & 3rd level
  CLSGRPS                 Service
   MAJORS                 Conservative     6.26    1.13     .64
   MAJORS                 Labour          -8.13   -1.43    -.84
   MAJORS        Liberal Democrat         -1.55    -.41    -.27
```

⇑
⋮

[The middle of this lengthy table has been abbreviated.]

⋮
⇓

```
EDQUAL        No qualifcation
 CLSGRPS                 Service
  MAJORS                 Conservative      .06     .02     .01
  MAJORS                 Labour        2.16E-03 6.68E-04 5.32E-04
  MAJORS        Liberal Democrat         -.92    -.53    -.50
 CLSGRPS                 Intermediates
  MAJORS                 Conservative     1.97     .42     .28
  MAJORS                 Labour         -12.68   -2.34   -1.48
  MAJORS        Liberal Democrat        -2.77    -.94    -.75
 CLSGRPS                 Working class
  MAJORS                 Conservative    11.63    2.43    1.49
  MAJORS                 Labour           1.18     .20     .09
  MAJORS        Liberal Democrat         1.53     .47     .32
```

- -

Figure 9.7 (*continued*)

```
Goodness-of-fit Statistics

                       Chi-Square      DF       Sig.

Likelihood Ratio        65.3506        40       .0069
        Pearson         65.0521        40       .0074
```

Including a quantitative variable in a general loglinear analysis

The 'general loglinear' analysis procedure allows one to construct more complex models than those possible with a 'hierarchical' loglinear analysis. One feature available in the inclusion of the effects of one or more quantitative variables into a loglinear model as covariates.

In an extension to the above example, we will bring across an interval/ratio variable, **rage** (respondent's age), as a **Cell Covariate**. *Covariates* are quantitative variables that are likely to affect the distribution of cases across the cells defined by the categorical variables in a loglinear model. Covariates must be *interval/ratio variables*.

Here, by including **rage** as a covariate, we are anticipating that the respondent's age may be affecting the associations between the other variables. For instance, for the variable **majors**, it may be that older respondents are probably more likely to identify with the Conservative Party. Including an appropriate quantitative covariate into a loglinear model can help improve its 'fit'.

Figure 9.8a General loglinear analysis with **rage** included as a covariate

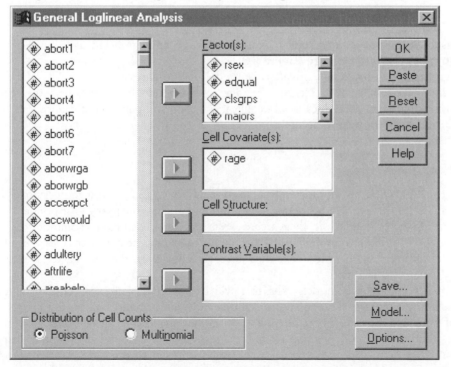

Figure 9.8a shows the window for a General loglinear analysis the same as before, only with **rage** included as a covariate. As can be seen in the subwindow in Figure 9.8b, the resulting model has a larger number of terms since the interactions of **rage** with the four other variables must be included.

Figure 9.8b Model for a general loglinear analysis of two-way interactions with **rage** included

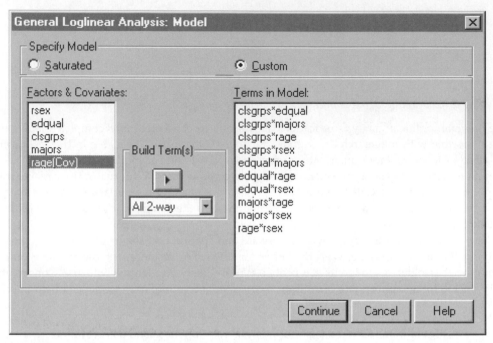

The resulting output is very similar except that **rage** appears listed as a covariate and the **Design** must also include **rage** (Figure 9.9).

When **rage** is included as a covariate, a model of two-way interactions 'fits' the data quite well (Sig. = 0.6798/0.6479). Hence, the age of respondents does affect the pattern of associations between sex, educational qualification, class and party identification markedly and its inclusion leads to a more accurate prediction of cell frequencies.

'Logit' analysis

In our third example, we demonstrate a 'logit' analysis to carry out a regression-style causal analysis. To do this we will introduce an additional variable, **burglary** ('Respondent's opinion of the incidence of burglary in their area: (1) Very common; (2) Fairly common; (3) Not very common; (4) Not at all common'). **burglary**, an attitude, may be considered logically to follow (or to be affected by) people's sex, their level of education, their social class, and/or their political party identification.

We will compare two models. The first will be the effects of **rsex**, **edqual**, **clsgrps** and **majors** upon **burglary** and the second will exclude **majors** and will be the effects of **rsex**, **edqual** and **clsgrps** only upon **burglary**. By comparing the fit of the two models, we are testing whether it is necessary to include the effects of a party identification upon **burglary** in addition to the effects of sex, education and class in order to produce an adequate model of **burglary**. (For example, Conservative Party supporters could be more likely than others to feel that burglary is more common in their area, regardless of their gender, educational level or social class.)

We pull down the **Analyze** menu, select **Loglinear** and this time choose **Logit**. The main window will come up as shown in Figure 9.10a. Here, we select **burglary** from the list of

Figure 9.9 Results for a general loglinear analysis with **rage** included as a covariate

- -
                    GENERAL LOGLINEAR ANALYSIS
- -

Data Information

     2433 cases are accepted.
      713 cases are rejected because of missing data.
  2433.88 weighted cases will be used in the analysis.
       72 cells are defined.
        0 structural zeros are imposed by design.
        3 sampling zeros are encountered.

- -

Variable Information

Factor   Levels   Value

RSEX   2   Sex of respondent by observation   Q32
                        1 Male
                        2 Female

EDQUAL   4   Recoded Ed qualification
                     1.00 Degree
                     2.00 A-level & 3rd level
                     3.00 O-level & CSE
                     4.00 No qualifcation

CLSGRPS   3   Class groupings
                     1.00 Service
                     2.00 Intermediates
                     3.00 Working class

MAJORS   3   Main parties
                     1.00 Conservative
                     2.00 Labour
                     3.00 Liberal Democrat

- -

Covariates
RAGE   Respondent's age in years   YY   Q33

- -

Model and Design Information

 Model: Poisson
Design: Constant + EDQUAL*CLSGRPS + CLSGRPS*MAJORS + CLSGRPS*RAGE + RSEX*CLSGRPS
        + EDQUAL*MAJORS + EDQUAL*RAGE + RSEX*EDQUAL + MAJORS*RAGE + RSEX*MAJORS
        + RSEX*RAGE

- -
                    GENERAL LOGLINEAR ANALYSIS
- -

Correspondence Between Parameters and Terms of the Design

Parameter   Aliased   Term

        1   Constant
        2   [EDQUAL = 1.00]*[CLSGRPS = 1.00]
        3   [EDQUAL = 1.00]*[CLSGRPS = 2.00]
        4   [EDQUAL = 1.00]*[CLSGRPS = 3.00]
        5   [EDQUAL = 2.00]*[CLSGRPS = 1.00]

⇑

Figure 9.9   (*continued*)

:

[The middle of this lengthy table has been abbreviated.]

:

⇓

```
61      x     [RSEX = 1]*[MAJORS = 3.00]
62      x     [RSEX = 2]*[MAJORS = 1.00]
63      x     [RSEX = 2]*[MAJORS = 2.00]
64      x     [RSEX = 2]*[MAJORS = 3.00]
65            [RSEX = 1]*RAGE
66      x     [RSEX = 2]*RAGE
```

```
Note: 'x' indicates an aliased (or a redundant) parameter.
      These parameters are set to zero.
```

- -

Convergence Information

```
Maximum number of iterations:           20
Relative difference tolerance:         .001
Final relative difference:      1.09700E-06
```

Maximum likelihood estimation converged at iteration 5.

- -
                    GENERAL LOGLINEAR ANALYSIS
- -

Table Information

Factor	Value	Observed Count	%	Expected Count	%
MAJORS	Conservative	30.64	(1.25)	21.35	(.87)
MAJORS	Labour	54.20	(2.22)	63.30	(2.59)
MAJORS	Liberal Democrat	17.51	(.72)	18.64	(.76)
CLSGRPS	Intermediates				
MAJORS	Conservative	2.19	(.09)	2.18	(.09)
MAJORS	Labour	3.83	(.16)	4.14	(.17)
MAJORS	Liberal Democrat	1.09	(.04)	.27	(.01)
CLSGRPS	Working class				
MAJORS	Conservative	.00	(.00)	.17	(.01)
MAJORS	Labour	2.19	(.09)	1.51	(.06)
MAJORS	Liberal Democrat	.00	(.00)	.08	(.00)
EDQUAL	A-level & 3rd level				
CLSGRPS	Service				
MAJORS	Conservative	99.89	(4.09)	100.43	(4.11)
MAJORS	Labour	89.17	(3.65)	89.31	(3.65)
MAJORS	Liberal Democrat	30.82	(1.26)	29.28	(1.20)

⇑

:

[The middle of this lengthy table has been abbreviated.]

:

⇓

Factor	Value	Observed Count	%	Expected Count	%
EDQUAL	No qualifcation				
CLSGRPS	Service				
MAJORS	Conservative	22.00	(.90)	20.66	(.85)
MAJORS	Labour	21.00	(.86)	19.28	(.79)
MAJORS	Liberal Democrat	3.00	(.12)	3.34	(.14)
CLSGRPS	Intermediates				
MAJORS	Conservative	59.00	(2.42)	57.92	(2.38)

Figure 9.9   (*continued*)

```
MAJORS              Labour     71.00 (  2.92)     75.95 (  3.12)
MAJORS   Liberal Democrat      16.00 (   .66)     17.09 (   .70)
CLSGRPS        Working class
MAJORS        Conservative     75.00 (  3.08)     69.55 (  2.86)
MAJORS              Labour    178.00 (  7.32)    183.65 (  7.55)
MAJORS   Liberal Democrat      28.00 (  1.15)     25.56 (  1.05)
```

- -

Table Information

			Adj.	Dev.
Factor	Value	Resid.	Resid.	Resid.
RSEX	Male			
EDQUAL	Degree			
CLSGRPS	Service			
MAJORS	Conservative	7.16	2.45	1.49
MAJORS	Labour	-9.02	-2.59	-1.16
MAJORS	Liberal Democrat	.13	.06	.03
CLSGRPS	Intermediates			
MAJORS	Conservative	-1.9E-03	-1.6E-03	-1.4E-03
MAJORS	Labour	.17	.13	.09
MAJORS	Liberal Democrat	.80	1.86	1.26
CLSGRPS	Working class			
MAJORS	Conservative	-.22	-.56	-.66
MAJORS	Labour	1.02	.87	.67
MAJORS	Liberal Democrat	-.04	-.21	-.29
EDQUAL A-level & 3rd level				
CLSGRPS	Service			
MAJORS	Conservative	6.27	1.42	.68
MAJORS	Labour	-3.18	-.67	-.34
MAJORS	Liberal Democrat	-1.37	-.41	-.25

[The middle of this lengthy table has been abbreviated.]

EDQUAL	No qualifcation			
CLSGRPS	Service			
MAJORS	Conservative	1.00	.32	.24
MAJORS	Labour	1.09	.39	.28
MAJORS	Liberal Democrat	-1.12	-.66	-.60
CLSGRPS	Intermediates			
MAJORS	Conservative	-.89	-.32	-.12
MAJORS	Labour	-1.00	-.23	-.12
MAJORS	Liberal Democrat	-1.00	-.35	-.28
CLSGRPS	Working class			
MAJORS	Conservative	5.54	1.42	.69
MAJORS	Labour	-6.29	-1.16	-.49
MAJORS	Liberal Democrat	2.65	.89	.55
```

- - - - - - - - - - - - - - - - - - - - - - - - - - - - - - - - - - - - -


Goodness-of-fit Statistics

|                  | Chi-Square | DF | Sig.  |
|------------------|------------|----|-------|
| Likelihood Ratio | 26.8469    | 31 | .6798 |
| Pearson          | 27.4796    | 31 | .6479 |
```

variables on the left-hand side and use the arrow button to insert it in the **Dependent** box. **rsex**, **edqual**, **clsgrps** and **majors** are inserted in the **Factor[s]** box.

Figure 9.10a   **Logit** main window

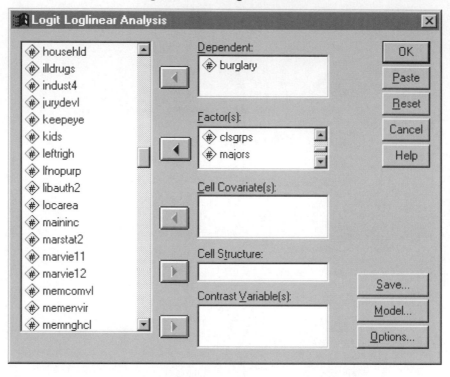

Then, you click on the **Model** button to set up the first model. When the subwindow in Figure 9.10b comes up, click the **Custom** button. Then, select **All 2-way** in the small pull-down list under **Build Terms**, highlight all four of the variables (**rsex**, **edqual**, **clsgrps** and **majors**) in the **Factors & Covariates** box on the left and click the right-hand **Build Terms** button to generate a model of all 2-way interaction of the 'causal' variables. Then, click **Continue**.

We decide to keep the output to a minimum since the purpose of this analysis is to compare the 'fit' of two models. To do this, you click on the **Options** button to bring up the **Options** sub-window (Figure 9.10c) and switch off the **Display** and **Plot** ticks. Press the **Continue** button in order to return to the main Logit window.

Once you return to the main window, you would click **OK** to run the first model. Its results appear in Figure 9.11.

You will now be familiar with the beginning of the output, which shows the numbers of cases in the analysis and the labelling of the variables included in the analysis.

The form of the model design is different. What a logit analysis does is model the interactions between the 'dependent' variable (here, **burglary**) and the 'independent' variables (here, **rsex**, **edqual**, **clsgrps** and **majors**). Since this Logit model is a 'causal' model of the effect of the four independent variables upon the dependent variable **burglary**, the only terms of interest are interactions between the **burglary** and the independent variables. All other interactions (which are those solely between the independent variables) are of no interest and, in effect, are allowed to take place without any limitations. For instance, if you had five independent variables, all of the logit analyses that you carried out would have (unseen)

Figure 9.10b **Logit Mode** with **majors** included

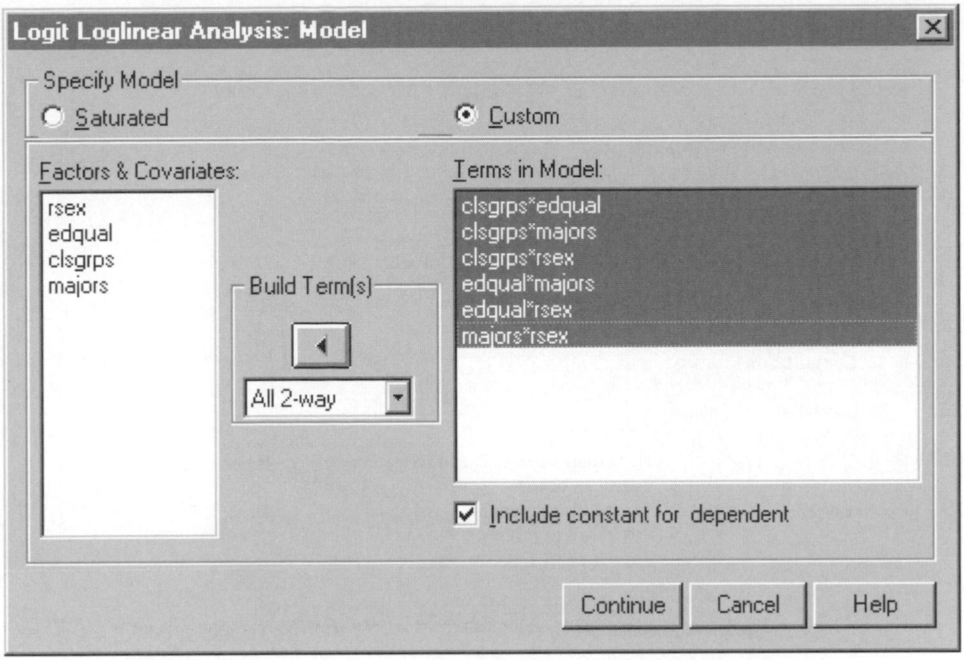

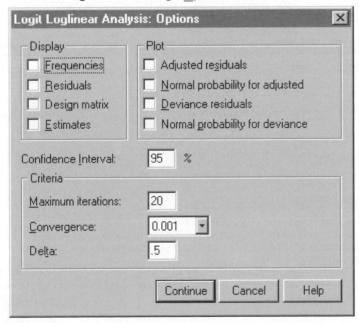

Figure 9.10c **Logit Options** subwindow

modellings of five-way interactions between the five independent variables – even if the interactions between the independent variables and the dependent variable were kept quite tightly restricted. You can see this in the **Design**, where all of the interactions shown include **burglary** (Figure 9.11).

Figure 9.11 Results for a **logit** analysis with **majors** *included*

- -
GENERAL LOGLINEAR ANALYSIS
- -

Data Information

```
    2393 cases are accepted.
     753 cases are rejected because of missing data.
 2412.79 weighted cases will be used in the analysis.
     288 cells are defined.
       0 structural zeros are imposed by design.
      50 sampling zeros are encountered.
```

- -

Variable Information

Factor	Levels	Value
BURGLARY	4	Incidence of burglary in this area Q142
		1 Very common
		2 Fairly common
		3 Not very common
		4 Not at all common
RSEX	2	Sex of respondent by observation Q32
		1 Male
		2 Female
EDQUAL	4	Recoded Ed qualification
		1.00 Degree
		2.00 A-level & 3rd level
		3.00 O-level & CSE
		4.00 No qualifcation
CLSGRPS	3	Class groupings
		1.00 Service
		2.00 Intermediates
		3.00 Working class
MAJORS	3	Main parties
		1.00 Conservative
		2.00 Labour
		3.00 Liberal Democrat

- -

Model and Design Information

```
 Model: Multinomial Logit
Design: Constant + BURGLARY + BURGLARY*EDQUAL*CLSGRPS + BURGLARY*CLSGRPS*MAJORS
        + BURGLARY*RSEX*CLSGRPS + BURGLARY*EDQUAL*MAJORS + BURGLARY*RSEX*EDQUAL
        + BURGLARY*RSEX*MAJORS
```

Note: There is a separate constant term for each combination of levels
      of the independent factors.

Figure 9.11   (*continued*)

- -
                    GENERAL LOGLINEAR ANALYSIS
- -

Correspondence Between Parameters and Terms of the Design

Parameter   Aliased   Term

        1   Constant for [RSEX = 1]*[EDQUAL = 1.00]*[CLSGRPS = 1.00]
                       *[MAJORS = 1.00]
        2   Constant for [RSEX = 1]*[EDQUAL = 1.00]*[CLSGRPS = 1.00]
                       *[MAJORS = 2.00]
        3   Constant for [RSEX = 1]*[EDQUAL = 1.00]*[CLSGRPS = 1.00]
                       *[MAJORS = 3.00]
        4   Constant for [RSEX = 1]*[EDQUAL = 1.00]*[CLSGRPS = 2.00]
                       *[MAJORS = 1.00]
        5   Constant for [RSEX = 1]*[EDQUAL = 1.00]*[CLSGRPS = 2.00]
                       *[MAJORS = 2.00]
        6   Constant for [RSEX = 1]*[EDQUAL = 1.00]*[CLSGRPS = 2.00]
                       *[MAJORS = 3.00]
        7   Constant for [RSEX = 1]*[EDQUAL = 1.00]*[CLSGRPS = 3.00]
                       *[MAJORS = 1.00]

                              :
       [The middle of this lengthy table has been abbreviated.]
                              :

      275   x   [BURGLARY = 2]*[RSEX = 2]*[MAJORS = 2.00]
      276   x   [BURGLARY = 2]*[RSEX = 2]*[MAJORS = 3.00]
      277   [BURGLARY = 3]*[RSEX = 1]*[MAJORS = 1.00]
      278   [BURGLARY = 3]*[RSEX = 1]*[MAJORS = 2.00]
      279   x   [BURGLARY = 3]*[RSEX = 1]*[MAJORS = 3.00]
      280   x   [BURGLARY = 3]*[RSEX = 2]*[MAJORS = 1.00]
      281   x   [BURGLARY = 3]*[RSEX = 2]*[MAJORS = 2.00]
      282   x   [BURGLARY = 3]*[RSEX = 2]*[MAJORS = 3.00]
      283   x   [BURGLARY = 4]*[RSEX = 1]*[MAJORS = 1.00]
      284   x   [BURGLARY = 4]*[RSEX = 1]*[MAJORS = 2.00]
      285   x   [BURGLARY = 4]*[RSEX = 1]*[MAJORS = 3.00]
      286   x   [BURGLARY = 4]*[RSEX = 2]*[MAJORS = 1.00]
      287   x   [BURGLARY = 4]*[RSEX = 2]*[MAJORS = 2.00]
      288   x   [BURGLARY = 4]*[RSEX = 2]*[MAJORS = 3.00]

Note: 'x' indicates an aliased (or a redundant) parameter.

     These parameters are set to zero.

- -

Convergence Information

Maximum number of iterations: 20
Relative difference tolerance: .001
Final relative difference: .0005

Maximum likelihood estimation converged at iteration 8.

Figure 9.11 (*continued*)

- -

GENERAL LOGLINEAR ANALYSIS

- -

Goodness-of-fit Statistics

	Chi-Square	DF	Sig.
Likelihood Ratio	136.8897	120	.1389
Pearson	134.4160	120	.1740

- -

Analysis of Dispersion

Source of Dispersion	Entropy	Concentration	DF
Due to Model	75.0004	28.4940	93
Due to Residual	2761.6750	1538.8947	7142
Total	2836.6754	1567.3887	7235

Measures of Association

```
      Entropy =   .0264
Concentration =   .0182
```

This first model with **majors** included gives a fairly satisfactory fit to the data (the significance of the Chi-Squares are 0.1389 and 0.1740, respectively).

The real question, however, is whether a model that excludes the effect of **majors** upon **burglary** will fit the data significantly worse. Let us look at how such a model would be constructed. After running the first model, you click on the **Model** button again in order to return to the Logit model subwindow. To produce a second model with the effects of **majors**

Figure 9.12 Logit Model with **majors** *excluded*

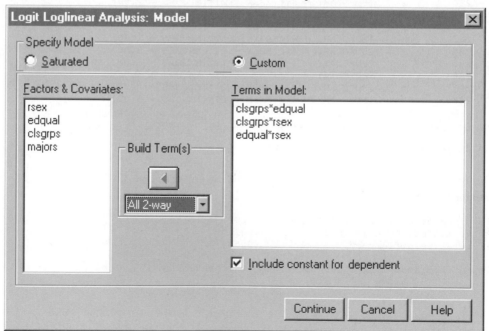

removed, you highlight the three interactions in the Logit model subwindow that include **majors** ('**clsgrps*majors**', '**edqual*majors**' and '**majors*rsex**') and click the *left-hand* pointing **Build Term[s]** button to remove them. The result is shown in Figure 9.12. You then return to the main Logit window and click on **OK** to run the second model.

(**Note** that it is important to construct the second, more restricted, model with **majors** excluded in this way, by *deleting* interaction terms from the original Logit model subwindow. If you were to attempt to do the equivalent by 'resetting' the Logit procedure and constructing a new Logit model from scratch by entering in only **rsex**, **edqual** and **clsgrps** (but not **majors**) as factors, the resulting Logit model would appear to be an equivalent, but would not be so. Leaving out **majors** altogether in that manner would mean that the people who do not identify with any of the three major political parties would be included in the second model (the number of cases would rise from 2393 to 2938 and the results would be substantially different). If effect, one would not be 'comparing like with like' and any differences between the two models could result solely from the inclusion of new cases in the second model.)

Once the two models have been run, they can be compared.

Most of the output from the second model will be almost identical to that of the first, so we will show only those portions which are significantly different.

First, note that the **Design** of the second model is considerably simpler since all of the terms that included **majors** are now absent (Figure 9.13).

(**Design**: **Constant + burglary + burglary*edqual*clsgrps + burglary*rsex*clsgrps + burglary*rsex*edqual**)

The second, simpler model with **majors** excluded actually produces a better fit to the data (the significance of the Chi-Squares are 0.2047 and 0.3530 respectively). So, we conclude that it is not necessary to know a person's party identification, only their gender, level of education and social class, in order to model their opinion about how common burglary is in their area.

Conclusion

As with most of the statistical procedures available in SPSS, more complex loglinear analyses are possible. For instance, it is possible to construct loglinear models in which the interactions in some cells are more likely than in other cells or to exclude cells from the analysis in which it is unlikely or impossible that anyone will be found.

What this module has done is give you an introduction to loglinear analysis with SPSS. Following its instructions, you should be able to carry out some basic multivariate analyses with categorical data, either:

- 'Disentangling' the complex interplay of associations between a collection of categorical variables, or
- Carrying out a simple causal analysis in which one categorical variable is seen as being potentially caused by some combination of a number of independent categorical variables.

Loglinear analysis exercises

- Try out some loglinear analyses for yourself.
  1. *Model selection.* Choose three or more categorical variable or ordinal variables that are made up of a small number of categories that you believe are related, one with the other.

Figure 9.13 Results for a **Logit** analysis with **majors** *excluded*

- -
GENERAL LOGLINEAR ANALYSIS
- -

[The first part of the table is identical to Figure 9.5]

Model and Design Information

 Model: Multinomial Logit
Design: Constant + BURGLARY + BURGLARY*EDQUAL*CLSGRPS + BURGLARY*RSEX*CLSGRPS
       + BURGLARY*RSEX*EDQUAL

Note: There is a separate constant term for each combination of levels
      of the independent factors.

- -
GENERAL LOGLINEAR ANALYSIS
- -

Correspondence Between Parameters and Terms of the Design

Parameter   Aliased   Term

        1   Constant for [RSEX = 1]*[EDQUAL = 1.00]*[CLSGRPS = 1.00]
                      *[MAJORS = 1.00]
        2   Constant for [RSEX = 1]*[EDQUAL = 1.00]*[CLSGRPS = 1.00]
                      *[MAJORS = 2.00]
        3   Constant for [RSEX = 1]*[EDQUAL = 1.00]*[CLSGRPS = 1.00]
                      *[MAJORS = 3.00]
        4   Constant for [RSEX = 1]*[EDQUAL = 1.00]*[CLSGRPS = 2.00]
                      *[MAJORS = 1.00]
        5   Constant for [RSEX = 1]*[EDQUAL = 1.00]*[CLSGRPS = 2.00]
                      *[MAJORS = 2.00]
        6   Constant for [RSEX = 1]*[EDQUAL = 1.00]*[CLSGRPS = 2.00]
                      *[MAJORS = 3.00]
        7   Constant for [RSEX = 1]*[EDQUAL = 1.00]*[CLSGRPS = 3.00]
                      *[MAJORS = 1.00]
        8   Constant for [RSEX = 1]*[EDQUAL = 1.00]*[CLSGRPS = 3.00]
                      *[MAJORS = 2.00]

⇑
:

[The middle of this lengthy table has been abbreviated.]

:
⇓

      169   x   [BURGLARY = 3]*[RSEX = 2]*[EDQUAL = 1.00]
      170   x   [BURGLARY = 3]*[RSEX = 2]*[EDQUAL = 2.00]
      171   x   [BURGLARY = 3]*[RSEX = 2]*[EDQUAL = 3.00]
      172   x   [BURGLARY = 3]*[RSEX = 2]*[EDQUAL = 4.00]
      173   x   [BURGLARY = 4]*[RSEX = 1]*[EDQUAL = 1.00]
      174   x   [BURGLARY = 4]*[RSEX = 1]*[EDQUAL = 2.00]
      175   x   [BURGLARY = 4]*[RSEX = 1]*[EDQUAL = 3.00]
      176   x   [BURGLARY = 4]*[RSEX = 1]*[EDQUAL = 4.00]
      177   x   [BURGLARY = 4]*[RSEX = 2]*[EDQUAL = 1.00]
      178   x   [BURGLARY = 4]*[RSEX = 2]*[EDQUAL = 2.00]
      179   x   [BURGLARY = 4]*[RSEX = 2]*[EDQUAL = 3.00]
      180   x   [BURGLARY = 4]*[RSEX = 2]*[EDQUAL = 4.00]

Note: 'x' indicates an aliased (or a redundant) parameter.
      These parameters are set to zero.

- -

Figure 9.11 (*continued*)

Convergence Information

Maximum number of iterations: 20
Relative difference tolerance: .001
Final relative difference: .0005

Maximum likelihood estimation converged at iteration 8.

- -
                    GENERAL LOGLINEAR ANALYSIS
- -

Goodness-of-fit Statistics

                  Chi-Square   DF   Sig.

Likelihood Ratio   176.6064   162   .2047
        Pearson   168.2044   162   .3530

- -

Analysis of Dispersion

Source of Dispersion   Entropy Concentration   DF

Due to Model   55.1420   20.3817   51
Due to Residual   2781.5334   1547.0070   7184
Total   2836.6754   1567.3887   7235

Measures of Association

    Entropy = .0194
Concentration = .0130

- -

    Carry out a 'model selection' loglinear analysis in order to establish the simplest set of associations between the variables that still gives close estimations of the true frequencies in each cell ('a good fit to the data').

2. *General.* Choose three or more categorical or ordinal variables that are made up of a small number of categories that you believe are related. Carry out two or more general loglinear analyses of these variables in which you set up at least two different models or descriptions of patterns of interrelationships that you believe may produce good descriptions of the data. Compare the results of the analyses to establish: (a) which of the models you have proposed produce good 'fits' to the data (some, none, or all of the models you test may fit the data well); (b) compare the results from each model to see which model (if any!) produced the best 'fit' to the data. You compare the models by: (i) seeing which model generates the 'P' value that indicates the best fit; (ii) if one model is a simpler set of relationships than another model, seeing whether the change in the rise in degrees of freedom when the simpler model is compared with the more complex model is greater than the rise in the value of Chi-square; (iii) if two models fit the data approximately equally well, choosing the model with the simpler set of interrelationships.

3. *'Logit'.* Select one categorical or ordinal variable that you believe may be affected by (or 'caused') by two or more other categorical or ordinal variables and carry out two or more probit loglinear analyses to see which is the simplest combination of 'causal' variables that can adequately model the distribution in the 'dependent' variable.

Hints:

- It is best to begin your experimentation with loglinear analysis by investigating simple or obvious relationships between a small number of variables. Try more complex models later on when you become more familiar with the technique.
- Do not expect the loglinear analysis technique to work miracles. A model with too many variables or two many empty cells will fail. Remember that the number of cells rises exponentially with each extra variable you add to a model. Similarly, a categorical variable with a large number of values greatly increases the complexity of model estimation. Keep the number of variables to a minimum and use **Recode** to combine categories in order to keep the number of categories in the variables that you include in your models at the minimum possible without losing significant information.

10 Multiple Response Sets

Introduction

Occasionally, the categorical responses to what is essentially a single question can be spread across a series of variables and the analyst may wish to combine these responses together. The British Social Attitudes data contains examples of these types of variables.

1. **Sets of 'dichotomous' variables**. A single basic question may be asked across a spread of categories with the answer for each category being either positive or negative (*YES/NO*). For instance, respondents to subsection C of the BSA survey were asked:
   'Here are a number of circumstances in which a woman might consider an abortion. Please say whether or not you think the law should allow an abortion in each case.
   a. *The woman decides on her own she does not wish to have the child*
   b. *The couple agree they do not wish to have the child*
   c. *The woman is not married and does not wish to marry the man*
   d. *The couple cannot afford any more children*
   e. *There is a strong chance of a defect in the baby*
   f. *The woman's health is seriously endangered by the pregnancy*
   g. *The woman became pregnant as a result of rape'*
   Respondents were to answer *YES* or *NO* to each subquestion. Seven variables result, **abort1** to **abort7**, which were coded '**1**' for 'Yes' and '**2**' for 'No'. These variables can each be analysed in their own right, such as in the seven **Frequencies** counts that appear in Figure 10.1a, but a researcher might wish to combine the responses across all seven items into a single item.

2. **Sets of categorical variables with each variable having a unique code.** A single basic question may be asked across a spread of categories with the answer for each category being given a unique code. For instance, respondents to the BSA Survey were asked:
   'Do you personally belong to any of the groups listed on this card?' Respondents were shown a card with a list of eleven organisations: The National Trust; the Royal Society for the Protection of Birds; Friends of the Earth; the World Wildlife Fund; Greenpeace; the Council for the Protection of Rural England, Scotland or Wales; Other wildlife or countryside protection groups; the Ramblers' Association; Other countryside sport or recreation groups; Urban conservation groups; the Campaign for Nuclear Disarmament. A person could be a member of one organisation, some combination of the organisations, or none. Twelve variables result, **club1** to **club12**, one for each of the eleven organisations plus a *'Belongs to none of these'* variable. Instead of dichotomous *YES/NO* codes, however, the variable for each organisation has a unique code for the 'presence' of that organisation. For example, as in shown in Figure 10.1b, respondents who said they were a member of the Royal Society for the Protection of Birds are coded as '*2*' in the variable **club2** and respondents who are members of CND are coded as '*11*' in the variable **club12**. While each variable can be analysed in its own right, again, the researcher might wish to combine the responses across all twelve **club** variables into a single item in order to see the aggregate pattern of membership.

Figure 10.1a Normal **Frequencies** counts of the seven abortion variables

ABORT1 Woman does not wish to have child C2.51a

		Frequency	Percent	Valid Percent	Cumulative Percent
Valid	1 Yes	484	15.4	56.7	56.7
	2 No	369	11.7	43.3	100.0
	Total	853	27.1	100.0	
Missing	-2 Skp,A+B versions	1657	52.7		
	-1 No self-completn	600	19.1		
	9 Not Answered	36	1.1		
	Total	2293	72.9		
Total		3146	100.0		

ABORT2 Couple agree they do not want chldC2.51b

		Frequency	Percent	Valid Percent	Cumulative Percent
Valid	1 Yes	536	17.0	63.2	63.2
	2 No	312	9.9	36.8	100.0
	Total	848	27.0	100.0	
Missing	-2 Skp,A+B versions	1657	52.7		
	-1 No self-completn	600	19.1		
	9 Not Answered	40	1.3		
	Total	2298	73.0		
Total		3146	100.0		

ABORT3 Woman is   not+doesn't want to marryC2.51c

		Frequency	Percent	Valid Percent	Cumulative Percent
Valid	1 Yes	454	14.4	53.6	53.6
	2 No	393	12.5	46.4	100.0
	Total	847	26.9	100.0	
Missing	-2 Skp,A+B versions	1657	52.7		
	-1 No self-completn	600	19.1		
	9 Not Answered	42	1.3		
	Total	2299	73.1		
Total		3146	100.0		

Figure 10.1a (*continued*)

ABORT4 Couple cannot afford more childrenC2.51d

		Frequency	Percent	Valid Percent	Cumulative Percent
Valid	1 Yes	500	15.9	59.1	59.1
	2 No	346	11.0	40.9	100.0
	Total	846	26.9	100.0	
Missing	-2 Skp,A+B versions	1657	52.7		
	-1 No self-completn	600	19.1		
	9 Not Answered	42	1.3		
	Total	2300	73.1		
Total		3146	100.0		

ABORT5 Strong chance of defect in baby   C2.51e

		Frequency	Percent	Valid Percent	Cumulative Percent
Valid	1 Yes	746	23.7	87.3	87.3
	2 No	108	3.4	12.7	100.0
	Total	854	27.2	100.0	
Missing	-2 Skp,A+B versions	1657	52.7		
	-1 No self-completn	600	19.1		
	9 Not Answered	34	1.1		
	Total	2292	72.8		
Total		3146	100.0		

ABORT6 Womans health   endangerd by pregncyC2.51f

		Frequency	Percent	Valid Percent	Cumulative Percent
Valid	1 Yes	814	25.9	94.6	94.6
	2 No	47	1.5	5.4	100.0
	Total	861	27.4	100.0	
Missing	-2 Skp,A+B versions	1657	52.7		
	-1 No self-completn	600	19.1		
	9 Not Answered	28	.9		
	Total	2285	72.6		
Total		3146	100.0		

Figure 10.1a (*continued*)

ABORT7 Woman pregnant as a result of rapeC2.51g

		Frequency	Percent	Valid Percent	Cumulative Percent
Valid	1 Yes	812	25.8	94.1	94.1
	2 No	50	1.6	5.9	100.0
	Total	862	27.4	100.0	
Missing	-2 Skp,A+B versions	1657	52.7		
	-1 No self-completn	600	19.1		
	9 Not Answered	26	.8		
	Total	2284	72.6		
Total		3146	100.0		

3. **Sets of categorical variables with a set of codes that is the same across all the variables**. Thirdly, a series of questions may all have the same set of potential response categories and the analyst may wish to combine the responses to all the questions. There are no suitable examples in the **Crime** dataset, but examples can be found in the **Politics** dataset; where, for instance, respondents were asked:

Figure 10.1b   Normal **Frequencies** counts of **club** variables

CLUB1 R belong to National Trust?   Q916

		Frequency	Percent	Valid Percent	Cumulative Percent
Valid	0	971	30.9	90.0	90.0
	1 National Trustm	95	3.0	8.8	98.8
	99	13	.4	1.2	100.0
	Total	1079	34.3	100.0	
Missing	-2	2067	65.7		
Total		3146	100.0		

CLUB2 R belong to R.S.P.B.?   Q917

		Frequency	Percent	Valid Percent	Cumulative Percent
Valid	0 No, not member	1017	32.3	94.2	94.2
	2 Yes, member	49	1.6	4.6	98.8
	99 Not answered	13	.4	1.2	100.0
	Total	1079	34.3	100.0	
Missing	-2 Skp,A+B versions	2067	65.7		
Total		3146	100.0		

Figure 10.1b (*continued*)

CLUB12 R belong to Campaign nuclear disarm.Q926

		Frequency	Percent	Valid Percent	Cumulative Percent
Valid	0 No, not member	1059	33.7	98.2	98.2
	11 Yes, member	7	.2	.6	98.8
	99 Not answered	13	.4	1.2	100.0
	Total	1079	34.3	100.0	
Missing	-2 Skp,A+B versions	2067	65.7		
Total		3146	100.0		

'Looking at the list below, please tick the box next to the one thing you think should be Britain's highest priority, the most important thing it should do.'
The respondents were shown a list with four options: '1) Maintain order in the nation; 2) Give people more say in government decisions; 3) Fight rising prices; 4) Protect freedom of speech.'
Then, they were asked . . .
'And which one do you think should be Britain's next highest priority, the second most important thing it should do?'
. . . with the same choice of options.

Normal Frequencies counts of the two resulting variables, **bprior1** and **bprior2**, are shown in Figure 10.1c. Instead of knowing whether an option was mentioned as most important or

Figure 10.1c Normal **Frequencies** counts of **brprior1** and **brprior2**

BRPRIOR1 1st priority Britain   shd do?A2.30Ab2.68a

		Frequency	Percent	Valid Percent	Cumulative Percent
Valid	1 Maintain order	634	20.1	39.0	39.0
	2 Ppl>say govt decisions	445	14.2	27.4	66.3
	3 Fight rising prices	192	6.1	11.8	78.1
	4 Protect speech freedom	156	5.0	9.6	87.7
	8 Can't choose	200	6.3	12.3	100.0
	Total	1627	51.7	100.0	
Missing	-2 Skp, C version	889	28.2		
	-1 No self-completn	600	19.1		
	9 Not answered	30	1.0		
	Total	1519	48.3		
Total		3146	100.0		

Figure 10.1c   (*continued*)

BRPRIOR2 2nd priority Britain   shd do?A2.30bB2.68 b

		Frequency	Percent	Valid Percent	Cumulative Percent
Valid	1 Maintain order	336	10.7	20.8	20.8
	2 Ppl>say govt decisions	360	11.4	22.2	43.0
	3 Fight rising prices	401	12.7	24.7	67.7
	4 Protect speech freedom	281	8.9	17.3	85.1
	8 Can't choose	242	7.7	14.9	100.0
	Total	1620	51.5	100.0	
Missing	-2 Skp, C version	889	28.2		
	-1 No self-completn	600	19.1		
	9 Not answered	37	1.2		
	Total	1526	48.5		
Total		3146	100.0		

second most important, however, an analyst may want to find out how often respondents simply mentioned the options as important.

Each of these situations is basically the same, in each instance the analyst has a range of variables that are all codings of a single basic question, and in each instance the analyst may wish to combine the responses across the range of variables. SPSS has a procedure, **Multiple Response,** that caters for this specific problem.

Using Multiple Response

Multiple Response is a procedure for combining the responses across a range of related variables and then displaying the result in the format of a frequency distribution and/or a crosstabulation table.

Multiple Response is selected by going to the **Analyze** menu, choosing **Multiple Response** and then **Define Sets** ... A **Define Multiple Response Sets** window will open up (Figure 10.3a).

The analyst must define the variables that will go into making up a 'multiple response set'. The set of variables can be either a group of dichotomous variables or a group of variables with a range of categories for codes. First, we will look at an example of a multiple response set that is defined by dichotomous variables.

Creating a multiple response set from a group of dichotomous variables

Figure 10.3a shows how this is done. Here, the seven variables that resulted from the abortion question are used to create a multiple response set called **$mrabort**. This is done by selecting the variables **abort1** to **abort7** from the list of variables in the **Set definition** column on the left-hand side of the window and bringing them into the **Variables in Set** box in the centre of

Figure 10.2 Selecting **Multiple Response** from the **A**nalyze menu

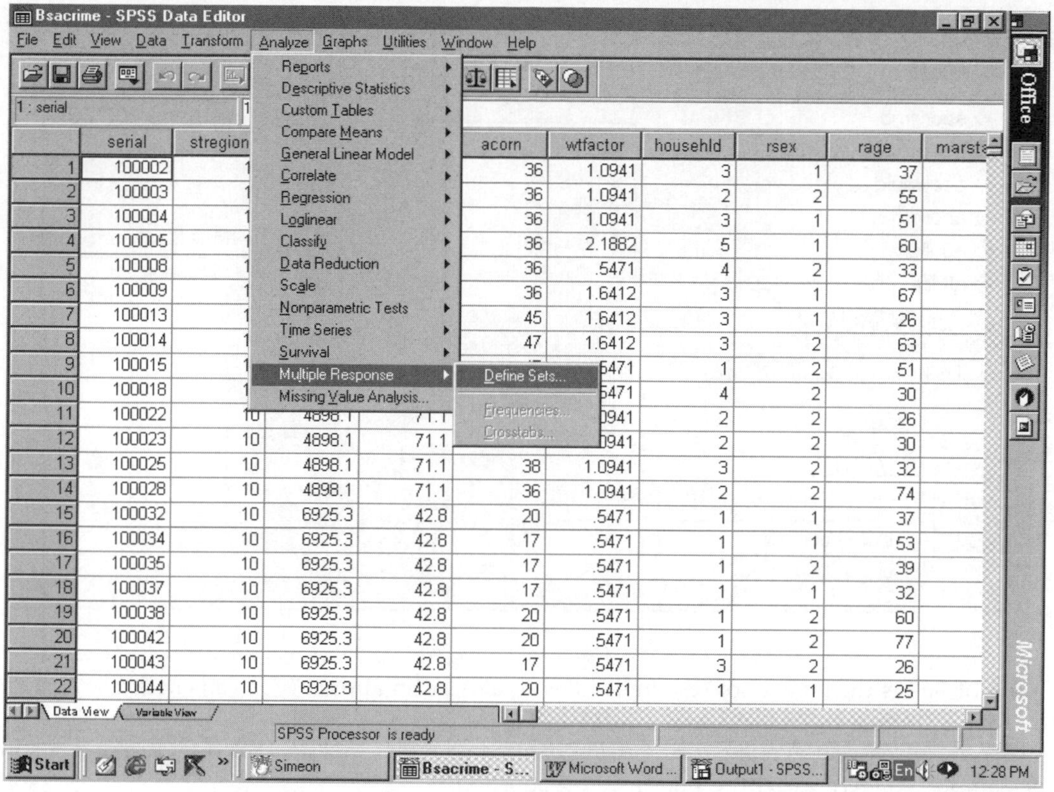

the window. SPSS has to be told which value to count as the dichotomous variable. This is done by ticking the **Dichotomies** option and entering in '**2**' as the **Counted value**. 'mrabort' is typed into the **N**ame box and the multiple response set is given the **Label** '*Against abortion if*'. Then, when the **A**dd button is clicked, **$mrabort** appears in the **Mult Response Sets** box on the right-hand side of the window. (The names of multiple response sets always have a '**$**' inserted at the beginning of their name.)

(**Note** that by choosing '**2**' (*NO*) as the counted value, we are counting responses where the respondent said abortion should *not* be legal and are creating an 'anti-abortion' multiple response set. Choosing '**1**' (*YES*) as the counted value, would have produced the mirror image, a 'pro-abortion' multiple response set.)

The resulting multiple response set can be seen at the top of Figure 10.3b, the frequency count for **$mrabort**. (Instructions on how to use SPSS to produce multiple response sets and then how to generate frequency tabulations and crosstabulations of them are given in the sections below.)

Since the frequency counts of multiple response sets are not based upon a single variable, interpreting them requires some care. In Figure 10.3, the name of the dichotomous multiple response set is given as **$mrabort** with the label '*Against abortion if*' and SPSS reminds us that the value tabulated to produce **$mrabort** was '**2**'.

For a multiple response set created from a group of dichotomous variables, the 'value labels' come from the variable label and name given to each variable that makes up the multiple response set. For instance, going across the first row of the table, the '**Dichotomy label**' is '*Woman does not wish to have child C2.51a*', which is the value label of the variable **abort1**. The

Figure 10.3a   Define Multiple Response Sets window for a group of dichotomous variables

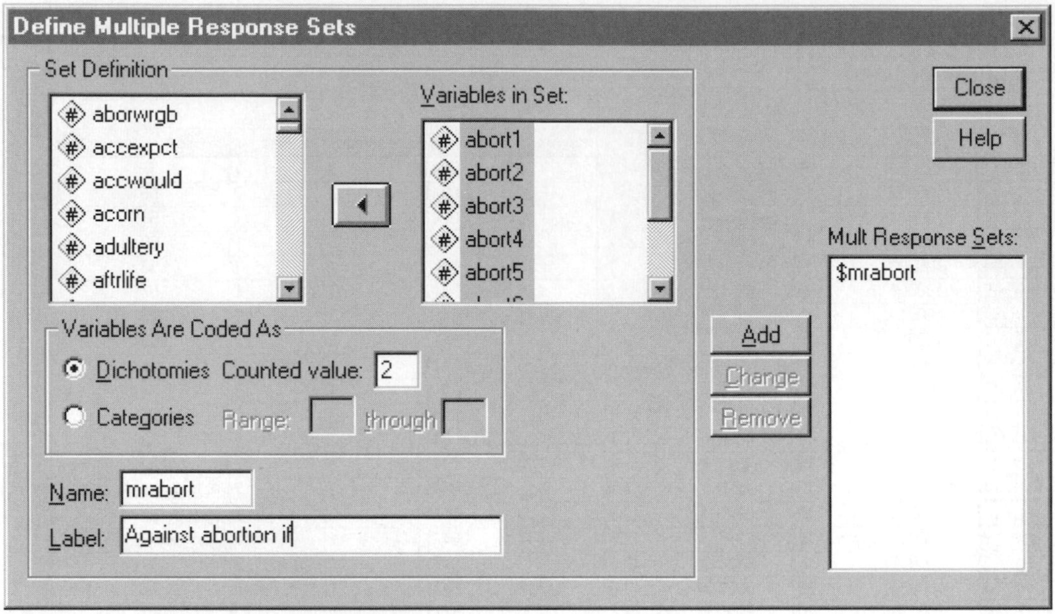

Count of 369 is the number of respondents who said '*No*' in **abort1** (you can check this against the simple frequency tabulation of **abort1** in Figure 10.1a).

(The main reason the number of missing cases is so high (2637) is that only respondents in sub-sample 'C' were asked the questions on abortion.)

The count column sums to 1626. This figure does not refer to individual cases but instead to the number of '*No*' responses that respondents gave to the variables **abort1** through **abort7**. Some respondents could have said '*No*' to all seven questions and have been 'counted' seven times, others could have said '*No*' to only one question and only have been 'counted' once, with the rest of the individual respondents falling somewhere in between, depending upon the number of '*No*' answers they gave. (In fact, quite a substantial number of respondents have

Figure 10.3b   Frequency count for a dichotomous response set (**$mrabort**)

```
Group $MRABORT  Against abortion if
     (Value tabulated = 2)


                                                      Pct of  Pct of
Dichotomy label                        Name   Count  Responses  Cases

Woman does not wish to have child C2.51a ABORT1  369    22.7    72.5
Couple agree they do not want chldC2.51b ABORT2  312    19.2    61.4
Woman is not+doesn't want to marryC2.51c ABORT3  393    24.2    77.2
Couple cannot afford more childrenC2.51d ABORT4  346    21.3    67.9
Strong chance of defect in baby   C2.51e ABORT5  108     6.7    21.3
Womans health endangerd by pregncyC2.51f ABORT6   47     2.9     9.2
Woman pregnant as a result of rapeC2.51g ABORT7   50     3.1     9.9
                                                ------- -----  -----
                             Total responses    1626   100.0   319.4

2,637 missing cases;   509 valid cases
```

given only 'Yes' answers and hence will not be included at all in the construction of **$mrabort**.) It is important to remember that the numbers in any tabulation or crosstabulation of a multiple response set can refer to the number of responses that fit the definition of the set rather than the number of cases.

The second column, 'Pct of responses', sums to 100.0 and is the percentage of responses coming from each variable that makes up the multiple response set. For example, the 369 'No' responses to **abort1** make up 22.7 per cent of the 1,626 responses.

Finally, the third column, 'Pct of cases', is the percentage of 'valid cases' that can be found in each variable that makes up the multiple responses set. The 369 cases that responded 'No' to **abort1** are 72.5 per cent of the 509 valid cases for **$mrabort**. Since quite a lot of cases had respondents who answered 'No' to more than one question, the number of responses is considerably higher than the number of valid cases. This is the reason that the sum of the 'Pct of cases' column adds to 319.4 per cent instead of 100.0 per cent.

Creating a multiple response set from a group of categorical variables

Multiple response sets can also be based upon a group of categorical variables. Figure 10.4a shows how this is done. Here, the twelve **club** variables are used to create a multiple response set called **$mrclubs**. As before, the variables **club1** to **club12** are selected from the **Set definition** column and brought into the centre **Variables in Set** box. The **Categories** option is ticked and SPSS is told the range of values to include in the multiple response set. (In this example, the range is 1 to 97; this includes the codes 1 to 11 for the eleven organisations plus a code '97' which was entered for respondents who did not belong to any of the eleven named organisations.) The name of the multiple response set is **$mrclubs**, which appears once the **Add** button is clicked (Figure 10.4b)

The resulting multiple response set can be seen in the top of Figure 10.4c, the frequency count for **$mrclubs**. What SPSS has done is look across the responses to the variables **club1** to

Figure 10.4a   Define Multiple Response Sets window for a group of category variables, each with a unique code

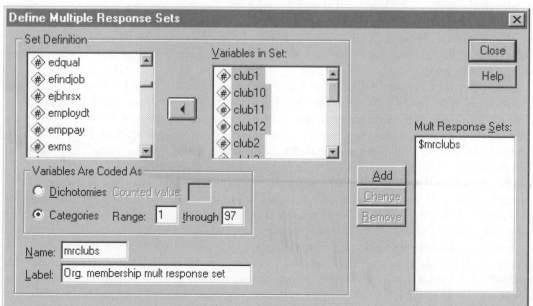

Figure 10.4b   Define Multiple Response Sets window for a range of category variables, each with the same code

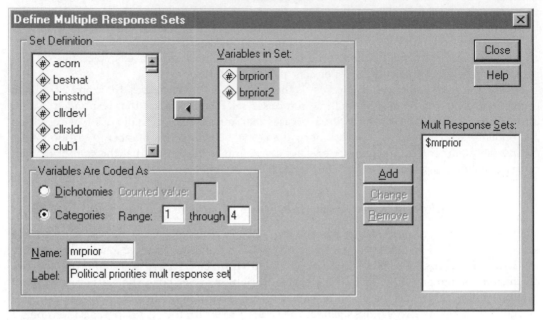

club12, including all the values in the range from 1 to 97 that it finds in the twelve variables and summarising all the responses it finds in **$mrclubs**. The frequency count for a multiple response set created from categorical variables more resembles a 'traditional' frequency count since each row in the table is based upon one value in the range of allowed values. In this example, since each variable only has one of the values in the range, an exact correspondence can be seen between the values and counts in the multiple response set and the values and counts of the individual variables that make up the set. For instance, row 1 is the 95 members of the National Trust and this corresponds with the 95 respondents coded as '**1 – belonging to the National Trust**' in **club1**, row 2 is the 49 members of the Royal Society for the Protection of Birds, which corresponds with the 49 respondents coded as '**2 – Yes a member of the RSPB**' and so on.

SPSS takes its **Category labels** from the value labels used in the first variable that defines the multiple response set. Hence, you must take care that the first variable has value labels defined for *all* values that will appear in the multiple response set, *even if some of these values are not present in this first variable*. (For instance, for the multiple response set **$mrclubs** to be fully labelled, we had to give the variable **club1** value labels for all twelve values that make up **$mrclubs** even though, in **club1**'s simple frequency tabulation, only code '**1**' is present.)

The 'Pct of responses' and 'Pct of cases' columns have the same meanings as before. In this example, since only a small number of valid cases have more than one value across the range of the **club** variables, the total number of responses (1154) is not much greater than the number of valid cases (1066) and the 'Pct of cases' column sums to only 108.2.

A second example of creating a multiple response set from categorical variables is shown in Figure 10.4b. In this instance, the categorical variables used to create the multiple response set, **bprior1** and **bprior2**, have the same range of values, from **1** to **4** (as can be seen in their frequency counts in Figure 10.1c). The multiple response set, *$mrprior*, adds together the responses across the individual variables.

The bottom frequency count in Figure 10.4c shows the result. *$mrprior* gives the combined distribution of answers that respondents gave when they were asked what should be Britain's most important and second most important priorities. This application of **Multiple Response** can be particularly useful when the goal is to discover the aggregate pattern of responses across a wide range of values over a large number of variables.

Figure 10.4c   Frequency counts for categorical multiple response sets (**$mrclubs** and **$mrprior**)

```
Group $MRCLUBS   Org. membership multiple resp set


                                                     Pct of   Pct of
Category label                        Code   Count  Responses  Cases

National Trustm                         1      95     8.2       8.9
RSPB                                    2      49     4.3       4.6
Friends of the Earth                    3      11     1.0       1.0
World Wildlife Fund                     4      38     3.3       3.5
Greenpeace                              5      15     1.3       1.4
Council Protection Rural                6       3      .3        .3
Other wildlife protection organisation  7      26     2.3       2.5
Rambler's Association                   8      11     1.0       1.1
Countryside sports & leisure            9      24     2.1       2.3
Urban conservation group               10       6      .5        .6
Campaign for Nuclear Disarmament       11       7      .6        .6
Belong to none                         97     867    75.2      81.4
                                            -------  -----     -----
                      Total responses        1154   100.0     108.2

2,080 missing cases;   1,066 valid cases
```

```
Group $MRPRIOR   Political priorities mult response set


                                                     Pct of   Pct of
Category label                        Code   Count  Responses  Cases

Maintain order                          1     970    34.6      66.9
Ppl>say govt decisions                  2     806    28.7      55.6
Fight rising prices                     3     592    21.1      40.9
Protect speech freedom                  4     437    15.6      30.2
                                            -------  -----     -----
                      Total responses        2805   100.0     193.5

1,697 missing cases;   1,450 valid cases
```

Tabulating and crosstabulating multiple response sets

Once multiple response sets have been created, they can be viewed through tabulations or crosstabulations.

Tabulations

The window for obtaining frequency counts of multiple response variables, is assessed by clicking on **Frequencies** ... on the **Multiple Response** procedure and a window like Figure 10.5 comes up. **Mult response** sets that already have been defined will appear in the left-hand box and are brought into the **Table[s] for:** box. Clicking on **OK** will then produce frequency counts like those in Figure 10.3b and 10.4c. The interpretation of these frequency counts already has been discussed at some length above.

Figure 10.5 Window for obtaining a frequency count of Multiple Response variables

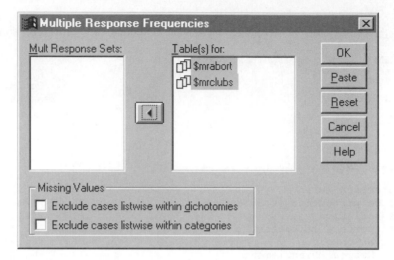

Crosstabulations

Multiple response sets also can be viewed in crosstabulations. The **Crosstabs** window is assessed by clicking on **Crosstabs** ... on the **Multiple Responses** procedure. A main window like that in Figure 10.6a will appear.

The multiple response sets and variables that will be used to make up the tables are defined in the same manner as for a normal **Crosstabs** table. Multiple response sets can be used to

Figure 10.6a **Multiple Response Crosstabs** window

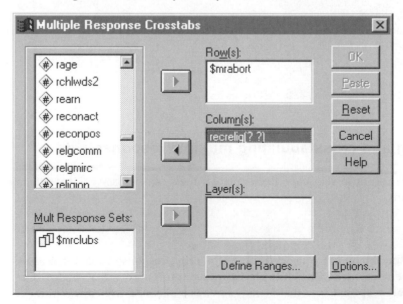

define the rows, columns and/or layers of the crosstabulation table. Any combination of multiple response sets and 'normal' variables are allowed (subject to the usual considerations of good table design). In the example here, the rows will be defined by the multiple response set **$mrabort**. In order to keep the example simple, no layers will be used and the columns will be defined by a 'normal' variable, **recrelig**, a recoding of religion into two categories: (1) 'Catholic' and (2) 'All others'.

The range of values that the 'normal' variable **recrelig** can take needs to be defined by clicking on the 'Define Ranges' button, bringing up the **Define Variable** subwindow and putting in '**1**' as the **Mi̲nimum** and '**2**' as the **Ma̲ximum** (Figure 10.6b).

Figure 10.6b   Multiple Response Crosstabs: Define Variable subwindow

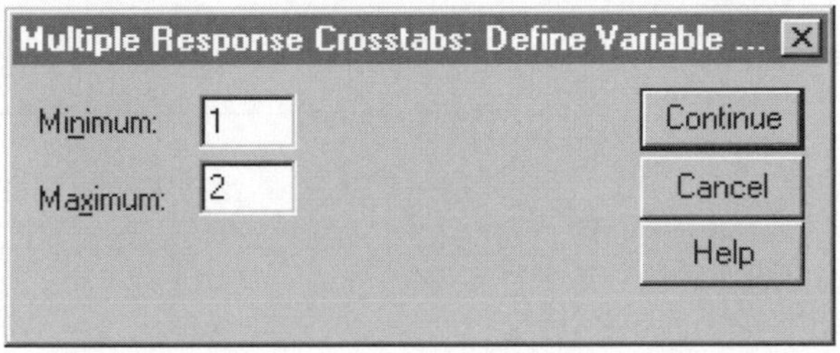

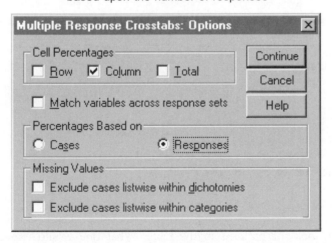

Clicking on the **Options** ... button brings up the subwindow in Figure 10.6c. Here, column percentages are chosen and the percentages will be based upon *responses* rather than cases.

Figure 10.6c   Multiple Response Crosstabs: Options subwindow with column percentages based upon the number of responses

To run the procedure, click on **OK**. Figure 10.7 is the result. The table has the same appearance as a 'normal' crosstabulation table, but there is an important difference. Since the crosstabulation is of a multiple response set, the numbers upon which the cell frequencies and percentages are based have only an oblique relation to the number of cases. A respondent can be counted up to seven times in the table depending upon the number of times they answered '*NO*' to the abortion questions (and respondents who did not answer '*NO*' to any of the questions will not appear in the table at all or even be counted as one of the valid cases).

Figure 10.7 Crosstabulation of a multiple response set (**mrabort**) by a categorical variable (**recrelig**), column percentages with percentages and totals based upon the number of responses

* * * C R O S S T A B U L A T I O N * * *

$MRABORT (tabulating 2) Against abortion if by RECRELIG Catholic or not

		RECRELIG		
	Count	Catholic	All others	
	Col pct			Row
				Total
		1	2	
SMRABORT				
ABORT1 Woman does not wish		37 17.9	332 23.4	369 22.7
ABORT2 Couple agree they do		38 18.2	275 19.4	312 19.2
ABORT3 Woman is not+doesn't		39 19.0	354 24.9	393 24.2
ABORT4 Couple cannot afford		41 19.8	305 21.5	346 21.3
ABORT5 Strong chance of def		24 11.6	84 5.9	108 6.7
ABORT6 Womans health endang		13 6.1	34 2.4	47 2.9
ABORT7 Woman preganant as a		15 7.4	35 2.5	50 3.1
	Column Total	207 12.7	1419 87.3	1626 100.0

Percents and totals based on responses

509 valid cases; 2,637 missing cases

That said, one can look for patterns in the table. What one would expect to find is that proportionately more Catholics will be against abortion in the more drastic situations — **abort5**, **abort6** and **abort7**. This is in fact the pattern that can be observed: 11.6 per cent of the 'Catholic' 'NO' responses are to making abortion legal even if there is the strong chance of a deformity in the baby, compared to only 5.9 per cent of the 'NO' responses of the others (and 6.7 per cent of the whole set of responses); 6.1 per cent of 'Catholic' 'NO' responses are to allowing abortion when the woman's health is endangered by the pregnancy, compared to only 2.4 per cent of the others; and 7.4 per cent of the Catholic 'NO' responses are against abortion even when the woman is pregnant as a result of rape, compared to 2.5 per cent of the others.

There is scope for altering the format of the table. Percentages can be based upon the number of *cases* instead of upon the number of *responses* and, as with 'normal' crosstabulation tables, percentages can be based upon columns, rows, or the total numbers in the table. Figure 10.8 requests a **mrabort** by **recrelig** crosstabulation table, only with row percentages which are based upon the number of cases in the table rather than the number of responses.

Figure 10.8 Multiple Response Crosstabs: **Option** subwindow with row percentages based upon the number of cases

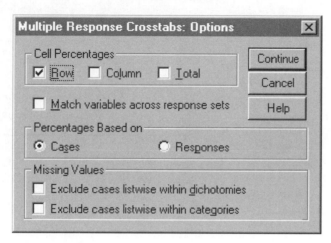

The result appears in Figure 10.9. The same pattern as before is visible, only displayed differently. Catholics make up 10.7 per cent of the respondents, or cases. The number of Catholics who gave 'NO' answers to the 'less drastic' situations in which a woman might seek an abortion are roughly equivalent to their representation in the number of cases. For the latter three instances, **abort5**, **abort5** and **abort7**, however, two to three times more Catholics gave 'NO' answers than would be expected from their overall representation in the table (22.2 per cent, 27.0 per cent and 30.4 per cent, respectively, compared to the 10.7 per cent of the number of cases that are Catholic in the table).

Summary

Using multiple response sets can be an effective way of seeking patterns in data in situations such as the above in which a series of variables all are responses to essentially a single question and the analyst wishes to combine the responses together in order to display their pattern. The multiple response procedure, however, does not provide facilities for hypothesis-testing based upon probability statistics. For instance, neither the Chi-square test nor other 'goodness-of-fit' statistics are available with the crosstabulation facility for multiple response sets, cell residuals cannot be calculated and the frequencies facility does not provide either measures of central tendency such as the mean or median or measures of dispersion such as standard deviation. Percentages are the closest that multiple response comes to statistical analysis.

The reasons for this stem from the basic premise that underlies probability-based statistical testing and the nature of the data that make up a multiple response set. All probability statistics

Figure 10.9 Crosstabulation of a multiple response set (**mrabort**) by a categorical variable (**recrelig**), row percentages with percentages and totals based on the number of cases

* * * CROSSTABULATION * * *

$MRABORT (tabulating 2) Against abortion if by RECRELIG Catholic or not

		RECRELIG		
Count Row pct		Catholic 1	All others 2	Row Total
SMRABORT				
ABORT1 Woman does not wish		37 10.1	332 89.9	369 72.5
ABORT2 Couple agree they do		38 12.1	275 87.9	312 61.4
ABORT3 Woman is not+doesn't		39 10.0	354 90.0	393 77.2
ABORT4 Couple cannot afford		41 11.8	305 88.2	346 67.9
ABORT5 Strong chance of def		24 22.2	84 77.8	108 21.3
ABORT6 Womans health endang		13 27.0	34 73.0	47 9.2
ABORT7 Woman preganant as a		15 30.4	35 69.6	50 9.9
Column Total		55 10.7	454 87.3	509 100.0

Percents and totals based on responses

509 valid cases; 2,637 missing cases

are designed to test whether a pattern observed in a sample of data accurately reflects the true pattern that would be observed if the researcher had access to complete information for the whole population. Since the number of responses that each case contributes to the construction of a multiple response set varies unpredictably (from zero responses up to the maximum possible), reliable generalisation from a multiple response set to a whole population is not possible. The basic premise of probability-based statistical testing does not hold for multiple response sets; hence, statistical testing cannot be valid. The multiple response procedure is basically a tool for data exploration.

Multiple Response Set exercises

1. Create a Multiple Response Set variable that is based upon a group of dichotomous variables. (Groups of variables suitable for this type of multiple response set are rare in the BSA data. Some groups of variables that are appropriate (aside from the abortion questions used in our examples) are: (a) the set of variables to do with membership in various types of community group (these all begin with the letters '*mem*' and (b) the sets of variables in the **Politics** dataset that relate to types of 'political' activism that the respondent may have been involved in (these variables all begin with either the letters '*do*' or the letters '*devt*'.))

2. Create a Multiple Response Set variable that is based upon a group of categorical variables in which each variable has a different code. (Group of variables suitable for this type of multiple response set are rare in the BSA data. A group that is appropriate (aside from the types of club membership used in our examples) is the set of variables in the **Politics** dataset that relate to things that the respondents may have done with regard to 'countryside' issues. These are the variables **ctrydon1** to **ctrydon8** (but note that **ctrydon7** and **ctrydon8** will need to be recoded before use because their codes are the same as those for **ctrydon1** and **ctrydon2**).)

3. Create a Multiple Response Set variable that is based upon a group of categorical variables in which each variable has the same code. (There are many such groups in the BSA data; for example, most of the batteries of attitudes questions. The difficulty here will be deciding upon a group for which it will be sensible to combine the responses into a multiple response variable.)

4. Produce frequency tabulations for the multiple response variables you have created. Note that two different frequency percentages are produced: one based on the percentage of *cases* and another based on the percentage of *responses*.

5. Generate crosstabulation tables using the multiple response variables you have created. You can crosstabulate the multiple response variables with each other or with a 'normal' variable. First, generate the tables requesting percentages based upon **cases**. Second, generate the same tables, only requesting that the percentages be based upon **responses**. Note that the percentages in the two tables will not be the same, and consider why they differ.

'Geometric' coding

The multiple response procedure can be a valuable tool for exploratory analysis where the researcher wishes to combine together responses across a range of variables but it does have some weaknesses. First, as noted above, multiple response sets cannot be used in a *confirmatory statistical analysis*. Second, sometimes the main reason a researcher wants to combine the responses across a range of variables together is to see which responses group together. Multiple response allows us to discover the gross numbers of responses to each category, but it cannot tell us whether linkages exist between the responses so that certain categories tend to fall together.

'Geometric coding' is a way of coding data that results in a single variable that displays the combinations of categorical responses to a question. This variable is amenable to confirmatory statistical analysis.

An example of 'geometric' coding

The British Social Attitudes datasets do not contain any examples of geometric coding, but the abortion questions can be adapted to show how the approach works. As explained above, respondents were asked whether abortion should be legal or illegal in seven types of circumstance. The example of **Multiple Response** that used the seven abortion variables demonstrated how the gross number of responses across the seven variables could be aggregated together into a single response set. When the resulting response set, **mrabort**, is displayed, the pattern of results suggests that there is a split between the response to the first four abortion questions which relate generally to 'abortion on demand' owing to relatively mild social or financial factors and the latter three abortion questions where the circumstances are more drastic (severe deformity, health danger, rape). With multiple response, however, it is not possible to examine directly whether the categories of response actually do 'hang together' in groups.

It is possible to code the responses to the seven abortion circumstances under a single 'geometric variable' which we will call **geoabort**. The seven circumstances in which a respondent might feel abortion should be illegal are given the values: **1**; **2**; **4**; **8**; **16**; **32**; **64**. This is a 'geometric progression', each value is a doubling of the previous value. But the value is not the code. To arrive at the coding of the variable **geoabort** for a respondent, the coder adds together the values of all the circumstances for which a respondent said abortion should be illegal. The *sum of the values* is the code of the variable **geoabort**. Each combination of circumstances will produce a unique sum that cannot come from any other combination. For example:

- If a respondent does not think abortion should be illegal in any of the seven circumstances, **geoabort** is coded as zero ('**0**').
- If a respondent believes abortion should be illegal if a woman does not wish to have a child, *but does not believe that abortion should be illegal in any of the other six circumstances*, **geoabort** is coded as one ('**1**').
- If a respondent believes abortion should be illegal if the couple agree they do not want a child, *but does not believe that abortion should be illegal in any of the other six circumstances*, **geoabort** is coded as two ('**2**').
- If a respondent believes abortion should be illegal if a woman does not wish to have a child *and also* that abortion should be illegal if the couple agree they do want a child, *but does not believe that abortion should be illegal in any of the other five circumstances*, **geoabort** is coded as **3** ('**3 = 1 + 2**'). There is no other combination of responses that can produce the code '**3**'.
- The coder follows that protocol for each respondent, adding together the values for the circumstances that a respondent thinks abortion should be illegal.

Figure 10.10, 'Frequency output for a "geometric variable", **geoabort**', shows the result when the resulting geometric code for the 846 respondents who answered all the abortion questions is tabulated. The combination of values that produced each unique code is given in the table. You may want to examine these.

344 respondents, 40.6 per cent of the 846 cases, have a code of '**0**'; that is, they said that abortion should be legal in all seven types of circumstances. 25 respondents, 2.9 per cent, said that abortion should be illegal only in the circumstance that a woman does not want a child (that is, **geoabort** is coded '**1**'). 19 respondents, 2.3 per cent, said that abortion should be illegal if a woman does not want a child *and* when the couple agrees they do not want the child (**geoabort** coded '**3**'). The most common code for a combination of categories is '**15**' (**1 + 2 + 4 + 8**): 139 respondents, 16.4 per cent of all respondents. This is the code produced by a combination of the four types of circumstances that are the relatively 'mild' social and financial reasons. Hence, the impression that the social and financial circumstances fall into a block appears to be confirmed.

Figure 10.10 Frequency output for a 'geometric' variable **geoabort** geoabort Abortion not allowed if

geobart Abortion not allowed if

	Frequency	Percent	Valid Percent	Cumulative Percent
.00 Legal in all 7 instances	344	40.6	40.6	40.6
1.00 Woman doesn't want child	25	2.9	2.9	43.5
2.00 Couple doesn't want child	4	.5	.5	44.0
3.00 1 + 2	19	2.3	2.3	46.3
4.00 Woman is single	29	3.4	3.4	49.7
5.00 1 + 4	23	2.7	2.7	52.4
6.00 2 + 4	9	1.0	1.0	53.4
7.00 3 + 4	28	3.3	3.3	56.7
8.00 Couple can't afford more children	16	1.9	1.9	58.6
9.00 1 + 8	8	1.0	1.0	59.6
10.00 2 + 8	5	.6	.6	60.2
11.00 3 + 8	7	.8	.8	61.1
12.00 4 + 8	31	3.7	3.7	64.8
13.00 1 + 4 + 8	22	2.6	2.6	67.3
14.00 2 + 4 + 8	11	1.4	1.4	68.7
15.00 1 + 2 + 4 + 8	139	16.4	16.4	85.1
16.00 Defect in baby	8	.9	.9	86.0
17.00 1 + 16	1	.1	.1	86.2
18.00 2 + 16	2	.2	.2	86.3
19.00 3 + 16	2	.2	.2	86.5
20.00 4 + 16	1	.1	.1	86.6
21.00 1 + 4 + 16	2	.2	.2	86.8
24.00 8 + 16	9	1.0	1.0	87.8
25.00 1 + 8 + 16	2	.2	.2	88.0
28.00 4 + 8 + 16	4	.5	.5	88.5
29.00 1 + 4 + 8 + 16	2	.3	.3	88.7
30.00 2 + 4 + 8 + 16	2	.2	.2	88.9
31.00 1 + 2 + 3 + 4 + 8 + 16	29	3.4	3.4	92.4
43.00 1 + 2 + 8 + 32 (Health endangered)	1	.1	.1	92.5
45.00 1 + 4 + 8 + 32	1	.1	.1	92.6
47.00 1 + 2 + 4 + 8 + 32	2	.3	.3	92.8
49.00 1 + 16 + 32	1	.1	.1	92.9

Figure 10.10   (continued)

60.00 4 + 8 + 16 + 32	1	.1	.1	93.1
61.00 1 + 4 + 8 + 16 + 32	1	.1	.1	93.2
62.00 2 + 4 + 8 + 16 + 32	2	.2	.2	93.4
63.00 1 + 2 + 4 + 8 + 16 + 32	5	.6	.6	94.0
64.00 Rape occurred	1	.1	.1	94.2
69.00 1 + 4 + 64	1	.1	.1	94.3
71.00 1 + 2 + 4 + 64	2	.3	.3	94.6
76.00 4 + 8 + 64	1	.1	.1	94.6
79.00 1 + 2 + 4 + 8 + 64	6	.7	.7	95.3
92.00 4 + 8 + 16 + 64	1	.1	.1	95.5
95.00 1 + 2 + 4 + 8 + 16 + 64	7	.8	.8	96.3
96.00 32 + 64	1	.1	.1	96.4
111.00 1 + 2 + 4 + 8 + 32 + 64	2	.3	.3	96.6
120.00 8 + 16 + 32 + 64	2	.2	.2	96.8
123.00 1 + 2 + 8 + 16 + 32 + 64	1	.1	.1	96.9
124.00 2 + 4 + 8 + 16 + 32 + 64	2	.2	.2	97.1
127.00 Illegal in all 7 instances (1+2+4+8+16+32+64)	24	2.9	2.9	100.0
Total	846	100.0	100.0	

24 respondents, 2.9 per cent, have a code of **127**, the code that results when a respondent states that abortion should be illegal in all seven of the possible circumstances ($1 + 2 + 4 + 8 + 16 + 32 + 64 = 127$). So, a blanket condemnation of abortion in all circumstances is rare.

Working with geometric codes

The ability to portray combinations of answers precisely is the great advantage of geometric coding. One should note, however, that the strategy of using geometric coding does have its limitations. In this example, the seven circumstances could in theory have produced as many as 127 unique combinations. Since the number of unique combinations doubles with each additional value, there are limits to the number of categories that can be used (8 values could mean up to 255 unique combinations, 9 values 511 and so on). (**Note**, however, that all of the combinations that are possible in theory may not actually come up. For instance, the seven circumstances in our example did produce less than half the possible combinations.)

When coding, it is good practice to give the options that are expected will occur most often the lower values. This should reduce the number of high codes, which are harder to interpret.

Also, giving adjacent values to responses that you expect to group together is good practice. (In our example, the 'social' circumstances were given adjacent values, as were the more 'drastic' circumstances.)

Figure 10.11   Crosstabulation of the recorded 'geometric' anti-abortion variable (**recgeoab**) by religion (**recrelig-Catholic or All others**)

| | | | recrelig Catholic or not | | |
| | | | 1.00 Catholic | 2.00 All others | Total |
			1.00 Catholic	2.00 All others	Total
RECGEOAB Recoded 'geometric' anti-abortion variable	1.00 Legal in all instances	Count	15	329	344
		% within RECRELIG Catholic or not	21.7%	42.3%	40.7%
		Adjusted Residual	-3.3	3.3	
	2.00 Illegal for social reasons only	Count	37	401	438
		% within RECRELIG Catholic or not	53.6%	51.6%	51.8%
		Adjusted Residual	.3	-.3	
	3.00 Illegal even for health & severe reasons	Count	8	32	40
		% within RECRELIG Catholic or not	11.6%	4.1%	4.7%
		Adjusted Residual	2.8	-2.8	
	4.00 Illegal in all instances	Count	9	15	24
		% within RECRELIG Catholic or not	13.0%	1.9%	2.8%
		Adjusted Residual	5.3	-5.3	
Total		Count	69	777	846
		% within RECRELIG Catholic or not	100.0%	100.0%	100.0%

When a geometric coding procedure does produce a variable with a large number of codes, it may be possible to simplify the analysis by recoding the rarer codes into groups. For example, many of the codes of **geoabort** have only a couple of cases. If we are interested in comparing the people who think abortion should be illegal only for 'social' circumstances with those who think abortion should be illegal even in some of the more severe circumstances such as when there are serious health considerations, patterns can be clarified by recoding (Figure 10.11).

Figure 10.11 shows the results of doing this. **geoabort** has been recoded into four categories: (1) the 344 respondents who feel abortion should be legal in all seven circumstances; (2) those who feel abortion should be illegal if the abortion is sought for some combination of 'social or financial' reasons only; (3) those who feel abortion should be illegal even if there are more severe reasons for seeking an abortion; (4) the 24 respondents who feel that abortion should be illegal in all circumstances. The association between religion and the recoded abortion variable is highly significant ($p < 0.001$). The 'All others' category is more likely to say that abortion should be legal in all circumstances. In contrast, the 'Catholic' group is more likely to say that abortion should be illegal even when there are serious health circumstances or other severe reasons and to say that abortion should be illegal in all circumstances.

Conclusion

In situations where a central goal of an analysis will be to identify the combinations of responses to a general question, geometric coding can be a solution. Unlike multiple response sets, a variable whose values result from geometric coding can be used in a confirmatory statistical analysis wherever categorical data are appropriate.

'Geometric' coding exercise

Design some hypothetical 'geometric' coding questions for a draft questionnaire on a topic of your choice. Note that the type of question that would be appropriate for a geometric code would be one for which: (1) respondents are likely to choose more than one answer out of a set of options and (2) the focus of the analysis would be more upon the *combinations* of answers people gave rather than a simple tabulation of the categories they picked.

Conclusion

You have now worked your way systematically through an introduction to the majority of features available with SPSS and have had practical experience of carrying out analyses. This final section collates the material that has been presented so that you will be ready to carry out a complete analysis from start to finish.

A central feature of this workbook has been its reliance upon the analysis of datasets drawn from the British Social Attitudes Survey. The suggested exercises at the end of each Module have dealt with the procedures covered in that section of the workbook. While this means that you have had experience of the genuine sorts of problems and issues that would confront a 'real' researcher, in one crucial respect all that you have done so far has been artificial. Each module has covered the conditions under which it would be appropriate to use its statistical procedure, both in terms of the problem that the statistics are designed to answer and the levels of measurement that the procedures require. While you have had to develop ideas for analyses and then choose appropriate variables from the datasets in order to test those ideas, the *type* of problem and *which* statistical tests to use have never been at issue in each Module's exercises.

A 'real' researcher, however, would not have these advantages. In 'real world' research, quantitative analysts will have an idea or research problem which leads them to develop anticipated empirical findings – hypotheses. Before any statistical analysis can even be contemplated, the analyst has to locate quantitative information that will shed light on their research problem. This may mean generating completely new quantitative information through a sample survey or some other means of generating primary data – or, if they are lucky, locating an existing quantitative dataset that already contains the information they need. The creation of a completely new dataset or the selection of an existing source of data for a secondary analysis involves the careful *operationalisation* of theoretical concepts – establishing variables in the dataset that validly represent the conceptual ideas which one wishes to test. Only when the information has been generated or located will the researcher have a dataset that contains quantitative information which can be analysed to establish whether hypothetically predicted findings actually are confirmed in a variable analysis. You have not had to face these problems here since several datasets have been provided 'ready-made' from the British Social Attitudes Survey.

Choosing the correct statistical test

Once a research problem has been identified, hypotheses have been derived, and a dataset that contains information which will allow the statistical testing of these hypotheses has been obtained, the researcher confronts a different kind of dilemma – which statistical tests from the extensive battery of those available should be used? It is not uncommon for a student to complete one or more statistics courses quite successfully, only to encounter an unexpected 'block' the first time they attempt to carry out an independent analysis as part of a dissertation project or thesis. The source of the problem is quite simple – during the stats courses, they always would have been told which statistical procedure to use in any given exercise. In a real

239

analysis, however, there is no one there to tell the researcher which procedures to apply — they have to work this out for themselves. If students have never faced this problem before, it can be a daunting task!

The process that one goes through in order to decide upon the correct statistical procedure for an analysis can be thought of as a triangular relationship. The researcher will have a 'research problem' — the question or hypothesis which they wish to resolve through their analysis. The information they use to resolve this research problem hopefully will be contained in the data that is available for their analysis. If the data cannot provide variables for analysis that are conceptually valid operationalisations of the ideas in the research problem, attempting an analysis is pointless. If the data is suitable, its characteristics (for instance, the level of measurement of each variable in the analysis) and the exact nature of the research question will determine which statistical test or tests that are chosen as being most appropriate (Figure C.1).

Figure C.1 The triangular relationship between 'research problem', data and statistical procedures

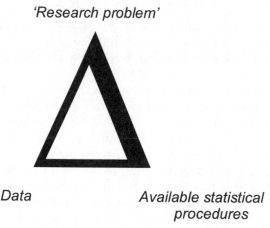

'Research problem'

Data   *Available statistical procedures*

The characteristics of the variables that will be used in an analysis and the exact nature of the statistical question that the analysis seeks to answer, taken together, determine the possible statistical procedures which are appropriate. Figure C.2 collates the requirements of each procedure together into a single table in order to make the task of selecting the appropriate statistic easier.

In order to use the table systematically to select an appropriate statistic, go through the following steps:

1. *Establish whether the 'analysis problem' involves looking at one variable at a time, or at a connection between two or more variables*
   If the 'problem' involves only one variable, the appropriate statistic or procedures should be found in the **Only one variable** column. If the 'problem' involves two or more variables simultaneously, the appropriate statistic should be located in one of the cells that are a combination of a '1st or *Dependent variable*' and '2nd or *Independent variables*'.
2. *Use the level of measurement of the variable or variables to select the appropriate cell of statistical procedures.*
   If the 'problem' involves only one variable, this is relatively simple. You go down the **Only one variable** column to the appropriate row. For instance, if the variable of interest is **rage**

Figure C.2 Choosing the correct statistical procedure

2nd or Independent Variables are:

1st or Dependent Variable:	Only one variable	Nominal/Categorical	Ordinal	Interval/Ratio
Nominal/Categorical	Frequency count Bar chart, Pie chart Mode	Crosstabs Chi-square (χ^2), Phi (ϕ), Cramer's V, Contingency coefficient, Lambda, McNemar's test, Uncertainty coefficient Loglinear analysis	Crosstabs Chi-square (χ^2), Phi (ϕ), Cramer's V, Contingency coefficient, Lambda, McNemar's test, Uncertainty coefficient Loglinear analysis	Probit analysis Logistic regression
Ordinal	Median (Md) Quartiles, Deciles, Interquartile deviation (dq) Box and dot plot	Crosstabs Eta Loglinear analysis	Crosstabs Kendall's Tau (τ), Gamma, Somer's d, Kappa, Spearman's correlation coefficient (Rho) Loglinear analysis	Scattergram plot Correlation coefficients Regression
Interval/Ratio	Histogram Mean Standard deviation (sd), Variance Skewness, Kurtosis Stem and leaf diagram Box and dot plot	*t*-test Analysis of Variance (ANOVA) Box and dot plot for two or more groups	*t*-test Analysis of Variance (ANOVA)	Scattergram plot Pearson's correlation coefficient (*r*) Regression

(Respondent's age), it is a interval/ratio variable, and the appropriate statistic will be one or more of those in the bottom row: Histogram; Mean; Standard deviation; Variance; Skewness, Kurtosis; Stem and leaf diagram or Box and dot plot.

If the 'problem' involves two or more variables, you have to decide whether one of the variables can be considered the 'first' or 'dependent' (*caused*) variable, while the other variable(s) can be considered the 'second' or 'independent' (*causal*) variable(s). You then establish the level of measurement of each variable and locate the appropriate cell in the table. For instance, if the 'first' and the 'second' variable are interval/ratio, you will be led to the statistics listed in the bottom right-hand cell: Scattergram plot; Pearson's correlation coefficient (*r*); Regression.

3. *Depending upon the nature of the 'analysis problem', select an appropriate procedure or statistic* Continuing with the above 'one-variable' example, if the 'problem' was to indicate the average or central point of the distribution of respondents' ages, you would select the mean. If the problem was to examine the distribution of ages around the central point, you could choose the standard deviation or the variance. If you wished to produce a visual depiction of the age distribution, a histogram, a stem and leaf diagram or a box and dot plot could be in order.

In the case of the 'two-variable' example above, if you believed that the second variable could be an independent cause of the first, dependent, variable, regression could be used to test this.

(Figure C.2 shows only the statistical and graphing procedures that are available in SPSS and covered in this workbook. You will have noted that there are other statistical procedures in SPSS that this workbook does not discuss. There of course are also many additional statistical procedures which SPSS does not cater for. Both of these groups of additional procedures can be considered comparatively exotic or specialised relative to those that we have covered.)

A note of caution

Finally, we would like to end with a note of caution. The process of becoming proficient in SPSS can be described as 'having a steep learning curve'. That is, at the beginning, the novice can feel overwhelmed by the amount of detail that must be absorbed in order to get SPSS to work and by the necessity of understanding all facets of carrying out even a simple statistical procedure before they can begin to gain an overall understanding of how to use the package. Very quickly, however, the basics of running an SPSS analysis begin to make sense and a feeling of mastery can follow quickly. This feeling of mastery, however, can be illusory. SPSS is the type of computer package that can be called a TOM (**T**otally **O**bedient **M**oron). It will carry out a completely nonsensical analysis in a very efficient and completely reliable manner. As long as the numerical characteristics of the variables specified in an analysis allow it, SPSS usually will produce the statistics that have been requested, even if the rationale underlying the analysis is completely nonsensical. It is rare that SPSS will give a warning equivalent to asking the researcher '*Are you really sure this is what you want to do?!*'

This is partially owing to SPSS being designed to cater to a very broad constituency of users who will working with many radically different types of data across a wide variety of disciplines, from the social sciences through marketing and commercial applications to the biological sciences. A manifestation of this is the tendency (which you may have noticed) of SPSS to provide more, rather than less, information in its output than most users will need. That, and the scientific appearance of an impressively designed bit of output, can impart a (perhaps false) sense of proficiency to the novice user. For example, if you asked SPSS to correlate the variables **religion** and **rempstat** (the respondent's economic status), both of which are multiple category variables in which the codes in no way fall into a interval or ratio or even an ordinal scale, SPSS would gladly oblige, reporting an correlation coefficient with its associated level of significance without any warning or indication that this was a completely invalid procedure to have carried out. SPSS leaves it up to the researcher to understand the characteristics of the variables in their data and to know enough about the statistical procedures they are requesting to realise when a procedure is utterly incorrect. While it is rewarding to carry out a SPSS analysis that 'works' in the sense of producing output without error messages, you must remember that it is up to you to request sensible tasks and to interpret the resulting output properly. The flexibility and ease of use of SPSS can be a mixed blessing.

That said, SPSS is first and foremost a very powerful and flexible tool for the analysis of social data. By the time you have completed the modules in this workbook and carried out analysis exercises using the practice datasets, you will have developed an important skill. The ability to analyse data using SPSS can provide an immediate 'payback' on the other courses that you will be taking as part of your degree – particularly if any of these require the analysis of quantitative data. Possessing knowledge of SPSS can be vital for the successful completion of a postgraduate degree. An even more significant area is that of employment. The SPSS package is, without doubt, *the* package for social science data analysis and is recognised as such throughout the world in academia, the public services and in private enterprise. Being able genuinely to claim and demonstrate a knowledge of SPSS can be the decisive factor in a job interview.

References

Comrey, A.L. (1973). *A First Course in Factor Analysis*. San Diego: Academic Press.

Jowell, Roger, Curtice, John, Park, Alison and Thomson, Katarina, (eds) (1999). *British Social Attitudes: The 16th Report: Who Shares New Labour Values?* Aldershot: Ashgate

Kuhn, Thomas S. (1962). *The Structure of Scientific Revolutions*. Chicago and London: University of Chicago Press.

Lin, Nan (1976). *Foundations of Social Research*. New York: McGraw-Hill.

Norusis, Marija J. (1988). *The SPSS Guide to Data Analysis for SPSS/PC+*. Chicago: SPSS Inc.

Norusis, Marija J. (2000). *Guide to Data Analysis SPSS 10.0.* New Jersey: Prentice-Hall.

SPSS Inc. (2000) *SPSS Base 10.0 User's Guide*. Chicago: SPSS Inc.

Tukey, John W. (1977). *Exploratory Data Analysis*. Reading, Mass: Addison-Wesley.

Appendix 1
The Dataset Variables Quick Look-Up Guides

The following Quick Reference Sheets provide summary information on the variables included within each dataset. The first column provides the variable name, variable label and the location of the question in the original BSA questionnaire. The second column gives a guide to the level of measurement of each variable (interval/ratio variables are categorised as 'scale' as they are in SPSS). The original questions and frequency tables (where appropriate) for each variable are included in Appendix 3 and relevant page numbers can be found in the final column. Where no page number is listed, the variable is most likely a derived variable — that is, one created from two or more questions.

BSACrime

Variable name and label	Level of measurement	Page number	Variable name and label	Level of measurement	Page number
abort1 Woman does not wish to have child C2.51a	NOMINAL	332	**aborwrgb** R thinks wrong very low income fam B2.06b	ORDINAL	326
abort2 Couple agree they do not want chld C2.51b	NOMINAL	332	**accexpct** Friend has right xpct R lie2police B2.35a	ORDINAL	330
abort3 Woman is not + doesn't want to marry C2.51c	NOMINAL	332	**accwould** Wd R lie police: friend hit pedestn B2.35b	ORDINAL	330
abort4 Couple cannot afford more children C2.51d	NOMINAL	332	**acorn** acorn Q16	NOMINAL	–
abort5 Strong chance of defect in baby C2.51e	NOMINAL	332	**aftrlife** R believe in life after death? B2.20a	ORDINAL	328
abort6 Woman's health endangerd by pregncy C2.51f	NOMINAL	332	**areahelp** Ppl help each oth.in area A2.01B2.36C2.01	NOMINAL	317
abort7 Woman pregnant as a result of rape C2.51g	NOMINAL	332	**attacks** People attacked in the street? Q144	ORDINAL	280
aborwrga R thinks wrong serious defect baby B2.06a	ORDINAL	326	**bencheat** Incorrect info 2 get govt benefits B2.09b	ORDINAL	327

Variable name and label	Level of measurement	Page number	Variable name and label	Level of measurement	Page number
bestnat Nationality best describes R Dv Q1002	NOMINAL	–	**club10** R belong to Rambler's Association? Q923	NOMINAL	–
biblfeel Closest to R's feelings about Bible B2.21	NOMINAL	328	**club11** R belong to Urban Conservation Group Q925	NOMINAL	–
burgarea Who burgles in this area? A2.03B2.38C2.03	NOMINAL	317	**club12** R belong to Campaign nuclear disarm. Q926	NOMINAL	–
burghelp Ppl see hous broken into? A2.02B2.37C2.02	NOMINAL	317	**club2** R belong to R.S.P.B.? Q917	NOMINAL	–
burglary Incidence of burglary in this area Q142	ORDINAL	280	**club3** R belong to oth wildlife protecn grp Q922	NOMINAL	–
censor Censorship uphld moral A2.40eB2.78eC2.54e	ORDINAL	324	**club4** R belongto cntryside sports, leis org Q924	NOMINAL	–
changbad Human chng nature make worse B2.61bC2.26b	ORDINAL	–	**club5a** R belong none of these, DK,NA [drop] Q927	NOMINAL	–
chattend R attend church apart frm spec.occas Q979	ORDINAL	–	**club6** R belong to Friends of the Earth? Q918	NOMINAL	–
chchconf Confidence in churches + religus org B2.12c	ORDINAL	327	**club7** R belong to World Wildlife Fund? Q919	NOMINAL	–
chchpowr Do church + rel.org. have 2much power? B2.17	ORDINAL	328	**club8** R belong to Greenpeace? Q920	NOMINAL	–
chngdo10 Would R keep 5gbp too much change? Q799	NOMINAL	305	**club9** R belong Council Protection Rural ? Q921	NOMINAL	–
chngkp10 Wrong man keep 5gbp too much change? Q798	ORDINAL	305	**clubs** Member of sports club/cultural group Q171	NOMINAL	281
chrchact Often take part church activities? B2.32	ORDINAL	330	**cnty** County	NOMINAL	–
			crime Perception of crime in local area	SCALE	–
club1 R belong to National Trust? Q916	NOMINAL	–	**curunemp** How long present unemploym[if unemp] Q600	SCALE	293

Variable name and label	Level of measurement	Page number	Variable name and label	Level of measurement	Page number
deathapp Death penalty approprt A2.40cB2,78cC2.54c	ORDINAL	324	**heaven** R believe in Heaven? B2.20b	ORDINAL	328
drunks Drunks/tramps on the streets ? Q137	ORDINAL	279	**hedqual** Highest educational qual. obtained? Q1078	ORDINAL	–
efindjob How long2find job,if start look[emp] Q591	SCALE	292	**hell** R believe in Hell? B2.20c	ORDINAL	328
employdt Time R been employed MMM[months] dv Q557	SCALE	292	**hmgdbad** Homes + gardens in bad condition? Q139	ORDINAL	279
emppay Employer should provide support scale	SCALE	–	**hometype** Type of accomodation Q173	NOMINAL	281
exms Is extra-marital sex wrong? Q965	ORDINAL	313	**homosex** Is sex between same-sex adults wrong? Q966	ORDINAL	313
fampay Family should provide support scale	SCALE	–	**househld** Number in household including R? Q30	SCALE	276
famrelig Religion respondent brought up in dvQ974	NOMINAL	–	**illdrugs** People dealing in illegal drugs? Q145	ORDINAL	280
fatalist People can do little 2 change life B2.22b	ORDINAL	329	**indust4** Mangmnt try get btr em A2.39eB2.77eC2.53e	ORDINAL	323
godbelf1 Closest to R's belief about God? B2.18	NOMINAL	328	**jurydevl** R trust jury to come to best view? Q849	ORDINAL	310
godbelf2 Best describes your beliefs abt God B2.19	NOMINAL	328	**keepeye** Anyone keep eye on home? A2.04B2.39C2.04	NOMINAL	317
godconcn God concerns Himself with humans? B2.22a	ORDINAL	329	**kids** Number of children in hhold	SCALE	–
godgmean Life meaningful because God exists B2.22c	ORDINAL	329	**leftrigh** Left-right scale(redistrb to indust4) dv	SCALE	–
govtpay Govt should provide support scale	SCALE	–	**lfnopurp** Life does not serve any purpose? B2.22d	ORDINAL	329
graffiti Graffiti on walls/buildings? Q135	ORDINAL	279	**libauth2** Libertarian-authort'n (tradvals/censor) dv	SCALE	–

Variable name and label	Level of measurement	Page number
locarea Eval of local area	SCALE	–
maininc Main source income R + partner now? Q1186	NOMINAL	315
marstat2 Respondent's marital status[full] Q109	NOMINAL	277
marvie11 All right couple live tog + nt marry B2.08a	ORDINAL	326
marvie12 Good idea liv.tog 1st if int. marry B2.08b	ORDINAL	326
memcomvl R member Oth. local community/voluty Q170	NOMINAL	281
memenvir R member Local conservation/envirnmn Q169	NOMINAL	281
memnghcl R is member Neighbourhd councl/forum Q167	NOMINAL	281
memnghwt R is member Neighbourhood Watch Schm Q168	NOMINAL	281
memnone Member of these local comm'ty group? Q161	NOMINAL	281
memparcl R is member of Parish or town councl Q166	NOMINAL	281
memplpty R is member of a political party Q165	NOMINAL	281
mempta R is member of Parent-teachers assoc Q163	NOMINAL	281
memresid R is member of Tenants/residents ass Q162	NOMINAL	281

Variable name and label	Level of measurement	Page number
memsclgv R is member of Board school governor Q164	NOMINAL	281
memsikvl R member of vol.group help sick + eldr Q170	NOMINAL	281
natresp Respect nature God created B2.61cC2.26c	ORDINAL	–
neigill Ask neighbour collect prescription? Q793	ORDINAL	304
neigmilk Ask neighbour loan 5gbp pay milkman? Q795	ORDINAL	304
neigsink Ask neighbour plunger unblock sink? Q794	ORDINAL	304
nghbrhd How long R lived in neighbourhood?yr Q150	SCALE	281
nhsscale Dissatisfied with NHS scale	SCALE	–
noisyngb Noisy neighbours/loud parties? Q134	ORDINAL	279
norooms How many rooms your household have? Q175	SCALE	282
numbcars How many vehicles in all? Q932	SCALE	313
numben Number of benefits received	SCALE	–
nwunempt Unemployd mnths last 5yr[able + activ] Q596	SCALE	292
obey School teach obey auth A2.40dB2.78dC2.54d	ORDINAL	324
ownfate We each make our own fate? B2.22f	ORDINAL	329

Variable name and label	Level of measurement	Page number	Variable name and label	Level of measurement	Page number
ownoccup Percentage owner occupied Q14	SCALE	—	**rchlwds2** Rich + poor diff.law/ same law[2pt sc] A2.44	NOMINAL	324
partyid1 R's political party identification Q125	NOMINAL	278	**rearn** R's gross earnings [if in paid wrk] Q1190	ORDINAL	315
pbylost Lost + ask passerby for directions? Q800	ORDINAL	305	**reconact** R's main economic activity last wk? Q497	NOMINAL	291
pbyphone Ask passerby2change 5gbp for phone? Q801	ORDINAL	305	**reconpos** Current economic position respondent Q527	NOMINAL	—
percap1 Percapita income/All	SCALE	—	**relgcomm** Turning point R made new relig.comm B2.23	NOMINAL	329
percap2 Percapita income/ Adults only	SCALE	—	**relgmirc** R believe in religious miracles? B2.20d	ORDINAL	328
pms Is sex before marriage wrong? Q963	ORDINAL	313	**religion** Religion of respondent? dv Q971	NOMINAL	314
poltrust Trust police not to bend rules? Q788	ORDINAL	303	**religius** R describe self as religious? B2.33	ORDINAL	330
popden Population density ⟨pers./sq.kilometr⟩ Q13	SCALE	—	**relprob1** Religions bring conflict > peace? B2.15a	ORDINAL	327
prayfreq About how often do you pray? B2.31	ORDINAL	329	**relprob2** Ppl strongrlgbelief often intolrnt B2.15b	ORDINAL	327
r11attach R age 11–12yrs,often attend church? B2.30	ORDINAL	329	**relprob3** GB better country if < rlg influence B2.15c	ORDINAL	327
raceglty White/black more likly found guilty? Q791	ORDINAL	303	**reltruth** R's view truth any/many/1 religion? B2.34	NOMINAL	330
raceori2 Respondent's race self-rated dv Q1003	NOMINAL	314	**rghclass** Respondent: Goldthorpe-Heath cls 1990 Q549	ORDINAL	—
racetens Insults/attacks because race/colour? Q141	ORDINAL	280	**richglty** Rich/poor more likely found guilty? Q792	ORDINAL	304
rage Respondent's age in years YY Q33	SCALE	276			

Variable name and label	Level of measurement	Page number
richlaw 1law fr rich/1law poor A2.39dB2.77dC2.53d	ORDINAL	323
rlginfgv Relg leaders shd not influenc govt B2.13b	ORDINAL	327
rlginfvt Relg leaders shd not influenc vote B2.13a	ORDINAL	327
rrgclass R.G.Social Class current/last job? Q548	ORDINAL	–
rseg2 Socio-economic group of R [20 cat] Q542	NOMINAL	–
rsex Sex of respondent by observation Q32	NOMINAL	276
rsic92gp Standard Indust. Class '92(comm) dv Q541	NOMINAL	–
rstatus Status rank of Respondent	SCALE	–
rsuper No. R supervises [if ever worked] Q504	SCALE	–
rubbish Rubbish or litter lying about? Q138	ORDINAL	279
sciebelf Belve science > feelings + faith B2.61aC2.26a	ORDINAL	–
scieharm Modern science do harm > good? B2.14aC2.26d	ORDINAL	327
scietrst Trust2much science,not enuf faith? B2.14b	ORDINAL	327
secontact Partners economic activity[mar/liv] Q1091	NOMINAL	–

Variable name and label	Level of measurement	Page number
seconpos Current economic position spous/prt Q1121	NOMINAL	–
sempnum Number employees R's work?[self-emp] Q513	SCALE	291
serial Serial Number Q1	NOMINAL	–
sexrole Man's job earn money,woman's famly B2.07a	ORDINAL	326
sghclass Spouse/partner Goldthorpe-Heath cls Q1143	ORDINAL	–
slfgmean Life meaningful,provid meaning slf B2.22e	ORDINAL	329
smokday Smoke how many cigarettes a day? Q1193	SCALE	316
soctrust R say most people can be trusted? Q790	NOMINAL	303
srgclass Spouse/partner R.G. social class? Q1142	ORDINAL	–
srinc Self-rated income group Q448	ORDINAL	287
srprej Describe your racial prejudice? Q860	ORDINAL	312
sseg2 Spouse:R.G. socioeconomic gr[cat 20] Q1136	NOMINAL	–
ssic92gp Spouse/partner SIC '92(compres)[mar Q1135	NOMINAL	–
sstatus Status score of Spouse	SCALE	–
ssuper Spouse:how many supervise at work Q1098	SCALE	–

Variable name and label	Level of measurement	Page number
stifsent Lawbreakr strictr sent A2.40bB2.78bC2.54b	ORDINAL	324
stregion Standard Region dv Q11	NOMINAL	276
taxcheat Taxpayer not report incom less tax B2.09a	ORDINAL	326
tea2 How old was R when R left school? Q1014	SCALE	315
teenonst Teenagers hanging round street Q136	ORDINAL	279
tenure5 Accommodation tenure(full) Q180	NOMINAL	282
tradvals Yng ppl not resp.tradval A2.40aB2.78aC2.54a	ORDINAL	324
tvconwk Days R watched TV news last week? Q121	SCALE	278
tvhrswk Hours TV R watch/day Monday-Friday? Q119	SCALE	277
tvhrswke Hours TV R watch/day at the weekend? Q120	SCALE	278
unionsa Now in trade union/Staff associatn? Q552	NOMINAL	292
vandals Vandalism + deliberate damage? Q140	ORDINAL	280
vatcheat Is it wrong to pay cash, avoid VAT? Q796	ORDINAL	304
vatdo Would R pay cash to avoid VAT? Q797	NOMINAL	305

Variable name and label	Level of measurement	Page number
vehtheft Cars broken into/stolen in this area Q143	ORDINAL	280
volun Vol org memberships	SCALE	–
wealth Wrk ppl nt get fairshr A2.39cB2.77cC2.53c	ORDINAL	323
welfare Welfare scale(welfresp to welffeet) dv	SCALE	323
welthds2 Fair share/rich too much[2pointsc] A2.41	NOMINAL	324
wkjbhrsi R work how many hours/week?[if work] Q520	SCALE	291
wwfamsuf Family life suffer woman works f-t B2.07b	ORDINAL	326
youngsex Sex wrong boy + girl both under 16yr? Q964	ORDINAL	313

BSAHealth

Variable name and label	Level of measurement	Page number
abdie R view abortion right kid die in 20s Q738	ORDINAL	298
abmental R view abortion right kid mental dis Q736	ORDINAL	297
abphys R view abortion right kid physic.dis Q737	ORDINAL	298
abshort R view abortion right kid 8yo height Q739	ORDINAL	298
acorn acorn Q16	NOMINAL	–

Variable name and label	Level of measurement	Page number	Variable name and label	Level of measurement	Page number
bestnat Nationality best describes R dv Q1002	NOMINAL	–	**club2** R belong to R.S.P.B.? Q917	NOMINAL	–
chgcanc Let change genes2reduc breast cancer Q753	ORDINAL	300	**club3** R belong to oth wildlife protecn grp Q922	NOMINAL	–
chgcleve Allow change genes increase intellig Q749	ORDINAL	300	**club4** R belongto cntryside sports,leis org Q924	NOMINAL	–
chgfat Let change genes2make average weight Q755	ORDINAL	300	**club5a** R belong none of these, DK,NA [drop] Q927	NOMINAL	–
chggay Allow change genes2straight/not gay? Q750	ORDINAL	300	**club6** R belong to Friends of the Earth? Q918	NOMINAL	–
chgheart Allow change genes2reduce heart dis? Q752	ORDINAL	300	**club7** R belong to World Wildlife Fund? Q919	NOMINAL	–
chgheig Allow change genes to change height? Q748	ORDINAL	300	**club8** R belong to Greenpeace? Q920	NOMINAL	–
chgsex Let change genes determine baby sex? Q756	ORDINAL	300	**club9** R belong Council Protection Rural? Q921	NOMINAL	–
chgstrai Allow change genes2gay/not straight? Q751	ORDINAL	300	**clubs** Member of sports club/cultural group Q171	NOMINAL	281
chgviol Let change genes2reduce aggr/violent Q754	ORDINAL	300	**cnty** County	NOMINAL	–
			crime Perception of crime in local area	SCALE	–
club1 R belong to National Trust? Q916	NOMINAL	–	**curunemp** How long present unemploym[if unemp] Q600	SCALE	293
club10 R belong to Ramblers' Association? Q923	NOMINAL	–	**ddaemp** Unlawful to refuse employ disabled? Q695	NOMINAL	294
club11 R belong to Urban Conservation Group Q925	NOMINAL	–	**ddashp** Unlawful to refuse2serve disabled? Q696	NOMINAL	294
club12 R belong to Campaign nuclear disarm. Q926	NOMINAL	–	**dentlimt** NHS dental treatment only fr low inc Q474	ORDINAL	289

Variable name and label	Level of measurement	Page number	Variable name and label	Level of measurement	Page number
dentothr Is R's dental treatment covered priv Q476	NOMINAL	290	**emppay** Employer should provide support scale	SCALE	–
dentsat How satisfied with NHS dentists Q456	ORDINAL	287	**fampay** Family should provide support scale	SCALE	–
disforcd Emp be forcd empl disb A2.26dB2.60dC2.25d	ORDINAL	321	**gencanc** What decide person's breast cancer? Q744	NOMINAL	299
disjob Much prej.in GB disabled getting job Q694	ORDINAL	294	**gencare** R cared family/friend genetic condn? Q758	NOMINAL	301
dislmt R's health/disab limit daily activty Q692	NOMINAL	293	**genchgin** Insurance cost dec.by genetic tests Q727	ORDINAL	296
disnew R has health problem/ disability >1yr? Q690	NOMINAL	293	**gencleve** What decides a person's intelligence? Q741	NOMINAL	298
disnoall Emp shd NOT make allow A2.26cB2.60cC2.25c	ORDINAL	–	**genempl** Employer have right see gene test? Q729	ORDINAL	297
disnteff Disabld wrkr not as ef A2.26aB2.60aC2.25a	ORDINAL	320	**geneyes** What decide person's eye colour? Q747	NOMINAL	299
disprejd Disabld wkproblem prej A2.26bB2.60bC2.25b	ORDINAL	320	**genfamil** Serious genetic condition R/family? Q757	NOMINAL	301
disprj Much prej in GB against the disabled Q693	ORDINAL	293	**genfat** What decide person's very overweight? Q746	NOMINAL	299
disservs Govt + LA serv.force easy A2.26fB2.60fC2.25f	ORDINAL	321	**gengay** What decid person being gay/lesbian? Q742	NOMINAL	298
disshops Shops + banks force easy A2.26eB2.60eC2.25e	ORDINAL	321	**genharm** Human genes resrch harm > good B2.65bC2.30b	ORDINAL	–
diswrk R's health/disab afffect paid work? Q691	NOMINAL	293	**genheart** What decides a person's heart disease? Q743	NOMINAL	299
efindjob How long2find job,if start look[emp] Q591	SCALE	292	**genheigh** What decides a person's height? Q740	NOMINAL	298
employdt Time R been employed MMM [months]dv Q557	SCALE	292			

Variable name and label	Level of measurement	Page number	Variable name and label	Level of measurement	Page number
genhope Human genes research give hope B2.66C2.31	ORDINAL	331	**househld** Number in household including R? Q30	SCALE	276
gennochd Genetic risk disease: no kids B2.65aC2.30a	ORDINAL	331	**hsarea1** GPs' appointmnt system A2.21aB2.55aC2.20a	ORDINAL	319
genpromo Employer see test result of employee Q733	ORDINAL	297	**hsarea10** Staffing doctors hospl A2.21iB2.55iC2.20i	ORDINAL	319
genrefin Let insurance comp. use genetic tests Q725	ORDINAL	296	**hsarea11** Quality hospl trtment A2.21jB2.55jC2.20j	ORDINAL	319
genresch Allow what humangenes research B2.64C2.29	NOMINAL	331	**hsarea12** Quality nursing hospl A2.21kB2.55kC2.20k	ORDINAL	319
gentaket Employer have right make R take test Q731	ORDINAL	297	**hsarea13** Waiting areas casualty A2.21lB2.55lC2.20l	ORDINAL	319
genviol What decide person's aggress/violent Q745	NOMINAL	299	**hsarea14** Waiting areas outpatient A2.21mB2.55mC2.20m	ORDINAL	320
govtpay Govt should provide support scale	SCALE	–	**hsarea15** Waiting areas GP surgery? A2.21nB2.55nC2.20n	ORDINAL	320
gpchange Difficult or easy to change GP? Q473	ORDINAL	289	**hsarea16** Waiting in outpatients A2.21oB2.55oC2.20o	ORDINAL	320
gpsat How satisfied with local doctors/GPs Q455	ORDINAL	287	**hsarea17** Waiting accidnt + emergency A2.21pB2.55pC2.20p	ORDINAL	320
gpuse Visited NHS GP in last yr:R/family? Q477	NOMINAL	290	**hsarea18** Waiting 999 ambulance? A2.21qB2.55qC2.20q	ORDINAL	320
healresp Who shld mainly pay for health care? Q436	NOMINAL	285	**hsarea2** Time GP gives patient? A2.21bB2.55bC2.20b	ORDINAL	319
hedqual Highest educational qual.obtained? Q1078	ORDINAL	–	**hsarea3** Being able2choose GP? A2.21cB2.55cC2.20c	ORDINAL	319
hometype Type of accomodation Q173	NOMINAL	–	**hsarea4** Quality of GP treatmnt A2.21dB2.55dC2.20d	ORDINAL	319
			hsarea5 Waiting non-emergency op? A2.21eB2.55eC2.20e	ORDINAL	319
			hsarea6 Waiting time consultants? A2.21fB2.55fC2.20f	ORDINAL	319
			hsarea7 Condition hosp.buildng A2.21gB2.55gC2.20g	ORDINAL	319

Variable name and label	Level of measurement	Page number	Variable name and label	Level of measurement	Page number
hsarea9 Staffing nurses hosptl A2.21hB2.55hC2.20h	ORDINAL	319	NOMINAL		
			marstat2 Respondent's marital status(full) Q109	NOMINAL	277
inpat1 Doc tell all you feel need to know? Q462	ORDINAL	288	**memcomvl** R member Oth.local community/volunty Q170	NOMINAL	281
inpat2 Doc take R's view treatmnt seriously Q463	ORDINAL	288	**memenvir** R member Local conservation/envirnmn Q169	NOMINAL	281
inpat3 Operation happen when booked for? Q464	ORDINAL	288	**memnghcl** R is member Neighbourhd councl/forum Q167	NOMINAL	281
inpat4 Home only when really well enough to Q465	ORDINAL	288	**memnghwt** R is member Neighbourhood Watch Schm Q168	NOMINAL	281
inpat5 Nurses take seriously any complaints Q466	ORDINAL	288	**memnone** Member of these local comm'ty group? Q161	NOMINAL	281
inpat6 Doctors take seriously any complaints Q467	ORDINAL	288	**memparcl** R is member of Parish or town councl Q166	NOMINAL	281
inpat7 Special nurse to deal w problems? Q468	ORDINAL	288	**memplpty** R is member of a political party Q165	NOMINAL	281
inpatsat How satisfied with being an inpatient Q457	ORDINAL	287	**mempta** R is member of Parent-teachers assoc Q163	NOMINAL	281
inpuse Been inpatient in last yr:R/family? Q479	NOMINAL	290	**memresid** R is member of Tenants/residents ass Q162	NOMINAL	281
kids Number of children in Hhold	SCALE	–	**memsclgv** R is member of Board school governor Q164	NOMINAL	281
leftrigh Left-right scale(redistrb to indust4) dv	SCALE	–	**memsikvl** R member of vol.group help sick + eldr Q170	NOMINAL	281
libauth2 Libertarian-authort'n(tradvals/censor)dv	SCALE	–			
locarea Eval of local area	SCALE	–	**nghbrhd** How long R lived in neighbourhood?yr Q150	SCALE	281
maininc Main source income R + partner now? Q1186		–			

Variable name and label	Level of measurement	Page number
nhsdnuse Had NHS dental trtmt last yr:R/fam? Q483	NOMINAL	290
nhslimit NHS only avail. to lower income group Q461	ORDINAL	288
nhssat How satisfied with NHS Q454	ORDINAL	287
nhsscale Dissatisfied with NHS scale	SCALE	–
norooms How many rooms your household have? Q175	SCALE	282
numbcars How many vehicles in all? Q932	SCALE	313
numben Number of benefits received	SCALE	–
nwunempt Unemployd mnths last 5yr[able + activ] Q596	SCALE	292
outpasat How satisfied with being outpatient? Q458	ORDINAL	–
outpat1 Appointment within 3 months back prb Q469	ORDINAL	288
outpat2 Wait to be seen less than 1-2 hr? Q470	ORDINAL	288
outpat3 Able to complain about treatment? Q471	ORDINAL	289
outpuse Been outpatient in last yr:R/family? Q478	NOMINAL	290
ownoccup Percentage owner occupied Q14	SCALE	–
partyid1 R's political party identification Q125	NOMINAL	278

Variable name and label	Level of measurement	Page number
percap1 Percapita income/All	SCALE	–
percap2 Percapita income/Adults only	SCALE	–
popden Population density ⟨pers./sq.kilometr⟩ Q13	SCALE	–
prdenuse Had priv.dental trtmt last yr:R/fam? Q482	NOMINAL	290
pregtest Offr all pregnant women genetic test Q735	ORDINAL	297
privmed R has private health insurance? Q459	NOMINAL	287
privuse Had priv.medical trtmt last yr:R/fam Q481	NOMINAL	290
raceori2 Respondent's race self-rated dv Q1003	NOMINAL	314
rage Respondent's age in years YY Q33	SCALE	276
rearn R's gross earnings [if in paid wrk] Q1190	ORDINAL	315
reconact R's main economic activity last wk? Q497	NOMINAL	291
reconpos Current economic position respondent Q527	NOMINAL	–
religion Religion of respondent? dv Q971	NOMINAL	314
rghclass Respondent: Goldthorpe-Heath cls 1990 Q549	ORDINAL	–

Variable name and label	Level of measurement	Page number	Variable name and label	Level of measurement	Page number
rrgclass R.G.Social Class current/last job? Q548	ORDINAL	–	**srprej** Describe your racial prejudice? Q860	ORDINAL	312
rseg2 Socio-economic group of R [20 cat] Q542	NOMINAL	–	**sseg2** Spouse: R.G.socioeconomic gr[cat 20] Q1136	NOMINAL	–
rsex Sex of respondent by observation Q32	NOMINAL	276	**ssic92gp** Spouse/partner SIC '92(compres)[mar] Q1135	NOMINAL	–
rsic92gp Standard Indust.Class '92(comm) dv Q541	NOMINAL	–	**sstatus** Status score of Spouse	SCALE	–
rstatus Status rank of Respondent	SCALE	–	**ssuper** Spouse:how many supervise at work Q1098	SCALE	–
rsuper No. R supervises [if ever worked] Q504	SCALE	–	**stregion** Standard Region dv Q11	NOMINAL	276
seconact Partners economic activity[mar/liv] Q1091	NOMINAL	–	**tea2** How old was R when R left school? Q1014	SCALE	315
seconpos Current economic position spous/prt Q1121	NOMINAL	–	**tenure5** Accommodation tenure(full) Q180	NOMINAL	282
sempnum Number employees R's work?[self-emp] Q513	SCALE	291	**trgencha** Charity scient truth dangerhumangene Q724	ORDINAL	296
sghclass Spouse/partner Goldthorpe-Heath cls Q1143	ORDINAL	–	**trgencom** drug scientist truth dangerhumangene Q723	ORDINAL	296
sickresp Who ensure sick ppl enough to live? Q438	NOMINAL	–	**trgengvm** Gvt health min. truth dangerhumangene Q720	ORDINAL	296
smokday Smoke how many cigarettes a day? Q1193	SCALE	316	**trgengvs** Govt scientist truth dangerhumangene Q722	ORDINAL	296
srgclass Spouse/partner R.G. social class? Q1142	ORDINAL	–	**trgenjou** Journlst truth danger humangene res? Q719	ORDINAL	295
srinc Self-rated income group Q448	ORDINAL	287	**trgenuni** Univ scientist truth dangerhumangene Q721	ORDINAL	296

Variable name and label	Level of measurement	Page number
tvconwk Days R watched TV news last week? Q121	SCALE	278
tvhrswk Hours TV R watch/day Monday-Friday? Q119	SCALE	277
tvhrswke Hours TV R watch/day at the weekend? Q120	SCALE	278
unionsa Now in trade union/Staff associatn? Q552	NOMINAL	292
visituse Visited NHS patient last yr:R/family Q480	NOMINAL	290
volun Vol org memberships	SCALE	–
welfare Welfare scale(welfresp to welffeet) dv	SCALE	323
whchhosp Can choose hospital for operation? Q472	ORDINAL	289
wkjbhrsi R work how many hours/week?[if work] Q520	SCALE	291

BSAPolitics

Variable name and label	Level of measurement	Page number
acorn acorn Q16	NOMINAL	–
bestnat Nationality best describes R dv Q1002	NOMINAL	–
binsstnd Govt/local cnl set rubbish collectn? Q847	NOMINAL	309
brprior1 1st priority Britain shd do? A2.30aB2.68a	NOMINAL	321

Variable name and label	Level of measurement	Page number
brprior2 2nd priority Britain shd do? A2.30bB2.68b	NOMINAL	321
cllrdevl R trust city cnl building developmnt Q848	ORDINAL	210
cllrsldr Clr > voter know best leaders? A2.36aB2.74a	ORDINAL	322
club1 R belong to National Trust? Q916	NOMINAL	–
club10 R belong to Ramblers' Association? Q923	NOMINAL	–
club11 R belong to Urban Conservation Group Q925	NOMINAL	–
club12 R belong to Campaign nuclear disarm. Q926	NOMINAL	–
club2 R belong to R.S.P.B.? Q917	NOMINAL	–
club3 R belong to oth wildlife protecn grp Q922	NOMINAL	–
club4 R belong to cntryside sports,leis org Q924	NOMINAL	–
club5a R belong to none of these, DK,NA [drop] Q927	NOMINAL	–
club6 R belong to Friends of the Earth? Q918	NOMINAL	–
club7 R belong to World Wildlife Fund? Q919	NOMINAL	–
club8 R belong to Greenpeace? Q920	NOMINAL	–

Variable name and label	Level of measurement	Page number	Variable name and label	Level of measurement	Page number
club9 R belong to Council Protection Rural? Q921	NOMINAL	–	**ctrydon6** Money to campaign cntryside issue? Q894	NOMINAL	313
clubs Member of sports club/cultural group Q171	NOMINAL	281	**ctrydon7** Campaign volnteer cntryside issue? Q895	NOMINAL	313
cntlcncl Shld councils be contrld by cent.gov Q803	ORDINAL	306	**ctrydon8** Protest march abt cntryside issue? Q896	NOMINAL	313
cnty County	NOMINAL	–	**ctrydone** Ever done anythn countryside issues Q888	NOMINAL	313
condevt R's concern abt housing development? Q870	NOMINAL	312	**curunemp** How long present unemploym[if unemp] Q600	SCALE	293
conroad R's concern about major new road? Q879	NOMINAL	312	**dcbcldr** R happen to know who leader council? Q812	NOMINAL	306
crime Perception of crime in local area	SCALE	–	**dcbcname** Do u know the name of dist.council? Q806	NOMINAL	306
ctaxref Inc.council tax > inflatn ref? A2.36bB2.74b	ORDINAL	–	**devtdo1** Take no action concrn housing devt Q871	NOMINAL	312
ctaxval Council tax is good value for money? Q805	ORDINAL	305	**devtdo2** Contact mp concern housing devt Q872	NOMINAL	312
ctrydon1 Contacted MP abt countryside issue Q889	NOMINAL	313	**devtdo3** Contact gov dept concern housing devt Q873	NOMINAL	312
ctrydon2 Contacted gov dept cntryside issue Q890	NOMINAL	313	**devtdo4** Contact media concern housing devt Q874	NOMINAL	312
ctrydon3 Contacted media abt cntryside issue Q891	NOMINAL	313	**devtdo5** Sign petition concern housing devt Q875	NOMINAL	312
ctrydon4 Signed petition abt cntryside issue Q892	NOMINAL	313	**devtdo6** Join consvtn grp concern housing devt Q876	NOMINAL	312
ctrydon5 Joined consvtn grp cntryside issue Q893	NOMINAL	313	**devtdo7** Money to campaign concrn housing devt Q877	NOMINAL	312

Variable name and label	Level of measurement	Page number	Variable name and label	Level of measurement	Page number
hometype Type of accomodation Q173	NOMINAL	281	**lgeffic8** Clr dont care what ppl think A2.37gB2.75g	ORDINAL	323
househld Number in household including R? Q30	SCALE	276	**libauth2** Libertarian-authort'n (tradvals/censor) dv	SCALE	–
idstrng How strong R's party identification? Q130	ORDINAL	279	**locarea** Eval of local area	SCALE	–
kids Number of children in hhold	SCALE	–	**locvoted** Did R vote? in local election? Q832	NOMINAL	–
laoth Local auth'ty inform R as resident? Q816	ORDINAL	307	**lords** Should House of Lords be changed? Q760	NOMINAL	301
laserv Local auth'ty inform R abt.services? Q815	ORDINAL	307	**lordshow** How changed[if Lord shld be changed] Q761	NOMINAL	301
lconsult LA btr decisions consult local A2.34B2.72	NOMINAL	321	**losetch** MPs soon lose touch with people? Q782	ORDINAL	302
leftrigh Left-right scale(redistrb to indust4) dv	SCALE	–	**lpolitic** R has much interest local politics? Q132	ORDINAL	279
lelects Hold LA elections every year? A2.35B2.73	NOMINAL	322	**maininc** Main source income R + partner now? Q1186	NOMINAL	315
lgeffic1 Votes decide how area is run A2.37aB2.75a	ORDINAL	322	**manyvote** So many vote not matter if R A2.36cB2.74c	ORDINAL	322
lgeffic2 No point voting;no diff. Who A2.37bB2.75b	ORDINAL	322	**marstat2** Respondent's marital status[full] Q109	NOMINAL	277
lgeffic3 Privat mor effic.thn council A2.37cB2.75c	ORDINAL	322	**memcomvl** R member Oth.local community/volunty Q170	NOMINAL	281
lgeffic4 Councilrs lose touch w.pepl A2.37dB2.75d	ORDINAL	322	**memenvir** R member Local conservation/envirnmn Q169	NOMINAL	281
lgeffic5 Local cnl electn complicated A2.37eB2.75e	ORDINAL	322	**memnghcl** R is member Neighbourhd councl/forum Q167	NOMINAL	281
lgeffic7 R do as good job as councilr A2.37fB2.75f	ORDINAL	322			

Variable name and label	Level of measurement	Page number	Variable name and label	Level of measurement	Page number
memnghwt R is member Neighbourhood Watch Schm Q168	NOMINAL	281	**nireland** Long-term policy for NI shld be? Q850	NOMINAL	310
memnone Member of these local comm'ty group? Q161	NOMINAL	281	**norooms** How many rooms your household have? Q175	SCALE	282
memparcl R is member of Parish or town councl Q166	NOMINAL	281	**numbcars** How many vehicles in all? Q932	SCALE	313
memplpty R is member of a political party Q165	NOMINAL	281	**numben** Number of benefits received	SCALE	–
mempta R is member of Parent-teachers assoc Q163	NOMINAL	281	**nwunempt** Unemployd mnths last 5yr[able + activ] Q596	SCALE	292
memresid R is member of Tenants/residents ass Q162	NOMINAL	281	**ownoccup** Percentage owner occupied Q14	SCALE	–
memsclgv R is member of Board school governor Q164	NOMINAL	281	**parlconf** How much confidence in parliament? B2.12a	ORDINAL	327
memsikvl R member of vol.group help sick + eldr Q170	NOMINAL	281	**partyid1** R's political party identification Q125	NOMINAL	278
monarchy R's view importance monarchy continu Q762	ORDINAL	302	**percap1** Percapita income/All	SCALE	–
mpstrust Trust any politicians to tell truth? Q789	ORDINAL	303	**percap2** Percapita income/ Adults only	SCALE	–
natbrit Does R think of self as British? Q989	NOMINAL	–	**politics** How much interest R has in politics? Q131	ORDINAL	279
nateuro Does R think of self as European? Q991	NOMINAL	–	**poltrust** Trust police not to bend rules? Q788	ORDINAL	303
nghbrhd How long R lived in neighbourhood?yr Q150	SCALE	281	**popden** Population density ⟨pers./sq.kilometr⟩ Q13	SCALE	–
nhsscale Dissatisfied with NHS scale	SCALE	–	**postvot** Let everyone vote by post/poll stat? Q836	NOMINAL	308
			postvtlk More likely R would vote if by post? Q837	ORDINAL	308

Variable name and label	Level of measurement	Page number	Variable name and label	Level of measurement	Page number
prejas Is there prejudice against Asians? Q854	ORDINAL	311	**rghclass** Respondent: Goldthorpe-Heath cls 1990 Q549	ORDINAL	–
prejblk Is prejudice against black people? Q855	ORDINAL	311	**rlginfgv** Relg leaders shd not influenc govt B2.13b	ORDINAL	327
prejfut Racial prejudice in future 5 yrs? Q858	NOMINAL	311	**rlginfvt** Relg leaders shd not influenc vote B2.13a	ORDINAL	327
prejnow Is more race prejudice than 5 yrs ago Q856	NOMINAL	311	**rrgclass** R.G.Social Class current/last job? Q548	ORDINAL	–
ptyntmat Doesn't matter which party in power? Q786	ORDINAL	302	**rseg2** Socio-economic group of R [20 cat] Q542	NOMINAL	–
raceori2 Respondent's race self-rated dv Q1003	NOMINAL	314	**rsex** Sex of respondent by observation Q32	NOMINAL	276
rage Respondent's age in years YY Q33	SCALE	276	**rsic92gp** Standard Indust. Class '92(comm) dv Q541	NOMINAL	–
rates Central,Local govt dec rates/countax Q804	NOMINAL	306	**rstatus** Status rank of Respondent	SCALE	–
readpap R reads newspaper 3+times a week? Q115	NOMINAL	277	**rsuper** No. R supervises [if ever worked] Q504	SCALE	–
rearn R's gross earnings [if in paid wrk] Q1190	ORDINAL	315	**rwdclead** R named leader correctly? DvQ	NOMINAL	–
reconact R's main economic activity last wk? Q497	NOMINAL	291	**schlstnd** Govt/local cnl set school standards? Q845	NOMINAL	309
reconpos Current economic position respondent Q527	NOMINAL	–	**seconact** Partners economic activity[mar/liv] Q1091	NOMINAL	–
regulds2 Big business be free/govt control? A2.48	NOMINAL	325	**seconpos** Current economic position spous/prt Q1121	NOMINAL	–
religion Religion of respondent? dv Q971	NOMINAL	314	**sempnum** Number employees R's work?[self-emp] Q513	SCALE	291

Variable name and label	Level of measurement	Page number	Variable name and label	Level of measurement	Page number
sghclass Spouse/partner Goldthorpe-Heath cls Q1143	ORDINAL	–	**tvhrswk** Hours TV R watch/day Monday-Friday? Q119	SCALE	277
shopvtlk More likly R wld vote if at shop/PO? Q838	ORDINAL	309	**tvhrswke** Hours TV R watch/day at the weekend? Q120	SCALE	278
smokday Smoke how many cigarettes a day? Q1193	SCALE	316	**unionsa** Now in trade union/Staff associatn? Q552	NOMINAL	292
srgclass Spouse/partner R.G. social class? Q1142	ORDINAL	–	**volun** Vol org memberships	SCALE	–
srinc Self-rated income group Q448	ORDINAL	287	**votecomp** Way of voting R prefer:ballot/button Q839	NOMINAL	309
srprej Describe your racial prejudice? Q860	ORDINAL	312	**voteduty** R's view on gen electin voting A2.29B2.67	NOMINAL	321
sseg2 Spouse: R.G.socio-economic gr[cat 20] Q1136	NOMINAL	–	**voteintr** Parties only interested in votes? Q783	ORDINAL	302
ssic92gp Spouse/partner SIC '92(compres)[mar] Q1135	NOMINAL	–	**voteonly** Vote way people like me have gov.say Q784	ORDINAL	–
sstatus Status score of spouse	SCALE	–	**votesyst** Should voting system be changed? Q763	NOMINAL	302
ssuper Spouse: how many supervise at work Q1098	SCALE	–	**welfare** Welfare scale(welfresp to welffeet) dv	SCALE	–
stregion Standard Region dv Q11	NOMINAL	276	**whpaper** Which paper? [reads 3 + times] Q116	NOMINAL	–
tea2 How old was R when R left school? Q1014	SCALE	315	**whynvt** Why did R not vote? dv Q833	NOMINAL	–
tenure5 Accommodation tenure(full) Q180	NOMINAL	282	**whynvt97** Why did R not vote in '97general elec Q822	NOMINAL	307
tusaever Have you ever been a member of a TU? Q553	NOMINAL	292	**wkendvot** Should hold local election weekend? Q834	NOMINAL	307
tvconwk Days R watched TV news last week? Q121	SCALE	278	**wkjbhrsi** R work how many hours/week?[if work] Q520	SCALE	291

Variable name and label	Level of measurement	Page number
wkndvtlk Wld R vote if local election weekend Q835	ORDINAL	307

BSAWelfare

Variable name and label	Level of measurement	Page number
acorn acorn Q16	NOMINAL	–
areahelp Ppl help each oth.in area A2.01B2.36C2.01	NOMINAL	317
bencheat Incorrect info 2 get govt benefits B2.09b	ORDINAL	327
bestnat Nationality best describes R dv Q1002	NOMINAL	–
bigbsds2 Big busn benefits bosses more/same? A2.46	NOMINAL	325
bigbusnn Big busn benft owners A2.39bB2.77bC2.53b	ORDINAL	323
careresp Who pay care of elderly resid.homes? Q440	NOMINAL	286
club1 R belong to National Trust? Q916	NOMINAL	–
club10 R belong to Ramblers' Association? Q923	NOMINAL	–
club11 R belong to Urban Conservation Group Q925	NOMINAL	–
club12 R belong to Campaign nuclear disarm. Q926	NOMINAL	–

Variable name and label	Level of measurement	Page number
club2 R belong to R.S.P.B.? Q917	NOMINAL	–
club3 R belong to oth wildlife protecn grp Q922	NOMINAL	–
club4 R belongto cntryside sports,leis org Q924	NOMINAL	–
club5a R belong none of these, DK,NA [drop] Q927	NOMINAL	–
club6 R belong to Friends of the Earth? Q918	NOMINAL	–
club7 R belong to World Wildlife Fund? Q919	NOMINAL	–
club8 R belong to Greenpeace? Q920	NOMINAL	–
club9 R belong Council Protection Rural? Q921	NOMINAL	–
clubs Member of sports club/cultural group Q171	NOMINAL	281
cnty County	NOMINAL	–
crime Perception of crime in local area	SCALE	–
curunemp How long present unemploym[if unemp] Q600	SCALE	293
distpnd Council spend > poorer? A2.09aB2.44aC2.09a	NOMINAL	317
dole Opinion on unemployment benefit level Q425	NOMINAL	283
dolefidl Ppl on dole are fiddln A2.38gB2.76gC2.52g	ORDINAL	323

Variable name and label	Level of measurement	Page number	Variable name and label	Level of measurement	Page number
efindjob How long2find job,if start look[emp] Q591	SCALE	292	**leftrigh** Left-right scale(redistrb to indust4) dv	SCALE	–
employdt Time R been employed MMM [months]dv Q557	SCALE	292	**libauth2** Libertarian-authort'n(tradvals/ censor)dv	SCALE	–
emppay Employer should provide support scale	SCALE	–	**locarea** Eval of local area	SCALE	–
failclm Many people fail to claim benefits? Q424	ORDINAL	283	**lowwage** Easy fr boss: govt top up? A2.18B2.53C2.18	ORDINAL	319
falseclm Many people falsely claim benefits? Q423	ORDINAL	283	**maininc** Main source income R + partner now? Q1186	NOMINAL	315
fampay Family should provide support scale	SCALE	–	**marstat2** Respondent's marital status[full] Q109	NOMINAL	277
govtpay Govt should provide support scale	SCALE	–	**memcomvl** R member Oth.local community/volunty Q170	NOMINAL	281
gvjbds2b Govt resp.provide job/own resp[2pt] A2.43	NOMINAL	324	**memenvir** R member Local conservation/envirnmn Q169	NOMINAL	281
healresp Who shld mainly pay for health care? Q436	NOMINAL	285	**memnghcl** R is member Neighbourhd councl/forum Q167	NOMINAL	281
hedqual Highest educational qual.obtained? Q1078	ORDINAL	–	**memnghwt** R is member Neighbourhood Watch Schm Q168	NOMINAL	281
hometype Type of accomodation Q173	NOMINAL	281	**memnone** Member of these local comm'ty group? Q161	NOMINAL	281
househld Number in household including R? Q30	SCALE	276	**memparcl** R is member of Parish or town councl Q166	NOMINAL	281
incomgap Gap between high and low incomes Q447	ORDINAL	286	**memplpty** R is member of a political party Q165	NOMINAL	281
indust4 Mangmnt try get btr em A2.39eB2.77eC2.53e	ORDINAL	323	**mempta** R is member of Parent-teachers assoc Q163	NOMINAL	281
kids Number of children in hhold	SCALE	–			

Variable name and label	Level of measurement	Page number	Variable name and label	Level of measurement	Page number
memresid R is member of Tenants/residents ass Q162	NOMINAL	281	**numben** Number of benefits received	SCALE	–
memsclgv R is member of Board school governor Q164	NOMINAL	281	**nwunempt** Unemployd mnths last 5yr[able + activ] Q596	SCALE	292
memsikvl R member of vol.group help sick + eldr Q170	NOMINAL	281	**ownoccup** Percentage owner occupied Q14	SCALE	–
morewelf Govt sh spend > on poor A2.38dB2.76dC2.52d	ORDINAL	323	**partyid1** R's political party identification Q125	NOMINAL	278
mstchild High earner entitled more child benf Q432	ORDINAL	285	**penspoor** Married couple living onstatepension Q442	ORDINAL	286
mstdisab Hi incom disabld entitled more beneft Q434	ORDINAL	285	**percap1** Percapita income/All	SCALE	–
mstretir High earner entitled bigger statepen Q430	ORDINAL	284	**percap2** Percapita income/ Adults only	SCALE	–
mstunemp High earner entitled more unemp.bene Q428	ORDINAL	284	**popden** Population density ⟨pers./sq.kilometr⟩ Q13	SCALE	–
nghbrhd How long R lived in neighbourhood?yr Q150	SCALE	281	**raceori2** Respondent's race self-rated dv Q1003	NOMINAL	314
nhslimit NHS only avail.to lower income group Q461	ORDINAL	288	**rage** Respondent's age in years YY Q33	SCALE	276
nhssat How satisfied with NHS Q454	ORDINAL	287	**rearn** R's gross earnings [if in paid wrk] Q1190	ORDINAL	315
nhsscale Dissatisfied with NHS scale	SCALE	–	**reconact** R's main economic activity last wk? Q49	NOMINAL	291
norooms How many rooms your household have? Q175	SCALE	282	**reconpos** Current economic position respondent Q527	NOMINAL	–
numbcars How many vehicles in all? Q932	SCALE	313	**redids2** Govt duty narrow incom gap/not? A2.45	NOMINAL	324
			redistrb Govt sh redistrib incm A2.39aB2.77aC2.53a	ORDINAL	323

Variable name and label	Level of measurement	Page number	Variable name and label	Level of measurement	Page number
religion Religion of respondent? dv Q971	NOMINAL	314	**sickresp** Who ensure sick ppl enough to live? Q438	NOMINAL	285
retresp Who ensure ppl enuf money retirement Q437	NOMINAL	285	**singmum1** Sng mum + yng chld duty2wrk A2.12B2.47C2.12	NOMINAL	318
rghclass Respondent: Goldthorpe-Heath cls 1990 Q549	ORDINAL	–	**singmum2** Sng + yng ch ptw govt ccare A2.13B2.48C2.13	ORDINAL	318
richlaw 1law fr rich/1law poor A2.39dB2.77dC2.53d	ORDINAL	323	**smokday** Smoke how many cigarettes a day? Q1193	SCALE	316
rrgclass R.G.Social Class current/last job? Q548	ORDINAL	–	**smumsch1** Sng mum + sch chd duty2work A2.14B2.49C2.14	NOMINAL	318
rseg2 Socio-economic group of R [20 cat] Q542	NOMINAL	–	**smumsch2** Sng + sch ch govt aftschool A2.15B2.50C2.15	ORDINAL	318
rsex Sex of respondent by observation Q32	NOMINAL	276	**sochelp** Ppl nt deservany help? A2.38fB2.76fC2.52f	ORDINAL	323
rsic92gp Standard Indust.Class '92(comm) dv Q541	NOMINAL	–	**socspnd1** Gvt spend on benefit for unemployed? Q417	ORDINAL	282
rstatus Status rank of Respondent	SCALE	–	**socspnd2** Gvt spend on benefit notwork disabld Q418	ORDINAL	282
rsuper No. R supervises [if ever worked] Q504	SCALE	–	**socspnd3** Gvt spend parents work on low income Q419	ORDINAL	282
seconact Partners economic activity[mar/liv] Q1091	NOMINAL	–	**socspnd4** Govt spend benefits for single parent Q420	ORDINAL	282
seconpos Current economic position spous/prt Q1121	NOMINAL	–	**socspnd5** Govt spend benefits for retired ppl? Q421	ORDINAL	282
sempnum Number employees R's work?[self-emp] Q513	SCALE	291	**socspnd6** Govt spend benefits for carers sick/disb Q422	ORDINAL	283
sghclass Spouse/partner Goldthorpe-Heath cls Q1143	ORDINAL	–	**srgclass** Spouse/partner R.G. social class? Q1142	ORDINAL	–

Variable name and label	Level of measurement	Page number	Variable name and label	Level of measurement	Page number
srinc Self-rated income group Q448	ORDINAL	287	**trnem2** Who shd pay helpful training nt nec? Q699	NOMINAL	294
srprej Describe your racial prejudice? Q860	ORDINAL	312	**trnem3** Who shd pay training for future job? Q701	NOMINAL	295
sseg2 Spouse: R.G.socioeconomic gr[cat 20] Q1136	NOMINAL	–	**trnun1** Who shd pay training for unemployed? Q703	NOMINAL	295
ssic92gp Spouse/partner SIC '92(compres)[mar] Q1135	NOMINAL	–	**trnun2** Who shd pay train employed help any job? Q705	NOMINAL	295
sstatus Status score of spouse	SCALE	–	**tvconwk** Days R watched TV news last week? Q121	SCALE	278
ssuper Spouse: how many supervise at work Q1098	SCALE	–	**tvhrswk** Hours TV R watch/day Monday-Friday? Q119	SCALE	277
stregion Standard Region dv Q11	NOMINAL	276	**tvhrswke** Hours TV R watch/day at the weekend? Q120	SCALE	278
taxcheat Taxpayer not report incom less tax B2.09a	ORDINAL	326	**ubpoor** Married couple living on unempbeneft Q441	ORDINAL	286
taxpoor Inc.tax betroff:spnd poor A2.10B2.45C2.10	NOMINAL	318	**unempjob** Most cld find job want A2.38eB2.76eC2.52e	ORDINAL	323
taxspend Govt choos taxation v.social service Q427	ORDINAL	284	**unemresp** Who ensure unemployed enuf to live? Q439	NOMINAL	285
tea2 How old was R when R left school? Q1014	SCALE	315	**unionsa** Now in trade union/Staff associatn? Q552	NOMINAL	292
tenure5 Accommodation tenure(full) Q180	NOMINAL	282	**volact1** Volunteer wrk: R did politicl A2.28aB2.16a	ORDINAL	–
topupchn Top up wages:2work + kids? A2.16B2.51C2.16	NOMINAL	318	**volact2** Volunteer wrk: R did charitab A2.28bB2.16b	ORDINAL	–
topupnch Top up wages:2work no kids A2.17B2.52C2.17	ORDINAL	319	**volact3** Volunteer wrk: R did religius A2.28cB2.16c	ORDINAL	–
trnem1 Who shd pay for necessary training? Q697	NOMINAL	294			

Variable name and label	Level of measurement	Page number	Variable name and label	Level of measurement	Page number
volact4 Volunteer wrk: R did oth.work A2.28dB2.16d	ORDINAL	–	**welfresp** Ppl not look aftr self A2.38aB2.76aC2.52a	ORDINAL	323
volun Vol org memberships	SCALE	–	**welfstig** SocSec ppl feel 2ndcls A2.38bB2.76bC2.52b	ORDINAL	323
wealth Wrk ppl nt get fairshr A2.39cB2.77cC2.53c	ORDINAL	323	**welthds2** Fair share/rich too much[2pointsc] A2.41	NOMINAL	324
welfare Welfare scale(welfresp to welffeet) dv	SCALE	323	**wkjbhrsi** R work how many hours/week?[if work] Q520	SCALE	291
welffeet Less benefit => own feet A2.38hB2.76hC2.52h	ORDINAL	323			
welfhelp WelfSt stops ppl helpn A2.38cB2.76Cc2.52c	ORDINAL	323			

Appendix 2
Scales

This Appendix gives information about the construction and format of a variety of scales – special variables that have been constructed from the responses to a group of questions. Some of these scales were developed by the original team that collects and codes the British Social Attitudes survey and others have been devised by the authors of this text to add to the teaching utility of the practice datasets.

Most of the variables contained in the British Social Attitudes data are based upon the responses to single questions. Take for example, the variable *graffiti*, which is the response of people to the following question: *'How common or uncommon is this in your area ... Graffiti on walls or buildings.'* By analysing the responses to this single item, you can comment on the sample's opinion about graffiti in their area. However, you can use this information for little else than this. You might be using the Crime dataset to examine people's opinions about problems in their area. The use of a single question, like the one on graffiti, might provide a misleading or inaccurate view. (For instance, you may want to use people's answers to the graffiti question as an indicator of whether people see their local area as having problems, but some people may *like* the graffiti in their area and not see it as a problem at all!)

However, it is also true to suggest that most respondents' attitudes can be expected to be similar on a number of related questions. For example, you might expect many respondents who see graffiti as a problem to see other things in their area – such as noisy neighbours or loud parties, teenagers hanging around on the streets, the presence of drunks or tramps, rubbish and litter, vandalism, etc. – also as problems. Though there may not be a perfect correspondence between respondents' answers to these questions (nor necessarily should there be), if these answers show enough of an association, they could be used together in a *scale* to reflect a broader construct (in this case, people's general perception about whether their area is 'problematic').

In this way you can use a scale to give a quicker and wider consideration of a person's view towards a general topic. The scale value should be both more valid and more reliable than their answer to a single question.

There are a number of scales within the practice datasets. These scales are made up of items that show an association with each other that can be linked to a wider construct. A description of each scale is provided below. It is useful to note that the actual scores, such as 22, do not mean anything concrete, as this value is merely a score that has been reached from a combination of different answers to the items that make up the scale. Therefore, your interpretation of scale scores really depends upon how the scores compare to the scores of other people. For instance, it may be that elderly people will score lower (a mean of 15) than the young (a mean of 35) on the scale *locarea* (the scale of respondents' perception of problems in their area). You could then conclude that the elderly more than the young feel, on average, that their area in general is more 'problematic'. (Lower scores on *locarea* indicate that respondents feel problems are *more* common.) This result should be more reliable and valid than a conclusion based upon just comparing the responses of the young and elderly to single questions.

The first three scales have been developed by the team at the National Centre for Social Research and each is designed to tap a different dimension of 'left'/'right' views.

leftrigh *'Left-right scale'* Based upon the responses to *five* variables in the BSA dataset: **redistrb**; **bigbusnn**; **wealth**; **richlaw**; **indust4**.

libauth2 *'Libertarian-authoritarian scale'* Based upon the responses to *six* variables: **tradvals**; **stifsent**; **deathapp**; **obey**; **wronglaw**; **censor**.

welfare *'Welfarism scale'* Based upon the responses to *eight* variables: **welfresp**; **welfstig**; **welfhelp**; **morewelf**; **unempjob**; **sochelp**; **dolefidl**; **welffeet**.

We will quote directly from the descriptions of the scales given by the National Centre:

> Each of these scales consists of a number of statements to which the respondent is invited to 'agree strongly', 'agree', 'neither agree nor disagree', 'disagree', or 'disagree strongly' ...
>
> The indices for the three scales are formed by scoring the leftmost, most libertarian or most pro-welfare position as 1 and the rightmost, most authoritarian or most anti-welfarist position as 5. The 'neither agree nor disagree' option is scored as 3. The scores to all the questions in each scale are added and then divided by the number of items in the scale giving indices ranging from 1 (leftmost, most libertarian or most pro-welfare) to 5 (rightmost, most authoritarian, most anti-welfare). (Jowell *et al.*, 1997: 244)

In addition, we have created a number of scales in order to extend the scope of possible analyses that you can carry out using the datasets.

Three scales were constructed from the responses to the variables **healresp**, **retresp**, **sickresp**, **unemresp**, **trnem1**, **trnem2**, **trnem3**, **trnun1** and **trnun2**. the ten original questions asked respondents whether the **government**, **employers**, or **people themselves** *'should be mainly responsible for'* respectively: (1) the cost of health care; (2) the retired; (3) the chronically sick or disabled; (4) the unemployed; (5) the elderly; (6) necessary training; (7) beneficial training; (8) career training; (9) job-specific training for the unemployed; (10) general training for the unemployed:

govtpay: A scale ranging from 0 to 10, based upon the number of questions for which the respondent said *'government'* should be mainly responsible.
emppay: A scale ranging from 0 to 9, based upon the number of questions for which the respondent said *'a person's employer'* should be mainly responsible.
fampay: A scale ranging from 0 to 9, based upon the number of questions for which the respondent said *'a person themselves and their family'* should be mainly responsible.

Two income scales were constructed. Each was based upon a variable in the original dataset that categorised each respondent's household income. The income categories were recoded into their median amount in pounds and that amount was divided by the total number of people living in the household or the number of adults living in the household. (Note that these scales were constructed to provide 'quantitative' variables for teaching purposes; the amounts in pounds and pence that these scales give are at most an approximation and should not be used in a published analysis.) Two scales result from this procedure:

percap1: Average annual income of each person in the respondent's household, based upon all the people living in the household.
percap2: Average annual income of the each adult in the household, based upon all adults aged 18 or more living in the household.

The detailed Census 'Standard Occupational Classification' code was used to construct scales of occupational status for the respondent and his or her spouse. The approximately 300 detailed occupational categories that appear in the dataset were recoded into status scores that ranged from a low of 11 to a high of 88. Two scales result:

rstatus: Status rank of the respondent's occupation.
sstatus: Status rank of the occupation of the respondent's spouse.

Other scales were constructed:

numben: The number of social benefits the respondent's household received; ranging from 0 to 7.
volun: The number of types of voluntary organisations the respondent was a member of, based upon the variables **memresid**, **mempta**, **memsclgv**, **memplpty**, **memparcl**, **memnghcl**, **memnghcl**, **memnghwt**, **memenvir**, and **memcomv1**. (The number ranges from 0 to 6.).

locarea: A scale giving the respondent's evaluation of his or her local area. Based upon adding together the responses to the six variables **noisyngh**, **graffiti**, **teenonst**, **drunks**, **rubbish** and **hmgdbad** plus responses to four questions not included in your practice datasets (questions about local transport (**loctrans**), local schools (**loceduc**), local job chances (**locjobs**) and suitability of the area as a place to bring up children (**locraise**)). The scale ranges from 17 to 40, with lower values indicating a more negative evaluation of the local area.

nhsscale: A scale giving the degree of the respondent's dissatisfaction with the National Health Service (NHS). Based upon adding together the responses to the variables **nhssat**, **gpsat**, **dentsat**, **inpatsat**, **outpasat**, **inpat1** to **inpat7**, **outpat1** to **outpat3** and **whchhosp**. The resulting scale ranges from 16 to 66 with higher scores indicating more dissatisfaction with the NHS.

crime: A scale giving the respondent's perception of crime in his or her own area. Based upon adding together the responses to six variables **vandals**, **racetens**, **burglary**, **vehtheft**, **attacks** and **illdrugs**. The scale ranges from 1 to 19 with higher values indicating a perception of *more* crime.

Reference

Jowell, Roger, Curtice, John, Park, Alison and Thomson, Katarina (1999). *British Social Attitudes. The 16th Report: Who Shares New Labour Values?* Aldershot: Ashgate.

Appendix 3
Questions Used to Generate Variables Used in the Practice Datasets[1]

British Social Attitudes: 1998 Face to Face Interview

Questionnaire

Q11   [*StRegion*]
  %   Standard Region
 8.2 Scotland
 6.0 Northern
 9.7 Yorkshire & Humberside
 8.6 West Midlands
 7.6 East Anglia
 4.7 East Anglia
 8.7 South West
19.7 South East
12.0 Greater London
 5.8 Wales

$\boxed{N = 3146}$

Q30   [*Household*]
      (You have just been telling me about the adults that live
      in this household. Thinking now of **everyone** living in the
      household, **including children:**)
      Including yourself, how many people live here regularly
      as members of this household?

      [*RSEX*]
  %   **PLEASE CODE SEX OF (name)** (*figures refer to [RSex]*)
44.9 Male
55.1 Female

      [*RAge*]
      FOR RESPONDENT: I would like to ask you a few details
      about each person in your household. Starting with
      yourself, what was your **age** last birthday?
      FOR 97+ YEARS, CODE 97.

---

[1] The authors are grateful to the National Centre for Social Research for permission to reproduce sections of the 1998 interview schedule and questionnaires. the tabulations and summary statistics appearing with the questions are as supplied by the National Centre.

% **Median: 45 years** (*figures refer to [RAge]*)
0.1 (Don't know)
0.2 Refusal

Q109 [*MarStat2*]
Can I just check, which of these applies to you at present?
% CODE FIRST TO APPLY
58.0 Married
8.0 Living as married
2.1 Separated (after being married)
5.5 Divorced
8.3 Widowed
18.0 Single (never married)
0.0 (Refusal/not answered)

NEWSPAPER READERSHIP & TELEVISION VIEWING

Q115 [*ReadPap*]
Do you normally read any daily **morning** newspaper at least
% 3 times a week?
57.0 Yes
42.9 No
0.2 (Refusal/not answered)

IF 'Yes' AT [ReadPap]
Q116 [*WhPaper*]
Which one do you normally read?
% IF MORE THAN ONE: Which one do you read **most** frequently?
4.3 (*Scottish*) Daily Express
9.0 (*Scottish*) Daily Mail
12.0 Daily Mirror (*Record*)
1.4 Daily Star
15.0 The Sun
4.6 Daily Telegraph
0.6 Financial Times
2.2 The Guardian
1.0 The Independent
2.8 The Times
0.0 Morning Star
3.3 Other Irish/Northern Irish/Scottish regional or local
daily morning paper (WRITE IN)
0.3 Other (WRITE IN)
0.4 MORE THAN ONE PAPER READ WITH EQUAL FREQUENCY
0.2 (Refusal/not answered)

Q119 [*TVHrsWk*]
How many **hours** of television do you normally watch on an
ordinary day or evening **during the week**, that is, Monday
to Friday?
INTERVIEWER: ROUND UP TO NEAREST HOUR
IF DOES NOT WATCH TELEVISION ON WEEKDAYS, CODE 0
IF NEVER WATCHES TELEVISION AT ALL, CODE 97
% **Median: 3 hours**
0.1 (Never watches television)

IF WATCHES TELEVISION (I.E. *NOT* 'Never watches television at all/DK/Refusal') AT [TVHrsWk]

N = 2067

Q120 [*TVHrsWke*]
How many **hours** of television do you normally watch on an ordinary day or evening **at the weekend?**
INTERVIEWER: ROUND UP TO NEAREST HOUR
IF DOES NOT WATCH TELEVISION AT WEEKENDS, CODE 0
% **Median: 3 hours**
0.1 Never watches television

Q121 [*TVConWk*]
On about how many **days** in the past week, that is, the seven days from last *day* until yesterday, did you watch all or part of the news on any television channel?
IF 'NONE', CODE AS 0.
ENTER NUMBER OF DAYS ON WHICH NEWS WATCHED
% **Median: 7 days**
0.1 (Never watches TV)

PARTY IDENTIFICATION

Q122 [*SupParty*]
Generally speaking, do you think of yourself as a
% supporter of any one political party?
41.9 Yes
58.0 No
0.0 (Don't know)
0.0 (Refusal/not answered)

IF 'No/Dk' AT [SupParty]
Q123 [*ClosePty*]
Do you think of yourself as a little closer to one
% political party than to the others?
26.0 Yes
31.9 No
0.1 (Don't know)
0.1 (Refusal/not answered)

IF 'Yes' AT [SupParty] OR IF 'Yes/No/Dk' AT [ClosePty]
Q125 [*PartyID1*]
IF 'Yes' AT [SupParty] OR AT [ClosePty]: Which one?
If 'No/DK' AT [ClosePty]:
If there were a general election tomorow, which political party do you think you would be most likely to support?
% DO NOT PROMPT
26.0 Conservative
44.7 Labour
10.3 Liberal Democrat
1.5 Scottish Nationalist
0.3 Plaid Cymru
0.4 Other party
0.5 Other answer
11.3 None
0.7 Green Party

  1.9 Refused to say
  2.3 (Don't know)
  0.0 Not answered

IF ANY PARTY AT [PartyID1]
Q130 [*Idstrng*]
  Would you call yourself very strong (*party given at*
  % [*PartyID1*]), fairly strong, or not very strong?
  7.4 Very strong (party at [*PartyID1*])
 28.3 Fairly strong
 48.1 Not very strong
  0.1 (Don't know)
  4.8 (Refusal/never answered)

Q131 [*Politics*]
  How much interest do you generally have in what is going
  % on in politics?
  7.5 ... a great deal,
 21.4 quite a lot,
 36.3 some,
 24.2 not very much,
 10.6 or, none at all?
  0.0 (Don't know)
  0.0 (Refusal/not answered)

N = 2067

Q132 [*LPolitic*]
  And how much interest do you have in **local politics?**
  %
  2.7 ... a great deal,
  8.0 quite a lot,
 27.8 some,
 36.5 not very much,
 24.9 or, none at all?
  0.1 (Refusal/not answered)

N = 3146

Q134 [*NoisyNgb*]
  Please use this card to say how common or uncommon each
  of the following things is **in your area.**
  Firstly, noisy neighbours or loud parties?

Q135 [*Graffiti*]
  (How common or uncommon is this **in your area**)
  Graffiti on walls and buildings?

Q136 [*TeenOnSt*]
  Teenagers hanging around on the streets?

Q137 [*Drunks*]
  Drunks or tramps on the streets?

Q138 [*Rubbish*]
  Rubbish and litter lying about?

Q139 [*HmGdBad*]
  Homes and gardens in bad condition?

Q140 [*Vandals*]
Vandalism and deliberate damage to property?

Q141 [*RaceTens*]
Insults or attacks to do with someone's race or colour?

Q142 [*Burglary*]
Homes broken into?

Q143 [*VehTheft*]
Cars broken into or stolen?

Q144 [*Attacks*]
People attacked in the streets?

Q145 [*IllDrugs*]
People dealing in illegal drugs?

	[*NoisyNgb*]	[*Graffiti*]	[*TeenOnSt*]
	%	%	%
Very common	4.4	3.4	13.3
Fairly common	8.3	11.1	30.0
Not very common	36.0	36.6	30.3
Not at all common	51.2	48.7	26.0
(Don't know)	0.1	0.2	0.4
(Refusal/NA)	–	–	–

	[*Drunks*]	[*Rubbish*]	[*HmGdBad*]
	%	%	%
Very common	2.8	12.4	3.6
Fairly Common	8.3	26.6	13.2
Not very common	31.4	38.0	49.9
Not at all common	57.2	22.9	32.7
(Don't know)	0.3	0.2	0.6
(Refusal/NA)	–	–	–

	[*Vandals*]	[*RaceTens*]	[*Burglary*]
	%	%	%
Very common	6.7	0.7	5.8
Fairly Common	15.2	3.7	23.6
Not very common	45.2	27.1	47.9
Not at all common	32.7	67.1	21.0
(Don't know)	0.3	1.4	1.8
(Refusal/NA)	–	–	–

	[*VehTheft*]	[*Attacks*]	[*IllDrugs*]
	%	%	%
Very common	8.8	1.5	7.2
Fairly Common	26.6	5.8	15.6
Not very common	43.4	35.4	27.3
Not al all common	18.8	56.5	41.8
(Don't know)	2.4	0.9	8.1
(Refusal/NA)	–	–	–

Q150 [*NghBrHd*]
Can I just check, how long have you lived in your present
neighbourhood?
ENTER YEARS. ROUND TO NEAREST YEAR.
PROBE FOR BEST ESTIMATE.
IF LESS THAN ONE YEAR, CODE 0.
% **Median: 13 years**
0.1 (Don't know)
0.1 (Refusal/NA)

Q161-Q170 Are you currently a member of any of these?
IF YES: Which ones? PROBE: Which others?
CODE ALL THAT APPLY
% Multicoded (Maximum of 9 codes)
73.8 (None of these) [*MemNone*]
4.9 Yes: Tenants'/residents' association [*MemResid*]
2.5 Yes: Parent-teachers' association [*MemPTA*]
1.0 Yes: Board of school governors/School Board [*MemScIEN*]
2.5 Yes: a political party [*MemP/Pty*]
0.7 Yes: Parish or town council [*MemParCl*]
0.5 Yes: Neighbourhood council/forum [*MemNghCl*]
13.5 Yes: Neighbourhood Watch Scheme [*MemNghWt*]
2.3 Yes: Local conservation or environmental
group[*MemEnvir*]
5.9 Yes: Other local community or voluntary group
WRITE IN WHAT IT DOES) *(MemComVl)*
1.8 Yes: voluntary group to help sick/elderly/
children/other vulnerable group [*MemSikVL*]
0.1 (Refusal/NA)

Q171 [*Clubs*]
And are you a member of any kind of local sports club, or
of a cultural group such as an art or drama club?
%
16.3 Yes, sports club(s) only
4.5 Yes, cultural group(s) only
1.7 Yes, both sports club(s) and cultural group(s)
77.5 No
0.1 (Refusal/NA)

N = 3146

Q173 [*HomeType*]
CODE FROM OBSERVATION AND CHECK WITH RESPONDENT.
Would I be right in describing this accommodation as a
% ... READ OUT ONE YOU THINK APPLIES ...
21.9 ... detached house or bungalow
36.8 ... semi-detached house or bungalow
27.6 ... terraced house or bungalow
9.8 ... self-contained, purpose-built flat/maisonette
(inc. tenement block)
3.0 ... self-contained converted flat/maisonette
0.3 ... room(s), not self-contained
0.5 Other answer (WRITE IN)
0.1 (Refusal/NA)

Q175 [*NoRooms*]
How many rooms does your household have for its **own use?**
Please exclude kitchens under 2 metres (6 feet 6 inches)
wide, bathrooms, toilets and hallways.
PROMPT ON HOUSEHOLD DEFINITION IF NECESSARY
% **Median: 5.0**
- (Don't know)
0.1 (Refusal/NA)

Q180 [*Tenure5*]
Does your household own or rent this accommodation?
IF OWNS: Outright or on a mortgage?
% **IF RENTS:** From whom?
28.6 OWNS: Own (leasehold/freehold) outright
43.4 OWNS: Buying (leasehold/freehold) on mortgage
15.5 RENTS: Local authority/council
3.3 RENTS: Housing Association/Housing Trust
1.2 RENTS: Property company
0.5 RENTS: Employer
0.8 RENTS: Other organisation
0.3 RENTS: Relative
5.5 RENTS: Other individual
- RENTS: Housing Action Trust
0.2 Rent free (other than squatting)
0.2 Squatting
0.2 Other answer **(WRITE IN)**
0.2 (Don't know)
0.1 (Refusal/NA)

PUBLIC SPENDING AND SOCIAL WELFARE
Q417 [*SocSpnd1*]
Some people think that there should be more government
spending on social security, while other people
disagree. For each of the groups I read out please say
whether you would like to see **more** or **less** government
spending on them than now. Bear in mind that if you want
more spending, this would probably mean that you would
have to pay more taxes. If you want less spending, this
would probably mean paying less taxes. Firstly:

**Benefits for unemployed people: would you like to see
more or less government spending than now?**

Q418 [*SocSpnd2*]
(Would you like to see more or less government spending
than now)
Benefits for disabled people who cannot work

Q419 [*SocSpnd3*]
Benefits for parents who work on very low incomes

Q420 [*SocSpnd4*]
Benefits for single parents

Q421 [*SocSpnd5*]
Benefits for retired people

Q422 [*SocSpnd6*]
Benefits for people who care for those who are sick or disabled

	[*SocSpnd1*] %	[*SocSpnd2*] %	[*SocSpnd3*] %
Spend much more	3.4	13.0	7.6
Spend more	18.3	59.0	60.7
Spend the same as now	40.0	23.4	25.8
Spend less	29.8	1.6	2.7
Spend much less	5.3	0.1	0.3
(Don't know)	3.1	2.8	2.9
(Refusal/NA)	0.1	0.1	0.1

	[*SocSpnd4*] %	[*SocSpnd5*] %	[*SocSpnd6*] %
Spend much more	5.0	16.6	17.9
Spend more	28.6	54.3	63.6
Spend the same as now	41.0	24.5	15.4
Spend less	17.6	2.1	0.5
Spend much less	3.6	0.1	0.0
(Don't know)	4.2	2.4	2.4
(Refusal/NA)	0.1	0.1	0.1

Q423 [*FalseClm*]
I will read two statements. For each one please say
whether you agree or disagree. Firstly ...
Large numbers of people these days **falsely claim
benefits.**
% **IF AGREE OR DISAGREE: Strongly or slightly?**
59.4 Agree strongly
24.0 Agree slightly
 7.7 Disagree slightly
 4.6 Disagree strongly
 4.3 (Don't know)
 0.1 (Refusal/NA)

Q424 [*FailClm*]
(And do you agree or disagree that ...)
Large numbers of people who are eligible for benefits
these days **fail** to claim them.
% **IF AGREE OR DISAGREE:** Strongly or slightly?
37.4 Agree strongly
42.0 Agree slightly
11.7 Disagree slightly
 3.0 Disagree strongly
 5.8 (Don't know)
 0.1 (Refusal/NA)

Q425 [*Dole*]
Opinions differ about the level of benefits for
unemployed people.
Which of these two statements comes closest to your own
view

%
29.0 ... benefits for unemployed people are **too low** and cause
hardship,
46.5 or, benefits for unemployed people are **too high** and
discourage them from finding jobs?
17.1 (Neither)
0.3 Both: unemployment benefit causes hardship but can't
be higher or there would be no incentive to work
1.2 Both: unemployment benefit causes hardship to some,
while others do well out of it
0.5 About right/in between
2.0 Other answer (WRITE IN)
3.3 (Don't know)
0.1 (Refusal/NA)

Q427 [*TaxSpend*]
Suppose the government had to choose between the three
options
% on this card. Which do you think it should choose?
2.9 Reduce taxes and spend **less** on health, education and
social benefits
31.7 Keep taxes and spending on these services at the **same**
level as now
63.0 Increase taxes and spend **more** on health, education and
social benefits
1.3 (None)
1.0 (Don't know)
0.1 (Refusal/NA)

Q428 [*MstUnemp*]
Suppose two people working for a large firm each became
unemployed through no fault of their own. One had a very
high income, one had a very low income. Do you think the
very high
% earner should be entitled to:
8.7 ... more unemployment benefit than the very low earner,
73.2 the same amount,
12.5 less benefit,
2.5 or, no unemployment benefit at all?
0.6 It depends
0.5 Other answer (WRITE IN)
1.9 {Don't know)
0.1 (Refusal/NA)

Q430 [*MstRetir*]
Now suppose a very high earner and a very low earner in a
large firm retired. Do you think the very high earner
should be
% entitled to:
12.2 ... a bigger **state** retirement pension than the very low
earner,
71.2 the same amount,

```
11.2  a lower state pension,
 2.6  or, no state pension at all?
 0.5  It depends
 0.6  Other answer (WRITE IN)
 1.7  (Don't know)
 0.1  (Refusal/NA)
```

Q432 [*MstChild*]
Now what about child benefit. Should very high earners be
%   entitled to:

```
 0.8  ... more child benefit than very low earners
45.3  the same amount,
26.7  less,
25.1  or, no child benefit at all?
 0.2  It depends
 0.5  Other answer (WRITE IN)
 1.2  (Don't know)
 0.2  (Refusal/NA)
```

Q434 [*MstDisab*]
Now what about disability benefits. Should disabled
people with
%   very high incomes be entitled to:

```
 3.5  ... more disability benefits than those with very low
      incomes,
58.2  the same amount,
27.1  less disability benefits,
 8.5  or, no disability benefits at all?
 0.4  It depends
 0.5  Other answer (WRITE IN)
 1.5  (Don't know)
 0.3  (Refusal/NA)
```

Q436 [*HealResp*]
Please say from this card who you think should **mainly** be
responsible for paying for the cost of health care when
someone is ill?

Q437 [*RetResp*]
Still looking at this card, who you think should **mainly** be
responsible for ensuring that people have enough money to
live on in retirement?

Q438 [*SickResp*]
And who do you think should **mainly** be responsible for
ensuring that people have enough to live on if they become
sick for a long time or disabled?

Q439 [*UnemResp*]
And who do you think should **mainly** be responsible for
ensuring that people have enough to live on if they become
unemployed?

	[*HealResp*]	[*RetResp*]	[*SickResp*]	[*UnemResp*]
	%	%	%	%
Mainly the Government	82.3	55.9	79.6	84.8
Mainly a person's employer	9.0	8.8	8.5	3.0
Mainly the person them-selves and Family	6.2	32.5	9.5	9.8
(Don't know)	2.2	2.5	2.2	2.2
(Refusal/NA)	0.3	0.3	0.2	0.2

Q440 [*CareResp*]
And who do you think should **mainly** be responsible for
paying for the care needs of elderly people living in
residential and
  %   nursing homes?
77.9 Mainly the government
17.7 Mainly a person themselves and their family
 4.0 (Don't know)
 0.4 (Refusal/NA)

Q441 [*UBPoor*]
Now for a few questions on state benefits.
Think of a married couple without children living only on
unemployment benefit. Would you say that they are:

Q442 [*PensPoor*]
Now thinking of a married couple living only on the state
pension. Would you say that they are:

	[*UB Poor*]	[*PensPoor*]
	%	%
Really poor	10.8	16.7
Hard up	44.8	55.6
Have enough to	33.5	22.8
Have more than enough	2.9	0.5
(Don't know)	7.7	4.1
(Refusal/NA)	0.3	0.2

Q447 [*IncomGap*]
Thinking of income levels generally in Britain today,
would you say that the **gap** between those with high incomes
and those with
  %   low incomes is:
80.9 ... too large,
13.5 about right,
 1.5 or, too small?
 3.9 (Don't know)
 0.3 (Refusal/NA)

Q448 [*SRInc*]
  % Among which group would you place yourself:
  4.2 ... high income,
 52.3 middle income,
 42.6 or, low income?
  0.5 (Don't know)
  0.3 (Refusal/NA))

HEALTH CARE

Q454 [*NHSSat*]
     All in all, how satisfied or dissatisfied would you say
     you are with the way in which the National Health Service
     runs nowadays?

Q455 [*GPSat*]
     From your own experience, or from what you have heard,
     please say how satisfied or dissatisfied you are with the
     way in which each of these parts of the National Health
     Service runs nowadays:
     First, local doctors or GPs?

Q456 [*DentSat*]
     (And how satisfied or dissatisfied are you with the NHS as
     regards ...)
     ... National Health Service Dentists?

Q457 [*InpatSat*]
     ... Being in hospital as an **in-patient?**

Q458 [*OutpaSat*]
     ... Attending hospital as an **out-patient?**

	[*NHSat*]	[*GPSat*]	[*Dent Sat*]	[*Inpat Sat*]	[*Outpa Sat*]
	%	%	%	%	%
Very satisfied	8.2	26.9	14.5	16.4	12.7
Quite satisfied	33.4	48.5	38.1	37.6	39.6
Neither satisfied nor dissatisfied	21.5	10.0	17.1	20.0	20.0
Quite dissatisfied	25.6	9.9	13.6	12.5	15.9
Very dissatisfied	10.7	3.6	9.5	4.8	5.9
(Don't know)	0.4	0.8	7.0	8.4	5.5
(Refusal/NA)	0.3	0.3	0.3	0.3	0.3

Q459 [*PrivMed*]
     Are **you yourself** covered by a private health insurance
     scheme, that is an insurance scheme that allows you to get
     private medical **treatment?**
     ADD IF NECESSARY: 'For example, BUPA or PPP.'
  % IF INSURANCE COVERS DENTISTRY **ONLY**, CODE 'No'
 17.2 Yes
 82.4 No
  0.2 (Don't know)
  0.3 (Refusal/NA)

Q461 [*NHSLimit*]
It has been suggested that the National Health Service
should be available **only to those with lower incomes**.
This would mean that contributions and taxes could be
lower and most people would then take out medical
insurance or pay for health care.
Do you support or oppose this idea?
  % IF 'SUPPORT' OR 'OPPOSE': A lot or a little?
10.0 Support a lot
16.1 Support a little
18.7 Oppose a little
52.9 Oppose a lot
 2.0 (Don't know)
 0.3 (Refusal/NA)

Q462 [*InPat1*]
Now, suppose you had to go into a local NHS hospital for
observation and maybe an operation. From what you know or
have heard, please say whether you think the hospital
doctors would tell you all you feel you need to know?

Q463 [*InPat2*]
(And please say whether you think . . .)
. . . the hospital doctors would take seriously any views
you may have on the sorts of treatment available?

Q464 [*InPat3*]
. . . the operation would take place on the day it was
booked for?

Q465 [*InPat4*]
. . . you would be allowed home only when you were really
well enough to leave?

Q466 [*InPat5*]
. . . the nurses would take seriously any complaints you
may have?

Q467 [*InPat6*]
. . . the hospital doctors would take seriously any
complaints you may have?

Q468 [*InPat7*]
. . . there would be a particular nurse responsible for
dealing with any problems you may have?

Q469 [*OutPat1*]
Now suppose you had a back problem and your GP referred
you to a hospital out-patients' department. From what you
know or have heard, please say whether you think . . .
. . . you would get an appointment within three months?

Q470 [*OutPat2*]
(And please say whether you think . . .)
. . . when you arrived, the doctor would see you within
half an hour of your appointment time?

Q471 [*OutPat3*]
... if you wanted to complain about the treatment you
received, you would be able to without any fuss or bother?

Q472 [*WhchHosp*]
Now suppose you needed to go into hospital for an
operation.
Do you think you would have a say about which hospital you
went to?

	[*In Pat1*]	[*In Pat2*]	[*In Pat3*]	[*In Pat4*]	[*In Pat5*]	[*In Pat6*]
	%	%	%	%	%	%
Definitely would	19.5	12.1	6.1	12.9	18.0	15.2
Probably would	52.4	52.4	43.6	39.9	59.0	57.8
Probably would not	21.4	27.2	36.9	35.6	17.6	21.0
Definitely would not	5.0	5.5	8.9	9.4	2.6	3.0
(Don't know)	1.4	3.3	4.3	2.0	2.6	2.7
(Refusal/NA)	0.3	0.3	0.3	0.3	0.3	0.3

	[*In Pat7*]	[*Out Pat1*]	[*Out Pat2*]	[*Out Pat3*]	[*Which Hosp*]
	%	%	%	%	%
Definitely would	12.5	9.8	4.4	10.0	4.1
Probably would	40.0	35.6	28.2	46.6	17.3
Probably would not	33.5	34.8	43.0	28.7	49.3
Definitely would not	6.1	14.9	21.6	8.7	25.1
(Don't know)	7.7	4.6	2.5	5.6	3.9
(Refusal/NA)	0.3	0.3	0.3	0.3	0.3

Q473 [*GPChange*]
Suppose you wanted to change your GP and go to a different
practice, how difficult or easy do you think this would be
to arrange?
% Would it be:
7.3 ... very difficult,
20.7 fairly difficult,
37.6 Not very difficult,
27.5 or, not at all difficult?
6.7 (Don't know)
0.3 (Refusal/NA)

Q474 [*DentLimt*]
Many dentists now provide NHS treatment only to those
with lower incomes. This means that other people have to
pay the full amount for their dental treatment, or take
out private insurance to cover their treatment.
Do you support or oppose this happening?
% IF 'SUPPORT' OR 'OPPOSE': 'A lot or a little?'
8.3 Support a lot
18.0 Support a little
20.2 Oppose a little

50.4 Oppose a lot
 2.9 (Don't know)
 0.3 (Refusal/NA)

IF 'No' AT [PrivMed] OR 'No' AT [DentInsu]
Q476 [*DentOthr*]
Is your **dental** treatment covered by any (*other*) private
 % insurance scheme?
 5.3 Yes
86.2 No
 3.0 (Don't go to the dentist)
 0.1 (Don't know)
 1.3 (Refusal/NA)

Q477 [*GPUse*]
In the last **twelve** months, have you or a close family
member visited an NHS GP?
PROBE AS NECESSARY AND CODE ONE ONLY

Q478 [*OutPUse*]
And in the last **twelve** months, have you or a close family
member been an **outpatient** in an NHS hospital?
PROBE AS NECESSARY AND CODE ONE ONLY

Q479 [*InPUse*]
And in the last **twelve** months, have you or a close family
member been an **inpatient** in an NHS hospital?

Q480 [*VisitUse*]   N=3146
And in the last **twelve** months, have you or a close
family member **visited** a patient in an NHS hospital?

Q481 [*PrivUse*]
And in the last **twelve** months, have you or a close family
member had any medical treatment as a **private** patient?

Q482 [*PrDenUse*]
And in the last **twelve** months, have you or a close family
member had any **dental treatment as a private** patient?

Q483 [*NHSDnUse*]
And in the last **twelve** months, have you or a close family
member had any **dental** treatment as an **NHS** patient?

	[*GPUse*]	[*OutPUse*]	[*InPUse*]	[*VisitUse*]
	%	%	%	%
Yes, just me	20.7	20.6	10.6	18.4
Yes, not me but close family member	17.5	26.7	21.7	9.1
Yes, both	54.3	13.7	2.9	32.7
No, neither	7.3	38.6	64.6	39.4
(Don't know)	–	0.1	–	0.1
(Refusal/NA)	0.3	0.3	0.3	0.3

	[*PrivUse*]	[*PrDenUse*]	[*NHSDnUse*]
	%	%	%
Yes, just me	3.8	8.5	13.6
Yes, not me but close	6.5	8.3	18.5
family member			
Yes, both	1.1	7.3	27.1
No, neither	88.2	75.2	40.2
(Don't know)	0.1	0.5	0.4
(Refusal/NA)	0.3	0.3	0.3

ECONOMIC ACTIVITY, LABOUR MARKET AND INDUSTRIAL RELATIONS

Q497 [*REconAct*] **(PERCENTAGES REFER TO HIGHEST ANSWER ON THE LIST)**
Which of these descriptions applied to what you were doing

% last week, that is the seven days ending last Sunday?

%	
3.3	In full-time education (not paid for by employer, including on vacation)
0.4	On government training/employment programme (eg. Youth Training, Training for Work etc)
56.1	In paid work (or away temporarily) for at least 10 hours in week
0.3	Waiting to take up paid work already accepted
2.8	Unemployed and registered at a benefit office
1.1	Unemployed, **not** registered, but actively looking for a job (of at least 10 hours a week)
0.6	Unemployed, wanting a job (of at least 10 hours per week) but **not** actively looking for a job
4.2	Permanently sick or disabled
20.4	Wholly retired from work
10.4	Looking after the home
0.3	(Doing something else) (WRITE IN)
0.3	(Refusal/NA)

ASK ALL SELF-EMPLOYED IN CURRENT OR LAST JOB

N = 220

Q513 [*SEmpNum*]
In your work or business, (*do/did*) you have any employees, or not?
IF YES: How many?
IF 'NO EMPLOYEES', CODE 0.
FOR 500+ EMPLOYEES, CODE 500.
NOTE: FAMILY MEMBERS MAY BE EMPLOYEES ONLY IF THEY RECEIVE A REGULAR WAGE OR SALARY.

%	Median: 0
-	(Don't know)
-	(Refusal/NA)

ASK ALL IN PAID WORK

N = 1764

Q520 [*WkJbHrsI*]
How many hours do you normally work a week in your main job - **including any paid or unpaid overtime?**
ROUND TO NEAREST HOUR.
IF RESPONDENT CANNOT ANSWER, ASK ABOUT LAST WEEK.

IF RESPONDENT DOES NOT KNOW EXACTLY, ACCEPT AN ESTIMATE.
FOR 95+ HOURS, CODE 95.
FOR 'VARIES TOO MUCH TO SAY', CODE 96.

% **Median: 40 hours**
1.9 Varies too much to say
0.4 (Don't know)
0.1 (Refusal/NA)

ASK ALL WHO HAVE EVER WORKED   N=3057

Q552 [*UnionSA*]
(May I just check) are you **now** a member of a trade union or
staff association?

%
19.1 Yes, trade union
3.6 Yes, staff association
76.8 No
0.1 (Don't know)
0.4 (Refusal/NA)

IF 'No/DK' AT [UnionSA]   N=3057

Q553 [*TUSAEver*]
Have you **ever** been a member of a trade union or staff
association?

%
27.2 Yes, trade union
2.1 Yes, staff association
47.5 No
0.1 (Don't know)
0.4 (Refusal/NA)

Q557 [*EmploydT*]
For how long have you been continuously employed by your
present employer?
% **Median: 60 months**
0.1 (Don't know)
0.1 (Refusal/NA)

IF 'Start looking' AT [ELookJob]
Q591 [*EFindJob*] **(NOT ON SCREEN)**
How long do you think it would take you to find an
acceptable replacement job? IF LESS THAN ONE MONTH, CODE
AS ONE MONTH. IF 'NEVER' PLEASE CODE 96.
% **Median: 2 months**
0.8 Never
2.9 (Don't know)
0.5 (Refusal/NA)

IF 'Yes' AT [NwUnemp] OR UNEMPLOYED
Q596 [*NwUnempT*]
IF 'Yes' AT [NwUnemp]: For how many **months** in total during
the last five years?
IF UNEMPLOYED: For how many **months** in total during the
last five years that is, since May 1993, have you been
unemployed and seeking work?
INTERVIEWER: IF LESS THAN ONE MONTH, CODE AS 1.

% **Median: 6 months**
0.2 (Don't know)
0.3 (Refusal/NA)

ASK ALL UNEMPLOYED   N = 139
Q600 [*CurUnEmp*] **(NOT ON SCREEN)**
How long has this present period of unemployment and
seeking work lasted so far? ENTER NUMBER, THEN SPECIFY
MONTHS OR YEARS.
% **Median: 8.58 months**
  - (Don't know)
0.3 (Refusal/NA)

Q690 [*DisNew*]
Do you have any health problems or disabilities that have
% lasted or are expected to last for more than a year?
35.1 Yes
64.4 No
0.1 (Don't know)
0.3 (Refusal/NA)

IF 'Yes' AT [DisNew]
Q691 [*DisWrk*]
Does this health problem or disability affect the **kind** of
% paid work or the **amount** of paid work that you might do?
17.0 Yes
17.9 No
0.2 (Don't know)
0.5 (Refusal/NA)

Q692 [*DisLmt*]
And does this health problem or disability limit your
ability to carry out normal day-to-day activities?
If you are receiving medication or treatment please
consider
% what the situation would be without it.
20.0 Yes
15.1 No
0.1 (Don't know)
0.5 (Refusal/NA)

ASK ALL
Q693 [*DisPrj*]
Generally speaking, do you think there is a lot of
prejudice in Britain against people with disabilities, a
little, hardly any,
% or none?
25.3 A lot
51.1 A little
14.6 Hardly any
6.4 None
2.3 (Don't know)
0.3 (Refusal/NA)

Q694 [DisJob]
And when it comes to **getting a job**, do you think there is a
lot of prejudice in Britain against people with
disabilities, a
%   little, hardly any, or none?
36.6 A lot
48.9 A little
 7.8 Hardly any
 2.9 None
 3.5 (Don't know)
 0.3 (Refusal/NA)

Q695 [DDAEmp]
As far as you know, is it against the law or not for an
employer to refuse to take on a person only because they
have a disability?
%   If you (Don't know), just say so.
70.1 Against the law
 7.7 Not against the law
 4.9 Depends
16.9 (Don't know)
 0.3 (Refusal/NA)

Q696 [DDAShp]
AGAIN, as far as you know, is it against the law or not for
someone providing goods and services to refuse to serve a
person only because they have a disability?
%   **AGAIN**, if you (Don't know), just say so.
67.5 Against the law
12.1 Not against the law
 2.3 Depends
17.8 (Don't know)
 0.3 (Refusal/NA)

Q697 [TrnEm1]
Now some questions about **training**. Please say who you
think should mainly be responsible for paying for
training for **employees**
... where the training is necessary for the work that
%   they do?
10.4 Mainly the government
84.1 Mainly the employer
 0.9 Mainly a person and their family
 0.0 Someone else (WRITE IN)
 3.3 (Mixture)
 1.0 (Don't know)
 0.3 (Refusal/NA)

Q699 [TrnEm2]
(And please say who you think should mainly be
responsible for paying for training for **employees**)
... where the training is **not** necessary for the work that
%   they do, but may help them do their job better?
14.8 Mainly the government
59.2 Mainly the employer

20.1 Mainly a person and their family
 0.1 Someone else (WRITE IN)
 3.7 (Mixture)
 1.8 (Don't know)
 0.3 (Refusal/NA)

Q701 [*TrnEm3*]
      (And please say who you think should mainly be
      responsible for paying for training for **employees**)
      ... where the training is **not** necessary for the work that
  %   they do, but may help them get better jobs in the future?
27.6 Mainly the government
13.6 Mainly the employer
53.6 Mainly a person and their family
 0.1 Someone else (WRITE IN)
 2.8 (Mixture)
 2.0 (Don't know)
 0.3 (Refusal/NA)

Q703 [*TrnUn1*]
      And please say who you think should mainly be responsible
      for paying for training for **the unemployed**
      ... where the training is necessary for a particular type
  %   of work that they might do?
70.3 Mainly the government
16.5 Mainly employers in the local area
 7.1 Mainly a person and their family
 0.1 Someone else (WRITE IN)
 3.9 (Mixture)
 1.7 (Don't know)
 0.3 (Refusal/NA)

Q705 [*TrnUn2*]
      (And please say who you think should mainly be
      responsible for paying for training for **the unemployed**)
      ... where the training is **not** necessary for a particular
  %   type of work, but may help them do **any** job better?
64.5 Mainly the government
 9.6 Mainly employers in the local area
19.4 Mainly a person and their family
 0.1 Someone else (WRITE IN)
 3.6 (Mixture)
 2.4 (Don't know)
 0.3 (Refusal/NA)

GENETICS RESEARCH   N=2120
Q719 [*TrGenJou*]
      Now some questions on research into human genes.
      How much trust do you have in each of the following to tell
      the **truth** about **any dangers** of research into human genes?

      Journalists on national newspapers?

Q720 [*TrGenGvM*]
Government health ministers?
(How much trust do you have in them to tell the **truth** about **any dangers** of research into human genes?)

Q721 [*TrGenUni*]
Scientists in universities?

Q722 [*TrGenGvS*]
Government scientists?

Q723 [*TrGenCom*]
Scientists working for drug or pharmaceutical companies?

Q724 [*TrGenCha*]
Scientists working for health research charities?

	[*TrGenJou*] %	[*TrGenGvM*] %	[*TrGenUni*] %
A lot of trust	2.2	2.5	22.2
Some trust	23.8	40.0	56.6
Very little trust	47.3	40.4	14.4
No trust at all	24.2	14.5	4.2
(Don't know)	2.0	1.9	1.9
(Refusal/NA)	0.6	0.6	0.7

	[*TrGenGvS*] %	[*TrGenGvS*] %	[*TrGenCha*] %
A lot of trust	6.3	9.3	26.7
Some trust	49.0	39.4	59.5
Very little trust	31.1	33.0	8.9
No trust at all	11.1	15.9	2.3
(Don't know)	1.8	1.7	1.9
(Refusal/NA)	0.6	0.6	0.6

Q725 [*GenRefIn*]
People can take genetic tests to tell them whether they are likely to develop a serious genetic condition in the future.
In your opinion, should such tests be used ...
... by insurance companies to **accept or refuse people** for life insurance policies?

Q727 [*GenChgIn*]
In your opinion, should such tests be used
... by insurance companies in deciding **how much to charge** people for their life insurance policies?

	[*GenRefIn*] %	[*GenChgIn*] %
Definitely should	4.2	2.8
Probably should	15.8	18.4
Probably should **not**	27.7	27.1
Definitely should **not**	47.8	47.4
(Other answer (WRITE IN))	0.2	0.1
(Don't know)	3.5	3.5
(Refusal/NA)	0.7	0.7

Q729 [*GenEmpl*] $\boxed{N = 2120}$
      Now suppose someone who is applying for a job **has had** such
      a genetic test. Should the employer have **the right** to see
      the result of this test, or not?

Q731 [*GenTakeT*]
      Now suppose the applicant has **never** had such a test.
      Should the employer have the right to **make** the applicant
      have a test?

Q733 [*GenPromo*]
      And what about an **existing employee** who has had such a
      test which shows that they **are** at risk of developing a
      serious genetic condition. Should the employer have the
      right to take the test result into account when the chance
      of promotion comes up?

	[*GenEmpl*]	[*GenTakeT*]	[*GenPromo*]
	%	%	%
Definitely should	5.9	2.4	4.4
Probably should	16.7	9.5	20.6
Probably should **not**	22.3	17.8	23.1
Definitely should **not**	49.6	65.7	46.6
(Other answer (WRITE IN))	0.3	0.3	0.6
DEPENDS ON THE JOB/TYPE OF WORK	2.0	1.3	0.5
(Don't know)	2.5	2.3	3.4
(Refusal/NA)	0.7	0.7	0.7

Q735 [*PregTest*]
      Genetic tests can also be taken from unborn babies while
      still in the womb, to show if the child is likely to be
      born with a serious medical condition, but such tests
      carry some risks.
      Which of the statements on this card comes closest to
   % your view?
44.7 **All pregnant women** should be offered such tests.
47.5 Only women where there is **special reason to suspect a
      problem** should be offered such tests.
 5.6 Such tests should **not be allowed** at all.
 1.5 (Don't know)
 0.7 (Refusal/NA)

Q736 [*AbMental*]
      Now suppose a woman had one of these tests and it showed
      that there **was** very likely to be a serious problem with
      her unborn child.
      Do you think it would be
      right or not for the woman to have a legal abortion . . .
      . . . if the child was very likely to be born with a serious
      mental disability and would never be able to lead an
      independent life?

Q737   [*AbPhys*]
  (Do you think it would be right or not for the woman to
  have a legal abortion . . .)
  . . . if the child was very likely to be born with a
  serious **physical disability** and would never be able
  to lead an independent life?

Q738   [*AbDie*]
  . . . if the child was very likely to be born with a
  condition that meant it would live in **good health,** but
  then would
  die in its twenties or thirties?

Q739   [*AbShort*]
  And what if the child would be healthy but would **never
  grow taller than an eight year old**?
  Do you think it would be right or not for the woman to
  have a legal abortion?

	[*AbMental*]	[*AbPhys*]
	%	%
Never right	8.0	10.2
Sometimes right	39.4	45.2
Always right	48.9	41.2
(Don't know)	2.9	2.6
(Refusal/NA)	0.8	0.8

	[*AbDie*]	[*AbShort*]
	%	%
Never right	35.4	47.5
Sometimes right	41.8	31.6
Always right	17.7	15.7
(Don't know)	4.3	4.4
(Refusal/NA	0.8	0.8

Q740   [*GenHeigh*] $N = 2120$
  Some things about a person are caused by their **genes,**
  which they inherit from their parents. Others may be to
  do with **the way they are brought up,** or **the way they live.**
  Some may happen just **by chance.**
  Please say what **you** think decides each of the things that
  I am going to READ OUT . . . . If you don't know, please just
  say so.
  . . . a person's height?

Q741   [*GenCleve*]
  Please say what **you** think decides . . .)
  . . . a person's intelligence?
  (If you (Don't know), please just say so).

Q742   [*GenGay*]
  Please say what **you** think decides . . .
  . . . being gay or lesbian?

Q743 [*GenHeart*]
And what do you think decides a person's chances . . .
. . . of getting heart disease?

Q744 [*GenCanc*]
. . . of getting breast cancer?

Q745 [*GenViol*]
. . . of being aggressive or violent?

Q746 [*GenFat*]
. . . of being **very overweight?**

Q747 [*GenEyes*]   N = 2120
. . .the colour of a person's eyes?

	[*GenHeigh*] %	[*GenCleve*] %	[*GenGay*] %
All to do with genes	40.0	12.0	15.5
Mostly to do with genes	35.9	24.1	18.2
Mostly to do with upbringing or lifestyle	1.1	17.6	6.8
All to do with upbringing or lifestyle	0.3	3.6	3.8
An equal mixture of genes and upbringing/lifestyle	9.9	32.8	13.0
Just chance	3.8	4.1	19.3
(Don't know)	8.2	5.0	22.6
(Refusal/NA)	0.8	0.8	0.8

	[*GenHeart*] %	[*GenCanc*] %	[*GenViol*] %
All to do with genes	9.9	12.7	2.7
Mostly to do with genes	19.2	35.5	6.6
Mostly to do with upbringing or lifestyle	15.5	2.5	32.7
All to do with upbringing or lifestyle	4.7	1.1	15.8
An equal mixture of genes and upbringing/lifestyle	37.7	19.0	28.5
Just chance	5.9	14.2	5.7
(Don't know)	6.2	14.2	7.1
(Refusal/NA)	0.8	0.8	0.8

	[*GenFat*] %	[*GenEyes*] %
All to do with genes	4.0	70.5
Mostly to do with genes	11.4	16.3
Mostly to do with upbringing or lifestyle	23.0	0.2
All to do with upbringing or lifestyle	11.1	0.0
An equal mixture of genes and upbringing/lifestyle	39.0	0.8
Just chance	4.5	5.3
(Don't know)	6.3	6.1
(Refusal/NA)	0.8	0.8

Q748 [*ChgHeig*]   N = 2120
Suppose it was discovered that a person's genes **could** be changed.
Do **you** think this should be allowed or **not** allowed to make a person . . .
. . . taller or shorter?

Q749 [*ChgCleve*]
Do **you** think this should be allowed or **not** allowed to make a person . . .)
. . . more intelligent?

Q750 [*ChgGay*]
. . . 'straight', rather than gay or lesbian?

Q751 [ChgStrai]
. . . gay or lesbian, rather than straight?

Q752 [*ChgHeart*]
And should changing a person's genes be allowed or **not** allowed to . . .
. . . reduce a person's chances of getting heart disease?

Q753 [*ChgCanc*]
. . . to reduce a person's chances of getting breast cancer?

Q754 [*ChgViol*]
. . . to make them less aggressive or violent?

Q755 [*ChgFat*]
. . . to make them of average weight, rather than very overweight?

Q756 [*ChgSex*]   N = 2120
. . . to determine the sex of an unborn baby?

	[*ChgHeig*] %	[*ChgCleve*] %	[*ChgGay*] %
Definitely allowed	5.2	5.0	6.1
Probably allowed	18.4	15.0	12.4
Probably **not** allowed	20.5	23.8	21.1
Definitely **not** allowed	52.9	53.3	54.4
(Don't know)	2.0	2.1	5.2
(Refusal/NA)	0.9	0.9	0.9

	[*ChgStrai*] %	[*ChgHeart*] %	[*ChgCanc*] %
Definitely allowed	1.0	27.3	35.5
Probably allowed	5.3	40.8	36.3
Probably **not** allowed	18.4	11.9	9.6
Definitely **not** allowed	69.7	16.4	14.8
(Don't know)	4.7	2.7	2.8
(Refusal/NA)	0.9	0.9	0.9

	[ChgViol]	[ChgFat]	[ChgSex]
	%	%	%
Definitely allowed	24.3	12.8	3.0
Probably allowed	34.3	32.2	9.3
Probably **not** allowed	16.8	23.2	16.1
Definitely **not** allowed	20.5	27.9	68.6
(Don't know)	3.1	3.0	2.1
(Refusal/NA)	1.0	0.9	1.0

Q757 [GenFamil]   N = 2120

Has a **doctor** ever advised you, or any member of your
immediate family, of a serious genetic condition in
your family?
%   FOR 'NOT SURE', CODE (DON'T KNOW).
8.0 Yes
90.3 No
0.8 (Don't know)
0.9 (Refusal/NA)

IF NOT REFUSED AT [GenFamil]
Q758 [GenCare]
And have you ever **helped care for** a family member or
%   friend, **born** with a serious genetic condition?
9.0 Yes
89.6 No
0.4 (Don't know)
0.9 (Refusal/NA)

CITIZENSHIP   N = 2067
Q759 [GovtWork]
CARD
Which of these statements best describes your opinion on
%   the present system of governing in Britain?
2.2 Works extremely well and could not be improved
43.4 Could be improved in small ways but mainly works well
40.3 Could be improved quite a lot
11.4 Needs a great deal of improvement
1.8 (Don't know)
0.8 (Refusal/NA)

Q760 [Lords]   N = 1026
Do you think that the House of Lords should remain as it is
%   or is some change needed?
23.1 Remain as it is
65.2 Change needed
11.2 (Don't know)
0.5 (Refusal/NA)

IF 'Change needed' AT [Lords]
Q761 [LordsHow]
%   Do you think the House of Lords should be:
16.1 ... replaced by a different body
13.1 abolished and replaced by nothing
33.9 or, should there be some other kind of change?

```
12.2  (Don't know)
11.6  (Refusal/NA)
```

Q762 [*Monarchy*]
      How important or unimportant do you think it is for
   % Britain to continue to have a monarchy?
27.7 ... very important
35.8 quite important
17.5 not very important
 6.8 not at all important
 9.9 or, do you think the monarchy should be abolished?
 1.9 (Don't know)
 0.4 (Refusal/NA)

Q763 [*VoteSyst*]   [N=1026]
      Some people say that we should change the voting system to
      allow smaller political parties to get a fairer share of
      MPs. Others say we should keep the voting system as it is,
      to produce more effective government.
      Which view comes closest to your own:
   % IF ASKED, REFERS TO 'PROPORTIONAL REPRESENTATION'
32.4 ... that we should change the voting system
62.8 or, keep it as it is?
 4.4 (Don't know)
 0.4 (Refusal/NA)

Q781 [*GovNoSay*]
      Please choose a phrase from this card to say how much you
      agree or disagree with the following statements.
      People like me have no say in what the government does

Q782 [*LoseTch*]
      (Please choose a phrase from this card to say how much you
      agree or disagree with this statement)
      Generally speaking those we elect as MPs lose touch with
      people pretty quickly

Q783 [*VoteIntr*]   [N=2067]
      Parties are only interested in people's votes, not in
      their opinions

Q784 [*VoteOnly*]
      Voting is the only way people like me can have any say
      about how the government runs things.

Q785 [*GovComp*]
      Sometimes politics and government seem so complicated
      that a person like me cannot really understand what is
      going on.

Q786 [*PtyNtMat*]
      It doesn't really matter which party is in power, in the
      end things go on much the same.

	[GovNo Say]	[Lose Tch]	[Vote Intr]	[Vote Only]	[Gov Comp]	[PtyNt Mat]
	%	%	%	%	%	%
Agree strongly	16.6	19.8	21.4	13.5	14.9	17.3
Agree	42.4	51.7	47.5	53.1	48.9	51.2
Neither agree nor disagree	15.0	15.1	13.7	10.7	11.2	6.9
Disagree	23.0	10.9	15.5	19.3	20.3	20.7
Disagree strongly	1.6	0.5	0.5	1.9	3.4	2.6
(Don't know)	0.6	1.2	0.6	0.7	0.4	0.5
(Refusal/NA)	0.8	0.8	0.8	0.8	0.8	0.8
	0.8					

Q787 [GovTrust]
   How much do you trust British governments of any party to
   place the needs of the nation above the interests of their
   own political party?

                                                    N=2067

Q788 [PolTrust]
   And how much do you trust British police not to bend the
   rules in trying to get a conviction?

Q789 [MPsTrust]
   And how much do you trust politicians of any party in
   Britain to tell the truth when they are in a tight corner?

	[GovTrust]	[PolTrust]	[MPsTrust]
	%	%	%
Just about always	2.0	5.8	0.6
Most of the time	26.5	42.1	8.0
Only some of the time	52.0	37.8	42.8
Almost never	17.2	10.9	46.4
(Don't know)	1.5	2.6	1.4
(Refusal/NA)	0.8	0.8	0.8

Q790 [SocTrust]
   Generally speaking, would you say that most people can be
   trusted, or that you can't be too careful in dealing with
 % people?
44.0 Most people can be trusted
54.4 Can't be too careful in dealing with people
 0.8 (Don't know)
 0.8 Refusal/NA

Q791 [RaceGlty]
   Suppose two people - one white, one black - each appear in
   court, charged with a crime they did not commit.
   What do you think their chances are of being found guilty
   . . .
 % READ OUT . . .
 3.2 . . . the white person is more likely to be found guilty,
41.0 they have the same chance,
50.8 or, the black person is more likely to be found guilty?
 4.0 (Don't know)
 1.0 (Refusal/NA)

Q792 [*RichGlty*]
Now suppose another two people from different
backgrounds - one rich, one poor - each appear in court,
charged with a crime they did not commit.
What do you think their chances are of being found guilty
...
%   READ OUT ...
1.2 ... the rich person is more likely to be found guilty,
33.1 they have the same chance,
62.5 or, the poor person is more likely to be found guilty?
2.3 (Don't know)
0.9 (Refusal/NA)

N=2067

Q793 [*NeigIll*]
Suppose that you were in bed ill and needed someone to go
to the chemist to collect your prescription while they
were doing their shopping.
How comfortable would you be asking a neighbour to do
this?

Q794 [*NeigSink*]
Now suppose you found your sink was blocked, but you did
not have a plunger to unblock it.
How comfortable would you be asking a neighbour to borrow
a plunger?

Q795 [*NeigMilk*]
Now suppose the milkman called for payment. The bill was
£5 but you had no cash.
How comfortable would you be asking a neighbour if you
could borrow £5?

	[*NeigIll*]	[*NeigSink*]	[*NeigMilk*]
	%	%	%
Very comfortable	47.0	53.5	17.6
Fairly comfortable	30.7	31.3	16.2
Fairly uncomfortable	10.3	7.4	19.5
Very uncomfortable	10.6	6.3	44.6
(Don't know)	0.4	0.5	1.2
(Refusal/NA)	0.9	0.9	0.9

Q796 [*VATCheat*]
Please say what comes closest to what you think about the
following situation.
A householder is having a repair job done by a local
plumber. He is told that if he pays cash, he will not be
%   charged VAT. So he pays cash.
26.1 Nothing wrong
30.5 Bit wrong
30.0 Wrong
7.6 Seriously wrong
3.7 Very seriously wrong
1.2 (Don't know)
1.0 (Refusal/NA)

Q797 [*VATDo*]
%   Might you do this if the situation came up?   N = 2067
70.5 Yes
25.4 No
 3.1 (Don't know)
 1.0 (Refusal/NA)

Q798 [*ChngKp10*]
     What comes closest to what you think about this
     situation?
     A man gives a **£5** note for goods he is buying in a big store.
     By mistake, he is given change for a **£10** note. He notices,
%   but keeps the change.
 7.7 Nothing wrong
19.8 Bit wrong
47.8 Wrong
14.5 Seriously wrong
 8.9 Very seriously wrong
 0.4 (Don't know)
 0.9 (Refusal/NA)

Q799 [*ChngDo10*]
%   Might you do this if the situation came up?
30.3 Yes
67.3 No
 1.4 (Don't know)
 1.0 (Refusal/NA)

Q800 [*PByLost*]
     Suppose you are in the middle of a town you do not know
     very well. You are trying to find a particular street and
     have got a bit lost. How comfortable would you be asking
%   **any** passer-by for directions?
41.8 Very comfortable
45.1 Fairly comfortable
 7.9 Fairly uncomfortable
 3.7 Very uncomfortable
 0.5 (Don't know)
 0.9 (Refusal/NA)

Q801 [*PByPhone*]   N = 2067
     AGAIN suppose you are in the middle of a town you do not
     know very well. You need to make an urgent 'phone call
     from a 'phone box but you only have a £5 note. How
%   comfortable would you be asking any passer-by for the
     right change?
14.1 Very comfortable
35.5 Fairly comfortable
28.2 Fairly uncomfortable
20.3 Very uncomfortable
 0.8 (Don't know)
 1.0 (Refusal/NA)

LOCAL GOVERNMENT
Q803 [*CntlCncl*]

N=2067

Now some questions about local government.
Do you think that **local councils ought to be controlled by**
% **central government** more, less or about the same amount as
now?
14.9 More
26.5 Less
50.7 About the same
 6.9 (Don't know)
 1.0 (Refusal/NA)

Q804 [*Rates*]
Do you think the **level of the council tax** should be up to
the local council to decide, or should central government
% have the final say?
59.3 Local council
33.5 Central government
 6.1 (Don't know)
 1.1 (Refusal/NA)

Q805 [*CTaxVal*]
And thinking about the level of the council tax in your
area, do you think it gives good value for money or not?
%
 1.6 Very good value
27.1 Good value
28.8 Neither good value nor poor value
28.6 Poor value
 8.0 Very poor value
 4.8 (Don't know)
 1.0 (Refusal/NA)

Q806 [*DcBcName*][1]
Do you happen to know the name of your **city, district or**
% **borough Council**?
79.7 Yes
18.7 No
 0.7 (Don't know)
 1.0 (Refusal/NA)

Q812 [*DcBcLdr*]
And do you happen to know who at the moment is the leader
of the largest party or group on your **city/district/**
% **borough** Council?
13.4 Yes
84.6 No
 0.9 (Don't know)
 1.0 (Refusal/NA)

---

[1] In this section the wording 'city, district or borough council' was replaced by 'borough council' in London.

IF 'Yes' AT [DcBCLdr]
Q813 [*DcLdrNam*]
   What is his or her name?
   ENTER NAME

Q815 [*LaServ*]
   Now just thinking about your local **city/district/borough**
   Council, how well would you say it keeps you informed
   about the services it provides? Please choose a phrase
 % from the card.
 8.3 Very well
44.1 Fairly well
34.6 Not very well
10.5 Not at all well
 1.5 (Don't know)
 1.0 (Refusal/NA)

Q816 [*LaOth*]
   And how well does your local council keep you informed
   about the things that are happening in your area that
 % affect you as a resident?
 6.5 Very well
42.1 Fairly well
36.8 Not very well
11.7 Not at all well
 1.8 (Don't know)
 1.1 (Refusal/NA)

VERSIONS A & B: ASK ALL
Q821 [*GEVot97*]
   Talking to people about the general election last year,
   we have found a lot of people didn't manage to vote. How
   about you – did you manage to vote in the general
 % election?
75.7 Yes
19.1 No
 0.9 Too young to vote
 2.0 Not eligible/Not on register
 1.2 Can't remember/ (Don't know)
 1.1 (Refusal/NA)

IF 'No' AT [GEVot97]
Q822 [*WhyNVt97*]
   Which of the explanations on this card best describes the
 % main reason why you did not vote in the general election?
 2.9 There was no one who I wanted to vote for
 2.2 I was too busy
 0.5 I/someone in my family was unwell
 2.7 I was away from home on election day
 4.1 I was not interested in the election
 2.6 I was not registered to vote
 3.1 I deliberately decided not to vote
 0.5 The polling station was too difficult to get to
 0.4 None of these (PLEASE SPECIFY)

```
    0.1  (Don't know)
    2.3  (Refusal/NA)
```

ASK ALL IN ENGLAND IF 'Yes' AT [GEVot97] AND IF   N=709
'No/Dk/Not answered' AT [VtMay98]
Q824 [*LocEl97*]
      And when you voted in the general election, did you also
   % have the chance to vote in local elections at the same
      time?
64.3 Yes
23.1 No
 6.7 (Don't know)
 5.9 (Refusal/NA)

Q834 [*WkendVot*]
      At present local elections are always held on a Thursday.
      Which of the statements on this card comes closest to **your**
   % views about the idea of holding them over a weekend
      instead?
29.5 Local elections should be held over a weekend because
      more people would be able to go and vote
20.4   Local elections should still be held on a Thursday
      because people have better things to do with their time at
      the weekend
48.3 I don't mind either way
 0.8 (Don't know)
 1.1 (Refusal/NA)

Q835 [*WkndVtLk*]
      And what about you? Do you think you would be more likely
      to vote if local elections were held over a weekend rather
      than on a Thursday, less likely, or would it not make any
   % difference?
16.2 More likely
74.8 Make no difference
 0.6 (Don't know)
 1.1 (Refusal/NA)

Q836 [*PostVot*]
      Which of the statements on this card comes closest to your
      view about voting in local elections?
37.6 Everyone should be allowed to vote by post in local
      elections because more people would use their vote
58.5 People should normally have to go to a polling station to
      vote because that is the only way we can be sure that
      elections are run fairly
 2.7 (Don't know)
 1.1 (Refusal/NA)

Q837 [*PostVtLk*]   N=2067
      And what about you? Do you think you would be more likely
      to vote if you could vote by post rather than go to a
      polling station, less likely, or would it not make any
   % difference?
```
```

19.7 More likely
70.5 Make no difference
 7.7 Less likely
 0.3 (Already has postal vote)
 0.6 (Don't know)
 1.1 (Refusal/NA)

Q838 [*ShopVtLk*]
     And what if you could vote at a local shop or post office
     rather than go to polling station? Do you think that you
     would be more likely to vote, less likely, or would it not
%   make any difference?
21.9 More likely
67.7 Make no difference
 8.5 Less likely
 0.7 (Don't know)
 1.1 (Refusal/NA)

Q839 [*VoteComp*]
     Which way of these two ways of voting would you prefer to
%   use?
31.1 ... filling in a ballot paper
10.9 pressing a computer button,
56.2 or, don't you mind either way?
 0.7 (Don't know)
 1.1 (Refusal/NA)

Q845 [*SchlStnd*]
     Thinking about how local councils run schools, which of
%   the statements on this card comes closest to your view?
67.2 The government should lay down standards for schools that
     all councils have to meet by law
28.5 Local councils should be completely free to decide for
     themselves how best to run their schools
 3.2 (Don't know)
 1.1 (Refusal/NA)

Q846 [*HelpStnd*]

N = 2067

     And thinking about how local councils decide who should
     get a 'home help', which of the statements comes close to
 %   your view?
48.8 The government should lay down standards for who gets a
     'home help' that all councils have to meet by law
47.9 Local councils should be completely free to decide for
     themselves who should get a 'home help'
 2.1 (Don't know)
 1.1 (Refusal/NA)

Q847 [*BinsStnd*]
     And thinking about how local councils run refuse
     collection, which of these statements comes closest to
     your view?
 %
37.2 The government should lay down standards for refuse
     collection that all councils have to meet by law

60.0 Local councils should be completely free to decide for
     themselves how best to run their refuse collection
 1.7 (Don't know)
 1.1 (Refusal/NA)

Q848 [*CllrDevl*]
     Say there was a proposal for a major new building
     development in your neighbourhood. Choosing a phrase
     from this card, please say how much you would trust the
     councillors on your **city, district, or borough** Council to
   % come to the best view about the proposal?
 2.1 Just about always
32.8 Most of the time
45.4 Only some of the time
14.9 Almost never
 3.5 (Don't know)
 1.1 (Refusal/NA)

Q849 [*JuryDevl*]
     And **AGAIN** choosing a phrase from the card, how much would
     you trust a 'jury' of (*twelve/fifteen*) ordinary local
   % people chosen at random to come to the best view?
 8.2 Just about always
54.5 Most of the time
26.8 Only some of the time
 6.3 Almost never
 3.1 (Don't know)
 1.1 (Refusal/NA)

Q850 [*NIreland*]

$\boxed{N = 1026}$

     Do you think the long-term policy for Northern Ireland
   % should be for it:
25.8 ... to remain part of the United Kingdom
51.9 or, to unify with the rest of Ireland?
 1.3 **EDIT:** Northern Ireland should be an independent state
   - **EDIT:** Northern Ireland should be split up into two
 4.1 **EDIT:** It should be up to the Irish to decide
 2.5 Other answer (WRITE IN)
13.3 (Don't know)
 1.2 (Refusal/NA)

Q852 [*ECPolicy*]
     Do you think Britain's long-term policy should be:
   %
13.9 ... to leave the European Union,
36.4 to stay in the EU and try to **reduce** the EU's powers,
22.5 to leave things as they are,
 8.5 to stay in the EU and try to **increase** the EU's powers,
 7.9 or, to work for the formation of a single European
     government?
10.0 (Don't know)
 0.8 (Refusal/NA)

Q853 [*EcuView*]
And here are three statements about the future of the
pound in the European Union. Which **one** comes closest to
% your view?
19.5 **Replace** the pound by a single currency
22.1 Use **both** the pound and a new European currency in Britain
53.3 Keep the pound as the **only** currency for Britain
 4.3 (Don't know)
 0.8 (Refusal/NA)

Q854 [*PrejAs*]
Now I would like to ask you some questions about racial
prejudice in Britain. First, thinking of **Asians** – that
is, people whose families were originally from India,
Pakistan or Bangladesh – who now live in Britain.
Do you think there is a lot of prejudice against them in
% Britain nowadays, a little, or hardly any?
52.8 A lot
38.2 A little
 5.6 Hardly any
 2.6 (Don't know)
 0.8 (Refusal/NA)

N = 1026

Q855 [*PrejBlk*]
And **black** people – that is people whose families were
originally from the West Indies or Africa – who now live
in Britain. Do you think there is a lot of prejudice
against them in Britain nowadays, a little, or hardly
% any?
45.4 A lot
43.1 A little
 8.3 Hardly any
 2.4 (Don't know)
 0.8 (Refusal/NA)

Q856 [*PrejNow*]
Do you think there is generally **more** racial prejudice in
Britain now than there was 5 years ago, **less, or about**
% the **same** amount?
19.6 More now
31.2 Less now
45.5 About the same
 0.1 Other (WRITE IN)
 2.8 (Don't know)
 0.8 (Refusal/NA)

Q858 [*PrejFut*]
Do you think there will be **more, less or about the same**
amount of racial prejudice in Britain in 5 years time
% compared with now?
23.3 More in 5 years
30.2 Less

40.8 About the same
 0.4 Other (WRITE IN)
 4.6 (Don't know)
 0.8 (Refusal/NA)

Q860 [SRPrej]
  % How would you describe yourself ... READ OUT ...
 1.9 ... as very prejudiced against people of other races,
23.9 a little prejudiced,
72.7 or, not prejudiced at all?
 0.3 Other (WRITE IN)
 0.4 (Don't know)
 0.8 (Refusal/NA)

COUNTRYSIDE

N=1079

Q870 [ConDevt]
      Suppose you heard that a housing development was being
      planned in a part of the countryside you knew and liked.
  %   Would you be concerned by this, or not?
78.6 Yes, concerned
19.3 No
 1.1 (Don't know)
 1.0 (Refusal/NA)

IF 'Yes' AT [ConDevt]
Q871-Q878
      Would you personally be likely to do any of these things
      about it?
      PROBE: Which others?
  %   Multicoded (Maximum of 8 codes)

 6.3 (No, would take no action)[DevtDo1]
31.0 Contact MP or councillor [DevtDo2]
17.0 Contact a government or planning department [DevtDo3]
 7.2 Contact radio, TV or a newspaper [DevtDo4]
65.0 Sign a petition [DevtDo5]
 9.8 Join a conservation group [DevtDo6]
17.2 Give money to a campaign [DevtDo7]
 8.9 Volunteer to work for a campaign [DevtDo8]
12.9 Go on a protest march or demonstration [DevtDo9]
 0.2 (Don't know)
 2.1 (Refusal/NA)

Q879 [ConRoad]
      Suppose you heard that a major new road was going to be
      built through a part of the countryside you knew and
      liked.
  %   Would you be concerned by this, or not?
75.5 Yes, concerned
21.4 No
 2.0 (Don't know)
 1.0 (Refusal/NA)

Q888 [*CtryDone*]
      Have you ever done any of the things on the card **to help**
  %   **protect the countryside**?
51.4 Yes
47.3 No
 0.2 (Don't know)
 1.0 (Refusal/NA)

      IF 'Yes' AT [CtryDone]
Q889-Q896
      Which have you ever done to help protect the countryside?
      Any others?
  %   Multicoded (Maximum of 8 codes)

11.6 Contacted an MP or councillor [*CtryDon1*]
 7.3 Contacted a government or planning department [*CtryDon2*]
 2.7 Contacted radio, TV or a newspaper [*CtryDon3*]
44.9 Signed a petition [*CtryDon4*]
 6.5 Joined a conservation group [*CtryDon5*]
13.3 Given money to a campaign [*CtryDon6*]
 3.4 Volunteered to work for a campaign [*CtryDon7*]
 5.2 Gone on a protest march or demonstration [*CtryDon8*]
 0.1 (Don't know)
  -   (Refusal/NA)

Q932 [*NumbCars*]
  %   How many vehicles in all?
43.2 One
26.2 Two
 8.0 Three
 1.9 Four
 0.7 Five or more
  -   (Don't know)
 1.2 (Refusal/NA)

SEXUAL RELATIONS   N=1079
Q963 [*PMS*]
      Now I would like to ask you some questions about sexual
      relationships.
      If a man and woman have sexual relations before marriage,
      what would your general opinion be?

Q964 [*YoungSex*]
      What if it was a boy and a girl who were both still **under
      16**?

Q965 [*ExMS*]
      What about a **married person** having sexual relations with
      someone other than his or her partner?

Q966 [*HomoSex*]
      What about sexual relations between two adults of the
      same sex?

	[PMS]	[YoungSex]
	%	%
Always wrong	7.6	56.2
Mostly wrong	7.8	24.1
Sometimes wrong	11.7	10.9
Rarely wrong	9.9	2.8
Not wrong at all	57.6	2.6
(Depends/varies)	2.9	1.2
(Don't know)	1.3	1.0
(Refusal/NA)	1.2	1.2

	[ExMS]	[HomoSex]
	%	%
Always wrong	51.8	38.5
Mostly wrong	28.7	11.5
Sometimes wrong	12.5	11.0
Rarely wrong	1.1	7.8
Not wrong at all	1.5	23.3
(Depends/varies)	2.0	3.9
(Don't know)	1.2	2.8
(Refusal/NA)	1.2	1.2

RACE, RELIGION AND CLASSIFICATION

N = 3146

Q971 [Religion]

Do you regard yourself as belonging to any particular religion?

IF YES: Which?

% CODE ONE ONLY - DO NOT PROMPT

45.1 No religion
 5.0 Christian - no denomination
 9.1 Roman Catholic
27.2 Church of England/Anglican
 1.1 Baptist
 2.3 Methodist
 3.6 Presbyterian/Church of Scotland
 0.3 Other Christian
 0.7 Hindu
 0.4 Jewish
 1.2 Islam/Muslim
 0.2 Sikh
 0.1 Buddhist
 0.3 Other non-Christian
 0.1 Free Presbyterian
 -   Brethren
 0.5 United Reform Church (URC)/Congregational
 1.3 Other Protestant
 0.2 (Refusal)
 0.2 (Don't Know)
 1.0 (not answered)

ASK ALL

Q1003 [RaceOri2]

% To which of these groups do you consider you belong?

 1.0 BLACK: of African origin
 1.2 BLACK: of Caribbean origin

```
 0.1  BLACK: of other origin (WRITE IN)
 1.3  ASIAN: of Indian origin
 0.5  ASIAN: of Pakistani origin
 0.1  ASIAN: of Bangladeshi origin
 0.1  ASIAN: of Chinese origin
 0.3  ASIAN: of other origin (WRITE IN)
92.4  WHITE: of any European origin
 0.7  WHITE: of other origin (WRITE IN)
 0.8  MIXED ORIGIN (WRITE IN)
 0.3  OTHER (WRITE IN)
 0.2  (Don't know)
 1.1  (Refusal/NA)
```

Q1014[*Tea2*]
How old were you when you completed your continuous
full-time education?
PROBE IF NECESSARY
'STILL AT SCHOOL' – CODE 95
'STILL AT COLLEGE OR UNIVERSITY' – CODE 96
'OTHER ANSWER' – CODE 97 AND WRITE IN
%   **Median: 16**
0.1 (Don't know)
1.1 (Refusal/NA)

Q1186[*MainInc*]
Which of these is the **main** source of income for you (*and
%   your wife/husband/partner*) at present?
62.1 Earnings from employment (own or spouse / partner's)
 8.5 Occupational pension(s) – from previous employer(s)
13.2 State retirement or widow's pension(s)
 2.5 Jobseeker's Allowance/Unemployment benefit
 4.7 Income Suppport
 0.4 Family Credit
 3.0 Invalidity, sickness or disabled pension or benefit(s)
 0.1 Other state benefit (WRITE IN)
 1.0 Interest from savings or investments
 0.9 Student grant
 1.6 Dependent on parents/other relatives
 0.5 Other main source (WRITE IN)
 0.3 (Don't know)
 1.2 (Refusal/NA)

ASK ALL IN PAID WORK   N=1764
Q1190 [*REarn*]
Which of the letters on this card represents your **own**
gross or total **earnings**, before deduction of income tax
and national
%   insurance?
 8.6 Q (Less than £3,999)
 9.1 T (£4,000-£5,999)
 8.2 O (£6,000-£7,999)
 8.4 K (£8,000-£9,999)
 8.4 L (£10,000-£11,999)
11.1 B (£12,000-£14,999)

```
 9.2  Z (£15,000-£17,999)
 6.0  M (£18,000-£19,999)
 6.0  F (£20,000-£22,999)
 6.2  J (£23,000-£25,999)
 3.3  D (£26,000-£28,999)
 2.1  H (£29,000-£31,999)
 1.3  C (£32,000-£34,999)
 1.4  G (£35,000-£37,999)
 0.3  P (£38,000-£40,999)
 0.6  N (£41,000-£43,999)
 3.2  Y (£44,000 or more)
 2.5  (Don't know)
 3.9  (Refusal/NA)
```

Q1193[*SmokDay*]
      About how many cigarettes a day do you usually smoke?
      IF 'CAN'T SAY', CODE 997
%   **Median: 15**
0.6 ((Don't know)/can't say)
1.3 (Refusal/NA)

Self-completion Questionnaire A

First a few questions about the area where you live.

[areahelp]

1. In some areas people do things together and try to help each other, while in other areas people mostly go their own way. *In general*, would you say you live in an area where . . .
   *PLEASE TICK **ONE** BOX ONLY*

	%
. . . people help each other,	28.3
OR people go their own way?	24.4
Mixture	44.4
Can't choose	1.7
(NA)	1.1

[burghelp]

2. Do you think you live in the sort of area where people who thought a house was being broken into would . . .
   *PLEASE TICK **ONE** BOX ONLY*

	%
OR . . . do something about it,	68.7
just turn a blind eye?	4.0
Mixture	22.3
No burglaries in this area	2.7
Can't choose	1.3
(NA)	1.1

[burgarea]

3. And do you think burglaries in *this area* are . . .
   *PLEASE TICK **ONE** BOX ONLY*

	%
. . . mostly done by people from other areas,	34.0
OR mostly done by people from around here?	16.4
Mixture	30.2
No burglaries in this area	9.7
Can't choose	8.4
(NA)	1.3

[keepeye]

4. If you were going away for a week, are there people living locally who you could ask to keep an eye on your home?
   *PLEASE TICK **ONE** BOX ONLY*

	%
Yes, friends/neighbours	57.7
Yes, family	12.8
Yes, both friends and family	22.6
No	3.1
Can't choose	2.7
(NA)	1.1

[distspnd]

9a. In your opinion, should your local council spend
   *PLEASE TICK **ONE** BOX ONLY*

	%	
. . . more money in the *poorer* parts of the district compared to other parts	39.8	**Answer b.**
. . . more money in the *better off* parts of the district compared to other parts	0	
. . . or should it spend its budget equally across the district?	54.1	**Go to**
Can't choose	3	**Question 10**
(NA)	1.7	

[areaspnd]

b. And do you think that your local council should be spending more money *in your area* compared to other areas, or not?
   *PLEASE TICK **ONE** BOX ONLY*

	%
Yes, more should be spent here	12.3
No, more should *not* be spent here	13.0
Can't choose	13.8
(NA)	2.3

EVERYONE PLEASE ANSWER
[taxpoor]

N = 2546

10. Which of these two statements comes closest to your own view?
*PLEASE TICK **ONE** BOX ONLY*

	%
The government should increase taxes on the better-off in order to spend more on the poor	52.7
OR The government requires people who are better-off to pay too much in taxes already	16.7
Can't choose	29.1
(NA)	1.4

[singmum1]

12. Thinking about a single mother with a child *under school age* Which one of these statements comes closest to your view?
*PLEASE TICK **ONE** BOX ONLY*

	%
She has a special duty to go out to work to support her child	16.5
She has a special duty to stay at home to look after her child	23.9
She should do as she chooses, like everyone else	51.2
Can't choose	7.8
(NA	0.6

[singmum2]

13. Suppose this single mother did get a part-time job. How much do you agree or disagree that the government should provide money to help with child care?
*PLEASE TICK **ONE** BOX ONLY*

	%
Agree strongly	27.0
Agree	47.8
Neither agree nor disagree	13.0
Disagree	7.4
Disagree strongly	1.3
Can't choose	3.0
(NA)	0.6

[smumsch1]

14. And what about when the child *reaches school age*?
Which one of these statements comes closest to your view about what the single mother should do?
*PLEASE TICK **ONE** BOX ONLY*

	%
She has a special duty to go out to work to support her child	44.0
She has a special duty to stay at home to look after her child	4.7
She should do as she chooses, like everyone else	45.1
Can't choose	5.2
(NA)	0.7

[smumsch2]

15. Suppose this single mother did go out to work. How much do you agree or disagree that the government should provide money to help with child care *outside school*?
*PLEASE TICK **ONE** BOX ONLY*

	%
Agree strongly	18.2
Agree	43.9
Neither agree nor disagree	17.9
Disagree	13.7
Disagree strongly	1.6
Can't choose	3.9
(NA)	0.7

[topupchn]

16. Some working couples with children find it hard to make ends meet on low wages. In these circumstances, do you think
*PLEASE TICK **ONE** BOX ONLY*

	%
... the government should top-up their wages,	56.1
or, is it up to the couple to look after themselves and their children as best they can?	31.0
Can't choose	12.0
(NA)	0.9

N=2546

[topupnch]
17. And what about working couples *without* children? If they find it hard to make ends meet on low wages, do you think ...
*PLEASE TICK **ONE** BOX ONLY*

	%
the government should top-up their wages,	25.4
or, is it up to the couple to look after themselves as best they can?	57.7
Can't choose	15.1
(NA)	1.7

[lowwage]
18. Please show how much you agree or disagree with the following statement?
If the government tops up people's wages, it makes it easier for employers to get away with paying low wages.
*PLEASE TICK **ONE** BOX ONLY*

	%
Agree strongly	24.8
Agree	48.4
Neither agree nor disagree	12.6
Disagree	9.0
Disagree strongly	1.1
Can't choose	3.3
(NA)	0.8

21. From what you know or have heard, please tick a box for *each* of the items below to show whether you think the National Health Service *in your area* is, on the whole, satisfactory or in need of improvement.

		In need of *a lot* of improvement	**In need of *some* improvement**	**Satis-factory**	**Very good**	**(DK)**	**(NA)**
[hsarea1] a. GPs' appointment systems	%	12.9	35.0	40.5	10.1	0.0	1.6
[hsarea2] b. Amount of time GP gives to each patient	%	7.1	25.1	56.3	9.8	0.0	1.6
[hsarea3] c. Being able to choose which GP to see	%	8.4	21.5	54.8	12.9	0.0	2.3
[hsarea4] d. Quality of medical treatment by GPs	%	4.7	17.7	55.4	20.0	0.1	2.1
[hsarea5] e. Hospital waiting lists for non-emergency operations	%	33.5	44.4	18.6	1.1	0.0	2.4
[hsarea6] f. Waiting time before getting appointments with hospita consultants	%	38.2	43.3	14.9	1.0	–	2.6
[hsarea7] g. General condition of hospital buildings	%	13.7	35.4	41.5	7.4	0.0	2.0
[hsarea9] h. Staffing level of nurses in hospitals	%	30.0	40.5	23.4	3.5	0.0	2.5
[hsarea10] i. Staffing level of doctors in hospitals	%	25.6	43.7	24.8	3.1	0.0	2.8
[hsarea11] j. Quality of medical treatment in hospitals	%	5.7	29.4	49.2	13.2	0.1	2.3
[hsarea12] k. Quality of nursing care in hospitals	%	7.1	25.0	45.9	19.7	0.1	2.3

[hsarea13]

N = 2546

		%					
l.	Waiting areas in accident and emergency departments in hospitals [hsarea14]	%	18.9	38.6	35.5	4.6	0.0	2.5
m.	Waiting areas for out-patients in hospitals [hsarea15]	%	13.4	36.7	42.6	5.2	0.0	2.1
n.	Waiting areas at GPs' surgeries [hsarea16]	%	4.1	16.7	61.8	15.4	–	2.0
o.	Time spent waiting in out-patient departments [hsarea17]	%	21.0	48.6	26.4	1.5	0.0	2.5
p.	Time spent waiting in accident and emergency departments before being seen by a doctor [hsarea18]	%	33.3	43.0	19.4	1.4	0.1	2.8
q.	Time spent waiting for an ambulance after a 999 call	%	6.0	25.8	51.5	11.3	0.2	5.1

22. In the last *two years*, have you or a close family member . . .
*PLEASE TICK **ONE** BOX ONLY ON EACH LINE*

			Yes	No	NA)
	[nhsdoc]				
a.	. . . visited an NHS GP?	%	94.8	4.3	1.0
	[nhsoutp]				
b.	. . . been an out-patient in an NHS hospital?	%	68.2	29.8	2.0
	[nhsinp]				
c.	. . . been an in-patient in an NHS hospital?	%	44.1	53.5	2.4
	[nhsvisit]				
d.	. . . visited a patient in an NHS hospital?	%	68.1	29.2	2.7
	[privpat]				
e.	. . . had any medical treatment as a private patient?	%	13.2	84.5	2.3
	[privdent]				
f.	. . . had any dental treatment as a private patient?	%	26.0	72.0	2.0

23. [govpower]
And what about the government, does it have too much power or too little power?
*PLEASE TICK **ONE** BOX ONLY*

	%
Far too much power	11.0
Too much power	25.2
About the right amount of power	46.6
Too little power	5.3
Far too little power	0.4
Can't choose	10.7
(NA)	0.7

26. Please tick a box for each statement to show how you feel about disabled people.

*PLEASE TICK **ONE** BOX ONLY ON EACH LINE*		Strongly agree	Agree	Neither agree nor disagree	Strongly Disagree	Can't disagree	choose	(NA)
	[disnteff]							
a.	In general, people with disabilities cannot be as effective at work as people without disabilities [disprejd]	%	4.6	20.5	24.1	34.9	10.9	3.5	1.5
b.	The main problem faced by disabled people at work is other people's prejudice, not their own lack of ability [disnoall]	%	4.6	20.5	24.1	34.9	10.9	3.5	1.5

N = 2546

		%						
c.	Employers should not make special allowances for people with disabilities **[disforcd]**	%	2.2	14.3	20.1	49.7	9.2	2.4	2.1
d.	Employers should be forced to employ more people with disabilities, even if it leads to extra costs **[disshops]**	%	6.9	33.6	29.3	22.6	2.2	3.7	1.7
e.	Shops and banks should be forced to make themselves easier for people with disabilities to use, even if this leads to higher prices **[disservs]**	%	16.9	58.1	14.0	6.6	0.8	2.0	1.6
f.	Services run by government or local authorities should be forced to make themselves easier for people with disabilities to use, even if this leads to higher taxes	%	14.8	54.4	18.3	6.6	1.1	2.8	1.9

[voteduty]
29. Which is these statements comes *closest* to your view about general elections?
*PLEASE TICK **ONE** BOX ONLY*

In a general election		%
	It's not really worth voting	7.9
	People should vote only if they care who wins	25.8
	It's everyone's duty to vote	64.8
	(Can't choose)	0.0
	(NA)	1.4

[bprior1]
30a. Looking at the list below, please tick the box next to the one thing you think should be Britain's *highest priority*, the *most* important thing it should do.
*PLEASE TICK **ONE** BOX ONLY*

Britain should ...		%
	Maintain order in the nation	38.2
	Give people more say in government decisions	26.9
	Fight rising prices	11.6
	Protect freedom of speech	9.4
	Can't choose	12.1
	(NA)	1.8

[bprior2]
b. And which *one* do you think should be Britain's *next highest* priority, the *second* most important thing it should do?
*PLEASE TICK **ONE** BOX ONLY*

Britain should ...		%
	Maintain order in the nation	20.3
	Give people more say in government decisions	21.7
	Fight rising prices	24.2
	Protect freedom of speech	16.9
	Can't choose	14.6
	(NA)	2.3

And now some questions about local government.
[lconsult]
34. Which of these two statements comes closest to your views?
*PLEASE TICK **ONE** BOX ONLY*

	%
Local councils would make better decisions if they made more effort to find out what local people want	86.2
OR	
Local councillors should just get on and make the important decisions themselves. After all, that's what we elected them for	6.9
Can't choose	5.0
(NA)	1.9

[lelects]

35. And which of these two statements comes closest to your views?
PLEASE TICK **ONE** *BOX ONLY*

N = 2546

%

Local elections should be held every year so we can soon make it clear if we think our local council is doing a bad job — 45.3

OR

Local elections should only be held every three or four years or else local councils will never get anything done — 42.0

Can't choose — 10.9

(NA) — 1.8

---

36. Please tick *one* box to show how much you agree or disagree with the following statements.
PLEASE TICK **ONE** *BOX* ON EACH LINE

		Agree strongly	Agree	Neither agree nor disagree	Disagree	Disagree strongly	(NA)
[cllrsldr]							
a.	Councillors know better than voters who is the best person to lead the local council	2.3	25.6	29.9	33.7	5.5	3.0
b.	A council that wants to increase the council tax by more than inflation should have to get a majority vote in favour through a local referendum	16.7	50.8	18.5	10.2	1.1	2.7
[manyvote]							
c.	So many other people vote in local elections it doesn't matter whether I vote or not	1.3	6.0	16.0	55.3	18.6	2.8

(% in each row)

---

37. Please tick *one* box to show how much you agree or disagree with the following statements.
PLEASE TICK **ONE** *BOX* ON EACH LINE

		Agree strongly	Agree	Neither agree nor disagree	Disagree	Disagree strongly	(NA)
[lgeffic1]							
a.	The way that people decide to vote in local elections is the main thing that decides how things are run in this area	4.2	46.7	29.4	16.9	0.7	2.1
[lgeffic2]							
b.	There is no point in voting in local elections because in the end it makes no difference who gets in	2.8	15.3	19.6	52.7	7.3	2.2
[lgeffic3]							
c.	Private companies can always run things more efficiently than local councils	2.6	17.1	36.5	36.3	5.1	2.5
[lgeffic4]							
d.	Generally speaking, those we elect as councillors lose touch with people pretty quickly	8.4	46.1	27.9	14.9	0.3	2.3
[lgeffic5]							
e.	Local council elections are sometimes so complicated that I really don't know who to vote for	3.9	28.1	23.0	37.4	5.1	2.4
[lgeffic7]							
f.	I feel that I could do as good a job as a councillor as most other people	5.4	29.0	30.6	29.2	3.4	2.4

(% in each row)

[lgeffic8]		Agree strongly	Agree	Neither agree nor disagree	Disagree	Disagree strongly	(NA)
g. Councillors don't care much what people like me think	%	6.6	33.6	29.6	26.6	1.4	2.2

N = 2546

38. Please tick *one* box for *each* statement to show how much you agree or disagree with it.
PLEASE TICK **ONE** BOX ON EACH LINE

		Agree strongly	Agree	Neither agree nor disagree	Disagree	Disagree strongly	(NA)
[welfresp]							
a. The welfare state makes people nowadays less willing to look after themselves	%	10.2	39.4	23.0	23.6	1.9	2.0
[welfstig]							
b. People receiving social security are made to feel like second class citizens	%	6.2	37.5	26.6	26.4	1.3	1.9
[welfhslp]							
c. The welfare state encourages people to stop helping each other	%	5.2	30.9	31.9	28.8	1.0	2.1
[morewelp]							
d. The government should spend more money on welfare benefits for the poor, even if it leads to higher taxes	%	6.9	36.0	29.2	22.9	2.9	2.1
[usempjob]							
e. Around here, most unemployed people could find a job if they really wanted one	%	11.4	42.4	22.2	19.9	1.9	2.2
[sochelp]							
f. Many people who get social security don't really deserve any help	%	5.1	27.0	29.4	32.1	4.2	2.1
[dolefidl]							
g. Most people on the dole are fiddling in one way or another	%	9.5	29.1	32.3	23.1	3.9	2.1
[welffeet]							
h. If welfare benefits weren't so generous, people would learn to stand on their own two feet	%	9.3	30.3	26.3	27.4	4.7	1.9

39. Please tick *one* box for *each* statement below to show how much you agree or disagree with it.
PLEASE TICK **ONE** BOX ON EACH LINE

		Agree strongly	Agree	Neither agree nor disagree	Disagree	Disagree strongly	(NA)
[redistrb]							
a. Government should redistribute income from the better-off to those who are less well off	%	8.2	30.4	28.1	26.8	4.6	2.0
[bigbusnn]							
b. Big business benefits owners at the expense of workers	%	11.2	42.4	29.1	13.5	1.0	2.7
[wealth]							
c. Ordinary working people do not get their fair share of the nation's wealth	%	12.2	51.4	23.3	10.5	0.5	2.1
[richlaw]							
d. There is one law for the rich and one for the poor	%	19.5	44.5	19.3	13.4	1.5	1.8
[indust4]							
e. Management will always try to get the better of employees if it gets the chance	%	14.0	45.8	23.4	14.2	0.8	1.8

40. Please tick *one* box for *each* statement below to show how much you agree or disagree with it.

N = 843

PLEASE TICK **ONE** BOX ON EACH LINE

			Agree strongly	Agree	Neither agree nor disagree	Disagree	Disagree strongly	(NA)
	[traduals]							
a.	Young people today don't have enough respect for traditional British values	%	16.4	47.8	23.9	9.4	0.8	1.7
	[stifsent]							
b.	People who break the law should be given stiffer sentences	%	29.4	48.9	15.9	4.0	0.3	1.5
	[deathapp]							
c.	For some crimes, the death penalty is the most appropriate sentence	%	28.9	29.7	15.1	15.4	9.3	1.6
	[obey]							
d.	Schools should teach children to obey authority	%	28.2	54.4	11.3	3.7	0.7	1.6
	[censor]							
e.	Censorship of films and magazines is necessary to uphold moral standards	%	23.9	45.0	15.2	10.3	3.8	1.8

[welthds2]

41. Which of these two statements comes closest to your own view?
PLEASE TICK **ONE** BOX ONLY

	%
Ordinary people get their fair share of the nation's wealth	11.3
OR	
A few rich people get too big a share of the nation's wealth	70.0
Can't choose	18.0
(NA)	0.7

[gujbds2b]

43. Which of these two statements comes closest to your own view?
PLEASE TICK **ONE** BOX ONLY

	%
It is the government's responsibility to provide a job for everyone who wants one	28.9
OR	
It is everyone's own responsibility to find a job for themselves and little to do with the government	53.0
Can't choose	17.8
(NA)	0.3

[rchlwds2]

44. Which of these two statements comes closest to your own view?
PLEASE TICK **ONE** BOX ONLY

	%
There is one law for the rich and one for the poor	63.2
OR	
Rich or poor, everyone gets treated the same	21.1
Can't choose	14.9
(NA)	0.7

[redisds2]

45. Which of these two statements comes closest to your own view?
PLEASE TICK **ONE** BOX ONLY

	%
It is the government's duty to narrow the gap in incomes between rich and poor	65.7
OR	
The government should leave the gap in incomes well alone	14.2
Can't choose	19.2
(NA)	0.8

[bigbsds2]

46. Which of these two statements comes closest to your own view?

    *PLEASE TICK **ONE** BOX ONLY*

	%
Big business benefits bosses at the expense of workers	53.8
OR	
Big business benefits bosses and workers alike	27.7
Can't choose	17.5
(NA)	1.0

[regulds2]

47. Which of these two statements comes closest to your own view?

    *PLEASE TICK **ONE** BOX ONLY*

	%
Big business should always be free to do what it thinks best	18.8
OR	
The government should set clear controls on what big business is allowed to do	64.5
Can't choose	15.9
(NA)	0.8

Self-completion Questionnaire B

N = 843

[Many questions in Questionnaire B are also in Self-completion Questionnaire A. The duplicated questions appear above.]

2. On the whole, do you think it should or should not be the government's responsibility to ...

PLEASE TICK **ONE** BOX ON EACH LINE		Definitely should be	Probably should be	Probably should *not* be	Definitely should *not* be	Can't choose	(NA)
[govresp1]							
a. Provide a job for everyone who wants one?	%	28.6	38.0	16.9	7.9	5.5	3.2
[govresp2]							
b. Reduce income differences between the rich and poor?	%	39.0	34.2	9.7	6.7	5.6	4.6

6. Do you *personally* think it is wrong or not wrong for a women to have an abortion

PLEASE TICK **ONE** BOX ON EACH LINE		Always wrong	Almost always wrong	Wrong only sometimes	Not wrong at all	Can't choose	(NA)
[abowrga]							
a. If there is a strong chance of serious defect in the baby?	%	7.3	4.5	22.4	58.4	5.3	2.1
[abowrgb]							
b. If the family has a very low income and cannot afford any more children?	%	23.6	12.0	20.5	29.9	7.4	6.7

7. Do you agree or disagree ...

PLEASE TICK **ONE** BOX ON EACH LINE		Strongly agree	Agree	Neither agree nor disagree	Disagree	Strongly disagree	Can't choose	(NA)
[sexrole]								
a. A husband's job is to earn money; a wife's job is to look after the home and family?	%	4.8	13.2	22.8	33.8	23.1	0.5	1.9
[wwfamsuf]								
b. All in all, family life suffers when the woman has a full-time job?	%	5.1	24.1	19.0	32.4	13.7	2.3	3.4

8. Do you agree or disagree ...

PLEASE TICK **ONE** BOX ON EACH LINE		Strongly agree	Agree	Neither agree nor disagree	Disagree	Strongly disagree	Can't choose	(NA)
[marvie11]								
a. It is alright for a couple to live together without intending to get married?	%	20.3	41.9	17.3	11.6	5.1	1.4	2.5
[marvie12]								
b. It's a good idea for a couple who intend to get married to live together first?	%	21.9	39.3	19.9	11.2	3.7	1.5	2.5

9. Consider the situations listed below. Do you feel it is wrong or not wrong if

PLEASE TICK **ONE** BOX ON EACH LINE		Not wrong	A bit wrong	Wrong	Seriously wrong	Can't choose	(NA)
[taxcheat]							
a. A taxpayer does not report all of his or her income in order to pay less income taxes?	%	2.6	23.4	51.1	19.3	1.8	1.8

N = 843

b.	**[bencheat]** A person gives the government incorrect information about themselves to get government benefits that they are not entitled to?	%	0.2	2.2	41.8	52.5	0.7	2.6

12. How much confidence do you have in . . .

PLEASE TICK **ONE** BOX ON EACH LINE		Complete confi-dence	A great deal of confi-dence	Some confi-dence	Very little confi-dence	No confi-dence at all	Can't choose	(NA)
a.	**[parlconf]** Parliament?	%	0.9	5.7	48.0	33.3	7.3	2.8	2.0
c.	**[chchconf]** Churches and religious organisations?	%	1.6	12.9	39.5	25.0	11.6	6.6	2.9

13. How much do you agree or disagree with each of the following?

PLEASE TICK **ONE** BOX ON EACH LINE		**Strongly agree**	**Agree**	**Neither agree nor disagree**	**Strongly Disagree**	**Can't disagree**	choose	(NA)
a.	**[rlginfvt]** Religious leaders should not try to influence how people vote in elections	%	39.5	31.2	9.3	9.9	5.2	2.1	2.6
b.	**[rlginfgv]** Religious leaders should not try to influence government decisions	%	31.5	31.3	11.6	15.4	5.4	2.0	2.9

14. Please consider the following statements and tell me whether you agree or disagree?

PLEASE TICK **ONE** BOX ON EACH LINE		**Strongly agree**	**Agree**	**Neither agree nor disagree**	**Strongly Disagree**	**Can't disagree**	choose	(NA)
a.	**[scieharm]** Overall, modern science does more harm than good	%	4.8	14.7	29.9	36.1	7.5	4.9	2.0
b.	**[scietrst]** We trust too much in science and not enough in religious faith	%	5.0	13.8	26.4	34.6	12.0	5.2	3.0

15. And do you agree or disagree with the following statements?

PLEASE TICK **ONE** BOX ON EACH LINE		**Strongly agree**	**Agree**	**Neither agree nor disagree**	**Strongly Disagree**	**Can't disagree**	choose	(NA)
a.	**[relprob1]** Looking around the world, religions bring more conflict than peace	%	26.9	48.0	12.2	7.3	1.1	1.9	2.6
b.	**[relprobe2]** People with very strong religious beliefs are often too intolerant of others	%	23.9	50.2	13.9	6.2	0.7	1.9	3.1
c.	**[relprobe3]** Britain would be a better country if religion had less influence	%	9.6	20.1	33.7	25.2	4.7	3.6	3.0

[chchpowr]

17. Do you think that churches and religious organisations in this country have too much power or too little power?
*PLEASE TICK **ONE** BOX ONLY*

	%
Far too much power	5.2
Too much power	19.6
About the right amount of power	46.8
Too little power	6.8
Far too little power	1.6
Can't choose	17.0
(NA)	3.0

[godbelf1]

18. Please tick one box below to show which statement comes closest to expressing what you believe about God.
*PLEASE TICK **ONE** BOX ONLY*

	%
I don't believe in God	9.9
I don't know whether there is a God and I don't believe there is any way to find out	15.0
I don't believe in a personal God, but I do believe in a Higher Power of some kind	13.5
I find myself believing in God some of the time, but not at others	14.4
While I have doubts, I feel that I do believe in God	22.8
I know God really exists and I have no doubts about it	21.4
(NA)	3.1

[godbelf2]

19. Which best describes your beliefs about God?
*PLEASE TICK **ONE** BOX ONLY*

	%
I don't believe in God now and I never have	13.2
I don't believe in God now, but I used to	11.6
I believe in God now, but I didn't used to	4.2
I believe in God now and I always have	47.6
Can't choose	21.7
(NA)	1.7

20. Do you believe in . . .

*PLEASE TICK **ONE** BOX ON EACH LINE*		Yes, definitely	Yes, probably	No, probably not	No, definitely not	Can't choose	(NA)
[aftrlife]							
a. Life after death?	%	20.8	29.5	19.8	15.3	11.1	3.6
[heaven]							
b. Heaven?	%	19.6	25.7	22.5	17.4	10.3	4.4
[hell]							
c. Hell?	%	11.2	15.8	27.5	27.5	11.6	6.5
[relgmirc]							
d. Religious miracles?	%	11.2	20.7	27.5	24.8	10.3	5.5

[biblfeel]

21. Which of these statements comes closest to describing your feelings about the Bible?
*PLEASE TICK **ONE** BOX ONLY*

	%
The Bible is the actual word of God and it is to be taken literally, word for word	4.1
The Bible is the inspired word of God but not everything should be taken literally, word for word	33.9
The Bible is an ancient book of fables, legends, history, and moral precepts recorded by man	43.6
This does not apply to me	8.3
Can't choose	8.0
(NA)	2.1

22. Do you agree or disagree with the following?

N = 814

PLEASE TICK **ONE** BOX ON EACH LINE		agree	Strongly Agree	Neither agree nor disagree	Strongly Disagree	Can't disagree	choose	(NA)
[godconcn]								
a. There is a God who concerns Himself with every human being personally	%	10.4	18.6	25.2	19.8	11.6	9.3	5.2
[fatalist]								
b. There is little that people can do to change the course of their lives	%	2.8	14.3	11.1	48.5	14.9	3.2	5.2
[godgmean]								
c. To me, life is meaningful only because God exists	%	5.9	8.8	21.2	32.6	19.1	6.1	6.3
[lfnopurp]								
d. In my opinion, life does not serve any purpose	%	1.4	4.0	9.4	46.7	27.9	4.4	6.1
[slfgmean]								
e. Life is only meaningful if you provide the meaning yourself	%	8.4	48.0	15.8	14.5	3.8	4.5	5.0
[ownfate]								
f. We each make our own fate	%	9.5	47.5	19.4	12.6	2.0	4.0	4.8

[relgcomm]

23. Has there ever been a turning point in your life when you made a new and personal commitment to religion?
PLEASE TICK **ONE** BOX ONLY

	%
Yes	15.1
No	82.1
(NA)	2.8

[r11attch]

30. And what about when you were around 11 or 12, how often did *you* attend religious services then?
PLEASE TICK **ONE** BOX ONLY

	%
Never	16.3
Less than once a year	6.9
About once or twice a year	7.0
Several times a year	9.4
About once a month	4.2
2–3 times a month	3.4
Nearly every week	21.7
Every week	20.9
Several times a week	4.1
Can't say/Can't remember	4.4
(NA)	1.8

[prayfreq]
Now thinking about the present ...

31. About how often do you pray?
PLEASE TICK **ONE** BOX ONLY

	%
Never	31.9
Less than once a year	6.3
About once or twice a year	9.3
Several times a year	11.9
About once a month	4.2
2–3 times a month	3.2
Nearly every week	6.4
Every week	4.8
Several times a week	5.7
Once a day	9.3
Several times a day	5.0
(NA)	2.0

[chrchact]

32. How often do you take part in the activities or organisations of a church or place of worship other than attending services?
   *PLEASE TICK **ONE** BOX ONLY*

	%
Never	63.4
Less than once a year	9.3
About once or twice a year	7.5
Several times a year	6.6
About once a month	3.7
2–3 times a month	0.7
Nearly every week	1.6
Every week	2.8
(NA)	2.7

[religius]

33. Would you describe yourself as ...
   *PLEASE TICK **ONE** BOX ONLY*

	%
Extremely religious	0.4
Very religious	5.9
Somewhat religious	31.4
Neither religious nor non-religious	29.8
Somewhat non-religious	13.2
Very non-religious	7.8
Extremely non-religious	6.5
Can't choose	2.8
(NA)	2.1

[reltruth]

34. Which of the following statements come closest to your own views:
   *PLEASE TICK **ONE** BOX ONLY*

	%
There is very little truth in any religion	11.7
There are basic truths in many religions	67.2
There is truth only in one religion	6.4
Can't choose	12.8
(NA)	1.9

[accexpct]

35. Suppose you were riding in a car driven by a close friend. You know he is going too fast. He hits a pedestrian. He asks you to tell the police that he was obeying the speed limit.

a. Which statement comes closest to your belief about what your friend has a right to expect from you?
   *PLEASE TICK **ONE** BOX ONLY*

	%
My friend has a *definite* right as a friend to expect me to testify that he was obeying the speed limit	2.1
My friend has *some* right as a friend to expect me to testify that he was obeying the speed limit	10.2
My friend has *no* right as a friend to expect me to testify that he was obeying the speed limit	79.9
Can't choose	6.2
(NA)	1.6

[accwould]

b. What would you do in this situation?
   *PLEASE TICK **ONE** BOX ONLY*

	%
Definitely tell the police that your friend *was* going faster than the speed limit	25.2
Probably tell the police that your friend *was* going faster than the speed limit	46.2
Probably tell the police that your friend *was not* going faster than the speed limit	10.4
Definitely tell the police that your friend *was not* going faster than the speed limit	1.3
Can't choose	14.4
(NA)	2.6

Note: questions B36 to B60 are the same as questions A1 to A19 and A21 to A26 of Version A of the questionnaire

$N = 814$

[genresch]

64. Do you think that ...
PLEASE TICK **ONE** *BOX ONLY* %

... scientists should *not* be allowed to carry out *any* research into human genes, 5.7

or, that the only genetic research that should be allowed is to help detect, prevent and cure diseases, 76.7

or, that scientists should be allowed to carry out whatever genetic research they choose to do? 7.7

Can't choose 8.3

(NA) 1.6

65. Please tick one box on each line to show how much you agree or disagree that

PLEASE TICK **ONE** *BOX* *ON EACH LINE*		agree	Strongly Agree	Neither agree nor disagree	Strongly Disagree	Can't disagree	choose	(NA)
[gennochd]								
a. ... people at risk of having a child with serious genetic disorder should not start a family?	%	13.0	27.1	29.7	18.7	3.1	6.2	2.1
[genharm]								
b. ... research into human genes will do more harm than good?	%	3.2	13.5	30.3	37.7	5.6	6.8	3.1

[genhope]

66. How hopeful or worried for the future do you feel about discoveries into human genes and what these may lead to?
PLEASE TICK **ONE** *BOX ONLY* %

Very hopeful about the future 7.5

Fairly hopeful 13.2

Hopeful about some things, worried about others 51.5

Fairly worried 8.4

Very worried about the future 3.6

Haven't really thought about it 8.7

Can't choose 5.6

(NA) 1.5

Self-completion Questionnaire C

N=814

[Most questions in Questionnaire C are also in Self-completion Questionnaires A and B. The duplicated questions appear above.]

51. Here are a number of circumstances in which a woman might consider an abortion. Please say whether or not you think the law should allow an abortion in each case.
*PLEASE TICK **ONE** BOX ON EACH LINE*

Should abortion be allowed by law?

				Yes	No	(NA)
a.	[abort1]	The woman decides on her own she does not wish to have the child	%	54.4	41.5	4.0
b.	[abort2]	The couple agree they do not wish to have the child	%	60.3	35.2	4.5
c.	[abort3]	The woman is not married and does not wish to marry the man	%	51.1	44.2	4.7
d.	[abort4]	The couple cannot afford any more children	%	56.3	38.9	4.8
e.	[abort5]	There is a strong chance of a defect in the baby	%	83.9	12.2	3.9
f.	[abort6]	The woman's health is seriously endangered by the pregnancy	%	91.6	5.2	3.1
g.	[abort7]	The woman became pregnant as a result of rape	%	91.4	5.7	3.0

Index